BORN IN THE RIGHT TIME

One Man's Journey Through the Generations

BY

Donald R. Yeager

BART
A Good read 50
Say Brother Mel
Happy Birthday

BORN IN THE RIGHT TIME

Published by
Right Time Publishing
Bellevue, Idaho 83313

Some names have been changed to
protect the innocent as well as the guilty.

Cover & Book Design
Mark Kashino Design - Hailey Idaho

Printed in the
United States of America

POD Fixed Format

Revision April 2021

ISBN: 978-0-578-87668-9

This memoir is dedicated to my loving parents, Henry and Rose.

Also to my son Don Jr., (DJ) for his character, strength and endurance!

PREFACE

YES! Unlike many of you red-blooded, born-on-American-soil-fortunates, my story begins with my grandparent's interesting history. So when I first thought about writing my memoirs, I wanted to get things straight—-straight from the horse's mouth—-right from the beginning—-so I consulted my mother, Rose, and picked her brain of the many stories she was always talking about–you know–about the old country and "when we were young." She seemed to be wanting to impress upon us children, how lucky we were to have been born in the US of A. When I mentioned to her that I was about to write a book about my life, she was most enthusiastic. I began to probe her mind– stories rolled out–and after many months of my note taking, her memory constantly sputtering out old thoughts—-here's what we came up with. ~

INTRODUCTION

Where did it all begin?

Well, I suppose we could go all the way back to Adam and Eve, but then that would be going too far. So, I'll begin my journey in the year 1939, the war years. Yes, I was born a "war baby", a coupling from WW II's greatest generation. Little did I know that their efforts in keeping us free from harm's way, their sacrifices of life, limb and mind would pave the way for future generations to thrive.

Fast forward–post war–1946–I am now of the Now generation, the so-called "golden years," the American people, recovering from the war, surged ahead. Leaping ahead–eighteen years to 1964–or there about, the "baby boomers" begin to arrive. Our economic growth leaps ahead with this generation gleaning the benefits from past recent discoveries and inventions. A generation gap is relevant and the era of "Sex, drugs and rock and roll" pops into our lives, and then–another war–Vietnam–again causes big changes in our lives.

So, yes, I feel fortunate, in feeling that I was "born in the right time" and to have been privy to the journey through these generations of the last (in my case) seven decades and I would like to share my adventures with you.

Getting into the heart of it—those of you who were fortunate to have been born during the 1930s, '40s, '50s, even into the '60s, will visualize within your minds the adventures of early youth. Remembering the first step to adult hood—your driver's license—so let's not forget getting the keys to Dad's car, the prelude to all the good times ahead involving hot rods, sports cars, motorcycles, speed boats and airplanes.

There were also our early loves, our college days and military tours (if you served) and perhaps the worldwide travels and escapades we encountered while roaming through different countries, especially those in Asia, the Far East and Europe.

Let's relive the years of the "flower children" that brought many of us into career changes, spurred on by a fast-revolving creative world that brought us into the Space Age. Remembering once again our youth and the feelings of strength, freedom and the competition that came with all the available sports or whatever might have suited our fancy or fantasies. So come along, and as you progress on from chapter to chapter, you may find yourself actually joining in and becoming a character in "our" story. Enjoy, share in my and your memories and please read on. ~

CONTENTS

BOOK THREE

BOOK FOUR

ACKNOWLEDGMENTS

Gary Sadler, U.S. Navy, LTCMD
The first to spark inspiration while sitting in my hairstyling chair,
getting a trim and swapping sea stories. "You should write a book!"

Bob Pearson, author.
For direction and enthusiasm.

Nat Young, author, and world-renowned surfer champion.
Proofreader, opinion; "A good story, don't change a thing!"

Alice Zyetz, author, editor, International Achievement Award, writing
teacher. 1st editing, "Great story, get it done!"

Jan Gillis, freelance editor, 2nd editing, thank you for your input!

Ron Weber, English major, actor, writer, editor, 3rd editing, comment
"After reading your book, you lived a life that many would have loved
to live!"

Karen Bossick, journalist, editor, reporter, and creator of Eye on Sun
Valley. 4th editing, interview pending when published.

Laurie Yeager, proofreader, fact finder, editing, 5th editing and final
approval to publishing.

Mark Kashino, graphic and fine artist, author, book design, publishing
director, t-shirt and cover design.
The last say, "5B or Not to Be!"

COMMENTS

*"You were true to your word, and delivered an
adventurous, well written, good read."* - Christine Kenck-
Courtright, editor of East Cape Periódico, Los Barriles, BCS, Mexico.

*"Read the book cover to cover in seven hours.
Couldn't put it down — good layout!"* - Steve King, artist.

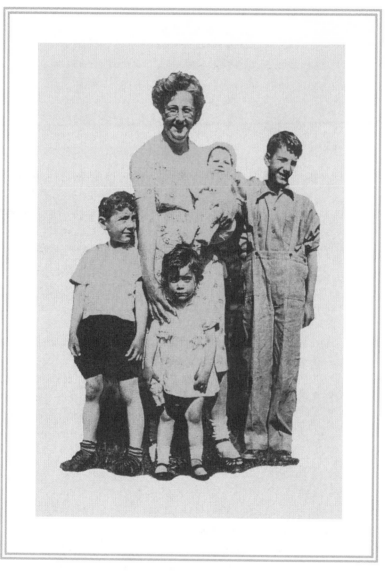

ROSE'S BROOD

A proud mother – with Dennis, Marilyn, Joyce
(in arms), and yours truly, Don.

BOOK ONE

Chapter 1: In The Beginning

In the early 1900s, in a small village lying on the Austria-Hungary border, a strong, built-like-a-bull young man was preparing for the journey of his life. At 19, Ignatius Steinhibel had lived all of his life in Tuzina, a picturesque hamlet lying in a valley in the shadow of the Carpathian Mountains. The soil was black as night and extremely rich. His family, farmers by trade, had survived for generations tilling the earth raising corn, potatoes and other vegetables for their own consumption and grains and oats for their domestic animals. Their daily lives were routine, simple, quiet and serene—very uneventful.

Ignatius, lured by the stories he'd read out of books from the village's one-room school library, grew restless. A wild imagination fed the wanderlust that lurked within his brain and body. He had recently married Johanna Greshner, a young lass he had grown up with in the village. She was now pregnant with their first child.

One morning after a fitful, mostly sleepless night, he awoke from a visionary dream. He saw himself sliding on his back down a bright, sparkling, silver stream of water that ran through the valley. There was no fear; only joy, as he cascaded feet first out of the mountains till his booted feet touched the ocean. Then he was sailing on a four-masted schooner into the unknown to a distant land he had only seen in picture books. When he awoke, he took it to be a sign for him to break tradition!

At the breakfast table, his heart beating fast, he announced his decision to leave the fatherland to venture out of his comfort zone and seek his fortune in the new frontier of the United States of America. His wife and child were to follow after he was settled and had made enough money to send for them.

Two years later, Ignatius accomplished his task. In 1908, Johanna and their son, "Igs," (Ignatius, Jr.) left their homeland and steamed across the ocean for the long-awaited reunion with husband and father. Arriving on Ellis Island with 600 other immigrants, mother and son were quickly processed through immigration. Clutching their pre-purchased train tickets sent from Ignatius, they were directed to the railroad station and were soon whisked away on their journey to the Midwest farming community of Walnut, Minn.

Ignatius anxiously awaited their arrival. As time drew near, he asked his employer for permission to take a horse and buggy to greet them. Refused, he grabbed the handles of a large wheelbarrow and wheeled it two miles down the dirt road to the railroad station where he greeted his new son and much missed spouse. After the initial hugs, kisses, and tears of joy, he loaded the large steamer trunk into the wheelbarrow, proudly placed his son upon his shoulders and, with Johanna's arm wrapped within his, made the return trip. Thus began a new adventure, another saga of European immigrants with hopes and dreams to be fulfilled.

After three years of subsistence farming, the family—now with an energetic bouncing, blue-eyed girl named Rose—decided to try city life. They moved to St. Paul, Minn., where Ignatius joined the city's police force. He cut a striking figure of a man in his blue and black, gold-trimmed uniform and soon worked his way up in the ranks to a special forces unit. Life was good, and soon he purchased a lovely brick home on Van Buren Avenue to house his growing family, which now included two more children, Lillian and Frederick.

Then tragedy struck. Ignatius was gunned down and died in the line of duty. His funeral was an elaborate procession, no different from a fallen soldier's. Long lines of uniformed men marched in cadence to a slow beating drum as the casket he rested in was ceremoniously carried down the steps of St. Agnes church and placed in a black Cadillac hearse. Johanna - left alone to raise the four children - took in laundry to supplement her pension from the Police Widow's Fund.

At the same time, in the small rural town of White Bear Lake, Minn., 45 miles away, Edward and Emily Yeager were busy raising their family of six children - five boys named Otto, Edward Jr., Walter, Arthur and Henry, and one girl named Agnes. The Yeagers had emigrated through Montreal, Canada, from a province in France, also wanting to better themselves in the New World.

With the money they had saved while working in Canada, they bought a small parcel on the outskirts of town and built a profitable milk and produce business. The children, all born on the farm, were first-generation American citizens. Otto drove the horse-drawn cart that delivered the milk and Walter was in charge of packing the chicken eggs in straw in wooden boxes to help protect them as they rode in the back. Arthur did all types of handyman jobs and Henry made golf clubs and caddied at the White Bear golf course.

In their early teens, the boys learned to play various instruments; saxophone, trumpet, tuba, and for percussion, a small snare drum and a washboard. They named their group "The Oompah Band" and played at local dance halls on Saturday nights. One night, while they were playing at the Como Lake open-air pavilion in St. Paul, Henry glanced down the polished length of his horn and noticed a tall, thin, good-looking girl, dressed in a brightly flowered dress dancing in the crowd. Spontaneously, he slipped off the stage onto the dance floor leaving his brothers to carry on without him.

Henry wasted no time in introducing himself to that girl by asking her for the pleasure of dancing the next waltz. That pretty girl was Rose Steinhibel, who had secretly admired Henry on stage from previous dances she had attended and was quite delighted when he approached. She giggled and leaped onto the dance floor at the touch of his hand. Henry and Rose danced themselves into a courtship and a marriage that would last 62 years. They raised four children. The first-born, a boy named Donald, arrived on Sept. 29th, 1939. ~

CHAPTER 2: THE EARLY YEARS

I, Donald. grew up as a typical American kid. By the time I was six, the war was over, and I was part of the postwar generation, maturing in the land of plenty, just as my grandfather had hoped.

I was born at Bethesda Hospital, in the city of St. Paul, Minn., the first child of Henry and Rose Yeager. I entered a world of chaos at 6:15 am, on the 29th of September 1939. My dad, Henry or "Hank" to his friends, was of French and Austrian descent, tall and handsome at 33 years of age. My mother Rose was 30, worked in a bakery, and was as Old Country German as they come.

My Dad had tried to serve his country during this WWII war and had registered for the draft but during his physical the doctors detected a slight heart murmur and rejected him. Disappointed, he served his country's war effort from the safety of its own shores. He finally found his niche in the printing world where ink, typesetting and the printing press became his forte.

Later, my mother bore three more children; my brother Dennis and my two sisters, Marilyn and Joyce. My mother was never one to spare the rod, nor was she an easy taskmaster. She took on most of the responsibility of raising us while my dad toiled at the presses. He worked the swing shift from 3 in the afternoon until midnight, sometimes pulling overtime and not arriving home till the wee hours of the morning, leaving only the weekends for us to get to know him. He was a good provider, keeping us clothed, fed and sheltered. We grew up in a comfortable, middle-class environment. These times were fun and innocent. We shared our free time with friends, neighbors and our closest relatives, Andrew (Bud) Licha and his wife Lillian, my mother's younger sister. On the weekends, we'd venture out in our autos to one of the many 10,000 lakes Minnesota is still famous for. While we children frolicked in the water, the adults enjoyed their quiet time together engaged in pleasant conversations. The men casually sipped on their beers - usually Hamm's, brewed in Minnesota, the land of sky blue waters - while the women kept one eye on us, but when someone yelled, "picnic's ready," we'd all rush to the table for some good ole' crispy Southern fried chicken, German potato salad and hot baked beans.

In addition to going to the lakes, we also looked forward to our yearly adventure of the visit to the Greshner's, my mother's cousin's dairy farm, about 150 miles away outside of the little town of Longwood, Wisconsin. I longed for this trip because it took me out of the city, placing me in a different environment filled with daily surprises, bringing me closer to my grandparents' beginnings as farmers. My cousins were a hardy lot, awaking at dawn to begin their daily farm chores and working long into the evening until dusk was upon them. John Greshner, my grandmother's brother, had also emigrated from Tuzina, Austria. He was the driving force of Longwood Farm, a short, stocky man with a barrel chest, strong shoulders, long arms and hands with immense strength in them. His fingers were shaped like sausages, acquiring their power from hand milking his dairy-producing cows twice daily for the last twelve years.

John's wife, Emma, was a small but most powerful woman. She had blessed him with two sons, John Junior and Stanley. John Junior, the oldest, was a real character, always kidding around, singing songs, telling us jokes or playing them on us. He became my Pied Piper - everywhere that John went - I was sure to follow.

Stanley, the second son, was exactly the opposite, lighter in frame, quiet and unassuming. He was hard worker and was destined to become the one who would carry on the family tradition of farming and animal husbandry.

John Senior's mother, Alice, was straight out from the Old Country. She was the true ruling hand and kept life harmonious. Everyone respected Great Grandma Alice. We all loved her dearly, always listened to her words of wisdom and never questioned her. I emphatically believed all she said and that belief eventually led me into one of my earlier hair-raising experiences.

The farm was pretty self-sufficient, with a large vegetable garden, a potato patch, and fields of corn, oats, hay and barley. Since dairy was their moneymaker, they had bought and raised a large herd of Holstein milking cows. Chickens ruled the farmyard, strutting, scratching, and roaming free. Some of the chickens were Rhode Island Reds, which laid creamy brown eggs and were my favorites because of their rich golden-orange yolks.

That week, spent at the Greshner's farm, always seemed to me to be a learning experience. Our two families shared in the chores, herding the cows to their milking stalls, slopping the hogs, collecting fresh eggs, picking tomatoes off the vine, pulling carrots and turnips, digging up potatoes, etc. etc.

I was only seven years old when I made my first, and last, attempt at killing for a meal. It turned out to be a chilling, unforgettable experience. It all began when great grandma Alice told me how to catch a chicken, fold its wings alongside its body and, while firmly locking it between my legs, stretch the head and neck out in front of me over a chopping block. "Don't be afraid." She said, and with one fast slam, I cut off the chicken's head with a very sharp, short-handled ax.

I was about to learn what the cliché "running around like a chicken with his head cut off" meant. As soon as the bird's head was separated from its body, its involuntary nervous system was immediately highly energized. Its strength greatly enhanced, the chicken bounced out from between my legs. The headless bird proceeded to put up such a fuss that it scared me almost out of my pants, raising my hair up on its ends. It crazily chased me around the barnyard, raising dust and scattering other animals in all directions. Hiding behind the barn, Grandma Greshner, along with my two cousins, howled with laughter at my wide-eyed fright and leaping antics as I ran around in circles.

The Sunday "farm" dinner was always a special event, in celebration of another satisfying week of hard work. Held promptly at noon, the dinner bell would ring out loud and clear. Sometimes if the wind was right, you could hear the neighboring farms' bells ringing as well, calling everyone to "chow time."

The dining room table would be laden with bowls of mashed potatoes mixed with our own rich milk and creamery butter, fresh peas, corn, squash and salad. The crispy chicken, country fried to perfection, was my favorite, but on special occasions, a roast with scrumptious mouth-watering gravy, would appear before our very eyes. Dessert followed with apple or peach pie, but my favorite dessert was "glorified rice," (nicely fluffed rice mixed in a huge bowl along with fruits, nuts, marshmallows, and real rich whipped cream, all blended together). Yum! Oh, those summer days! How I never wanted them to end. But, end they did, and you know what that meant, back to school and, in my case, church also. In our city, most neighborhoods had their little church on the corner—many with their own schools. I was raised in a predominantly Catholic diocese and attended both the church and school, located a half a block down our street on LaFond Avenue. For thirteen years I prayed and studied under the strict dominance and guidance of our priests, and the nuns of Notre Dame.

My eighth-grade homeroom teacher, Sister Mary Aquinas, was beautiful! Her angelic face was encased in white under a stiff black habit. Her form floated down the school's hallways, her body hidden from all but herself and God. She was my first infatuation and has remained forever in my memory. Years later I found out that she left the order to marry - I always thought that would happen!

Religion was a very important part of raising a family in the forties and fifties, and my parents were ever so proud in escorting us, their off-spring, down the center aisle to their favorite pew just in time for 8 a.m. mass on Sunday mornings. Lots of our activities were also centered on the church and school, such as fairs, fundraisers, dances, and basketball and football games. Yes! Life was good.

As I grew older, my leash was lengthened, and I was allowed to venture further away from my immediate neighborhood. On the corner of University and Dale Streets, about a mile away, was the Faust Theater. On Saturday afternoons, after I'd cut the grass, my buddies, "Little Joe" Tishida and "Chucky" Neidermeier, would meet me at the gas station up on the corner. Each of us held a treasured quarter in our hot little hands. Jumping up and down with excitement, we would skip up University Avenue and spend ten cents for the matinee, leaving us fifteen cents for an ice-cream soda after the show. It was our allowance for the week, and we loved spending it in this manner.

The Faust movie house was a fun gathering place for all the neighborhood kids. Kids my age would rush for the very front row where the large images on the screen would whisk us away into a fantasy world. Loaded up with bonbons, popcorn, red-hots and a soda, we would sit for hours, mesmerized with the flashing, (mostly black and white,) moving pictures that appeared on the screen.

The World News flashed first, delivering strange tales of what was going on in other countries far away—usually about some war or another disaster. Then a cartoon or two would follow.

We laughed at the crazy antics of the Disney cartoons and learned to mimic certain characters. My favorites were Donald Duck, Yosemite Sam, the Road-runner, (beep, beep!) and Bugs Bunny, (What's up Doc?) Then came the long-awaited serial feature. This enticed you to come back every week to catch the continuing sagas of Hopalong Cassidy, the masked Zorro, and the Lone Ranger with his trusted Indian sidekick, Tonto. I would sometimes dream all week about what was going to happen next in the next episode. I also liked the crazy antics of Bud Abbot and Lou Costello and the slapstick, head banging humor of the Three Stooges. Saturday afternoons at the movies were always a fantasy adventure, especially for us younger ones.

After the show we would wander back down Dale Street to Thomas Avenue, drop into the corner drugstore; spend the rest of our weekly allowance on a cherry-chocolate coke, a banana split, or that creamy ice cream soda, then home for a Saturday night bar-b-que dinner.

At the age of fifteen, I got my first job carrying and delivering the St. Paul Pioneer Press and Dispatch newspaper. At first, I had to toss the news to houses in the Rondo district where most of my customers were black. My father, when he could, would accompany me on my rounds until he felt it would be safe for me to go it alone.

Being a rather friendly fellow, my customers soon began to take a liking to me. Some cheerfully greeted me on my deliveries. Once a month I had to collect the money for the papers I delivered, and that was not always easy in this district. I found myself riding my bike into the "hood" sometimes late at night trying to catch my clients at home. One of those evenings, I stumbled upon one hell of a ruckus. Out of a ramshackle house, its screen door barely hanging on to its hinges and a seriously listing front porch, emerged a screaming black man, blood streaming down his face, being chased by a big black woman with a huge butcher knife in her hand screaming loud obscenities. Chills ran up my spine and my hair seemed to stand on end. Needless to say, that was the end of that paper route for this kid. I refused to go back on the job on that "side" of the street.

A short while later, the newspaper relocated me in my own backyard and I soon built up my route from 47 deliveries to over 156. There was no problem collecting here in my neighborhood, in fact, I even started to receive tips. My mother was very supportive of me, extending her long household working hours to help me out in the early mornings. She also helped me obtain new subscribers, which won me many contests, giving me numerous prizes, fun trips and more cash. Again - life was good.

Seeing as how I got to keep pretty much most of my hard earned money, which made me crave for more so I took on a second job, setting pins at the University bowling alley a few week nights. Then on Sundays, after delivering my papers, and after Mass, I set pins in the basement of our school under our basketball gym. My dad, Hank and my uncle "Igs" and their bowling partners had teams with colorful shining silk shirts embossed with the team's name. Their team was called "The Aggies," appropriate, considering that they all belonged to the St. Agnes parish. I always asked, and usually got to set pins on the two lanes that they bowled on. By sixteen I was very fast and proficient in sending the balls back to their rack and resetting the pins. I would work up a pretty good sweat, as lifting those balls and resetting those pins was no easy task, and besides - it was hotter then hell back there in those pits. In the beginning, I smashed my fingers a few times sending those heavy bowling balls back and "Oh Lordy," the pain would ring in my head, but I would bear it as best I could and carry on. I had a job to do and at 25 cents a line, I was making quite a few bucks!

With my own hard-earned cash in my pocket, a new sense of independence was born within me. My first purchase was a new 1954 Whizzer Motor Bike. Now, with power between my legs, I started taking trips further out into the country, and with the wind in my hair, a big smile on my face, glee in my heart and an occasional bug in my teeth, I reveled in this new sense of freedom.

The Whizzer enabled me to finish my paper route in record time. I'd begin by sitting on the corner with the other paper boys, fold up all my papers for throwing, pack them in the basket that hung from the handlebars and motor my way up and down the streets tossing the papers at a rapid pace, most of which hit their mark.

My paper route continued to grow and, with the extra money I earned and saved, more doors seemed to open up to me. I traded the Whizzer in for a 125cc Harley Davidson motorcycle. With the new ride came the ducktail hairdo, tight Levis, a leather jacket and engineer boots. I was growing up! Suddenly the world seemed to widen, ownership brought pride, pride brought new strength, and strength brought confidence.

Around the same time, I got interested in birds - racing homing pigeons to be exact. There were a lot of lofts around the neighborhood and I started hanging out in the backyards of some of the fanciers.

George Klingelhoffer, an older gentleman who lived a city block away, raised the nicest homers and he offered me a pair of "blue barbs" to start off with. Blue barbs had smoky blue bodies with two black horizontal lines on their wings. They are the most common color of the "scrub" pigeons that we see nesting under bridges and up in church steeples. My church, St. Agnes, had a flock of them nesting in theirs.

"Now," I thought, "I have to talk Dad into helping me build my own loft." My Dad loved his garage, his bit of solitude where he hung up his pinup girls from the print shop and shelved all of his experimental automobile polishes. He loved to disappear there to spend his early Saturday mornings polishing his car with the latest wax. I was overjoyed when I approached him to ask him if he could help me build a loft for pigeons above the garage, and he said, "Yes." Not only did he help build the coop, but he pursued the hobby along with me.

Raising and training the homers became a real involved undertaking and my Dad started spending more and more time with me, which was good for us both.

The loft was built and young birds were born. After six to eight weeks, before they got their flight wings, we would familiarize them with their surroundings by placing them outside of the flight cage near the "trap." The trap was an opening located on the landing where the birds entered the loft after their nightly or morning exercise flights. First, there was a large landing, then the opening with the trap that let the birds drop into the loft. Thin steel rods they pushed against let them enter, but they could not exit this way.

Soon the young birds felt at home and began to test their wings, they also soon learned to recognize my calling whistle and the sound of feed rattling in an old coffee can. These two sounds would bring the birds out of the sky when I wanted them to return to the loft. Usually, I flew the birds hungry so that they were excited to return home and "trap." For further training we placed them in carrying cages, took them a few blocks away and released them. The best birds usually beat us home. Then we extended them a mile away from home, then five miles, then ten and, finally, up to one hundred miles away.

We joined a homing pigeon racing club with a bunch of Italian guys who had lofts down in the levee along the Mississippi River. We were the outsiders, but they welcomed us with open arms. These guys loved to get together on Saturday nights before race day, talk pigeons, drink red wine and smoke cigars. They were a real comical group always pulling gags on each other. Dad never smoked in his life but he sure could match them in stories.

As our flock grew to more than 50 birds, feeding them got pretty expensive. I discovered that the railroad cars sitting on the side rails of the grain elevators held more pigeon feed that we could ever hope to use and began to sweep the left-over grain into gunnysacks. My old friend Chucky Neidermeyer had a large Red Flyer wagon with big hard rubber tires - perfect for hauling the sacks of grain home.

Thanks to the pigeons and the grain elevators, the tracks became our new playground, and we soon started hopping freights. This new thrilling and somewhat dangerous sport was the first of my many real adventures. I loved this excitement and never thought about the risks involved, except for the thrill of it.

The Northern Pacific's railroad tracks were only about half -mile away from home, and soon Chucky and I learned the freight train schedules - when they stopped, when they moved on, where they came from and where they went. The seven o'clock evening freight, one of our favorites, always had a hundred cars or more. It always arrived on time and switched over to a sidetrack, stopping to let a fast-moving passenger train go by in the opposite direction, then it would resume its journey on to Hudson, Wisconsin. When the wheels once again started to turn, the boxcars would bang against each other, the wood and steel creaking from the sudden movement and we would run alongside, grab the iron ladders and pull ourselves up and ride the rails. Usually, we would only ride to the Rice Street yard; about two miles down the tracks where the train would start to pick up speed. Hopping off, we'd hang out and catch the slow moving 8:30 freight going the other way back home. One time, however, with three engines pulling the train, it picked up speed much faster than usual and we had to ride it all the way to Hudson Wisconsin before it was safe to hop off. It took us over three hours to hitchhike home that evening. Chucky and I were grounded for a week.

The tracks became a favorite playground for my buddies, Chucky and Bob "Punchy" Miller and me. A fourth friend, Florian Shoena, joined us.

Florian, nicknamed "Flow-Joe," lived near the tracks at the end of a road that led into a closed sand pit. The pit housed abandoned sand trucks and an old steam shovel that had been left behind to rust. We loved to climb up into the cab, get behind the steering wheel and pretend we were the long-gone heavy equipment operators. We could make the still gauges and silent controls come alive with our vocal growls and our simulated foot and arm movements. One time we found a box of dynamite caps in an old shed and discovered that if we placed them on the tracks, they would explode with a bright blue and red flash when the train's heavy wheels came in contact with them. They were only igniters, not explosives, so they couldn't possibly do much harm. We also had fun flattening pennies and other coins. Little girls had their dolls, and we had our real freight trains and giant sand trucks to play with. Boys will be boys.

Many people lived along the tracks in what were then known as shanties or row houses. Built in the early 1940s for the railroad yard's working class, they were little one-bedroom shacks, tiny boxes with upside down V-shaped roofs. An early edition of the housing developments called suburbs that were now springing up all over America. Each one had its own little garden plot, tended lovingly by the occupants.

In August and September, when the gardens were at their peak of harvest, we loved to nab watermelons, corn, tomatoes, rhubarb, and whatever other goodies were available for our own dinner tables. The pilfering was not so much getting the fruits or vegetables stuffed into the small gunny sacks we carried, but just seeing if our timing would be right to get away with it. It was just a game we played, staking out our objectives days before our plunder, then trying to outsmart the watch dogs and hoping the tenant wasn't home to catch us in the act. We had heard rumors of other raiders being fired upon with shotguns loaded with salt and pepper. Our butts itched with the very thought. We were often yelled at, "Hey you kids!" or "Come back you little S.O.B.s," but we were never shot at or caught. But you'd be surprised at how fast your legs can move when someone's in hot pursuit. Most of them gave up easily, running out of breath or figuring it wasn't worth the effort for a few garden vegetables. Crunch, crunch, great carrots - right?

We loved to build forts, deep in the woods away from the tracks. They were usually dug into the earth and shored up with random lumber and an old blanket hiding the entrance. These secret hovels, lit by candles, were spartanly furnished with an old wooden chair or two, or a back seat from a car. They were great places to hide out while we read girly books and smoke cigarettes. The allure of the fort was its secret location and our hope that no one would ever discover it. Simple pleasures.

Other forts in the area had hidden entrances. Some had extensive tunnel systems and rear exits for fast escapes in case of invasion - part of the imaginary war games we played. Some of the more affluent kids had their forts equipped with signal flags, binoculars, BB guns, spare clothes for disguises, shovels, flashlights, dirty picture magazines and, maybe a pint of whiskey, "Ugggggh." Occasionally, a railroad tramp would discover one and settle in and that took care of that!

Tramps, bums and hobos made their homes either alongside the tracks or inside the boxcars, hidden behind boxes or stacks of hay. They cooked inside the cars and rode the rails from city to city, getting their food from the fields and orchards that they passed en route. Bums were feared and avoided, as they were usually intoxicated with cheap wine or whiskey, unshaven, and dressed in dirty, mismatched rags.

Tramps and hobos on the other hand, were friendly, always ready to work for a meal, traveling on the rails from camp to camp all over the country. During the depression years, when over a third of America was out of work, it was estimated that about four million people crisscrossed the country on freight trains in search of food, work or adventure. Of that number, more than 250,000 were teenagers - so we weren't doing anything new. We were just a little behind the times.

Since 1900, a group of hobos who called themselves "Tourist Union No. 93," have held a convention each year in Britt, Iowa, called "The National Hobo Convention." They would meet to spin yarns, share their cooking skills, play music, and choose a king. The king would be crowned with a silver two-quart pan with a handle with a tassel hanging off its end. It was their cooking utensil of choice - a can of beans, you know.

It became so popular that the Britt Chamber of Commerce has sponsored the annual event as an allure to tourists since 1934.

My buddy, Chucky and me, met one of these hobo kings one night as we were walking down the rails heading home. He was traveling through our area and had camped for the night under the Dale Street Bridge. When he saw us, he motioned us over to join him around his small campfire. We approached him hesitantly, but he seemed placid enough and he was by himself, and there were two of us, so we felt somewhat safe. We sat down and he held out his hand to shake. He was elated to meet two kids who still considered the rail yards and the tracks their playground. As he ate his pork and beans, heated over the fire in the can, he spilled out his story. We sat enthralled and took it all in.

His name was Rambling Rudy; he was around thirty years old and had been traveling the rails since he was fourteen. He'd been to all 48 states, jailed a few times for vagrancy, and was the 45th king of the hobos. He was traveling west to a camp on the Snake River in Idaho. As we sat and listened, he rolled a cigarette and drank a cup of coffee, made hobo-style with hot water in a tin cup and grounds on the bottom. In between puffs and sips, he played the harmonica. He said it was his favorite instrument as it was easily carried in his pocket. He wailed out some fine blues, the sounds of which have stuck in my head all these years. That night, at that very moment, I promised myself that one day, I too would play the blues harp. Chucky and I sat there for a long time, completely mesmerized with this adventurous soul until he said, "Don't you kids need to get home?" And off we went. Later that night, snug in bed, I fell asleep with his notes ringing in my head.

Besides the bums, we had to be on the lookout for the railroad detectives. " Dicks," we called them. They didn't like anyone flipping their freights and getting a free ride. They walked the tracks and rode the rails looking to nab offenders or hitchhikers. This intensified our adventure, challenging us to be ever more daring, trying different ways to dodge them. The fear of being nabbed drove us, but - not being nabbed - was our reward.

It was kind of a dangerous little game, being illusive, but one that we loved to play. But as we grew older, the sound and motion of riding steel wheels would be replaced by the driving wheels of rubber -automobiles!

As I look back on those days, I realize now how lucky we were to have the freedom to explore our little world of adventures - small, but large for us in that time. ~

CHAPTER 3: HOT RODS

I was very young, only four or five years old, when my proud father first placed me between his legs and put my hands on a steering wheel of his cruiser. From that moment on during our weekly Sunday drives in the country, I would wait patiently for the words, "Come on up son, and help me drive."

Hank, my dad, had a true passion for automobiles, and it rubbed off on me, creating many a pleasurable moment for the two of us. Dad had owned Model T's in his youth, and a Model A or two, but the first one I would get to enjoy was a 1938 Plymouth - the car that took us to our first Minnesota Twins baseball game together.

Before I turned sixteen, the legal age to get a driver's license in 1955, Dad took me out to the massive parking lot at the Minnesota State Fairgrounds for my first test drive. The blacktop was empty as I sat behind the wheel of my father's recently purchased 1948 Plymouth Special Deluxe. I followed his instructions: clutch in, turn the key to "On," press down on the starter, shift to low, ease the clutch out and press the gas pedal carefully, as if it had a egg below it, and with a little squeak of laid rubber, off we'd go. Dad helped me to shift into second gear with a little urging from his leading hand, then down into third, which was easy as pie. Column shifts were called "three on a tree" back then. A few practice drives and I got my license. It was a giant step for me.

From then on it was, "Hey Dad, I'll wash the car if you let me drive it down to the end of the block and back." Driving the Plymouth bonded us even closer together. My love and infatuation of automobiles grew and grew and would become a special hobby of mine throughout my life.

One Friday night, while cruising on my Harley, I spotted a clean little 1935 five-windowed Ford coupe sitting under the lights of a used car lot on University Avenue in Minneapolis. "Tomorrow that little honey is going to be mine," I thought.

I anxiously awaited the morning so I could drag my dad over to the lot to sign on the dotted line. I dreamed of the spinner hubcaps that would go on the wheels, the chrome bell air cleaner on the carburetor, chrome acorn nuts on the heads, slap-on whitewalls and teardrop flared skirts covering the back wheels. Wow! Another young hot-rodder was born into the craze.

The '35 Ford was a good beginning car with a small 85 horsepower V-8 engine, an H-pattern floor stick shift, and a crank down back window so you could talk to the friends that you had tucked into the rear rumble seat. I'd discovered that if they bent into ball, you could close the lid and hide two people within its folds. Now four could watch a drive-in-movie for the price of two. It was a cute coupe, painted back-yard fence green, with bright yellow skirts. I'd just finished detailing it to my taste when disaster struck. A bad wiring job was the culprit. While I was having fun, roller-skating at the rink, it caught fire and became a dark, shriveled, metal skeleton. My heart sank, but not my spirit, as I watched the wrecker haul it off to the junkyard. I was real upset for a while - until I found my '29 Model A roadster. Now I had a project, and my real hot-rodding urge would begin. Powered by a 1948 Mercury flathead, with a Columbia two speed rear-end, sitting on top of a 1939 Ford chassis, and weighing next to nothing, this little puppy could lay a lengthy patch of rubber, its tires squealing all the way. Getting those revs up, popping the clutch and laying a scratch of rubber became one of my favorite fun things to do. It definitely caught everyone's attention, especially the girls - and every now and then - the police!

Officer Skelly, the neighborhood patrol cop, became my worst nightmare. He was rather ugly with a long horse face, capped on each side with elephant-looking ear lobes. He was tall and skinny and had big hands. He would hide from view and lie in wait to catch anyone showing off, spinning his or her wheels while speeding down the street.

One day, while out cruising together in the "A," with my father and my girlfriend, Patty, all squeezed together on that small, skinny bench seat, I approached an arched bridge that went high over the railroad tracks. Looking for that extra thrill, I put the pedal to the metal just as the "A" reached the apex of the arch. Airborne for a moment, the stress was too much for the bolts holding the body to the frame, and when we slammed down we could feel that the body had slipped slightly to one side.

"Boy, we sure got to see her skirt fly on that one!" My comic of a dad said. Later that day, he suggested that I get rid of it before I hurt someone. So, the "A" had to go.

Next, came a 1936 five-window Ford coupe that I had spotted a week before the "A" incident. The '36 sported an Auburn overhead valve conversion kit, a Stromberg 3 carburetor setup with progressive linkage, and exhaust system with a set of headers that gave off a low growling sound.

Putting the pedal to the metal, I found out that the coupe could reach the century mark (100mph) in no time flat, so now I was out to drag race who ever pulled up to me at a stop sign. Unfortunately, one day while I was street dragging a supercharged deuce roadster, I over revved the engine and the '36 blew a rod through its side block when forced to perform beyond its limits. I sold it to another street-rodder who knew how to rebuild engines and off I went in search of a new ride.

My search ended with the purchase of a 1941 Ford business coupe. It was painted robin's egg blue and had little jump seats in the back. This was by far the cleanest vehicle that I had owned up to this date, and it seemed like I was finally stepping up a notch or two.

I soon began to customize the coupe to my satisfaction, never one to leave well enough alone, and the amazing thing is that I did all of this on the small amount of money that I got from delivering newspapers and setting bowling pins. But in those days older cars didn't cost very much - a hundred bucks or two, sometimes less. And if I had to rebuild one, I could always find used parts from old wrecks at the junkyards, no problem.

Now that I had a nice-looking car, my romancing the opposite sex seemed to bounce ahead and parking at night at a "Lovers Lane" became a favorite nightly pastime. Cherokee Park, in West St. Paul, had the most romantic setting. It overlooked the Mississippi River and had big rolling lawns that met the cliff faces high up on a bluff. With a full moon shining on the river below, this spot was very busy, and you were lucky to find a parking spot to squeeze into. You'd turn your headlights off as soon as you pulled into the parking area, so as not to shine the lovers already there. It was a fun experience - those were the days!

Oops, now guess what? Yup, I got in an accident with the coupe - unfortunately. One afternoon while driving my girlfriend Patty home, my left hand doing the steering and my right arm around her, cheek rubbing cheek, inattentive driving I think the ticket I got said. Anyway, I t-boned a chicken farmer's pickup truck on its way to market. The impact caused a quite a commotion, with chickens busting out of their smashed cages and flying all over the place, squawking loudly as they ran around in confusion. Crates of eggs were destroyed and some of the eggs were crazily rolling down the street. The poor farmer was in a daze, and my crumpled hood was looking him in the face.

What a scene that was! People came running out of their houses, quickly gathering up all the unbroken eggs, grabbing what chickens they could catch, and then they just vanished. We were in the poorer side of town, and it was like a scene straight out of a movie. When the police arrived, there was not a single witness to interview - they had all disappeared with the spoils. After the accident the coupe never acted the same, it heated up; it rattled and just became unreliable, so off it went.

Enter my first 1940 Ford, a two-door deluxe, I say first, because this was one of the seven 40' Fords I would own. It was my ticket into another part of the hot-rodding world—the hot rod club. So, remember the black leather jacket that I bought when I got the Harley? Now the back of it was hand-painted with a 1932 Ford deuce roadster, along with my new club's name, the "Devil's Deputies." The '40 soon received a new paint job of vivid turquoise blue (God, I loved that color) over its freshly customized, smoothly leaded, trunk lid and bull-nosed hood. Hanging from the rear bumper with two chains, the embossed aluminum "Devil's Deputies" club plaque swung happily between dual chrome-tipped pipes. It was a statement of belonging and a sign of the camaraderie between guys who loved hot rods.

Every Tuesday night, at the Como Park pavilion, the "Devil's Deputies, would hold their meetings. After hashing over new projects on each other's cars and telling fun stories, we would line up and cruise down Lexington Avenue to the main drag, University Avenue. Then we'd all cruise up University to the local hangout, Porky's Drive-In, where girls on roller skates, delivered hamburgers and malts on trays that hung from our front doors. We sat in the back, munching, while we showed off our wheels to the endless parade of other cars that passed by in front of us. The whole back row of parking spaces was reserved for our club on Tuesday nights. It was a real gas just being there. We loved having something to do and a special place to meet and eat.

Other clubs in the area frequently joined the "Devil's Deputies" at Porky's. The "Pharaohs" from the Ramsey School District, had a few more "bucks" in their wallets than most of us, and had the latest, newer machines that were extensively customized. They also had the most expensive and sexiest paint jobs. They sat very low to the ground and bore the name, LEAD SLEDS.

The "Stokers," another neighborhood group had the most members, almost thirty of them, and they had the hottest cars - built more for the drag strip then the street.

The father of one member of the "Stokers" owned a large garage on Nicollet Island, under the Hennepin Avenue Bridge, that crossed over the Mississippi River. He was my good friend. His name was, Doug Wally, and he was nicknamed "Dougie Dynamo" mainly because of his never-ending energy. He was the president of the "Stokers" car club and he drove a '32 Deuce roadster, just like the one painted on the back of my leather jacket.

The "deuce" was a real smooth ride - painted a bright two-toned white and antacid pink, (you know - the pill) - quite shocking, to say the least. The engine, a 1957 Oldsmobile J-2, came stock from the factory with three Stromberg carburetors, but Dougie, always seeking more power, more "cubes" (cubic inches) for that ultimate surge, tore down the engine when he bought it, ported and relieved the piston chambers and completely balanced all its moving parts. He also threw in a 3/4 racing cam, then reassembled it and stuffed it under the hood of the Deuce. I was there at the garage the day he fired it up and observed the inaugural test-drive. I watched as the roadster screamed down the river road, growing smaller and smaller until Dougie and his ride disappeared from sight, but the exhaust pipes could still be heard - rumbling in the distance.

One Sunday a month, us local boys could grudge race at the Bloomington drag strip located just outside of Minneapolis. Some of our rival car clubs would also get together to settle their differences. It was a good thing, as it really was too dangerous for some of the hotter cars to drag race from the stoplights. For five dollars a run, we'd line up our cars two abreast and patiently wait our turn to go off the line. It was like a scene from Rebel without a Cause. I always thought I was pretty cool while waiting my turn. But every time I approached the line and revved up my engine, my clutch foot would shake so badly that you would've thought I had a case of palsy. My heart would beat fast and my mouth would go dry, but, as soon as the starter leaped into the air and dropped his flag, I'd pop the clutch, slam the gas pedal to the floor, and speed shift through the gears, for the race to the finish. I never did beat anyone to the end of the line. I always seemed to get "nosed" out. But - aaahhh - that was okay, I still had a hell of a lot of fun.

Stillwater Speedbowl, an oval half-mile dirt track in Stillwater, Minn., was where we raced jalopies. Jalopies were stripped down late 30's and 40's coupes and two doors, their bare bodies racing on fender less, hoodless, glassless frames. The windshield had welded screening to protect the driver from flying dirt clogs.

My friend, Val Kresback and his father, had an auto repair garage half a block down from my house; it was a dilapidated wood and tin structure, which was stuck in the alleyway, across from our church. It always seemed cold and dark inside, and it smelled like old used oil. The floor was crusted with tarred blacktop, caked with years of grease. Dirty benches covered with gasoline-soaked parts lined the walls. The small office was stacked with old billings, parts orders, unopened mail, a spittoon, and a smoke blackened, old-fashioned coffee maker sitting on top of an ancient wood stove.

Completely opposite from all the confusion and dirt, there was always a stack of fresh laundered, blue-black striped work coveralls, wrapped in brown paper, tied up with a brown string. These coveralls, along with matching folding cloth hats, were the mechanic's uniforms. Every Monday morning they would slip into a fresh uniform with pride to begin their week's labor.

Val, like his father, was small in stature; they were true grease monkeys and jalopy dirt track racers. His father always had a smile upon his face and a good attitude. Val was always coiffed with the most perfect flattop hairdo, with longer side fenders, all slicked back with Dippity Do, the styling gel of the time.

They prided themselves in their profession. They were hard workers and they would spend all day on customers' cars until five or six o' clock, have a quick snack, and then would stay late into the night slaving on their stockcars, readying them for the weekend races.

On Saturday afternoons my dad and I would help Val and his dad tow their iron steeds to the races at Stillwater. We would assist them a little in the pits and then go to the grandstand to watch the action.

The races never got started until early evening, so the last race, the trophy run, always ran under the lights. The cars, with their engines roaring and radiators steaming, would chase each other around the tight-circled bowl until one of them would get the checkered flag. Many were smashed up or rolled over in the process. This was a poor man's sport, but it was exciting and many a spectator choked on his hot dog or spilled his Coca-Cola on the person sitting in front of him while exuberantly watching the action.

Val, a natural at sixteen, often won his race. He would drive his sometimes limping, banged-up jalopy to the award stand, crawl out of the driver's side window opening, (the doors were always welded shut in case of a rollover.) His face blackened with dirt, grease and soot from the dusty race track, flashing the biggest white-toothed smile you could ever imagine, he would leap up to the awards stage, accept his prize and welcome the kiss on the cheek from that week's trophy queen. Afterwards, at the pizza parlor, there would be a lot of whooping and hollering, and "Boy, did you see that!?"

Blowing an engine was a real drag, and a spare re-built one would have to be installed for next week's race. I remember spending many an evening helping Val and his dad swap an engine. It involved disassembling the radiator, headers, transmission, motor mounts, and the wiring to get it ready for the hoist and the pull out. A new engine would then be dropped back in.

There were always one or two spare short blocks around in various stages of rebuilding. Val and I, with help from his dad and older brother, could pull a motor swap in a little less than four hours. All in all, it was a fun learning experience, a talent I would find useful in later life.

I always had one car that my parents knew about, but what they didn't know was that I had others stashed all over the place. At one time I had a '40 Ford coupe as my driver and a '48 Plymouth four-door hidden down the alley, that I used for racing around the back roads. At Val's dad's garage, I had a channeled-down 1928 roadster I was working on, another funky '40 Ford four-door, and a non-running '39 Ford Junker. I was always taking something from one and putting it on another or trading up or trading down - (we did a lot of that.) In those days, insurance was not a concern, and hardly any of the cars were registered in my name, except the one I drove. License plates traveled back and forth from car bumper to car bumper. Life was so easy, uncomplicated, and innocent back in the '50s.

Junkyards back then were virtual treasure chests, holding row upon row of cars, so many that some were stacked up on each other. They drew my car buddies and me like a giant magnet. During the light of day when they were open, we would scope out the parts we needed, buy what we could afford and scheme how to get the ones we couldn't. That's when the term, "Midnight Auto Supply" entered our vocabulary - a very dangerous means of appropriation.

Most junkyards were protected at night by fierce, teeth-baring, hair-raising, growling mongrels. Before you dared to climb over the fence, they somehow had to be preoccupied.

Our junkyard of choice, Ace Auto Parts, was the biggest and most spread out, located along the railroad tracks at the end of a road down near Rice Street. We became very efficient in our looting of this place, small stuff mostly, but it still took careful planning and at least three guys to pull off a safe job.

My buddy Punchy, chosen because he could cool the vicious beasts with his soft convincing voice and a bag of smelly old rib bones, would go to the opposite end and occupy the dogs' attention. When he thought it was safe, he would whistle softly to us and we would climb the fence on the other end and rush to grab what we had staked out earlier in the day.

Sometimes, we still had to unscrew or unbolt a part and that created too much noise, making the dogs look up from the bones in front of them. When that happened, Punchy would send out a loud warning whistle that the dogs were forgetting about the meat and thinking about returning to their job. We never thought twice, we quickly dropped what we were doing and beat feet. We always planned a quick escape route over the fence before we got the pants torn off us. And we never tried to sneak into a junkyard that had Dobermans. We knew those black and brown attack animals with the yellow-gold eyes were seriously scary. After a few close calls, we decided this sport wasn't much fun any more, and we started purchasing our needs from the local auto store. ~

CHAPTER 4: WEST SIDE STORY REVISITED

Every city has its gangs, and growing up in St. Paul, Minnesota, I had to deal almost daily with the guys that belonged to the Deibel Drugstore gang. They usually hung out at the soda fountain after school and on into the night. They weren't really a bad bunch, but they were annoying and were to be avoided, if at all possible. Big bad bullies they were, their two main threats, humiliation and bodily harm. But you could buy your way out if you had a spare nickel, dime or quarter in your pocket.

I didn't mind paying my passage out of my paper route earnings but, if I were on an errand for my mother and carrying the milk money, I would have to choose an alternative route to reach my destination.

I had to sneak across the street, run through the neighbor's yard, cross the alley, jump a fence, go through another yard, run across Thomas Avenue, climb a hill and go through yet another yard just to reach the alleyway that led up to the back door of the store. This maneuver was reversed in order to get back home - all for a gallon of milk, a loaf of bread and a pound of margarine.

When you traveled outside of your immediate neighborhood and entered someone else's turf, you had to play it cool. If you had a friend who lived in the area, you usually would be allowed safe passage. Otherwise, you had to hope and pray no one would take any notice of you as an intruder. Luckily, since I was a member of the Devil's Deputies hot rod club, with a very cool "short," (another name for a car in those days, as it took only a "short" time to get from point A to point B,) I was rarely hassled.

The bigger gangs were all older guys and they meant business. The Hell's Angels motorcycle club were bad news in the '50s, as The Wild One movie mildly showed. Marlon Brando was a pussycat compared to what some of them were really like.

If a girl wanted to be included in the club, her initiation was that she had to have sex with every member. Only then was she allowed to be someone's old lady. These gals were tough cookies, dressed in leathers and marked with tattoos. You were better off just stepping out of their way. Often though, they would lure some innocent dude, ("Hey baby, come here, I got something for you!") into some dark alley where he would be ambushed and relieved him of his valuables.

I got involved in one big gang war, when a girl from the West Side was picked up downtown one night and raped by one of the guys from Frog Town, my turf. There was going to be hell to pay.

Minnehaha Park was designated as the spot where the two gangs would meet and rumble. It was a huge park with lots of open space right next to the railroad tracks. Discreetly, the word was passed around, and the Frog Town boys began to prepare for the invasion onto our home turf.

Around 9:30, they started to come in droves. Some came in their "shorts," others arrived by a slow-moving freight train that was passing through, hopping off at the edge of the prairie. More came on motorcycles or loaded in the back of pickup trucks. It looked like it was going to be one hell of a fight!

In the dark we waited for the invaders to leave their cars and trucks unattended so we could slash all their tires so they couldn't escape. But the cops came before we could, which I was thankful for - I really didn't want to be bad that night.

The cops converged on the scene from all directions, their red, white and blue lights flashing, and their sirens wailing. Pandemonium erupted as guys from both gangs tried to escape. Tires squealed and rubber burnt. As we lay hidden behind the bushes across the street from the park, my buddies and I watched the excitement; thankful we didn't need to get involved.

The next morning, news of the event was splashed all over the front page of the St. Paul Pioneer Press. It was also reported that the Frog Town boy responsible for the incident had been stabbed and was in critical condition. Justice had been served and everyone laid low for a long time after that. Another lesson in life learned.

As I grew older, I belonged to a small gang of my own, formed with my different buddies from neighborhoods all over. There was Val Kresback from the west side, Moose Monahan from Lake McCarran, Bob "Punchy" Miller and Bob Hanson from Frog Town, the boys in the Devils Deputies hot rod club, and Butch Flanagan from the south side. With this territorial might, we were pretty much left alone, free to travel at will on both sides of the Mississippi - safety in numbers. ~

CHAPTER 5: ART OF THE CHASE

Ahhhhh - high school, the fun times, those years were precious, a time that we would forever hold dear to our hearts. Our first loves, our very own music - Rock and Roll - the songs that we would never forget, and friends - who at the time - we thought would last forever. Then there were the sporting events we loved to cheer for - and oh, let's not forget - the PROM!

I never excelled in my studies, squeaking by with a high C average was effort enough for me. Girls, cars, and tipping the fun scale were my top priorities. Scholastic achievement, hopefully, would come later in life.

Friday night was teen night at the famous Prom Ballroom on University Avenue and, with no school the next day, my buddies and I prepped up to WOW the chicks, so we would head over to Minneapolis to score a couple of six-packs.

Hennepin Avenue, sometimes known as Bum's Row, had down-and-out winos always out panhandling for a bottle of red. We would try to find one of these characters near a liquor store and offer him a few bucks to make a purchase for us. In all the times that we pulled this caper, we only chased one bum trying to get away with our money. Needless to say, with four angry teenagers in pursuit, he soon gave up.

Stout Malt Liquor was our drink of choice - a strong beer that came in small green and silver cans. "Three gulpers," we called them, as that was all it took to finish one off. It was powerful - at close to 12% alcohol content.

After making our score, we'd head back down University Avenue to the Prom Ballroom for the teen night dance. We'd park way in the back of the large parking lot in the shadows. While the radio blasted out the top hits of the day - Elvis Presley's "Hound Dog," Screaming Willie Jon's "Bad Boy" or Jerry Lee Lewis's "Great Balls of Fire"- we'd line up the small cans on the dashboard, pull their tabs, and chug them down. Three beers each would leave us light-headed with a good beer buzz. Finished, we'd toss the empties in one of the green dumpsters in the parking lot. Then we'd get our tickets and sashay into the massive ballroom looking for action.

Once inside, we'd pop some Sen-Sen breath fresheners into our mouths. Then we'd strut our stuff, looking for single girls to dance with.

Some of the hottest acts of the time played at the Prom ballroom. Upcoming stars like Jerry Lee Lewis, Gene Vincent and the Big Bopper knocked out tunes, and the dance floor was always crowded. The "Chicken" was the latest dance craze, and I was born with shuffling feet - and like Elvis - I could throw in some sexy hip movements. There were times I could gather as many as five or six girls in a circle around me, and "Chicken" it out with all of them, stopping the rest of the dancers on the dance floor as they gathered around the circle to cheer us on, clapping and bouncing to the rhythm. With my black slacks, pink shirt, and perfectly coifed pompadour duck-tailed hairdo, I cut quite a rug out there under the lights, winning many a young lady's interest with my crazy moves. At least one or two names and their phone numbers, written on a matchbook cover or napkin, found their way into my pocket.

As Billy Joel was to one day sing, "Catholic girls wait much too late," I passed up the girls I went to school with. Instead, I liked to meet girls from the public high schools; they seemed to be a little looser.

Roller-skating rinks were also great spots to impress the young ladies. Melody Roller Rink, a giant Quonset hut converted airplane hangar, was my favorite with its polished oak floors, and an impressive huge pipe organ for music, while we all skated along.

With my black leather skates, equipped with flashing lighted wheels, I commanded many a smooth move, showing off, in hopes of being picked out of the crowd by some beauty during the "ladies' choice" skate. I usually won out - thank you!

Another one of the favorite places to woo gals was at the drive-in movies, otherwise known as the "Passion Pits." A good romantic movie could help inspire some heavy petting, and soon the windows would fog up, especially in the cool Minnesota late summers. The movie outside would become a blur and its image would be blocked out of sight and mind. Being part contortionist really helped out on this casting couch. You hoped no one recognized your car and came tapping on your window to spoil the mood.

Car hopping was another favorite pastime at the drive-ins, especially if you didn't have a date. Some cars sat empty, while others filled up with guys and gals hopping from car to car. Many a new romance started out this way.

My first real love was Patricia Shelling, who I met one Sunday afternoon, ice-skating at an indoor rink. My friend Punchy and I noticed two cute blondes skating together, one dressed rather plain in a blue sweater and plaid skirt, the other in a tight pink fuzzy sweater.

The one in the pink sweater caught both our eyes, and we raced to see who would get to her first. Punchy won that toss, and I reluctantly skated off with plainer of the two. But, as it worked out, the girl in the sweater, with the rather large boobs, turned out to be only thirteen years old while her sister Patricia was sixteen. A romance bloomed that afternoon and Patricia and I would discover for the first-time what love was.

A year later, when Patricia turned 17, she and her family moved to the South Side, where they opened a small neighborhood store. Punchy and I had to travel onto dangerous turf to date our girlfriends, and we soon found out that we would have to fight for the right to be accepted into the Roosevelt High school district.

The initiation rites were held in the empty lot located behind the store. I had to fight Butch Flanagan, who was also interested in Patricia. The rules were that the winner would get the girl and the other would leave. Patricia didn't want me to lose, and she made the other gang members promise to be fair and not butt in if Butch looked like he was getting the worst of it. Needless to say, I was scared shitless. When Butch attacked me, I quickly put a headlock on him and a scissor lock with my legs around his mid-section. I hung on for dear life as if I were riding a wild bull.

Butch hit me with hard short punches over and over, but I gritted my teeth, held on tight and squeezed harder. He threw me on the ground, rolling around trying to break my vice-like grip, but I just squeezed harder. Soon he was exhausted. Blood started to come out of his nose, and he started to gasp and wheeze, but I still held on, not about to let loose of him. Feeling him weaken, I let loose with one hand and began to bang his head into the ground. Much to my surprise and relief, he yelled a muffled cry, "I give, I give up, you win, and she's yours!"

"Promise?" I asked, looking for reassurance.

"I promise, I promise. You win!"

We got off the ground, laughed, shook hands and became friends. Punchy and I were never bothered in that neighborhood again. Patricia and I started going steady, and she remained my girlfriend for the duration of high school.

Going steady, back in those days, was like wearing a feather in your cap. A couple going steady were idolized, having found young love together. Your popularity seemed to rise, due to the fact you were no longer available. You were admired, somewhat envied and often whispered about. ("Don't you know? They're going steady!")

Those of us who were going steady had special codes to announce the fact to our schoolmates, while keeping it secret from our parents and teachers who frowned on such things. If you were Seniors, the girl would wear the boy's graduation ring on her finger, the band would have a wad of chewing gum stuck to the bottom edge of it with string wrapped around. And if her boyfriend was athletic, she would wear his letter jacket, which was more obvious and generally more accepted by the adults.

I attended St. Agnes High School, a Catholic parochial school taught by Notre Dame nuns. We wore uniforms. The boys wore dark blue pants, light blue shirts and dark blue ties, black shoes with blue socks. The girls were attired in dark blue jumpers with a white blouse, and white socks and blue and white saddle shoes. There were many rules and regulations at the school, designed,

I suppose, to keep us "Aggies" in line and prepare us for college and later life.

One of those rules was that if you attended the high school prom, the boys weren't allowed to bring girls from other schools as their dates. The girls, on the other hand, were allowed to invite outsiders. Discrimination? I think so, it was a stupid rule, but this situation gave me an opportunity to pull off one of the highlights of my senior year.

A week or so before the Senior prom, as Eddie Baker and I were standing next to each other at the urinals in the boy's bathroom, we talked about how unfair it seemed. "This is bullshit," he whined, "We can't take our girlfriends to the prom because they don't go to this damn school, but the girls can bring their boyfriends from no matter where!"

"Yeah, and you know why, don't you?" I said.

"Give me a clue."

"Because most of the girls have boyfriends outside of this school, who attend St. Thomas Academy, and our girlfriends go to public schools. I think the nuns don't want us to bring in any "riff-raff."

"I never thought of it in that way, but you're right now that I think about it."

"I got it handled, though," I said.

"How's that?" Eddie asked.

"Well, the other day, Sister Augustus, my homeroom teacher, told me that if I took Mary Jean to the prom, she'd give me an A in homeroom study and religion class."

"Ya gonna do it? You'd take her to the prom?"

"I think so. I told Patty about it and she said it wouldn't bother her and, besides, it would make my mother happy. I know Mary Jean's friends would appreciate my gesture even though they know it's only that - a gesture."

Eddie snapped his finger and thumb up in the air next to his forehead like he was turning a light bulb on.

"Hey, you just gave me an idea. How's about I ask Ginny, Mary Jean's girl-friend, to the Prom. I'm sure she doesn't have a date yet either, and we can double date."

"Cool man. Let's take it one step further. Why don't we go super casual, you know, like no tuxedos, just our Levis, T-shirts, and leather jackets."

"You mean, like rebels?"

"Yea, kind of like James Dean, and I'll comb my hair into a pompadour on top with a ducktail back." I said.

"I dare you," Eddie challenged.

"And I double dare you," I challenged back.

We shook hands to seal the pact and, with our arms around each other, we laughingly left the lavatory.

For all of the next week leading up to the Prom night, we quietly told our schoolmates about our protest. It soon turned into the Senior Dare of the Year, and we were now truly committed. The rumor traveled into the girl's bathroom, and our dates found out about it, but they weren't offended. In fact, they thought it was cool. It even traveled as far as Sister Augustus's ears. I know that for a fact because the day before the Prom I saw her shake her index finger at me, indicating our naughtiness, but with a smile on her lips.

That Saturday night I "duded" myself up in a pair of fresh Levis, a nice clean white T-shirt, blue suede shoes and my black leather jacket. I combed my hair somewhat like Elvis's, with a high pompadour in the front and a nice tight ducktail line down the back. I was checking myself out in the mirror, looking very cool, when my mother walked through the door.

"Donald, just what do you think you're doing?" she asked, her body blocking the doorway, her hands planted firmly on her hips.

"Going to the Prom," I replied.

"Dressed like that?"

"Well it's kind of hard to explain, Mom. You see it's a small protest, because I'm not allowed to take my girlfriend to our Prom because she doesn't go to our school."

"Donnie, Donnie (she always used those words when she wasn't quite happy with me,) you are the renegade of the family." She shook her head back and forth in desperation, turned and left.

"Whew!" I said to myself. I thought for sure she was going to go through the roof and raise hell with me, but as I had grown older, she slowly relinquished her control of me. She had been a hard taskmaster.

Dad was working over time, so I didn't have to deal with him. He'd already left me his car to use, so I was ready to boogie. I went to the refrigerator and took out Mary Jean's corsage, still fresh in its small plastic container. Condensation had deposited little silver droplets of moisture on the underside of the lid nourishing the pinkish white flower, its crimson colored nodules in the center standing straight up at attention.

"Bye, Mom." I said, as I left the house.

"Have fun and drive careful," she said.

"Thanks, I will." The screen door slammed behind me.

I hopped behind the wheel of my dad's two-toned green 1955 Ford four-door, started the engine and pulled away from the curb. A giddy feeling ran through my body as I anticipated the evening's upcoming event. I arrived at Mary Jean's at 7:30, a half - hour before the dance began. I'd never met her parents and wondered how they would accept my casual appearance. Walking up to the front door, I did a final primp, took a deep swallow and rapped upon the door. Immediately, the door swung open, and there was Mary Jean's father - bigger than life. He stood there, one hand holding a Meerschaum pipe. The ivory bowl was carved in the form of an eagle's claw grasping an egg. Extending out of its base, like a twig from a tree, was a long-curved stem that swooped up to where it was clenched in the right side of his mouth. He puffed out a small amount of grayish white smoke as he spoke.

"Aren't you a little underdressed young man?"

"Not really, sir, I'm dressed in the uniform of the days. It's everyone else who'll be in costume tonight."

"Ummmmm," he pondered that one, took another puff and said, "You kids are just a little too rebellious these days, but - I remember when I was young - oh, here's Mary Jean now. My, doesn't she look pretty?"

"Hi Don. Oh, God, look at you, you're a regular hipster. How Cool!," she exclaimed, tossing her head back in laughter. I found out about the Senior Dare through the grapevine, you know, and I think it's really a cool thing you're doing, you rebel, you. Dad and Mom know, the whole school knows, and in fact, I think the St. Paul Pioneer Press is going to be there to cover the event.

"Oh?" I said, "I thought it was going to be a surprise."

"No, Yeager man, you've been found out," her dad said to me as he took another pull on the "claw" through smiling lips.

"Well, now that it's out in the open, I'll have no worries," I sighed.

Mary J's mother, who had been quietly standing behind her, reached out and took the corsage from my hand. I'd forgotten I even had it. She pulled it out of its container, and using the long straight pin it came with, pinned it on the right side of her daughter's dress. She gave her a kiss on the cheek, put her hand in mine, patted my shoulder and said, "You kids have fun tonight." With that, she shooed us out the door. We skipped down the sidewalk to the car feeling very devious.

That night turned out to be one of the best evenings of my high school career. And that adolescent practical joke got me voted in as the "Most Humorous Senior" in the 1957 yearbook.

Getting back to Patricia, we parted ways after my graduation. She still had a year left in high school and was pinned by her school's football quarterback, leaving me in the cold. I guess it wasn't meant to be. ~

CHAPTER 6: THE ESCAPE

After graduating from high school in June 1957, I still had no idea of what I wanted to do with my life. My first job was as a file clerk, and policy printer at State Farm Insurance's home office. However, little if any challenges presented themselves there, especially to one as active and creative as I was. I stuck it out for a year and found out that joining the ranks of the white-collar working force at the age of eighteen was not for me. I soon became bored and mischievous.

Wandering away from my workstation during slack periods, I started fraternizing with the secretaries, policy writers, file clerks, and other ladies that literally carpeted the massive office space. I became known as a free spirit, rather than a company man, and the ladies elected me as their communicator, passing on to me the gossip, rumors, and jokes, for me in turn to pass on to others. My supervisor caught me one day in the act of reproducing a batch of smutty office jokes. I was reprimanded and banned to a far dark corner and watched very closely. My freedom had been jeopardized. Feeling trapped and controlled prompted me to look elsewhere for employment. Besides, working in a window-less building and wearing a white shirt and tie every day, certainly was not my style.

My interest in cars quickly landed me my second job. Now employed by the Ford Motor Manufacturing Company, rebuilding generators and starters, I was introduced to the middle America realm of the working-class generation. Soon I was brown bagging it, punching the clock at 8 am, working side by side with a bunch of good ole' boys and eagerly awaiting the 10 o'clock break. Two hours more, and noon would arrive, and the whistle to stop work would blow. We would shut down our machines, lay down our tools, and rush outside to the loading docks where we each had our favorite spot to lounge while eating our lunches. Each lunch bucket and brown bag held various sandwiches, fruits, cakes and cookies. Sometimes Bill's or Joe's would appear more appetizing to me and lunches would be traded.

"Oh no, not baloney again, trade yah for yer egg salad." (Minnesota twang.)

A few months went by, and this dirty, menial, repetitious job also lost its luster. I became robot-like. Soon, the only thing to look forward to was the paycheck at the end of the week. Bob "Punchy" Miller, my running mate, was experiencing a similar dilemma. We were developing bad smoking and drinking habits, constantly getting into trouble, chasing after girls and left with little or no direction. One Saturday afternoon, while cruising the downtown area, we saw a recruiting poster of Uncle Sam, whose pointed finger seemed to beckon us. "I WANT YOU" was the message. Punchy and I looked at each other and in unison said, "Why not? Let's go!"

We parked my street rod and walked down the sidewalk to the long stairs leading up to the massive doors of the Federal Building. Pushing the steel doors apart, we entered its hallowed halls. Recruiting offices bordered both sides of a long hallway. We slowly walked past each entryway, closely scrutinizing each poster displayed. The Army was still drafting, so we quickly eliminated the foot soldiers. The Marines seemed too polished, and strictly regimented. Besides, we had heard stories of the harshness of their boot camp at Parris Island, where a recruit had recently died. Thanks, but no thanks.

The Navy, in comparison, looked inviting. Leaping out of the poster, a striding sailor appeared, a cocked white hat atop a smiling face. His bell-bottom, thirteen-button tailor-made trousers snapped in the wind as he stepped forward. "Sailing the oceans, a girl in every port, shur'nuff partner but, heck, looks like they're closed for lunch," I said to Bob.

Across the hallway, an Air Force sergeant, leaning on the side of his open door, noticed us meandering around and summoned us in with a wave of his hand. After twenty-five minutes filled with promises of "Up, up, and away into the wild blue yonder," we had visions of ourselves in smart blue uniforms with polished black brimmed caps displaying winged insignia crowning our heads. We were soon added to the recruiting list of the United States Air Force, and we were to report in two weeks.

Shaking the hand of the recruiter, we skipped down the hallway to large double doors that led back out to the street. Pushing them wide open, we went racing down the long staircase whooping with glee, slapping each other on the back, exclaiming, "All right man, all right, cool man, yahoo!"

Now, what to do for two weeks? Monday morning, I called my supervisor at the Ford plant and officially quit my job.

"I've joined the service, see ya!" I said, rather cocky and proud of myself. He wasn't impressed. I thought, "Hey, I'm starting a new career. Might as well take the next two weeks off."

And then the trouble began. ~

CHAPTER 7: TROUBLE

The short vacation that followed became a turning point in my life. I no longer held a valid driver's license, having had it suspended a few weeks before for drag racing and other traffic violations. To get around I used my bicycle and depended upon my friends for transportation. It was okay for a while but grew old with the passing of the first week.

To kill time, I started hanging out with Tom Schmaltz, a recent acquaintance I'd met when he first joined the Devils Deputies car club. He was a tall lanky guy and loved to talk shop with me. His father owned a junkyard and mechanics shop down near Rice Street, where we used to get off the trains when we were hitching them.

He'd been working on an old 1934 Ford coupe that sat way back in a corner of the yard. It didn't have any windows, floorboards or fenders, but the engine was still in it, so we pulled up our shirtsleeves and went to work.

Three evenings later with the tires re-inflated, army surplus aircraft bucket seats welded to the frame, pieces of plywood inserted for floorboards, exhaust coming straight out of the block and one hot wire leading from the battery to the coil, we cranked her up. She came alive in an instant, hitting on all eight, but slightly out of time, causing blue flames and smoke to come blasting loudly out of the exhaust ports.

The power waited to be unleashed with the release of the eleven-inch clutch, passing through the three-speed floor transmission, reawakening the slick tires mounted on the recently installed 1946 Mercury rear end. Oh, we had a ball, racing that fender-less, hood-less hot rod around and around and up and down the junkyard's aisles. Soon, that game became boring, also.

"Let me sneak it out on the side road alone," I said.

"All right," Tom said. "Give her hell!" and he hopped out.

Out the gate I went, tires smoking a blue white cloud as they laid rubber on the smooth pavement. As I recklessly spun around the corner and onto Minnehaha Avenue, a black and white cop cruiser immediately spotted me. A siren started wailing and a flashing red light lit up as the '57 Ford gave chase. "Oh, shit," I thought. "If they catch me, I'm in deep trouble." Driven by fear and adrenaline, I increased my speed, trying to outrun him. Stupid!

Out into the prairie I raced, over the railroad tracks, down the opposite embankment, where I thought I would be able to evade my pursuers. But the police had radioed for backup. A second patrol car appeared up ahead. It was getting dark, and I had no lights to guide me. I thought it would be wise to abandon the car in the deep brush of a gully and run for my life. I dumped it as quick as I could, but I was spotted almost immediately. The patrol car slammed on its brakes, and I could hear the siren winding down. I ran, and behind me I could hear a door open, then pounding footsteps following in my fleeing path.

"Hey, kid, stop! You're only making it worse for yourself." Closer, and closer, the man in blue came.

My mind was racing, "What to do?" Then I remembered an evasive tactic I had seen in a movie. I stumbled and dropped to the ground, just as an arm reached out to grab me. The cop tripped over my body, and sprawled out on all fours, smashing his face into the dirt.

"Jesus Christ," I thought, "I'm really in trouble now."

Scrambling to my feet, I started to run in the opposite direction. I only got off one step before he grabbed me by my ankle. Terrified, I tried to shake off his grip, accidentally kicking my captor in the process. He held me firmly, and I found myself face-to-face on the ground with a very angry servant of the law.

"Don't ever try to out run an ex-Marine, you little shit," he said angrily.

Holding me firmly by the scruff of the neck of my gathered t-shirt, he pushed me into the back seat of the cruiser. Twenty minutes later at the police station, the bars clanged behind me. Allowed one phone call, I called Punchy, explained my situation, and told him to contact my parents and tell them we were going camping together and we'd be home in a couple of days. I told Punch that they'd probably let me out in a day or two when I explained to them that I was joining the Air Force the next week.

Of course, my parents didn't believe a word Bob told them and soon got the truth out of him. And the police, they didn't give a rat's ass that I was joining the service. I was being charged with driving without a license, eluding an officer, resisting arrest and assault and battery to an arresting officer. The next morning, I was loaded into the paddy wagon they called the Black Maria and hauled off to municipal court. They did things fast in those days, no lawyers involved. You did something wrong, you went to court, you were sentenced, and you did your time. Period, amen, end of story!

When my case was called, I was escorted to the bench. The charges were read, and I was asked how I pleaded. Hoping for leniency, I replied, "Guilty, your honor, sir, but . . . "

"No buts, son. Ninety days," he said, slamming his gavel on the desk. "Next case."

"But, Judge," came a pleading, voice from the back of the courtroom.

Oh, oh, it was my Mom.

"Please, ma'am, approach the bench," he ordered.

A hurried whispered conference was held, my mother's tears softening the judge some as she asked for his forgiveness and encouraged him to let me off since I would be joining the Air Force with my high school buddy within the next few days.

"Sixty days," said the judge.

"But, Judge." This time it was I pleading, thinking that if it worked for my mother, well . . .

"All right, thirty days and not a day less." The judge voiced his final verdict and off to the Como Park Workhouse I went. ~

CHAPTER 8: JAIL HOUSE BLUES

Iron gates clanged behind me, and I was escorted into the inner chambers of the walled prison. I was about to experience a rude awakening to another way of life. Hell of a thing to be discovered by an eighteen-year-old youth. I was stripped of my street clothes and issued bright orange, prison coveralls, already stamped with the number 901.

Entering the main cell block area, I was greeted with humiliating catcalls, whistles, and shouted profanities, as I was paraded in front of the cells on the way up to the third tier and cell number 32. As the sliding iron door closed behind me, I took in my new home, an 8-foot-by-6-foot cell.

My first night was frightening. I couldn't sleep. Strange noises kept coming from the cells around me. Sexual invitations were whispered, coming from all directions.

"Hey, pretty boy, we're going to get you!"

"Oh, dear God, what did I do to deserve this?" I thought, as I nervously waited for the morning to come.

In the next few days I became more acquainted with prison life. I discovered the hole (solitary confinement) was a place to avoid being thrown into. Then I met some older inmates, who were seemingly concerned individuals and who took me, the younger one, under their wings. They were the fatherly types who put it upon themselves to protect us, the innocents, from the gang members that grouped around ready to pounce upon the newbies to see what we were made of.

The food wasn't bad, and kitchen duty was one of the few safe jobs available. I was soon put to work peeling the outsides off cabbages, dumping them in huge boiling pots of water, where they were slowly steamed down and processed into sauerkraut.

Entertainment was almost non-existent. There were a few inmates who had their own radios, so there was always music of some sort, drifting through the echoing halls. No television, no exercise yard, only a card room where the guys gambled for cigarettes, and whatever. Fill in the blanks!

Luckily, Lamar Pensile, the warden of the work farm, was a professional bowler, as was my Uncle Igs. Within two days of my confinement, I was transferred to the trustees' cellblock unit, thanks to my uncle's comradeship with Lamar. Now I was allowed to go outside under guard and do maintenance chores. I got to eat earlier, and I could lock myself up in the evening when I was ready to go to bed. We had a nice shower area and our own toilets in a larger cell. It was reassuring and being separated from the more hardened criminals was a welcome relief.

Five days into my thirty-day sentence, I received an unexpected visitor. Knowing it wasn't my parents or girlfriend, I anxiously waited for the door to be opened to the visiting booth. After seating myself in front of the small viewing window, I was surprised to find a man in uniform seated on the opposite side. Picking up the telephone that allowed the two of us to communicate, the Navy Chief Recruiting Petty Officer spoke first.

"Hi, son," he said. "My name is Chief Campbell Stowe. Your friend, Bob Miller, recently joined the Air Force across the hall, and we heard about your dilemma from the rumors floating around. We have very thin walls."

Knowing that the Air Force wouldn't allow me to enlist with them for at least six months of proven good behavior, Chief Stowe took it upon himself to visit the judge, whom he knew personally, and inquire about the possibilities of me being released to join the Navy instead.

I listened to his proposition. The Navy would assume complete responsibility for me if I agreed to join up. The judge would wipe my record clear, bury the file and release me from the remaining twenty-five days of jail time. "My God," I thought, "was I born under a lucky star!" Was there any question about what I would do?

I quickly accepted all terms and within the hour, after gathering up my meager belongings from my cell, and trading in my orange uniform for my own clothes, I hopped into the awaiting gray Navy vehicle, and was transported downtown to the municipal courthouse.

In the judge's chambers overlooking the Mississippi River, I was given a second chance. All of my juvenile infractions were dismissed - stricken from the record. With a clean slate, on November 24, 1959, I was sworn into the United States Navy.

I called my parents and informed them of the "contract." Even over the phone, I could feel a sense of relief drifting through my parents' living room. Good!

They made arrangements to meet with me downtown at the railroad station before I boarded the train to Chicago and the Naval Training Center. Tears of joy and relief were shed as I hugged and kissed my mother, Rose. I squeezed my brother and sisters, with a giant bear hug. I shook my father's hand goodbye.

"Good luck, son," he said, putting his other large, rough hand over our shake. I followed suit and capped his with my left hand. I could feel the warmth, and he lifted his cheeks in a small smile. I felt my tear ducts activating.

It all had happened so fast. Life can change in an instant - mine just had. I breathed a deep sigh of relief as I watched the skyline of St. Paul, Minnesota, disappear in the distance, the clattering of the steel wheels beneath me increasing their tempo, repeating to me: freedom, freedom, click clack, click clack. ~

CHAPTER 9: BOOTCAMP

Arriving in Chicago, I boarded a Navy-blue bus, its motor idling, already filled with recruits who had arrived there from all parts of the Midwest. I nervously smiled to a few as I walked to the rear of the bus, receiving small waves and weak responses from some. The door shut behind me, the emergency brake released, the driver grinded the shift lever into first gear and the bus wrenched forward to the Great Lakes Training Center.

On arrival we passed through the steel gates, guarded by white-helmeted sailors with the letters SP (Shore Patrol) painted in black letters on them. Black-belted holsters hung from their hips. A nightstick stuck on one side and a 45-hand gun on the other. I felt relieved, rather than frightened, knowing it was for our protection and security.

The bus continued into the center of a large parade ground where we disembarked and were systematically lined up into two ranks. Next, we were given our welcome speech, which was supposed to make us feel at home. We were then marched straight to the barbershop.

One by one, our heads were buzzed, immediately creating a similarity, a oneness by removing any personal traits that our former hirsute adornment might have suggested. We all became "skin heads" for the first time in our lives. Most of us gazed into the mirrors in disbelief, running our hands over our shiny, domed surface, feeling the prickly stubble left behind. Laughter and jokes soon followed. "You're so ugly, man, you look like you got whooped with an ugly stick."

They marched us into the adjoining Quonset hut, where we were commanded to strip down to our skivvies. Standing near-naked in a long line, each of us was examined by probing hands. Then the needles came, and we received the first of many military shots to come.

Alcohol wipe, punch, push, wipe, apply cotton and "Hold this, next!" That's how it went, with production line efficiency. Then, out the door, down the stairs, and into another building where the smell of leather, and fresh, new dungarees greeted us. We were asked our sizes as each piece of Navy issue was piled upon our outstretched arms. We were issued a duffel bag, asked our name and serial number, and received our stencils so that we could mark all our clothing. Mine was DONALD R. YEAGER 518-21-85. This was a much better number than I had received back in the St. Paul prison, and it gave me a proud new identity. Loaded up with our gear, we were next designated a barrack, assigned a bunk, called to attention and introduced to our platoon leader. He was the first in a long line of yelling, rough-voiced, Petty Officers who were soon to dominate our every move for the next six weeks. They wanted to impress upon us in the very early stages who was the boss and whom we'd be taking orders from. "Yes, Sir!" was the unified cry that would echo throughout the halls.

Names were now randomly called, and their owners were issued mess duties, compartment cleaning jobs, and guard duties. Groans of disappointment were emitted from the throats of those chosen for unfavorable jobs. I tried to be invisible, or absent, during the pickings. I started to learn the ropes at an early stage, volunteering ahead of time for lesser duties and being available to help the platoon leader or barracks officer whenever they were looking for a "rabbit" to run their errands.

I took pride in my new role and worked hard to make sure I passed every inspection. My locker was always in order, each item placed meticulously in its proper space, and my dress shoes were spit shined to a high-mirrored gloss. My bunk had all its corners tucked properly, and the blanket was stretched so tight you could bounce a quarter off it, which sometimes the barrack inspectors liked to do. This, along with my loud and clear, "Yes, Sirs!" kept me in the good graces of my superiors. I followed the rules, worked hard and was always in bed at night "Taps." "Lights out and quiet on all decks."

I escaped most of the guard duties. We had guards for everything - barracks, latrine, dumpster, gate, fence and more. As stupid as they may have seemed to us, they were taken very seriously by the officers on duty.

You were to challenge anyone who approached your post with the words, "Halt! Who goes there? Advance and identify yourself!" These watches were to prepare you for the more serious ones that you would stand later at your next duty station or on the ship you might be assigned to.

Within three weeks we were beginning to look like sailors. Our blue dress uniforms seemed to fit better, our marching moves were more precise, and we learned to "snap to" with our salutes and to stand at attention ramrod straight.

After a month our families were allowed to visit. Dad drove the Plymouth down from St. Paul and parked it outside the gate in the visitor's parking lot. Then my family boarded a waiting Navy bus that would be their transportation in and around the base. I met them at the visitor's reception building. We were all excited to see each other.

We attended services with the Catholic chaplain (I knew this would make points with my mother.) Then we went to the commissary, where we were treated to a roast beef dinner with lots of potatoes, gravy, peas, and homemade biscuits served up on steel trays.

Next, the families toured the barracks, where we could show off the "spit and shine" tidiness of a Navy recruit. The newfound sense of organization was very impressive to most parents. Next, it was off to the parade grounds.

Seated on wooden bleachers, parents now watched their sons proudly performing marching maneuvers to the commands of their platoon leaders. The Navy band played, and commanding officer, Capt. Russell Meyers made a small speech. We put on a good show.

Later, they showed Elvis Presley's new movie, "Jail House Rock," which hit home with me and my father, as he ribbed me in the side with his elbow. "Ya, sure," he said in his Minnesota twang, with a little hint of humor. I loved my dad even more when I knew I had pleased him.

Sunday afternoon ended with good wishes, hugs and kisses as the now proud and reassured parents left their sailors on base and began their journeys back home.

Basic training was soon over and I spent a two-week leave at home strutting my stuff in my dress blues, the envy now of a lot of my friends. Next stop: Norman, Oklahoma, and aviation electronics school. ~

Chapter 10: School Daze

Norman, Oklahoma, located just a few miles from Oklahoma City, was a naval prep school that taught basic electronics: Ohm's law, introduction to resistors, capacitors, sound waves - all the early stages of what was to evolve into the computer technology of present day.

Unfortunately, I did not excel in my studies. Try as I might, I was just too preoccupied with finding ways to have a good time, whenever and wherever I could. My weekend liberties in Oklahoma City were the beginning of a series of escapades as a sailor.

I had begun weight training in a gym in St. Paul while still in high school. My Minnesota membership was honored at the Oklahoma facility, so I continued to pump iron. One day, as I was loading weights onto the bar on the bench press, a fellow lifter offered to spot for me. Accepting the offer, I continued my two-hour session along with a new friend named Michael, a lieutenant colonel who was stationed nearby at Tinker Air Force Base.

Soon we were meeting every weekend to work out together. Michael loved showing me new exercises to help build up my body faster. He helped me with my sets and taught me different strength poses to show off my muscle definition. Little did I realize that Michael had a little bit more on his mind!

About three weeks into the "friendship," Michael invited me to join him as a guest at the officer's club at Tinker. He suggested that I dress in the civilian clothes I kept in my locker at the health club. Innocently, I accepted the invita-

tion, thinking it a nice gesture to be invited to eat and drink in an officer's club.
After a nice dinner and quite a few cocktails, the colonel's true intentions slowly began to reveal themselves.

As we became more intoxicated, Michael's touching became far more than just buddy-like. It brought back the memories of my experience with "Pops" in San Francisco, so I decided to bolt and pull a disappearing act. Excusing myself to go to the men's room, I slipped out the back door of the club. Half smashed, but with enough sense of mind to know that I must escape the bizarre situation I'd fallen into, I ran and boarded a blue Air Force liberty bus that was just leaving for Oklahoma City, luck and timing again being on my side.

I eventually made it back to Norman, vowing never to return to the health club for fear of running into him. I remained on base, worked out there and finally graduated - barely - and was transferred to my next school for training to be an Aviation Electronics Technician in Memphis, Tennessee.

Arriving at Memphis NAS (Naval Air Station,) I was excited about finally being stationed on an actual air base; one with planes, hangars, runways and lots of action. Introduction Week consisted of barracks assignment, school assignments, general familiarization of the base, its rules and regulations, and warnings about going on liberty.

Being an aviation electronics technician striker, I reacquainted myself with Ohm's Law and other earlier phases of electronics. Since it was only 1958, the studies were really quite simple compared to what would come later. But I was still in my rebel phase, and once again I failed to pay attention, and began to flunk out. I'd become infatuated with a well-built blonde that I'd met at the base pool, and my mind was again lost in dreamy pursuit. It was the beginning of another one of my downfalls as far as schooling was concerned.

I flunked my first exam but was given a second chance. I blew that one, also. The head instructor, realizing that he would never hand this sailor a diploma, dismissed me from further studies. He sent me compartment cleaning, dropping me from the school ranks.

Transferred from the school barracks to the transient barracks, I reported to a laid-back, tattooed, Camel straights-chain-smoking Third Class Petty Officer nicknamed "Skirts," because he loved chasing after women. Finally, here was someone in the chain of command that I could relate to.

Skirts and I soon bonded, becoming good friends, and started going on liberties together. I was no longer in school, so I didn't have to observe the midnight curfew, and Skirts had access to all kinds of liberty passes, which he fanned out to me.

Memphis, Tennessee was a hot town in the late fifties, loaded with good looking southern belles. It was also the present residence of Elvis Aaron Presley, the hot white boy with a black sound. He was influenced by the soul music derived from the blues that the local Negroes sang in and around the countryside of East Tupelo, Mississippi, his birthplace. But it was in the Memphis recording studio of Sun Records where he recorded his first song, "That's All Right, Mama," dedicated to his mother, whom he loved dearly.

By 1957 he had hit the charts big time with "Blue Suede Shoes," a Carl Perkins original. Soon, other hits followed like "Heartbreak Hotel," "Hound Dog," "Love Me Tender," "Don't Be Cruel," and on and on. Admirers (we call them "groupies, these days,) were flocking to his Graceland estate. They would stand for hours outside the gates, peering inside in hopes of catching a glance of the "King" as he came and went in his new white Cadillac convertible.

Skirts and I loved to cruise out to Elvis's home in Skirts' low, sexy-looking 1954 red Ford convertible, hoping to share the common admiration of the singer with a couple of those "groupies." If we failed to score there - we'd head on down to Beale Street, Memphis' main drag. With the top down, the radio blasting rock and roll and the bright lights shimmering off the polished car's surface and its flashy chrome spinner hubcaps, it was pretty easy to pick up a chick or two.

"Hey, ladies, want a ride? We got the King playing," I'd call out to them as I cranked up the volume on the radio. Some would be too cool, coy or phony, and we'd dump those ones in a hurry. "Out of the car." Then there were others, who would slide right on over close to me, and the flirting games would begin. These hot little numbers loved to neck and pet and loved to go out and park. One of our favorite places was Promontory Point, a bluff way out in the boondocks, overlooking the Mississippi River. Just like good ole' Cherokee Park back in the homeland of St. Paul, Minnesota.

The Memphis USO was also a great place to meet girls, get something good to eat, play pool, or shoot darts. Saturday nights they always had a dance, and the hostesses were in abundance. Most of the girls were local debutantes, with very proper upbringings and mannerisms. They were only interested in being big sisters or mothers to the homesick boys in the military. But - sometimes - a marriage stemmed from a relationship that had begun with a nice slow dance at the USO.

On the other hand - across the Mississippi - a bridge led into a forbidden zone, to the Cotton Club in Little Rock, Arkansas where black musicians played great jazz, which attracted older women who loved to drink, dance and get involved.

One Saturday night Skirts and I romanced a surprising duo, a lusty young mother and her equally seductive 18-year-old daughter. After a few drinks and sensual close dances, we left the club together. The four of us hopped into the convertible, and slowly cruised the back roads of the surrounding bayou countryside, a full moon lighting our way. We were the only car on the road, so Skirts doused the lights and we lazily rolled along. A canal, next to us, threw out a silver shaft of light on the water that shimmered far down the blackened lane.

It was very exciting and romantic and created two torrid affairs: Skirts with Lillian, the mother, and me with Bonnie Mae, the daughter. Skirts and Lillian soon married, (it was meant to be,) and my relationship with Bonnie Mae led me into a bizarre series of events that would eventually prove somewhat disastrous to my military career. ~

CHAPTER 11: BUSTED

For an eighteen-year-old Southern lass, Bonnie Mae was far more a woman than any of the other girls I had previously been involved with. Perhaps it was her sister-like relationship with her young mother. What I do know was that her noticeable bust, slim waist, long legs, strawberry blonde hair, blue eyes, and full lips drove me wild. We had hot and heavy make-out sessions, but we never went "all the way." I'd lay awake at night, trying to figure out ways to impress her.

On April 19, 1959, Hurricane Hilda, speeding its way up the peninsula driven by winds reaching up to 100 miles an hour, was due to hit the east coast of Florida. At the Pensacola Navy Airbase, an emergency flyaway was ordered to completely evacuate all its aircraft. The aviators and their flight instructors took to the air, flying inland in group formations to a safer haven - namely - our NAS training station at Memphis.

Skirts had assigned me to an empty barracks used primarily for transients and named me Master-at-Arms. It was an easy task. I had my own private quarters, and I was put in charge of the sailors that were transferring into or out of our schools. At this particular time, however, I had an empty house.

Around 3 pm, I was notified of the need for my barracks to be ready with fresh linens and blankets for the arriving Pensacola aircrews. Wow! How cool for me, I thought. I would feel very important greeting the relocated air-men.

When they arrived and started to fill the empty bunks in the barracks, I was introduced to an overwhelming group of excited hot shots, ready to hit the streets of Memphis for a three-day liberty, now that their planes were safe.

Two officers took over the extra bunks in my private Master-at-Arm's room. After settling in, one of them pulled out a bottle of Vodka from his flight bag. With a sly smile, he invited me to join them in a celebration drink.

"Here, buddy, we all deserve this. It's been one hell of a day," he said, taking a huge gulp, shaking his head from the jolt and passing the bottle to me sitting on the edge of my bunk. Well, heck, it was Friday night, no duty tomorrow, so why not? We proceeded to raid the cold pop machine for mix, and the three of us, hidden from view in my private quarters, proceeded to get slightly inebriated. Soon the bottle was empty, and the two aviators joined the rest of their cohorts heading into Memphis or off to dinner at the officer's club.

I was left alone, feeling quite cocky. So, with a few Vodka cocktails messing with my head, I did a stupid stupid thing. I decided to play dress up to see how I would look in an officer's uniform. The one I picked fit nicely and, my, was I handsome! I slipped on a light jacket with small gold bars on each shoulder and cocked a brimmed hat with gold braid over the top of my eyebrows. I admired myself in the mirror on the wall. "Wow," I thought, a light bulb flashing on and off in my brain, "This is how I can impress Bonnie Mae."

Dialing her phone number, my heart nearly pounded out of my chest as I waited while the phone rang - way too many times - on the other end. Finally, it was answered by the voice I was waiting to hear.

"Bonnie Mae, it's me, Don. What're you doing?"

"Hi, Donnie, sweetie, I'm all alone. Skirts and Mom went to a movie, so come on over, if you can."

Her invitation rang in my ears and took away my breath. "Cool, give me about an hour or so. I've got to figure out how to get there," I said, my mouth starting to go dry.

"OK, I'll be on the porch looking for you," she said breathlessly, softly returning the phone to its cradle.

After hanging up, I checked myself out one more time in the mirror. "Damn, I look dashing, how can she resist?" She'd never seen me in uniform before, only in my civvies - surely, she would succumb to an officer, even though she knew I wasn't one. I couldn't wait to see her eyes when she opened the door, and I stood there shining in brass. I needed to get off base, but how? I knew that no one was normally checked on passing out of the gates, but coming back through, everyone was stopped for identification and purpose.

"I'd better take a change of clothing, my I. D. and a car. Got to have a car," I said, muttering to myself. My mind continued to race, "Can't borrow Skirt's, he's already in town." Then I remembered a gray 1952 Chevy Navy truck parked behind the commissary that always had its keys in it. Dressed in the ensign uniform, civvies in a bag tucked under my left arm, I stepped out of the barracks front door, brave but stupid. On my way to the commissary, off-duty sailors in their whites saluted me as we passed each other.

"Great!" I thought, returning the salutes, "Got them fooled already. This'll be a cinch."

I found the truck in its usual place. I peered through the window and saw the keys hanging from the ignition, so far, so good. Quietly, I bent the chrome door handle down, slowly opened the door and slid behind the steering wheel. I turned the key on and pushed the starter button. The starter groaned apprehensively against the six cylinder flywheel. After a few revolutions, the engine coughed to life, its old lifters clattering away.

"No warm up needed in this climate," I thought, as I backed out of the parking spot, shoved it into low gear, and headed out to Wright Boulevard, named for the first aviators. I was feeling confident that tonight was going to be "the night!"

Reaching the stop sign, I shifted into second, pulled a rolling "California stop," spinning my wheels as I slipped a right-hand turn, and headed towards the gate. Approaching the Marine-guarded gate with liquored confidence, my mind was fogged with the images of Bonnie Mae's face and her full wet lips - I was removed from present time and not paying attention.

All of a sudden, oops, bad timing. I hadn't been watching close enough, and the light on the road outside the gate was turning red. "Shit!" I'd have to stop almost directly next to the guard shack. My heart began to race, my stomach knotted up as fear and anxiety grabbed me. I'd have to play it real cool.

The light changed and, as I started to roll, the corporal on duty saluted me. I reached up to return the recognition, and also to lower the brim of the officer's cap to cover my eyes a little under the bright security lights, but not soon enough!

Avast, aghast matey! I was horrified to see my Chief Master-of-Arms driving into the entrance opposite me. In an instant, our eyes met. The Chief did a double take, not believing his eyes. He pointed at me and yelled, "Stop that sailor, corporal!"

My heart dropped to my toes and a few seconds later I felt myself being lifted out of the cab of the truck as the combat-trained Marine wrenched open the door and grabbed me. The Shore Patrol arrived in an instant and I was thrown into the back seat of their jeep, flanked on both sides by two huge arm banded toughs. I was escorted to the duty office to be interrogated, my Chief following, looking very upset.

Stripped of my short lived "commission," I was charged with impersonating an officer, being drunk on duty, wrongful appropriation of a military vehicle, and, when asked to turn over my credentials, I was found to be in possession of twenty blank overnight liberty cards.

Shit, oh shit, oh man, throw away the key! Slam! For the second time, a set of bars clanged behind me. This time, though, was much more serious and life threatening, being in a military brig run by tough Marines.

You can be punished in many ways in the military. You could have a Captain's Mast, usually a slap on the wrist and maybe a little extra duty. Or, if it's a little more serious, you could get a Summary Court Martial. If it's more than serious, how about a General Court Martial?

The news of my arrest soon spread through the school, the base and the squadron that had just flown in.

Two days later I was in court. The trial was open to spectators, and they filled every available chair.

I had no representation, so I had my chance to explain myself. I did it tearfully with sorrowful overtones, knowing that I'd really messed up big time, but to little avail. They were going to make an example of me.

The trial was quick. I appeared beaten. "Please rise," the head of the committee commanded.

I faced four impeccably dressed uniformed officers, chests adorned with ribbons and medals. My head drooped as I was read the decision of the Court Martial board. I received the maximum! I was downgraded in rank to airman recruit. I lost all pay for two years, and I got one year in the brig.

How was I going to live this one down? My life, hardly in its beginning, seemed to be at its end and Bonnie Mae was now definitely out of the picture.

But wait! Seated on the board that had just handed down the harsh sentence was a sympathizer, a young Lt. JG, Samuel Goodfellow, (rightfully named.) Sam, unknown to me at the time, was also a native of my hometown, St. Paul, Minnesota, go figure? He was fresh out of law school and he turned out to be a "good fellow" for me - that's for sure!

Sam went to bat for me. He felt that I had been a victim of the Court. He also knew that I had acted impulsively under the influence of liquor and youthful desire and that I was being made an example of.

Visiting me in the brig, he offered to approach the ruling officer, ask for leniency, and quickly have me reassigned to a ship stationed in San Diego.

How this stroke of Lady Luck smiled on me again I'll never know. I was given another opportunity to change my ways. The ruling officer agreed that it was probably best that I was transferred out.

I reappeared before the Base Commander, along with my savior, and received a much more acceptable reprimand. I would instead serve thirty days of kitchen duty, without confinement, be broken to airman recruit, and lose all pay, except for fifty dollars every pay period, for one year. After serving my sentence of thirty days, I would then be transferred to sea duty. I spent the next month in the galley making box lunches for the flight crews.

Time flew by and I soon received my new orders. I was to report to the USS Kearsarge, an aircraft carrier berthed in San Diego. I had three days travel time and a military pass for transportation on the Southern Pacific railroad. I caught the bus to Memphis, made my connection and rattled my way across six states: Arkansas, Oklahoma, the tip of Texas, New Mexico, Arizona and across California to the ocean city of San Diego, thanking my lucky stars for the chance to move on once again. ~

CHAPTER 12: WEST COAST FIRSTS

I had never seen the ocean or palm trees before. Even the air smelled different - so heavy with moist humidity that there seemed to be a special fragrance to it. I was mesmerized by the brightness of the bay's silver-blue water as it reflected the sun's rays in the form of millions of flickering intense dots of brilliant light.

With my duffel bag slung over my left shoulder and the sealed brown envelope with my orders in my right hand, I waited anxiously for the Kearsarge liberty launch to ferry me across the bay to Coronado Island where the ship was berthed. When the motor launch arrived, about fifteen liberty "hounds," laughing, talking, and gesturing, had to disembark before those of us who were waiting could board for the return trip.

Reloaded, the launch reversed the engine's propellers, and we slowly backed away from the dock. Once clear and again in open water, the helmsman spun the large nautical steering wheel, pushed the throttle full ahead, and the launch's nose rose up and surged forward, sweeping into a 180-degree turn pointed towards the giant, gray mass of metal, that awaited us on the far side.

The ship grew larger and larger as the launch approached the boarding gangway that hung from its side. Hidden in its shadow, I lifted myself onto the iron platform, boarding my first ship, the USS Kearsarge - Attack Carrier - CVA 31. Shivers of delightful anticipation ran through my body as I reached the top of the ladder. I stepped onto the deck and faced aft to salute the Ensign flag, a military tradition when boarding a vessel. Then, holding the salute, I turned and addressed the Officer of the Day.

"Airman Recruit, Donald Yeager, reporting for duty, as ordered sir," I said in a strong and affirmative voice.

The Master-at-Arms Second Class, on duty with him, looked at me then glanced down at the clipboard held in his left hand. He ran his forefinger down the list of names until he found Yeager, Donald R., AR. 518-21-85, V-2 division, Catapults.

"Report to V-2 Division, towards the bow," he said, handing me a sheet of paper showing the layout of the ship with its different divisions and locations. The Kearsarge had recently returned from a six-month tour in the West Pacific and was in the process of transferring men. Some of those who had served on its recent tour were dismissed with thirty days leave before reporting to their next duty station. Others, like me, were replacing them.

Both the catapults and the arresting gear mechanisms were in the process of being torn down in preparation for the refitting that would take place in the next month or so. The ship was designated to head north to Long Beach soon and into a dry dock for up to six months, before heading out to the West Pacific again. This was a relaxing, no-hurry time for the crew and the duties were very light, allowing plenty of liberty and beach time.

How lucky could a guy be! Out of the frying pan, and assigned to a marvelous, mammoth of the sea, docked within sight of the great city of San Diego.

Soon I found myself roaming Broadway, the main drag in San Diego, looking for action. Pretty Mexican girls seemed to be everywhere and were easy to get to know. After a few liberties, I became more acquainted with the city life and I latched onto a beauty - or maybe she latched on to me. Lupe was her name and she was six years older than me - and about twenty years more streetwise.

Since Lupe knew all the bouncers on the strip, I had no trouble getting into the bars and jazz joints that lined both sides of Broadway, even though I had just turned nineteen. It was another interesting encounter.

San Diego was the first place that I took an off base/ship residence. With two new sailor buddies, John Stiganga, and Will "Wolfie" Rau, we rented a small stucco bungalow high in the hills of Old Town overlooking the old Convair airplane plant.

From our patio we could see the bay and across it - the Kearsarge - docked at Coronado Island. It was a real party pad, where my girlfriend, Lupe, introduced her seemingly endless supply of girlfriends to my sailor buddies.

Weekly poker parties were a highlight at the pad. A lot of guys lost their two-week paychecks to Wolfie, who was the card shark of our trio. Wolfie was good at getting money in other ways too. Since I had lost most of my pay as a result of my court martial, I joined him in trying various ways to earn extra money.

Gambling was heavy on the ship also; poker games, dice shooting, baseball pools, boxing predictions and so on. Sometimes just the heavy drinking, along with the prostitutes in town, took a lot of the sailors' money, leaving many of them looking for a loan to tide them over till the next pay period.

To fill the need, Wolfie and I organized a slush fund, taking on a third partner, Tim Kooke, a very big, strong, and slightly dumb country boy from Georgia as our enforcer.

We pooled a hundred dollars each, then loaned the money out to the broke sailors. Wolfie was the lender, I was the bookkeeper, and Tim was the collector.

The fund loaned $5 for $7, $10 for $13, $20 for $25 and so on. The debts were due on payday. We three would wait outside the Paymasters Office and collect our "just-due." This was usually not a problem, as those who were in debt to us would take one look at 'big" Tim, with his "you better pay up" look on his face, and the "green" would land in either my hands or Wolfie's.

The slush fund soon grew and each of us was pocketing around two hundred dollars profit every other week. I invested my share in the ship's banking office, telling the accountant that it was money from home so as not to arouse suspicion. Fortunately, especially for me in my present probation period, we never got caught pulling that scam.

During the late fifties, Tijuana, Mexico, only a short distance from San Diego, was a wild, wide-open border town. It was a snake pit of raw sex, tequila and preying hustlers, ready to pounce upon you to relieve you of your money, your car, your clothes and, on occasion, your life.

The night that Jon, Wolfie and I hit the strip it was especially vibrant with action and come-ons. The first sex bar we literally fell into was the then infamous Blue Fox. Next to the main door, off to the side of it, was a highly polished, silver, steel slide that readily deposited you onto a mass of soft, colored cushions, one floor beneath street level. Scantily clad prostitutes greeted you at the bottom and immediately began to pet you, closely whispering to you promises of more to come.

On stage, the strippers gyrated, gestured and did unbelievable tricks with their bodies. My wide, disbelieving eyes were zeroed in on one of the girls on the stage and she immediately singled me out, and coaxed me to come on up on stage and dance with her.

My tequila high was rushing through me and, egged on by my buddies, I joined her on the raised stage and proceeded to try to follow her suggestive movements - it was exciting.

That scene soon started to get out of hand and the place erupted into complete bedlam, sailors and Marines all going wild. The upstairs bouncer blew his whistle and immediately some of the local police stormed in. They held clubs in their hands, raised above their heads, turning them in circles, threatening us, yelling orders in Spanish - we all got the message - this party's over!

The bar emptied out fast, with women screaming and running around in various stages of undress. We crammed up the staircase, pushing each other in our rush to get the hell out of there. Total confusion was the only thing that saved me from the slammer that night - that - and a quick twenty-dollar cab ride back to the border where our cars were waiting for us on the other side. Whoa-ho, another exciting escape into the night. We left Tijuana alone after that heart-pounding episode.

The San Diego "experience," proved to be an eye opener for me and I was somewhat relieved when it came time for us to ship out to Long Beach. Three days after our Tijuana liberty, two large tugs arrived to pull the ship away from its moorings and direct it out into the shipping channel in the middle of the bay.

We all stood at attention up on the flight deck in formation ranks for the "Leaving Port Muster," as our ship slowly slipped out of the harbor. As I watched the city grow small in the distance, my mind raced back, replaying my recollections of all that I had encountered while in San Diego. Then they were stored away in my memory bank as we rounded Pt. Loma, and the city's skyline disappeared.

Although Long Beach wasn't that far up the coast as nautical miles go, the U.S.S. Kearsarge was required to head out to sea, therefore avoiding any possible contact with any other ships that may be traveling the coastal shipping lanes. The ship maneuvered throughout the day and into the evening. A couple of days later - mid-afternoon - images of towering ship cranes, intermingled within a forest of oil derricks, began to appear on the horizon as we drew closer to Long Beach. A short while later we were in a holding position offshore, still in deep water as our ship waited for the harbor pilot to arrive. Once aboard, he would direct our helmsman into the shipyards.

Excitement grew as the Kearsarge approached its dry dock berthing. Upon entering the steel enclosure, the engines were silenced. Huge ropes were secured from ship to dock to strategically place the mammoth V-shaped hull back into its skeletal ribbed womb. Once in position, the gates were closed behind it and the water was slowly - very slowly - pumped out until the keel of the ship fitted into its resting place where it would lie for the next few months. This very interesting to observe as it was very technical.

As soon as we were more stabilized, large gangplanks were wheeled up to the ship, allowing ship-yard workers aboard to start their tasks, and also allowing some of us to go on liberty. The shipyards were actually located in San Pedro and you had to catch the bus to Long Beach.

Sections Two, and Four had the first liberty call. I was in Section Four, and I anxiously waited for 1600 hours (4 pm), to disembark, pass through the gates, and grab the shuttle to town.

A new city to discover! How exciting, I thought, as I stepped off the bus onto Ocean Boulevard, Long Beach, California. There was no hesitation on my part to find out what the lure of this city was as the lights of the Pike Amusement Park drew me down the hill into an area alive with activity.

Drinking bars were interspersed amongst fast food stands, and carnival attractions. The Pike area was known as a "meat market," slang for easy pickups. It had also become a refuge for runaways from the Midwest and further east. The allure of beautiful warm weather and soft sand beaches beckoned to these lost souls searching for a life change, and it was known to be a runaway's haven.

Another attraction was the "West Pac Widows." These were women who were left alone on the shore while their mates were out to sea and they frequented the various clubs and bars. Some, desperate for companionship, took on part-time lovers until their husband's ship returned.

Quick marriages, and quick divorces, were common amongst the military personnel. Some of those women were like parasites, looking for the benefits that came with being married to a service man.

A motorcycle gang called the "Devil's Advocates" hung out at the Pike, creating general havoc whenever they showed their presence. They cruised Broadway Avenue and the semi-circled rainbow pier, picking up girls who looked like easy bait. They disappeared with them into the concrete jungle of hotels and little beach houses that dotted the area.

The use of drugs and booze was strongly evident, and prostitution ran rampant. The police and the Shore Patrol were kept busy raiding these hovels, breaking up fights, hauling in juvenile prostitutes and trying to keep things in order. It was a wide-open town back then. Sirens rang out at all hours of the day and night. But steps away - out on the beach - you could always find peace and serenity.

I bought some new civvies, a beach towel, a bathing suit, some flip-flops and I got a locker at the Anchor Locker Club on Broadway. There I kept my off-duty gear and had a place to hang my uniform while on liberty. I sometimes missed the last bus back to the shipyards and I would find myself out on the street in front of the club with my thumb held up in the air - hitchhiking.

Late one Sunday night, a rather strange one picked me up. When we reached the dark parking lot outside the gate, he stopped the car and made a move on me. Jesus! I thought, not again! I was repulsed and scared at the same time. What to do? I reacted quickly and smashed my fist into his nose! I heard a crack and blood and tears spurted from the surprised face of the now uninterested assailant. I guess he never expected that reaction, but it was an adrenaline fueled defense reaction. I "slammed" out the door and beat feet to the guard gate. The sound of squealing wheels faded behind me as the jilted wannabe lover sped away. Out of breath, my right-hand throbbing from the punch, I made for the safety of the guardhouse.

The Marine on duty observed it all from his post and he laughingly said, "Well, it looks like we won't be seeing that guy around here for a while. Good job, Sailor!" That made me feel good, and it was to be the last time I would hitchhike or take the bus into town. Instead I took some of the "slush money" I had hidden away and went out and bought a black 1940 Ford two-door for a hundred and fifty bucks.

The beach at the Pike attracted a great variety of people. I soon had a favorite spot picked out to watch people and still be close to everything. It was up against the wooden fence that separated the beach from the boardwalk. After three weeks of the ship being in dry-dock, I melted into the local scene. My body took on a beautiful golden color and I'd become a pretty good beach volleyball player.

I spent lots of hours on the beach, which made the locker club scene inconvenient. So, I rented a small one-room apartment at the Breeze Inn located at the end of Rainbow Pier, one block off Ocean Boulevard.

I loved having my own pad again. A place to eat, keep my clothes, lie back and relax, spend the night and entertain the ladies. Thus, began a series of romances with various girls, all of whom I met at the beach or while strolling the Pike Amusement Park.

One day, while taking my daily stroll up and down the beach, I was stopped in my tracks by a wolf whistle. I looked around, and found the compliment came from a petite, nicely built, redheaded girl in a pink bikini with a come-on smile on her face.

"Me?" I asked, pointing my finger at myself.

"Yes, you - you've got a great pair of legs," she said, winking playfully.

"Well, thank you, I've always considered them too thin - bird legs."

"Not hardly, come sit down and join us."

There were the two of them, Sharon, and Gretchen; her companion from Germany. The two began to show up at the beach every weekend. Sharon and I hit it off and she started spending Saturday nights at my place. I hooked Gretchen up with my shipmate John Stiganga and we became a happy foursome.

Sharon was a real kick, one of a kind. She would drive in from Torrance in her 1948 Plymouth coupe street rod named "Mr. Peanuts." It was a lot fancier and faster than my stock '40 Ford, as it sported a Chrysler Hemi engine under its hood. Her father had done all the work - lucky her.

We spent weekends cruising in the Plymouth up and down the Coast Highway to a lot of the other beaches along the California coastline. She always gave the driving privileges to me, and she loved to sit close to me, her arm around my neck. I'll never forget her joyful smile and bright eyes, nor her admiration and love.

Of all the beaches, we loved Hermosa the best, with its muscle beach weight lifters, sparkling, white sand, and pounding surf. Here we would spend most of the day sunbathing and frolicking in the water.

Around five o'clock, we would pack up our beach gear and leave the soft sand. Next, we would drift off the boardwalk onto the back streets and spend the early part of the evening in one of the beatnik coffee houses. The "Light House" was our favorite. Laying back, sipping on a hot cup of java, we'd spend a couple of hours listening to the beat of bongo drums intermixed with piano, flutes, and saxophones, all creating funky, jazz music.

It was hard for us to end our weekends. We were truly enamored with each other. We would tenderly hug and kiss until the very last moment when we had to finally go our own ways - Sharon, back to Torrance - and me, back to the ship.

That summer ended too soon for the two of us. Sharon left for college in Santa Barbara, leaving me without a woman. I replaced her with a new car - no comparison - but it would help keep my mind occupied - at least for a short while.

I sold the '40 Ford two-door; to a shipmate for triple what I had in it and with the proceeds bought a hot custom 1939 Ford. It had a perfectly balanced engine and literally would scream down the road when pushed to its limits. I started hanging out further down the coast, near Seal Beach's, "Tin Can Beach." The beach got its name from all the temporary shacks and shelters that would spring up between the beach and the coast highway during the annual grunion run.

Grunions are small silvery fish that would blanket the shallow water, near the shore. It was a great sport to net them, and a lot of people made a big party out of the annual event. The beach would come alive at night with bonfires burning, and people hanging out in their tin and cardboard shacks, excitingly comparing each other's catch after wading knee deep in the water with their flashlights, torches, and nets. It was great fun - short lived - but fun.

The Park Service would come in after the run and dismantle whatever was left, hauling it all away in big green trucks, restoring the beach back to its original state, for the surfers and sun worshipers. It was like the grunion runners came, and went, along with the tides, and then disappeared into thin air.

About this time, I started racing my '39, on Sundays at a drag strip on the outskirts of Pismo Beach. I ran in the AO class, which was stock gas, but - because of its perfectly balanced and tuned engine - I walked away with a few trophies. The trophy girl, Gay Louise, on one of these Sundays, was truly a knockout, with a perfect hourglass figure, 36-21-36.

After eliminating all my competitors, (there weren't that many,) I leaped up on to the podium to receive my trophy from her and the winner's kiss. I couldn't help myself. I slipped my arm around her slim waist and immediately got a feeling that she just might be my next girlfriend.

Gay was only eighteen years old but already had a baby named Sparky, who was almost a year old. Her brother, Lem, was very protective of her, but he took to me quickly because he admired my affection towards the little boy.

We started dating, and I would drive down every weekend I had off just to be with her. The local boys of Seal Beach started to give me a hard time every time I came into town.

They didn't like a stranger, much less a sailor boy, beating their street rods in the drags, nor did they like him having one of the sexiest blondes in town in his arms.

Especially threatening was Lenny, the father of Gay's child. He made it known to me that if I continued to hang out around Seal Beach, I could be in deep trouble.

I'd gotten into trouble before because of my passion for the opposite sex, and I thought, "I'd better leave this one alone." So, I stuffed Gay, Sparky, and brother Lem, into my '39 Ford, and snuck out of Seal Beach early one Sunday morning while the local boys were still busy dragging their cars at the strip.

I drove to the Long Beach shipyards, where I sold the coupe to Lem right there in the parking lot. Kissing Gay and Sparks good-bye, I was once again leaving a love behind. With a lump in my throat and a pain in my heart, I watched as they turned and waved, dust flying from the back wheels of the coupe. I went through the guard gate and boarded my ship.

The Kearsarge had been refitted, repainted, and was ready to re-enter the water for its shakedown cruise, before heading out to the West Pacific.

At 0600, the next morning, revelry was whistled in along with the command, "All hands on deck." I ran up to the flight deck for morning muster.

0800, more whistles, and the call, "Make preparations for getting underway. All hands report to their duty stations."

The dry dock's locks had been opened, letting the lock fill with ocean water allowing the Kearsarge to get its feet wet, so to speak. Two huge Coast Guard tugs had connected to the stern of the ship via four thick towing ropes and guided the aircraft carrier slowly out of its cradle. Reentering the ocean, the end of the pier slowly slipped away. A crowd stood and watched, waving small American flags, and handkerchiefs, as the friends, families, and lovers were left behind. Foghorns wailed, and the ships bell rang, as we slowly turned our bow once again out towards the open ocean for our shakedown cruise to San Francisco. ~

CHAPTER 13: SAN FRANCISCO

The ship, powered by four monstrous rotating blades, spinning beneath in the depths, slowly picked up speed, its hull vibrating with the increased power. Later we went to full power; a shudder ran through its length, leaving a large wake behind us, diminishing as it disappeared into the horizon.

One hundred miles from land in the vast dark blue ocean, the Kearsarge hit a storm so violent that the bow of the ship met the crest of the waves as it plunged itself into the valleys created by the enormous swells. Our accompanying destroyers disappeared for long seconds in the waves, rolling twenty to twenty-five degrees and taking on water over their bridges. I was observing the scene from the pitching catwalk and pitied the men on those ships, especially those who were experiencing their first time at sea.

The storm increased its intensity as darkness fell. Soon it was so black you couldn't see your hand in front of your face. I was in the bridle locker, which had no access to the interior of the ship, so I had to cross the flight deck to reach the fo'c'sle. I crawled out onto the catwalk; my eyes wide open to nothing but total darkness and vast emptiness. I felt the rain blasting into my face and heard the roar of the wind deafening my ears. I slowly lifted myself up onto the rolling and pitching flight deck. I closed my eyes tight and pictured within my brain the path across the deck. Flat on my belly, I reached blindly in front of me for the circular tie-down rings that were embedded in the steel plates that ran along side of the catapults, knowing that when I reached the end of the cable slit, I would be almost opposite the hatch that opened into the fo'c'sle.

It seemed to take forever; I was in my own world, a world of fear, but only fear of the moment. I felt as if someone was washing me with a powerful fire hose, slowing my progress. Soon I felt the slit - I opened my eyes. Shining above the hatch leading into the fo'c'sle was a red light, barely visible, but there. Reaching the bulkhead, its dark mass hidden in the darkness, my fingers searched for the handle on the hatch. Groping for a moment or two, the red light my only guide, I found it. Opening the portal ever so slowly so the winds wouldn't tear it from my grasp, I slipped within its chambers - safe.

The lights were dimmed within the ship and it had an eerie feeling. Through the silent corridors I wandered, encountering only one other sailor as I worked my way down and forward to the catapult hydraulic room and the security of my bunk.

"Where the hell have you been?" my friend and lower bunkmate John asked. "You're soaked to the skin."

"You wouldn't believe me if I told you," I whispered so I wouldn't wake the others. "I'm just lucky to be here. I fell asleep in the upper deck bridle locker and just crawled on my flat belly across the flight deck. Let's just keep this between you and me - OK?"

John just looked at me with bewilderment in his eyes and said, "You right, that's hard to take - but knowing you."

"Let's just leave it at that." I answered.

I crawled into my bunk, which hung off the bulkhead, close to the water line. The movement of the ship, along with the sound of the ocean slapping against its steel hull, slowly soothed me into a deep exhausted sleep.

The next morning in the chow hall, as I ravenously consumed a tray full of fried eggs, toast and "shit on the shingle" (creamed chip beef on toast), I replayed to a few of my trusted wide-eyed mates at the table a step-by-step account of my perilous nocturnal experience, (sorry John, I just can't keep it to myself,) but before I could finish my story, I was interrupted by the news being blasted over the loudspeakers that we had lost singers Buddy Holly and the Big Bopper in a plane crash.

An hour later, adding to the tragedy, we were informed that one of our own was also not so lucky. Missing from his midnight watch was Corporal Walt Penney, a marine guard I had lifted weights with. Apparently, he had ventured too close to the edge of the open fantail on the hangar deck level and had lost his footing on the wet deck, slipping beneath the safety chain.

"Wow, man, you were lucky," my friend John exclaimed, his eyes big as we took everything into account. I crossed myself, silently thanking God for my reprieve. Once again, I had lucked out.

Midday, the storm subsided, but the ocean was still shrouded in fog, and a misty rain slowly descended onto the deck. We never searched for Walt, assuming he was "lost at sea." Normal activity had resumed, and the ship's crew readied for entering San Francisco Bay. Sections Two and Four were to stand in formation on the deck. John and I, both in Section Four, were putting on our dress blues when the Kearsarge made a distinctive turn to port. We smiled at each other, excited to see a new city.

Racing to "entering port quarters" we grabbed a ride on an airplane elevator as it whooshed its way from the hangar deck up to the flight deck where we were greeted by a lifting fog. The ghostly shape of the ship slowly emerged from the fog bank and was instantly transformed from a dark gray mass into bright silver gray. As our ship slipped under the Golden Gate Bridge, the morning sun shadowed its image onto the ship's deck and our uplifted faces. The Navy band played as we stood at attention and saluted the raising of the flag to morning colors. Quarters were then dismissed in preparation for docking. Since this did not involve us, we walked forward towards the bow, admiring San Francisco's skyline as it grew larger before our very eyes.

One advantage to standing quarters upon entering port was that Sections Two and Four got rewarded with first liberty call. Once the ship was docked, secured again by giant hawsers fore and aft, the boatswain's whistle blew and the call "Commence liberty" came across the loud speakers. John, who was broke, traded his liberty for cash and took over the duty of one of the guys in Section Three. Already wearing my dress blues, I walked down the gangplank, joining others boarding the bus to the city.

Grouping in twos and threes, everyone got off when we hit Market Street and spread out up and down the bustling main fare. I let them disappear, slowly meandering by myself, gaping at the canyon of tall buildings. There was just too much to take in all at once, but then I noticed a beautiful woman window-shopping a few stores up ahead. Slowing down, as I drew closer to her, hoping to catch her eye, I was almost knocked down by a much larger, rougher, masculine-looking woman with short-cropped hair emerging from within the same store. She, in turn, whisked away the object of my intention, stopping me in my tracks and leaving me standing in bewilderment. I had never seen that before.

I did know one person who lived in the city, Pops, who had befriended me in Long Beach. He was about sixty years old and an ardent sun worshiper who spent some of his free time on the Pike. He also had his favorite spot next to the wall facing the beach. He was a slim man with wrinkled skin the color of creamed coffee. Some of the boys and I would often have lunch with him, which he always paid for. Afterwards, he would watch us as we played beach volleyball. When I told Pops that the Kearsarge would be in San Francisco the same time he was going to be there, he said I should look him up.

Dialing his number, I was surprised when it was answered by a voice saying, "Front desk, Holbrook Hotel."

"Uh," I hesitated. "I'm looking for a fellow named Pops."

"Oh yeah, a guy named Pops lives here sometimes. Ya want ta leave a message?"

"Just tell him that Don from the Pike in Long Beach is in town. He'll know who it is."

"He should be back around two o'clock. I'll tell him."

"Could you give me directions? I'll meet him."

New to the city, I didn't know that I had been directed to a small hotel in the Tenderloin District, known for its prostitution, drugs, drifters, vagabonds, etc. In broad daylight, its true colors were hidden. As I approached the lobby of the hotel, I was unaware of any of the dangers that could possibly lurk behind its closed doors. Pushing the large double glass doors inward, I entered the main lobby and was greeted by Pops who leaped up from a well-worn brown leather chair.

"Don, how great to see you. Come up to my room and we'll get you out of that silly uniform and into some fancy duds."

Up the stairs to the third floor we went. Once inside his room, Pops slid open his closet door and told me to find something that fit me. I replaced my dress blues for a silk multi-patterned shirt, a pair of khakis, braided brown belt and a blue suede jacket.

"Well, kid, you look great. Come on and let me show you some San Francisco action. Oh, by the way, everyone in the city knows me as Michael, not Pops, Okay?"

First, we had a great dinner at Original Joe's, a local Italian restaurant where all the waiters were dressed in black tuxedos. Michael seemed to know everyone. As we sat across from each other in a small booth across from the bar, our waiter, Otto, kept our wine glasses full of red Chianti. After dinner, Michael shelled out cash for the bill and we left OJ's around nine. The streets were alive with people of all nationalities, San Francisco being the cosmopolitan city it is. Flashing lights over marquees invited us to partake of the entertainment they offered within: music, plays, movies, food, drink, and strippers. Hawkers stood outside the strip joint entrances enticing us to "Come on, take a peek, no cover charge."

Michael was greeted with a knowing smile, and the curtained entrance was hastily drawn aside as we entered the first nightclub. Inside, there were women all over the place, sitting at the bar, standing against the walls, lounging in leathered upholstered booths and sitting at tables. A lot were with customers, most of whom were sailors and marines. We picked a vacant table and sat down. Immediately, two girls approached us. "Hello Michael, who's the cute guy you got with you?" one asked, running her hands softly over my shoulders.

"A friend of mine up from Long Beach," he answered, "Go on, and dance with him. I hear tell he's a great dancer!"

The two girls kept me occupied. Michael didn't participate, just lingered with a smile on his face, ordered drinks and observed. I was getting a little buzzed and started to get more than friendly with one of the girls when Michael decided it was time to go.

"Come on, Don," he said, "I know another hot spot." Reluctant at first, I finally complied, excusing myself as I crawled out from under the girl's arms ready to continue the night's excitement. The next bar was a disappointment. The music wasn't as good and there were fewer women but - I noticed - more men. I voiced a complaint, but Michael paid no attention. Instead, he put his arm around my shoulders and said, "Have another rum and coke and we'll leave in a minute or two." By now I was really getting inebriated and totally oblivious to Michael's overly friendly attentions.

"Let's go back to the other bar," I said. "I liked those girls."

"Hey, don't worry buddy, trust me," Michael answered, "I know an even better spot."

Next bar, same story, the booze was slowly taking over my senses. By now I didn't really care that I was being dragged into a bar that was all men. My first exposure to a gay bar was neither frightening nor threatening. Everyone was very huggy and attentive. Most of the little innuendoes flew over my head as I observed the action through slightly blurred eyes. Around two in the morning, Michael called a taxi, pushing me into the back seat with him for the ride back to the hotel.

The night desk clerk gave a knowing wink as the two of us climbed the stairs to Michael's room. All I wanted to do was go to sleep, but Michael had other things on his mind. Breaking out a box of photos from underneath the bed, he began to show me pictures of some very explicit sex scenes. First, they were of men and women, but as the pile dwindled, they were of men and boys.

"Sorry, Mike, not my bag."

Uninterested, I yawned and rolled over to the far side of the bed, closed my eyes and drifted away.

I don't know how long I lay in that stupor, but I awoke with a funny, sickening feeling that something was not quite right. Michael's arms and legs were wrapped around me! Shocked, I leaped out of bed. Disoriented, I was calmed by Michael reassuring me that it was just something I had imagined. I slipped back under the covers, asking Michael to stay on his side of the bed. Minutes after falling back to sleep, the same funny feeling again awakened me. "Wait a minute," I thought, "This guy wants something that I'm not ready to give." I roughly pushed his body off me and I leaped out of bed and immediately began to put on my uniform.

Michael apologized innocently for his sleeping habits and tried to talk me into returning to bed. Realizing the predicament, I was in, all I could think of was getting out of that room, out of that hotel, and back to my ship. It was time to get out of Dodge.

"See ya," I said, as I slammed the door behind me and raced down three flights of stairs, two at a time, my heart in my throat. Glancing at the clock in the lobby, I noticed that it was four a.m. Outside, it was very still on the streets, and the dark of night still enveloped the city. I wasn't pursued and sighed a breath of relief, glad once again to have escaped a potentially embarrassing situation. I hailed a cruising cab, "Pier 54 and hurry." I said as I scrunched down deep in the corner of the back seat. Hello, San Francisco - Good-bye, San Francisco! Another crazy lesson in life, when would I ever learn? ~

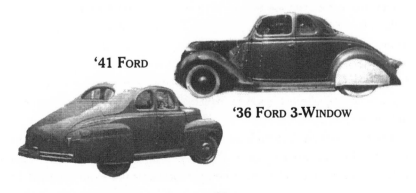

'41 FORD

'36 FORD 3-WINDOW

BOOK TWO

CHAPTER 14: WEST PAC

The Kearsarge spent six days in San Francisco taking on stores and mustering in the support crews that would service the squadrons of aircraft, which would be flown in from Alameda Air Station once we were at sea. The catapult crew was complete now, three petty officers and twelve airmen. My airman stripes were reissued and I was back on payroll. I was assigned to the flight deck crew, along with another sailor from my hometown; Tom Langhorne. Tom came from the East Side and had attended Roosevelt High, a neighboring school.

On Sept. 5, the ship hauled up anchor and headed out into the West Pacific Ocean for maneuvers on its way to Pearl Harbor. I was especially eager for the trip that would take 24 days for the crossing, arriving the day after my nineteenth birthday. That would be the extent of my sea duty. My new orders would disembark me in Hawaii, on the island of Oahu, for three years at Barbers Point Naval Air Station.

We were at sea for two days when we were joined by two destroyers and a light cruiser, our support and rescue ships. Later, other ships of the Seventh fleet would link up with us - a supply ship to replenish the perishables, an oil tanker for fuel, and a submarine. Our task force would then be complete.

On the morning of the third day, around 1100 hours, the call, "Ready to receive incoming aircraft," came across the loudspeakers. Tom and I rushed aft to watch the action as the arresting gear crew readied their cables to hook the planes as they landed on the flight deck.

On the far aft port side hung the arresting gear officer's landing platform. Here he would give the orders to the jet pilots directing their speed and approach angle. Aided by direct contact through earphones, lights, a giant reflective mirror and a flag man adjusting horizon and wing accordingly, he would accept the landing or wave off the aircraft for a flyby and another attempt. He was kept busy as a lot could happen within a few seconds. The ship could dip deep into a wave trough or the wind could change direction or speed, so he had to be right on the money, bringing in planes worth millions of dollars.

Once the task force was fully assembled, the war games began. As the impressive flying V shaped ship sliced its way through the deep dark blue water, I found myself truly enjoying being involved in naval operations. For an eighteen-year-old, this was indeed a real adventure.

The days and nights rushed by as the Kearsarge practiced its maneuvers far out at sea. The ship, darkened at night, practiced silent running, changing headings constantly, zigzagging to elude its Phantom pursuers. The catapults could launch planes within minutes of an "attack" warning. I had to learn all the catapult flight duties, starting with being the holdback man. Here I would slip titanium-breaking bars into a holdback cable that was attached to the aircraft's tail section, then into a connecting cable that was secured into a slot in the catapult. A sling harness attached to the plane's nose hook until the right tension was achieved then drew the plane forward. At a forward sign, the catapult would inch forward until stretched between the two in a "squat" position as it readied itself for the launch. I did a short stint, working jobs, holdback and harness. It was tough, hard work. Timing had to be right on, you had to watch your hands and your head all the time as you scurried under the active jet, most of the time in a low crouched position. It was hard on the knees and legs, and I was relieved when I was promoted to catapult launcher.

My new position was on the catwalk that hung off the flight deck. I had a panel of white, green and red colored buttons in front of me and huge headphones on my head, giving me direct contact to the catapult firing room lying deep in the belly of the ship.

Night launchings were the most spectacular to witness, and they could also be dangerous. Totally dependent on the lighted wands held in the catapult officer's hands, the pilots would be directed to center their aircraft on to the catapult. Once in position, the bridle was attached simultaneously with the hold back bar. That done, I would push the "Forward" white button, which would put pressure on both, the plane would squat down, now ready to be flung forward like a slingshot. The air officer's hands would then reach high over his head, the red lighted wands would be circled faster and faster, indicating to the pilot to rev up his engines in preparation for launch.

You could hear and feel the increase in power. When it reached a certain crescendo, the pilot in his dimly lit cockpit would give the "thumbs up" signal. The air officer would then point to me. I would push the "Ready" green button, a green light would flash on my panel, telling me the giant hydraulic piston below was up to pressure. I would raise both my arms high in the air with two thumbs up, the air officer would then genuflect towards the bow, his wands following in a swinging arc pointing forward. I would hit the red "Fire" button, the plane would surge forward, leaving behind the titanium bar, snapped in two pieces, spinning on the deck. All this happened within seconds, as it was crucial during wartime maneuvers to put as many planes in the air as quickly as you could launch them.

The plane, its afterburners aglow, would scream towards the sky, gaining altitude as fast as it could climb. The next plane would already be approaching the "cat," as the sound of the jet just launched diminished, now a silent speck of red and yellow glow, far away into the black sky.

We were constantly reminded of the danger we lived with. Sometimes night operations went on for a long time, launching and landing, launching and landing, and the men, very tired, sometimes grew careless. It was during one of these extended exercises that a bridle man, after his hookup on a "prop job" (propeller driven airplane), got too close to the spinning blades and was decapitated. Night operations were canceled the rest of that evening. If it had been wartime, they would have gone on, and he would have been considered a "war casualty."

Sometimes there would be a break, and it would be two or three hours between launches. During those times my buddy John Stiganga and myself would hole up in the bridle locker. We had temporary cots stashed there where we could cop a few Z's. We also had a small table where we could while away the hours playing pinochle. When we had left San Francisco, the two of us had made a bet; we would play a hundred games of pinochle at a dollar a game during the crossing. I would eventually collect eighty-five dollars.

The ocean was a truly wondrous thing to behold, especially from the vantage point of a large aircraft carrier. I loved to spend part of my time just gazing out at the total infinity. Many an evening I would go down to the hangar deck, walk back to the fantail and join my fellow sailors in sharing the disappearance of day's light. Sometimes I would miss evening's chow call just to watch the massive wake that the huge propellers created, pencil-lined out at the horizon, fading away in the brilliance of that day's sunset. On Sunday evenings, classical music would be piped out over the ship's loud speakers in celebration of the event.

After more than three weeks at sea, I noticed more birds beginning to appear, a sign that we were getting closer to land and our destination. Two days later, a small dark dot popped up, just a pimple on the horizon. Nobody called "Land ho" like in the early pirate days, but there it was: land. It remained black for the longest time, but as the ship drew closer, it grew larger and its color materialized into a vivid, lush green. And there it was: Kauai, the garden island, and the first of seven volcanic cones that formed the Hawaiian chain. Soon the famous Na Pali cliffs could be distinguished, and the mountains behind them took shape as the Kearsarge headed southwest through the Kauai channel.

The island behind us faded from view as the ship turned south and soon a larger spot appeared on the horizon: Oahu. Rounding the tip of Barbers Point, the ship came closer to Honolulu. The palm trees began to take shape, and the beaches took on a bright white/beige color.

The engines clanged back to slow as once again a harbor pilot boarded the ship, and we entered the famous Pearl Harbor. As we passed the battleship Arizona, which was sunk on December 7th, 1941, the word was passed to "render honor to port." The men, in their dress whites, saluted from the flight deck as we slowly, silently slipped by the great battleship, its flag still flying from the mast that protruded from the twisted mass of steel lying in the depths below. As we paid tribute to the 2,000 or so sailors still entombed in the bowels of the sunken hulk, a tear came to my eye as a bugler played taps.

Moments later, the Kearsarge berthed at Pier 37, ending my sea duty on Sept. 30, the day after my twentieth birthday. What a wonderful birthday present it was: Aloha, Hawaii! John Stiganga, Tom Langhorne, my hometown friend, and I disembarked to new duty stations on the island. I took the Navy bus to Barbers Point Naval Air Station, vowing to reconnect with John and Tom once we all were settled. Little did I know that some relationships are short-lived, and that I would never see these guys again. ~

CHAPTER 15: ISLAND DUTY

The transport squadron, VR 21, was considered preferred sea duty. Its barracks held around 150 men, was very clean with long shiny halls and walled cubicles off to sides, each bunking four men and their lockers. They had large communal showers with private heads, a TV room with posh leather chairs and a great recreational room with pool tables, table tennis, a library, and food and drink dispensers.

As soon as I checked in, I introduced myself and began inquiring about the squadron and its many billets, trying to finagle myself into a good job position. I wanted to fly a lot, if at all possible, and after asking around I found out getting into the Aero Equipment division would be the ticket. I studied up on what would be required of me at AE and made a mental note to myself to beat the system by assigning myself.

Early the next day, about an hour before morning muster, I walked into the giant Quonset hut that housed Aero Equipment and its crew and asked to see the duty officer. I was directed to a small office along the side and could see two khaki-clad chief petty officers talking to each other over their morning "cup of Joe." Knocking politely, I received permission to enter. I stepped smartly into the room, snapped to attention and, with a "Good morning sirs, Don Yeager, Airman," I confidently introduced myself.

I explained that I had just joined the squadron and had not been assigned any duties as of yet. I expressed my interest in becoming a part of Aero Equipment since I had performed similar duties while stationed at NAS Memphis. I continued, rattling off what I had studied up on the night before and it worked!

Whether they believed me or not or just gave it to me because of my forwardness, nerve and guts, I'll never know. But it didn't matter. What mattered was that Chief Harris and Chief Segona requested that Airman Don Yeager be assigned to Aero Equipment! I would spend the next three years being part of this wonderful team.

Reporting to duty the very first day was both intimidating and exciting. After morning muster, I was introduced around and placed in Section One under 1st Class Petty Officer Stan Able. VR 21 had fourteen shiny aluminum-sheeted R6Ds, each powered by four Pratt and Whitney reciprocal engines. They were wonderful aircraft and usually flew with a crew of eight - two mechanics, two radiomen, two orderlies and two officers (the pilot and co-pilot,) the latter doubling as navigator.

The squadron's main duties were to transfer men to and fro across the Pacific Ocean. They also flew secret missions, transporting confidential material and special arming devices, known only as "bird cages." Aero Equipment's duties to the aircraft were confined to the interior of the fuselage. They included cleaning and disinfecting, erecting seats for passengers or removing them for cargo, supplying freshly packed and inspected parachutes. They also provided clean bedding for the four bunks in the forward cabin, fresh water and coffee, food for the galley, and last but not least, fresh "honey buckets" (port-a-potties,) with plenty of hand towels and toilet paper.

The pre-flight duties of AE were most important, all pre-calculated with a special weight and balance slide rule. The mechanics had to be conferred with as to the amount of aviation fuel pumped into each wing tank. The radiomen had to be checked, in case they were carrying any extra gear. The cargo had to be properly placed and tied down, and the passengers and seats had to be counted and put in the proper position. Then the center of gravity was re-checked, using the special slide rule to determine the final weight and balance of the aircraft. At times, something or someone had to be bumped to satisfy the crew chief before take-off was approved.

Before I could be put up on the board for flight duty, thus enjoying the benefit of extra flight pay, I had to attend flight orderly school. There, I learned all about the R6D, its limitations and its peculiarities. I learned all about the specially designed slide rule needed to balance the aircraft. I studied hard and passed the two-week course with an excellent score. I had finally found something I wanted to learn.

And last, but most importantly, before any airman could get his wings in the squadron, he had to go through Survival School. This proved to be extremely intense.

The first day we were ferried far out to sea and dropped off in a life raft out of sight of any land. We had 24 hours to reach land, using the knowledge we'd acquired in Flight Orderly School. We had small nautical sextons to read the sun and the stars to guide us. We ate out of emergency ration cans and de-salted our own water with the survival kits provided. However, we never reached land but did survive the 24 hours.

A helicopter, locating our position the next day hovered above us, and we were commanded to slip over the side of the raft into the ocean and one by one we would be rescued by the helicopter that would lower down a rescue harness. Once properly secured in the life-saving device, we were lifted to the open door. Once we were all "rescued" we were flown to and deposited on the deck of a waiting ship. The sailors aboard congratulated us warmly of our "survival at sea" and immediately escorted us down for a hot shower, dry clothes and some good food, which - by the way - the Navy was famous for.

The next day back on the island, we were issued combat clothing for the next test of pain. We painted our faces and hands black and green and were given a rifle without any ammunition. We rode in a Marine bus to the Kamaileunu Ridge, outside the Schofield Barracks Marine Reservation. There, we were given a map and a canteen of water. Our objective was to safely cross the ridge through the jungle and underbrush using wild pig trails or whatever evasive tactics we could conceive to elude the "enemy." The Marines - the enemy - were dressed in North Korean uniforms and had previously hidden themselves in foxholes and pillboxes that dotted the ridges and the valley in between them.

In the hot and humid air, sweat was running off my forehead into my eyes when I encountered my first hidden pillbox. I had detected a movement in a thicket, and I froze immediately. I waited, heart pounding, daring not to cough or rustle any brush to give away my position. Soon, they started to talk in low voices to each other. I decided to slowly back away from the sound. I came upon a pig run hollowed out in the thick brush and proceeded to crawl on my belly, elbows, and knees through the tunnel almost directly under the noses of the enemy. Luckily, I didn't come face-to-face with one of the wild pigs, although I thought I heard one grunting as he rutted somewhere near me, but my mind was just playing tricks on me. Adrenaline peaking, I worked myself down off the ridge and found a small creek that was indicated on my map.

Following its downward path, I finally broke out of the dense undergrowth and found myself on a bright white sandy beach. I detected voices slightly muffled by the crashing surf and crept closer to their source. Peering over the edge of the sand dune, I saw a friendly sight - my survival group! With my rifle held high over my head, I stood up, showed myself and, with a smile of relief, joined them.

"Hey, you guys, ya got a beer?" I kidded them.

"Dino, you made it, man!" (They called me by my newly acquired nickname that would stick with me throughout my Navy days.) "And without a red ribbon," another one of my comrades chirped in. Some of us had made it to the rendezvous area without being tagged with a red ribbon, which meant we'd been shot. Others had as many as two or three of them tied to their arms. I was exuberant, exchanging slaps on the backs in congratulations.

On the beach was a large table set up with food brought in from the base commissary, along with fresh water and coffee. A truck had brought in some field tents and sleeping gear. We were ordered to build a pit fire and set up camp for the night. Once this was accomplished, we had some free time to strip down and go for a swim. Later that evening we all sat around the fire, exchanging our day's experiences with each other. Around nine o'clock, a night watch was set and we retired, completely spent.

It seemed that my head had hardly hit the pillow when I was awakened by gunshots, and loud growling voices speaking an unrecognizable foreign language. All of a sudden, the flap of my tent was thrown open and a bright flashlight blinded me. I felt the business end of a rifle poke my chest. We had been systematically captured. It all seemed so real, and these guys were not kidding. They were rough and lined us up with our hands clasped together behind our heads. Most were of Japanese/Hawaiian descent, dressed in North Korean uniforms with red stars on their hats. They spoke loud and harsh and shoved everyone into a covered troop carrier. Packed tightly together, the back flap came down, and in the darkness we were all driven to a "prisoner of war" camp.

Bright lights, a barbed wire compound with tin huts and manned machine gun towers greeted us as we were lined up in the dry dirt, dusty enclosure. Interrogating officers with riding crops in their hands, using broken or "pidgin" English, started asking us, "Who are you, where did you came from and what was your mission?"

Our answer? According to the Geneva Convention and our prior training, we could only give our name, rank, and serial number. As each answered, we were either sent off to carry rocks, threatened and poked in the stomach with the riding crops, spat upon in the face, or had obscenities yelled at us, using our mothers as the top ridicule. Others simply disappeared into a tunnel at one end of the compound.

My turn came and the cold red blood-streaked slanted eyes of one of the officers looked angrily into my eyes. His bad smelling, hot breath hit my face as he yelled the question "WHAT'S YOUR MISSION?"

"Donald R. Yeager, Airman, United States Navy, 518-21-85," I replied.

"Throw the son-of-a-bitch into the hot box," he screamed, his spittle spraying me in the face. I was pushed into a small stifling hot tin box, smaller than the size of a one-hole backyard outhouse. My arms touched the burning sides and my head banged the top. I began to perspire immediately as the heat was unbearable. The sweat ran off my forehead and into my eyes, the salty liquid making me squeeze them shut tight.

"I can make it through this," I thought. "I can, I know I can!"

I started to collect as much saliva I could in my mouth to help satisfy my thirst. I could hear others in their boxes, pleading to be let out. I heard the banging of flimsy tin doors opening and shutting. Soon my door opened, "WHAT'S YOUR MISSION?"

"SPLAT." I blew the saliva into my tormentor's face. Two can play at this game - I thought - wrong! SLAM went the door, then it reopened, and a can full of red ants joined me. They began to climb up my legs. They weren't biting, just climbing. I clenched my teeth as the aggravation grew more intense, then I started silently praying, "Please God, make it end."

My ears started to ring, and I grew dizzy. My mouth was now parched and it hurt. I was just about to give up, when the door opened and a soft, kind forgiving voice said, "Come on out, Sailor, you've had enough."

The fresh air and a breeze from the ocean revived me enough to make it to the underground tunnel. Once inside I was greeted with helping hands that supported me and led me to a cool cot to rest on. I was given water and assured that the test was over. The next day I received my survival card along with my wings.

I soon got into the swing of things - enjoying my duty on base. I had a great crew to work with. I loved racing around the tarmac, servicing the different planes in my electric go-cart. The Navy had electric-powered vehicles long before electric golf carts became popular. The food at the chow hall was great, especially for someone like me who'd come from a family of six with a limited income. At mealtime I'd load up my light tin plate to capacity. Meat, mashed potatoes, gravy, vegetables, loads of bread, plenty of milk, great desserts, and there was always a "surprise" daily special.

I even got to continue my love affair with cars. When I was on call, I spent my free time on base at the automotive hobby garage with my buddies, building custom cars, hotrods and dragsters. My compartment bunkmate and new best friend, Steve Boecher, and I were building identical matching 1950 Mercury convertibles. They were both bull-nosed, (no hood ornaments) and had smooth, leaded in trunk lids. They sat low to the ground, had white tops with red interiors, and were sprayed dark gray primer with wide white sidewalls, and spinner hubcaps. When off-duty, the two of us would cruise side by side down Nimitz highway to Waikiki Beach. We constantly got the double take. Life was sweet. ~

CHAPTER 16: WACKI-WACKI (WAIKIKI)

By March 1960, I'd been on Oahu for six months and in the Navy for almost half of my hitch. Tired of living on base, Steve and I rented half of a small two-bedroom duplex on Royal Hawaiian Ave, one block off Kalakaua Boulevard, the main drag of Waikiki. The Ala Wai canal was just down the block the other way. Two large traveler-palm trees framed the front yard. The musical group, The Kingston Trio, lived behind us on the next block. In the afternoons you could hear them practicing songs that they would become famous for, especially Tom Dooley. "Hang down your head, Tom Dooley. Hang down your head and cry. Hang down your head, Tom Dooley, poor boy you're bound to die." They performed at the Coconut Grove, a small open-aired dinner club located on the left side as you entered the International Market Place.

I bought a baritone ukulele as my interest in Hawaiian songs grew. I learned how to strum tunes like "Going to a Hookielau," "The Hawaiian Wedding Song," and many more, including the un-Hawaiian Elvis Presley song, "Blue Suede Shoes." Every Tuesday night, on the beach in front of the Reef Hotel under its huge banyan tree, the local beach boys attired in bright flowered Aloha shirts would show up just before sunset. They had crazy nicknames, just like me. There was Splash Lyons, Fat Kala, Panama Baptiste, Squeeze Kamana, and Jimmy Hakuoa, among others. Some were Hawaiians, some Samoan, some Portuguese, and every now and then a haole (white person) like me was invited to join in. They would become my "bros," my Hawaiian buddies. They would gather driftwood and build a large campfire on the beach. As the crackling inferno shot sparks onto the star-filled night, they would strum on their guitars and ukuleles while the flames reflected off their smiling teeth.

I would sit quietly on the outskirts and softly strum my ukulele, keeping my eyes on the fingers of the entertainers for chord changes. I felt privileged to be accepted into their realm and proud to be part of an old tradition. I practiced every day at home and on the beach and soon accumulated a repertoire of about 20 songs. Eventually, I was invited to join in on the jam sessions, entertaining the tourists and college girls that flew in for the summer to attend the University of Hawaii.

I loved living near the beach and I spent long periods of time off base because of my accumulated "crew's rest." What was "crew's rest?" Well, before you left on a flight you got one day's crew's rest. For every three days you were gone, you got one day, also, and when you returned you collected another day. Timed right, you could come and go, enjoying beach time and seldom work on base. As I gained seniority and recognition as a seasoned orderly, my flight trips became more exotic and longer, allowing me all kinds of free time. It was like being on vacation, lots of R&R.

One of my greatest trips, a traveling dream come true, was the Admiral's yearly Pacific base inspection tour. It required many stops in a 30-day time frame. It was considered a special privilege to be chosen for such a flight. The flight board on the wall of the Operations Department read like a travel brochure. Leave Barbers Point on May 17, land at Johnson Island, then on to Wake Island, Guam, into Subic Bay in the Philippines, then on to Okinawa; Taipei, Taiwan; Hong Kong; China; Atsugi, Japan; Kodiak, Alaska; and down to Alameda, Calif., arriving back at Barbers Point on June 17. Many stops - many overnighters - many new adventures.

One month, but it felt like a lifetime, flying to all those exotic places, walking the crowded Asian streets in my Navy uniform or civilian attire, feeling proud, safe and important.

Our crew had been handpicked. Most of us had flown together on trips before, with two exceptions; the two new orderlies that I would have under my watchful eye. Capt. Jones, our commanding officer, wanted this trip to go off without a hitch.

In preparation for the jaunt, the interior of the 427 was stripped naked and a special VIP package was installed. Mahogany woodworked panels separated each of the inspection officers' individual quarters that were decorated with leather seats, carpeting, desks, bed, and wardrobe. The officers were watched over, cooked for, and generally catered to by their own Philippine stewards. Their food, wine, liquors, and after dinner cigars were kept stashed away from the flight crew's provisions and guarded jealously by the stewards. My orderlies and I avoided contact with the guys dressed in white, each of us taking care of our own.

On May 17th our supplies were all aboard, sleeping quarters made up and the wing tanks were filled with aviation fuel. The chief's pre-flight inspection showed no hydraulic or oil leaks, and our cargo and passenger load was balanced out on the slide rule. Number 427 sat ready to go, its polished aluminum skin shining in the gleaming sun, waiting silently for the Admiral's entourage to arrive.

Capt. Jones and Commander Sullivan, our pilot and co-pilot, soon appeared out of the briefing room on the side of the hangar, striding together, flight plans in hand, their luggage already stowed aboard. As they approached, Chief Segona held up the final check papers to be okayed and signed by the co-pilot. Minutes later, two dark midnight blue 1960 Cadillacs, with small American flags flapping on the top of each front fender pulled up to the on ramp leading up to 427's rear entry door. The Marine driver leaped out of the driver's seat and stepped to the rear to open the doors for the VIPs. Our crew stood rigid at attention, saluting each of them as they approached the aircraft. They smiled, returned the salutes and proceeded up the ramp into the aircraft that would carry them halfway around the world in the next 30 days.

Once everyone was in, I closed the hatch and secured it. Outside, the steel ramp was wheeled away. The Admiral and his officers were immediately seated in their plush leather seats, their seatbelts fastened. The engines coughed, spitting out clouds of blue-black smoke as each was fired up and idled out. Within seconds, all four were humming in unison. Capt. Jones looked out the window and pulled his thumbs out opposite to each other, the sign to the ground crew to pull the chocks holding the wheels. Once free, he released the brakes and the plane taxied forward. Reaching the end of the runway, Captain Jones applied the left brake and held it firm as he applied power to the two right engines, and the plane turned 180 degrees, facing the length of the runway. With no hesitation, he applied full power to all four engines, and we roared down the runway and were soon airborne. The wheels thumped into the wheel wells as they tucked themselves away in the belly of the silver tube. We were on our way.

Our first stop was Johnston Island, 170 degrees longitude, and 17 degrees latitude from the equator. It was a short leg, taking only four hours to reach the small Pacific atoll. As we touched down, we could see three military vehicles with large white stars on their sides, sitting at the end of the runway waiting to greet and ferry off the inspection team. After taxiing to a designated spot, the engines were shut down, but not before each one burped out a final fart, emitting a puff of blue smoke.

The jeeps were there an instant after the ramp was in position and soon whisked away the Admiral and all the officers. A fuel truck pulled up as the jeeps left and our fuel tanks were topped off. Chief Segona signed the gas chit and we were relieved of duty, with most of the day to kill. We roamed the rocky beach aimlessly, had lunch at the mess hall and made idle conversation with the sailors stationed there. We had a few beers at the enlisted men's club, watched the sunset and turned in for the night. Departure time was scheduled for 0900 hours the next morning.

Early the next day, about 10 minutes before take-off, our pilots and passengers arrived. Within minutes after boarding, we were soon airborne, all anxious to get this trip on the road. It would be a nice daylight flight, about six hours to Wake Island, another beautiful atoll way out in the middle of the Pacific Ocean with sandy beaches.

I took the first four-hour watch, busying myself by teaching the other orderlies advanced weight and balance and keeping the crew happy. Afterwards, I slipped into one of the bunks in the forward crew's cabin for a catnap and drifted off to sleep, lullabied by the droning of the four reciprocal engines.

I woke when I felt the aircraft drop its nose for descent. I pulled on my dungarees while still lying prone and then swung my legs over the edge of the bunk, slipping my feet into my shoes. I took a few steps forward and poked my head through the heavy black cloth curtain that separated the cockpit from the navigation and radio tables, just in time to see Wake Island appear four miles ahead and about 3,000 feet below.

Captain Jones invited me to lower the middle jump seat down between him and the co-pilot and watch the approach. I secured and readied myself for touchdown, in awe of the island protruding out of the deep water ahead. As we descended, passing over the surf splashing onto the breakwater that protected the runway, we could see hundreds of "gooney birds" (albatrosses) nesting along the sides of the runway. The roar of the approaching R6D's engines disturbed their solitude and they began running in all directions, frantically flapping their wings, trying to get enough air under them to lift them into the sky and out of danger. Later, after landing, the crew and I would pass many hilarious moments observing the birds' acrobatic antics while we guzzled cold beer at the enlisted men's club. Albatrosses are most beautiful in flight, but when they land, they usually tip over in front. They don't seem to be too bothered by their clumsiness. They just shake their heads a little and squawk at each other after hitting the ground, a real comedy act, which they too seem to enjoy.

During WWII, a great naval battle had been fought on Wake Island. Many historical plaques placed in different areas reminded everyone of how close we had come to becoming Japanese-ruled. That evening we enjoyed the evening sun setting behind some of the beached rusting hulks lying silently on their sides.

The next morning, slightly hung over from too many beers while watching the gooneys, we gassed up, replenished the water supply, got fresh box lunches for the crew from the galley, and left at 1100 right on schedule. The R6D taxied down to the end of the runway for takeoff, and we roared down the center yellow line lifting into the South Pacific's robin's egg blue sky. We immediately rolled into a slow banking turn in a semi-circle around the island. As I glanced out the window, I could see the coral reefs below revealing soft, muted colors of blue and green that slowly dissipated as the plane gained altitude and the island disappeared.

Flying southwest directly in line with the Philippines, we headed for the Far East. Our next stop was Guam, the southernmost landmass of a chain of volcanic islands known as the Marianas. I checked on the two orderlies, who were performing all their duties perfectly. Continuing to the cockpit, I was thrown off balance by a sudden drop in altitude. We had been hit with a strong crosswind tipping the plane five to ten degrees. A typhoon was brewing somewhere and coming at us. Having gone more than half way, Capt. Jones opted to continue, rather than turning back. We all trusted in his decision, but I silently uttered a prayer. The DC-6 dropped closer to the water, flying below the cloudbank that lay black and ugly above us.

I hit the sack but was constantly being thrown into the air with the rise and fall of the airplane as it tipped its wings from one side to the other, trying to stabilize. I crawled out of the bunk and went aft, slipping quietly along the corridor of mahogany panels, checking on the safety and comfort of the passengers.

Peering in on the Admiral, I reported softly, "Captain says we should be touching down soon, Sir, sorry for the turbulence."

"That's all right, son. It's only Mother Nature playing her silly games on us," he replied nonchalantly, peering up at me over the glasses perched on the end of his nose.

I continued on with my check. All were securely strapped into their chairs - some with pillows tucked under their heads - others asleep, a few reading by very small lights. Reaching the rear of the plane, I sat down in my seat, secured my waist and shoulder harness and promptly drifted off.

When we finally landed at Agana Naval Air Station on Guam, the wind outside was howling fiercely. The palm trees were leaning over from its force, their fronded leaves doing a St. Vitus dance. Freshly fallen coconuts were strewn all over the ground. Because of the high-ranking officials we had on board, we were immediately directed to taxi to a large hangar at the far end of the airfield. As we drew near, its huge doors slid open, covering us in safety. There were two other aircraft already harbored within and, surprisingly, they were both civilian. Forced down in winds of typhoon strength, an American Airlines jet and a similar Pan Am airliner would also be waiting out the storm, compliments of the U.S. Navy.

A bus soon arrived to take everyone to our respective quarters. Because of the approaching storm, the enlisted barracks were already filled with more 120 passengers from the two civilian planes. The officers were dropped off at special guest quarters that had been set up. We continued to the recreation hall, where two large television rooms had been converted into emergency lodgings.

Disembarking from the bus, our small overnight suitcases in hand, we faced away from the howling winds, squinting our eyes and holding onto our white hats as we walked up the steps leading to the door of the recreation building. It was late, so when we opened the door we were surprised to find a "typhoon party" going on at the bar. An even bigger surprise - there were quite a few women.

"All right," I thought, "This is going to be all right!"

Hurriedly, we claimed our room, threw our gear on the bunks that had been set up for us and headed back to the bar.

Four stewardesses from the Pan Am and American Airlines planes occupied the stools at one end of the bar. They smiled as Jerry Burke, the first radioman, and I walked into the room. All the other stools were filled, so I headed straight toward the girls who - still in their stewardess uniforms - looked professionally sexy.

Squeezing up to the end of the bar along the side of the wall next to a pretty brunette on the stool to my left, I ordered up a rum and coke for myself and a beer for Jerry.

The brunette smiled and said. "Any port in a storm, sailor?"

Her voice was slightly slurred, indicating that she and her friends had probably been there for quite a while.

"No pun intended, I'm sure," I laughingly replied.

"What's your name?" She asked.

"Don Yeager, but my friends call me Dino."

"Well, I'm Annie Williams, and these are my friends, Linda, Peggy, and Norma." We're all home based in Honolulu."

"No kidding? Jerry and I are stationed at Barbers Point."

"Do you know Commander Harry Sullivan?"

"Do I? He's our co-pilot and navigator on this 30-day flight that we're on."

Small world. We exchanged phone numbers and promised to rendezvous on Oahu when we got back. Sweet!

The next day around 1100 hours the weather calmed, allowing both the Pan Am and American Airlines to take off. Jerry and I went to wave off the stewardesses we had met the night before. We would remain on Guam for another four days until the inspection team was satisfied before heading on to the Philippines.

Guam was very hot and humid, and warnings were painted "Wear a Hat - Wear a Hat - Wear a Hat" on every cement post all the way down the corridor to the chow hall. I dearly loved the tropical weather and, coming from Hawaii, I acclimated quickly, remembering to drink a lot of fluids and not to over-exert. Jerry and I hung out together, becoming close friends and spending a lot of beach time together. We acquired a small jeep from the Navy motor pool and explored the many beautiful hidden coves that the island had to offer, where we swam and snorkeled among the reefs. We had to muster in every morning but had no duties on these "no flight" days and were usually free around 10:00 am to explore this exotic island all day.

On May 24, a week into the trip, we left Guam. Looking out the window, I observed a phenomenal light show on the ocean below. The bright sunshine bounced off the water below, hitting the underside of our aluminum wings, which mirrored the reflection back onto the water in brilliant silvery white explosions as they hit the shoreline surf below. It only lasted for a moment, but I caught it. I closed my eyelids, the flashes still there, slowly disappearing into smaller and smaller dots.

Next stop: Olongapo in the Philippines, gateway to the Orient. ~

CHAPTER 17: FAR EAST EXPLOITS

We landed at Subic Bay, the American stronghold in the Philippines for the Seventh Fleet. After post-flight duties, I could hardly wait to get outside the gate. According to Navy lore, the Philippine women were known for their beauty and sexual allure. Liberty call in the small town of Olongapo was considered to be the best in the Pacific. After securing the aircraft and stashing our gear in the visitor's quarters, Jerry and I obtained a liberty pass from Chief Segona.

"You guys be careful out there," the Chief warned us, with a mischievous wink in his eye. We slipped into our civilian togs, aloha shirts and tight-fitting khaki chinos. With our signed passes, we slipped out of the gate onto the streets of the unknown. We were soon immersed in a different culture - a moving mass of humanity. There were people everywhere. Typical of the times, their economy depended on the military bases. They were anxious to please the "round eyes" that the guarded gates of the base spewed forth. The action began almost immediately with hawkers calling from both sides of the dusty, unpaved street as we strolled anxiously from stall to stall, shopping and eating along the way.

You could see the difference in the generations. The old men and women were always bowing their upper bodies slightly, their arms crossed in front of them stuck within their sleeves, smiling widely as they greeted you, their eyes lighting up. The young men, more hip to our culture, tried to entice the dollars out of our pockets, but in a friendly manner. And the girls, ah yes, the girls. These young women with their giggles, smiles and laughter knew how to come on to a young serviceman. Some displayed enticing sexuality, while others were shy and demure.

After an hour of feeling the place out, we began to be more comfortable with our surroundings and decided to find a clean looking bar with food, music and, of course, ladies! Jerry spotted it first. "Hey Dino, look!" He said, pulling me around, placing me in the direction he was pointing.

"MOM'S PLACE, BEER, WINE, FOOD, GIRLS," the sign read in big red letters. Standing outside of its entrance, posing on the sidewalk, were three darling Philippine girls dressed like stateside high school girls in bobby socks, saddle shoes, short pleated skirts, and tight furry pink sweaters. Go figure?

"Cool, man," I said, "Let's go," and we skipped across the street to the other side, dodging bicycles, jitneys, and motor scooters. The girls saw us coming and grabbed us by our arms and escorted us into the bar. Once inside, two more girls joined us. Then Mom, a very large Samoan-Philippine woman, came over to introduce herself and made us feel right at home.

"You boys come to right place for good time," she said in Pidgin English. "We have best food, good clean girls, rock and roll, and very cold beer." "Okay," I thought, "Do we need to go any further? Guess not!"

Around seven o'clock, the bar started to fill up with marines and sailors who were stationed there. You could tell by their comfort and friendliness towards Mom and the girls that this was home base to them. Apparently, they were there to pick up their girlfriends. They ignored us, had a few beers and left with their girls. Jerry leaned over and whispered in my ear. "I'm going upstairs with this girl. See you back on base."

I was left alone with Camellia, a small 4-foot-11-inch, 102-pound doll-like creature, with whom I had spent the last 30 minutes dancing, joking and playing darts with. She clung to me and made me feel like I was something real special.

Mom noticed the two of us sitting alone and invited us to join her at the bar.

"Camellia, bring your lover boy over here and let's see if he has a strong stomach," she said with a chuckle in her voice.

"Come on, Dino, this'll be a test of your manhood," Camellia said, smiling wickedly with her eyes open wide.

Not knowing what I was getting into but always willing to accept a challenge, I followed her and sat down on one of the wicker stools that lined the dark mahogany bar.

"Tabat, Tabat, you get you butt out here!" Mom called into the kitchen through a small window opening behind the bar. "And bring me a balut."

Instantly, the small cook came running, a wide toothy grin on his face, holding a small egg between his forefinger and thumb, his arm extended at full length, as if he couldn't get it to Mom quick enough. Mom took the egg, reached under the bar, pulled out a powerful flashlight and lit up the thin shell, exposing its contents. Inside, I could see a small bird embryo, not yet quite fully developed, all contained within a yolk sac with tiny blood veins and curled up in a fetal position.

"This is a balut, a delicacy amongst our people," Mom explained. "The poor creature has been dead for some time, buried beneath the earth under the hot sun. It is said to contain special aphrodisiac powers, and it would please Camellia and myself if you would devour the little creature and make him become a part of you."

"Eeee—God!" I thought. "They're serious, but I'm sure it'll be worth it in the long run." Of course, another part of me was asking. "Why me? What is it about me, that gets me into these situations?"

Mom poked a large hole in one end and a smaller one in the other. I was instructed to put the bigger holed end into my mouth, suck the little creature out and swallow quickly. I sucked hard and the unborn fetus shot down my throat, a rancid smell accompanying it as it left the shell. Mom poured me a shot of Jack Daniels and set a cold beer on the bar in front of me as a chaser.

I could feel the eyes upon me as I picked up the shot glass. I'm sure they were all wondering if I was going to upchuck it. Without thinking, I downed it straight away after swallowing the fetus. I slammed the empty glass down on the bar top, shook my head, clenched my teeth, and yelled, "All right!"

They all waited in silence, eyes upon me, the first belch came from deep within my stomach cavity. I could feel its rumble. A second burp came and this time I could feel its heat in my throat and a sharp rush in my nostrils fired by the whiskey. I grabbed the beer, tipping my head as I chug-a-lugged it. Another burp, this one milder and one of satisfaction, it immediately soothed the nausea that I was beginning to feel. "Whew!" I breathed out. I'd made it. A cheer went up from the group that had surrounded me at the bar. They applauded my performance. I was proud of myself. I clasped my hands together and raised them over my head in victory. It wasn't that bad. Mind over matter, but later I would wonder how the hell I kept it down.

Camellia and I slipped off the bar stools and with a wave good-by, we pushed the swinging doors open that led out into the street and disappeared into the night.

Camellia had a small room in her family's house, with her own entrance to avoid bothering anyone else, she told me, and that's where we would spend the night together. Leaving the safety of the main drag with its bright lights and the protectiveness of the roaming Shore Patrol, Camellia led me through a maze of side streets and alleyways, each step unknowingly drawing me deeper and deeper into forbidden territory. Local young hoods, most dressed in white tank tops and baggy black pajama-like trousers, hung out on the street corners, cigarettes dangling from their lips. Old men squatted in the open doorways of their small shacks or apartments, backlit by the glare of black and white television sets and dangling bare light bulbs.

They stared silently at my invasion into their world. But I seemed safe alongside Camellia as she called out greetings to some and yelled out what seemed to be warnings to others. She appeared to be in complete control. I followed her lead like a little puppy, apprehensive about going beyond her protective aura.

"Dino, honey, buy my family some food, and my love tonight is yours," she said as she dragged me into a neighborhood grocery store. She shopped enthusiastically, carrying the deep, white, rough cotton bag that she had grabbed off a hook as we'd entered the store. She chose the staples she needed - milk, rice, assorted vegetables, a couple of large Philippine beers and a pack of Pall Mall cigarettes. "For my father," she said of the last two items. I paid seven dollars in American money to the happily, smiling, continuously bowing proprietor of the store. I felt welcomed.

It was pitch black when we arrived at the elevated stick structure that Camellia called home. I blindly ascended the rickety stairs, following Camellia's voice and whispered directions, my arms full of groceries.

"Be careful." she said, "I can do this in my sleep. Take one step at a time, there's four of them.

The squeak of rusty hinges announced our arrival at the entryway. I immediately bumped my head on the low doorway, not being able to judge its height in the darkness. She hastily lit a jumble of candles that surrounded the small bedroom, each in their own stage of burn-off revealing to me Camellia's cramped world.

In a corner was a small four-drawer dresser, its top filled with photographs of memories, with a mosquito-netted canopied bed reflected in its mirror. A washstand with a bowl, pitcher of water, soap and towels, a narrow cardboard closet filled with colorful hostess dresses, a wicker nightstand with a lamp completed the room.

With a whisper for me to get undressed and slip under the mosquito netting into the bed, Camellia opened an adjoining door and stored the food we had brought home. She was back in a minute and began to disrobe, unveiling her curvaceous young body. Dancing teasingly, she blew candles out for each piece of clothing she discarded. She was having fun and giving me a little show.

Her lovemaking was tender, sweet and comforting. I felt I had known her forever, and she was mine. Only mine. Our love lasted for what seemed hours. We couldn't get enough of each other. We finally slipped into wasted unconsciousness, folded up in each other's arms. It was sweet, to say the least.

I woke with a start in the morning. "Holy Mackerel," I exclaimed, "It's morning, and I'm not supposed to be here. Oh-oh, I'm in deep shit."

Jumping out of the short bed, my feet hit the wooden floor and instant pain greeted me. Looking down I noticed my feet from the ankles down were covered in a mass of tiny red bites. After the exhausting love making the night before, I had fallen into a coma-like sleep and, being six-foot-one and sleeping in a slightly shorter bed, my feet and ankles had extended out of the netting, exposing them to all the little creatures that loved warm flesh and the blood. My feet had been their dinner table for most of the night. I frantically dressed and then, lovingly, Camellia applied a lotion to my feet, soothing the pain enough that I could put on my socks and shoes. She quickly gave me directions back to Main Street, kissed me good-bye -forever - and watched me disappear.

I walked fast, sometimes breaking into a run, until I saw the sign, "MOM'S PLACE." I turned right and found myself bouncing up and down among a mass of shorter people all heading to work at the base.

Arriving at the gate, pass in hand, I was instantly taken inside the guard shack to the Marine duty officer.

"Where the hell have you been, sailor?" he asked, his eyes blazing.

"Overnight liberty, sir," I answered.

"Didn't you know overnights were canceled?" the officer questioned.

"No sir, I wasn't informed," I said innocently.

"There's been some gang trouble out there. You could have been messed up good! Do you know how lucky you are to be standing here this minute, this day?" The Marine officer's face turned red as he screamed at me.

"Guards, take him away!" he said.

I was escorted to the Navy's duty office. After explaining who I was, whom I was with and what I was doing there, Chief Segona was notified and I was placed back under the Admiral's command, protecting me from any further disciplinary action. I was, however, refused any more passes and had to remain on base the remaining two days that we were in the Philippines.

The crew, however, was once again entertained by my misadventures. They shook their heads, wondering how I managed to keep screwing up and then lucking out - escaping disciplinary action. I wondered myself - and how many more incidents like these was I to fall into before I got into real trouble - again?

"Can't believe how you slip by, Dino," my friend Jerry commented. "You must have been born under a bright star."

"It's the luck of the draw, my friend, the luck of the draw," I answered him, mimicking the voice of W.C. Fields. Two days later, the inspection completed, we continued our tour, taking off and flying to Okinawa. ~

CHAPTER 18: OKINAWA-TAIWAN-HONG KONG

Naha, Okinawa, one of the strongholds of the Japanese during the Second World War, is in the East China Sea, six hours flight time north of the Philippines. The Navy had a small installation there held under the command of a much larger Marine division. The inspection tour's stop here was purely a statement, a show of Admiralty power, checking up on the chain of command. The tour spent the night here while the crew checked over the aircraft, and the officers inspected both the Marine and Navy operations.

Fuel tanks topped off once again, we were ready to roll at 0700 the next morning. Everyone was anxious to leave Okinawa, as the next two legs of the trip would be purely sightseeing. Soon after takeoff, the plane banked into a turn that headed us back southeast towards Taipei, Taiwan, a short flight of about two hours. Taiwan was historically called Formosa, meaning "beautiful island." We landed at the civilian airport. There were no marine or naval bases on Taiwan, but the U.S. Air Force had a small transport operation located in the far corner of the airport. We taxied over to their hanger area, parked and secured the aircraft and were then shuttled to hotels in the capital city of Taipei.

Our crew was given twenty-four hours crew's rest. After checking in at our hotel, the two radiomen, Jerry Burke, Rudy Lee, and I headed out into the street action. It was mid-afternoon and the streets were bustling with activity. Strange music drifted in the air, different smells attacked our nostrils, and an unfamiliar language that sounded like gibberish rang in our ears. A lot of the people lived in the streets. Their laundry hung everywhere like flags indicating territorial boundaries. Ducks, chickens, goats and pigs were caged or tethered next to the cooking pots of the small living quarters of the massive hordes. The atmosphere held a feeling of constant commotion. This energy was transferred to us three young sailors, as we floated from stall to stall, shop to shop.

We wandered the streets and alleyways till dark, eating from the street vendors an array of fresh vegetables, goat meat, chicken, and some things we didn't recognize (snake, dog?) They all had their own flavors -some very interesting - but most were tasty! At seven o'clock we returned to our hotel and were picked up in a Cadillac limousine flying two American flags on the front fenders. We were driven outside of the city into the countryside where we joined the rest of the crew and officers at a dignitary's private residence for a cocktail party and a special showing of the 1959 hit movie, On The Beach. A midnight buffet was served after the viewing and we were back in our hotel rooms at around two o'clock in the morning. Again, we were living the good life that was available to visiting dignitaries.

We slept in the next morning, pick up time was at 1300 hours, and take off to the mainland of China was at 1400 hours. It would be a short hop with three days layover for liberty and Gedonk shopping - a Navy term for sailors on a shopping spree when overseas. We landed at the New Kowloon International Airport just as the sun was setting. We parked next to a Continental Airlines jet, which was on its inaugural flight to the Orient. As we disembarked, I stopped for a moment to take in a deep breath and the view. The air smelled pure, freshly washed by a recent rain. The hills and valleys rising out of the city were shrouded in clouds, lending a certain mystique to this Far Eastern land, all new and exciting to most of us. We wondered why we were there. But, evidently, we didn't need to know. For all we had been told was that it was a high-ranking diplomatic assembly.

We checked into the Royal Ambassador Hotel that bordered the port of New Kowloon across the bay from Hong Kong - a government perk with all expenses paid. All we had to do was to sign chits and everything would be taken care of. Did I love this or what? Another free ride!

Our rooms were on the tenth floor, each suite having adjoining doors to each other. My two orderlies, Ken Logan and Mick Farr, and I decided to bunk together this time. I had some bookwork to go over with them, plus I wanted to get to know them, as I had been avoiding them socially most of the trip.

They seemed enthusiastic about sharing quarters with the "hot dog rebel" of the crew, as I had become known on this trip. Utilizing my rank status, I claimed the bed nearest the window with its panoramic view of the Hong Kong harbor where we could see the nightlights just starting to illuminate the still water. We decided to have dinner first, then take care of business, get a good night's rest, and then party on for the next couple of days.

Arriving downstairs in the dining room, dressed in our civvies, white shirts and sport jackets, we looked quite dashing. Putting on the Ritz and acting the part, I requested a table with a view from the maître d'. We were seated where we could observe everybody coming and going, while enjoying a splendid view of the harbor.

"Well, boys, here we are, and the tab is on Uncle Sam, so enjoy!" I exclaimed.

We were about to order from the menu when the rest of the crew showed up all spiffed out, looking quite different in their civilian clothes. Chief Segona, our crew chief, with a chest like a round barrel, a nose red and bulbous, a face topped by a wrinkled brow, pockmarked cheeks and a cleft chin, was dressed in a black suit pinstriped with silver. He appeared to be in costume, portraying a 1930's Mafia godfather. His second, 1st class Dennis Hangit, had on a similar outfit. Jerry and Rudy, the two radiomen, were dressed more like us, in dress shirts and sport coats. Before this tour had begun, we had all been told that this mode of dress might at some time be required so we all had packed accordingly.

"Wow, look at you guys," I said, directing my comment to the Chief and to Dennis, "You're dressed to kill - pun intended."

"To the nines, my man, to the nines," the Chief answered, his bright eyes twinkling. "And we aim to complement these duds with a couple of beautiful ladies later tonight. But, meanwhile, let's put on the grub-bag."

Everyone scooted into the booth, and the waiter brought two more chairs to accommodate all of us. We ate American food, rather than Asian, putting down huge T-Bone steaks, baked potatoes, veggies and salad. We drank beer and Jack Daniels whiskey, laughed and told stories. The Chief, having been to the Orient many times before, gave advice to us first-timers. He also gave us his tailor's name and address in Kowloon, a short rickshaw ride away. In the same breath, he offered up the name of his favorite nightclub, guaranteed to offer whatever pleasures we might be seeking.

I took notes: Tommy Wong, tailor, 1100 Kings Boulevard, and Suzanne Chung, Madame of the Chi-Chi Club, just around the corner. We finished dinner and I excused myself, and my orderlies, to go to our room.

"Hey, thanks, you guys, we're going to rest tonight and go over some bookwork, but we'll be hitting the streets first thing tomorrow," I said.

"You do that. We'll pave the way for you tonight," the Chief said. "Leave a little for the waiter, and I'll sign for the bill."

Everyone popped a five-dollar bill onto the now stained white linen tablecloth and the party broke up. I had momentary second thoughts about joining the others and continuing the party. "But, no," I thought, "I'd better stick to plan A and get the work done."

It was around two o'clock in the morning before my updated reports were completed. I evaluated Ken and Mick and told them how they were faring. Next, I taught them a few tricks on the slide rule to compute more accurately the weight and balance of the aircraft. This was going to become very important since, beginning with this stop, the belly of #427 and every available nook and cranny would be filled with Asian treasures. We fell asleep exhausted, but ready for the next day's adventures.

Dawn broke early for me, first light being my alarm clock. I rose with the birds. The fog in the harbor hadn't lifted yet and the morning stillness was broken periodically by the mournful sounds of freighters' bells, whistles, and foghorns. I slipped out of bed and pulled back the drawstrings of the partially opened red velvet drapes revealing the scene outside. Misty gray light entered the room. I was excited, wanting to roam the streets of this enchanting and mysterious city as soon as possible.

"Come on you guys, get your butts out of the rack, and let's go spend some of that per diem (extra flight pay) we're getting. I hit the shower first, shaving close under the hot spray. After patting my face with some stinging, spicy aftershave lotion that was provided by the hotel, I pulled on a pair of khaki chino pants, white socks, penny loafers, and a Hawaiian Aloha shirt.

"See you guys downstairs for breakfast." I yelled, as I opened the hotel room's door, bent down to pick up the British newspaper left outside of it, and headed on down the hallway to the elevator.

It was quiet in the dining room. I settled into the same booth we had occupied the night before. I ordered a Bloody Mary and settled back to read the morning paper, postponing breakfast until Kenny and Mick joined me. That solitude only lasted a moment when a familiar voice broke the stillness.

"Yo, Dino." It was my friend Jerry, the first radioman.

"Yo, Jerr, have a seat." I answered.

"Wow, you should have been at the Chi-Chi Club last night," Jerry said with a wide grin as he slid in opposite me.

"They have some beautiful women there," he continued. "And the good news is Suzanne, the madam, has set up a special flying-off party for our crew tomorrow night, starting at seven. Wait till you see these ladies! They are truly exotic. It seems like over the years, because of British rule and because of the worldly importance of this city, a lot of European men married Chinese women, and some of Suzanne's girls are offspring of these encounters. They're tall and sleek, some with brown eyes, some with blue eyes, some slightly slanted, some more round. These are not run-of-the-mill prostitutes. They are true ladies of the night."

"You got me all excited and I can't wait till tomorrow night. I'm going to see the Chief's tailor, Tommy Wong, right after breakfast and get me one of those Italian silk suits made, just for those ladies," I said.

"Think I'll go along with you, okay?"

When Kenny and Mick arrived at the table, Jerry filled them in on the happenings they missed the evening before. After breakfast the four of us hired two bright red rickshaws with yellow wheels, and we were swiftly whisked away down the boulevard to Tommy Wong's.

Kings Boulevard, the street that the tailor shop was on, was like Fifth Avenue in New York City. British police wore white uniforms with gold braid hanging off their shoulders, their heads adorned with white pith helmets topped with tall red plumes that swayed with their movements. They directed traffic standing on square box cubes, one hand waving in the air, the other with a whistle held to their lips, each putting on his own show from his pedestal. Long black limousines, Mercedes and Cadillac have seemed to be the norm. But the red rickshaws, pulled by mostly skinny men with their fares, skirted around the motorized traffic with amazing skill and grace. Some store windows were filled with diamonds and jewels while others had women's furs displayed on slim mannequins. Money exchangers were everywhere, and stores galore, offering everything you could imagine.

We finally arrived at the 1100 block and the store "Wong's for Men," with its sign written in English, Chinese, and French, stood out on a corner. We entered to the sound of a tinkling bell. A small Chinese man with a mouth full of smiling teeth, his white shirt sleeves rolled halfway up his arms, and a cloth measuring tape hanging over his shoulder greeted us.

"Ah so, welcome my friends, you be sailor boy or Marine?" He asked.

"We're sailors, and our chief, Chief Segona, told us about you," Jerry said, "Are you Tommy?"

His language sounded like it came out of a post-war B movie about the Orient. For all I knew, he could have spoken the Queen's English, but he played the part perfectly.

"Yes sah, you betcha. I be Tommy Wong, at your service. Chieffie Segona, velly good customer, he buy plenty suits. Tommy take velly good care of you." His arms crossed in front of him and his body bowed up and down.

"Well, Dino here wants one of your fine Italian-styled silk suits." Jerry said, pointing at me.

"Velly good. This be latest, only arrive Tommy's yesterday, fresh from the finest of silk worms," he explained, as he folded out a sample yard from a roll of light brown, silk fabric, with a hint of gold specks interwoven into it.

"You've sold me," I said, "Guess I don't need to look any further."

"Velly good." Tommy replied. He got down on his knees, snapped the measuring tape off his shoulder and started measuring my inseam.

"32 long leg, 33 round waist, 34 long arm, 42 regular shoulders," Tommy muttered as he mentally recorded each measurement moving swiftly around my body.

"You want three-piece suit? Coat, pant, and velly nice vest?"

"Sounds good to me, how much will it be? And how long will it take to make?" I asked.

"For you, today, velly special price, only forty-five American dollar. My girls work velly fast, only take twenty-four hours, you come back tomorrow, same time, suit done."

"You want too?" He turned and asked Jerry, in the same breath.

"No, Tommy, the rest of us are just tagging along, but I would like to know where to find some nice jade and some semi-precious stones."

"Oh Tommy have velly special place for you, plenty jade, rubies, black onyx, pearls, anything you like. Tommy close shop and take you special tour."

The four of us glanced at each other, shrugging our shoulders with questioning looks. Tommy moved his tiny feet, short stepping them to the front door. He flipped the "Open" sign to "Closed," and with a wave of his small hand and a sly smile on his face, he said, "Please to follow."

We followed him to the rear of the shop where he drew aside a set of drapes exposing a hidden door. He opened it, entered the semi-darkness beyond and proceeded down a narrow staircase. We hesitated, unsure of where he was leading us. Looking back at us, continually moving his hand back and forth, he beckoned us to follow him.

"Come forth, come forth please," he kept repeating.

Descending the staircase, we were surprised at what we saw in the room below. There, crowded close together were eight young girls, each hunched over a sewing machine intensely engrossed in the hard work of garment making. Tommy stopped to talk briefly to an older, grandmotherly-looking woman sitting on a high stool facing the girls. He gave her the measurements he had just taken and a sample of the material for the suit, all the while pointing and smiling at me. That taken care of, he then headed to a small wooden door in the far rear of the shop.

"Please to follow," he said, opening the portal that led to an underground tunnel system. One by one we followed, ducking our heads through the low door as we entered a dimly lit cave with corridors. I'd read about the underground systems that the Chinese had built in San Francisco, St. Louis, Chicago, Boise, Seattle, and other cities in the United States, and now I was experiencing one first hand, right here under the streets of Hong Kong.

"How exciting," I thought as my heart picked up its pace in anticipation.

Bare bulbs lit the way, hanging loosely from the wooden beams supporting the boards that held back the earth above. The air was humid, damp, musty, and mysteriously silent like a tomb - a little bit scary.

After walking hunched over for three or four minutes to avoid the low ceilings, we passed by numerous other doors encased in the earth walls, each somewhat like the one we had just come from. Suddenly, a rather strange smell hit our nostrils.

"What's that sweet odor?" Jerry asked.

"A mixture of opium, incense, and - and the smell of the living dead," Tommy whispered, raising his eyebrows high to accentuate his meaning.

"Really?" we exclaimed in unison. Our hearts started to race.

"Many men come to opium dens, they smoke, have velly sweet dreams, eat rice, have little tea, then smoke again. Many drift away into death - it is traditional for many to do. Nobody talk bout it, is part of life -death is," he explained to us in a hushed voice, sharing the secrets of the mysterious East.

Tommy stopped at a shiny enameled black door with a red and golden dragon painted on it, its tongue lashing out viciously.

"You like see?" he asked. "Yang San, proprietor, friend of mine, but you no talk, only look, okay?"

"Okay," we whispered back.

He knocked - boom, dot, dit, dit, dot, dot, boom - undoubtedly a special code. The door opened a slit, exposing a shadowy figure lit by a dim light behind him. An earthy sweet smell hit our nostrils.

"Yang San, is Tommy Wong, have curious American sailor boys want quick look-see," he said, his voice softly asking permission.

"Only for you, Master Wong, only for you." Yang San opened the door inches more. "Must be quick, though." Tommy smiled his approval at us and stepped aside.

First to peek in was Jerry. "Wow," we heard him whisper to himself, increasing our curiosity. After a moment, the door closed back to a slit, indicating his time up, and I stepped up and took his place. The door reopened enough to allow me to slip my head partially into the room. Amazed, I breathlessly took in the calm, spell-like, narcotic scene exposed to me.

Men were stacked in bunks that lined the walls, mostly naked except for a white loincloth that each had tied through their crotches, then wrapped around their waists. One was hunched on the floor, busily working a pair of chopsticks thrust into a bowl of rice cupped within his hand. Two others were sitting on short wooden stools around a small table. In the center of the table was a tall water pipe, filled with a brownish-white substance. A four-foot long tube was attached mid-length, the drawing end capped in a decorative silver flute. The two were silently passing it back and forth, taking large hits of sweet smoke, as if in slow motion. They all appeared to be emaciated and spaced out - far removed from their present surroundings.

The door squeaked back to a slit, almost biting my nose, as I backed away to let Kenny and Mick take their turns. Their peeks were quicker, and after a minute or so, the door closed to a small crack and Yang San's face filled it. Tommy stepped close to the opening and whispered something to Yang San in a strange dialect. Yang San answered him with a grunt and the door shut in front of him, ending our encounter.

"Jeez," Mick said, his eyes wide with disbelief. "They looked like zombies."

"Please not to say to anyone, okay?" Tommy asked us.

"We won't," Jerry answered for all of us.

Continuing, we turned right down another dimly lit long corridor extending deeper into the labyrinth. We approached another door, this one painted green with a yellow star on it. Tommy smiled, his eyes lit up. "Jewels," he said, while slowly rapping his knuckles upon its surface, again in a code. A moment of anticipation passed. Soon the door opened wide and a smiling face greeted us, a large gold tooth flashing out from the middle of pearl-like teeth, enhancing his grin. He was a large man dressed in a fluorescent blue suit, white shirt and matching tie. Three of the fingers on his left hand and four of the fingers on his right were ringed with diamonds and jade.

Behind him, under black lights, were cases filled with jewels lying on black velvet cloths. Four more men were in the room, sitting on stools behind the cases, each with jeweler magnifiers attached to bands encircling their heads.

Tommy bowed, said a few words to the suited one, and then stepped aside. We entered the room.

"Welcome, welcome, gentleman," the big one said, in perfect Queen's English. "And how we may be of service to you today?"

Jerry spoke up first. "I'd like to see some jade rings and some black onyx."

"Me, too," I added.

We were led to two brightly polished, wooden mahogany stools with red leather seats that sat on our side of the cases. Behind sat the four displayers, ready to satisfy our every whim. We each pointed to different pieces in the cases and one by one they were brought out for us to view. Kenny and Mick stood behind us, breathing over our shoulders.

After some finagling, Jerry finally laid out three hundred dollars for a variety of stones and jewelry that he knew he could resell and possibly triple his money back in Oahu. I purchased a beautiful emerald green jade ring set in gold and a black onyx one in silver. Kenny and Mick, caught up in the action, spent a hundred dollars each for some jade stones.

When the dealing was finished and our purchases were wrapped in clumps of tissue paper and stuffed deep in our pockets, we were led up a flight of stairs and through a door that entered a legitimate street level jewelry store. We walked through and nobody paid any attention to us as we exited the store. Back into the light of day, we were surprised to find ourselves still on Kings Boulevard, about a quarter a mile down the street from Tommy's. We all acted very cool and expressed our thanks to Tommy for his tour into the unknown, but once we left him, we all took a deep breath and exalted in our safe return to reality. We all laughed, high-fived each other and skipped happily down the boulevard, each fingering the new jewels in our pockets.

The day had cleared. A beautiful azure blue sky shone above the waters of the harbor. We stopped at an open-air sushi restaurant adjacent to the dock for the harbor cruise ferry.

"Who wants sushi?" Jerry asked.

"I'll join you," I answered.

Mick and Kenny decided to pass. We agreed to meet later for the three o'clock harbor cruise. Jerry and I ate a couple of different types of sushi, topping it off with a couple of fish eyes, a real delicacy in the Orient. We popped them into our mouths, washing them down with a couple of tall British ales. We heard the bell ring from the cruise boat and ran across the street to catch it. Mick and Kenny were already there.

Seeing the Hong Kong skyline with the mountains behind it from the water was truly spectacular and observing the lifestyle of the boat people was interesting. We got back to the hotel around six that evening, totally beat from the long day's activities and decided on an early dinner in the dining room, then just vegging out in front of the small screen television in our room. We wanted to save our energy for more shopping the next day and the party at Chi-Chi's before we flew off to Japan.

I guess I was more tired than I realized, I had overslept, not awaking until around eleven o'clock the next morning. The room was silent and empty as my roommates had slipped out. I heard a knock at the door and went to open it. Standing in the hallway was Tommy Wong, the tailor, with a shiny new suit held in the air on a wooden hanger.

"You no come, so Tommy deliver," the little man said, flashing his toothy smile.

"Great, Tommy, come on in," I said, opening the door wider. I tried on the suit. A perfect fit, just as I'd been promised.

"Fits great, looks good, and thanks for bringing it by." I said, going to the dresser to get my wallet. I returned, handing Tommy two twenties and a ten-dollar bill. That done, I spent the rest of the day shopping for gifts. For my mother, Rose, I chose a beautiful embroidered silk house robe. For my sisters, Marilyn and Joyce, I purchased two white-faced porcelain Geisha dolls, elaborately dressed in ceremonial costumes, bewigged with authentic oriental black hair piled high upon their heads, adorned with jewels and silk flowers and held together with a pair of crossed black ebony wooden hair picks. Both were enclosed in separate glass cases.

The afternoon was turning into evening when I tired of roaming the streets of Kowloon and hailed a rickshaw to carry me back to the hotel. Up in the room, Kenny and Rick were trying to decide what to wear for the party.

"Hey, I'm sure anything will work," I said. "As for me, I'm dressing up." They finally donned slacks and sport jackets; I, my new Italian silk suit. Around six thirty we took the elevator down to the lobby, running into the rest of the crew as we stepped into the lobby.

"Hey Chief, hey guys, ready to party?" I asked them in greeting, slapping Jerry and Rudy on the shoulders. They all laughed at my enthusiasm and complimented me on my new suit. We pushed the hotel's heavy glass doors open, strolled out into the street, and headed to the Chi-Chi Club.

Arriving at the club, we stormed through the door a-hootin'and a-hollerin.'
"Let's party, ladies," we all yelled in unison, and with that a group of girls immediately leaped up to join us. They interlinked their arms with ours and led us to the cozy little booths that lined the walls of the club.

Suzanne had decorated the club with crepe paper and balloons, giving it a festive atmosphere. Luscious food was spread around, and a bottle of champagne was at each table.   "Dream Lover" was spinning on the record player and a stack of 45's waited on the spindle above it.

The evening was totally riotous, reminding me of a house of ill-repute back in the days of the Old West. Everyone was wild and having fun in so many ways.

Close to midnight, Chief Segona got on top of a table, clanged a spoon against a glass and asked for our attention. "You guys got half an hour to say your good-byes. We got a plane to fly tomorrow, and you'll need to sober up and get your rest. I don't want a hung-over crew, got it? There was a lot of feverish hugging, kissing and touching shoved into the next half hour. When the Chief yelled, "Time's up," we reluctantly tripped out of the club. The Chief and his second, Dennis Hangit, urged us on our way with gentle pushes and tugs. When we returned to our hotel rooms and finally fell between the clean sheets, we all welcomed the end of the Hong Kong experience. Next stop on the agenda was Japan, land of the rising sun. ~

CHAPTER 19: JAPAN, LAND OF THE RISING SUN

Heading north, flying over the Pacific Ocean, we crossed the imaginary line of the Tropic of Cancer heading towards Japan. We were heading for Naval Air Station Atsugi, which is located west of Yokohama. The flight was uneventful. After landing and securing the plane, we took up our temporary quarters, changed into civilian clothes, and grabbed the bus to the little town of Sagamihara. We were getting used to this "gedonk flight" schedule and wasted no time in taking advantage of our time off, cramming in sightseeing, shopping, drinking and carousing. God, it was fun! We were of the privileged few, specially picked, and we took full advantage of our position, as it was a once-in-a-lifetime adventure.

After passing through the gates, the bus roamed the countryside, revealing another culture to me. Rural life appeared to be placid and slow moving - it was like watching a documentary movie as we whizzed by.

Women dotted the rice fields, wading in calf-deep water, their backs bent 90 degrees as they reached for rice stalks which they carried in the woven baskets resting on their backs. Their hands disappeared past their elbows as they pushed each plant into the soil below. Up on the levies, children with long switches in their hands drove slow plodding oxen hitched to water wheels, walking around and around in circles, transferring water from one level to another as each bucket dipped and poured.

We went by villages with small houses, each with their meticulously cared for gardens. In their yards, tethered goats kept the grass and weeds in check, while chickens, geese, ducks, and pigeons shared the ground grit.

As we drew closer to the city of Sagamihara, the road became busier. Bicycles and carts of every shape and size carried unbelievably large loads, seemingly perfectly balanced as they were pedaled, pushed, or pulled by small, somber-faced men taking their wares to market.

All of a sudden the bus jerked to a stop and the driver swung open the doors, got up out of his seat, walked down the steps, went to the back of the bus and relieved himself. OK! "They say man is his own master if he can piss in his own back yard," I noted. We all chuckled.

We soon arrived at the bus station in Sagamihara, and Jerry, Kenny, Mick, and I swung off the bus and grabbed the first taxi waiting alongside the curb for the ride into Yokohama.

It was traditional that the "rookie" experiencing his first time in Japan was given the shotgun position next to the driver. Mick was the only member of the crew who had not been to Japan before, so Jerry quickly dumped him into the front seat. "Here, Mick, first-timers ride shotgun, hop in." Laughing, the three of us crowded into the small back seat, knowing that Mick was in for the ride of his life.

"Downtown, to the Blue Moon hotel," we ordered, and then we urged our cab driver to "hayaku, boysan, hayaku" (go fast, boy, go fast.) He responded enthusiastically, realizing that he had a "virgin" sitting next to him and knowing us guys in the back would tip better for a good show.

Mick's eyes grew wide and his knuckles turned white as he grasped the small bar on the dash, holding on as our driver careened his hack fearlessly in and out the heavy traffic. He put on a great show, honking his horn, yelling out the window all the way, while we sat in the back seat urging him on by chanting, "Hayaku, boysan, hayaku!"

We arrived at our destination out of breath, hearts racing, tears in our eyes and cheeks hurting from laughing so much. Mick was visibly shaken; several times having missed possible injury just inches away. He had to be helped out of the cab. Jerry gave the cabbie double the amount of yen that was displayed on the cab's ticker for his excellent performance.

We had three days of liberty and planned to spend every moment we could in and around Yokohama. The chief was the one who clued us in on the hotel, The Blue Moon. He said it was run by a good Mamma-San with a stable of good clean girls, and it turned out to be all that one could ask for.

The bottom floor was a small bar with cozy booths where we could get to know the girls. It also had a barbershop with women barbers, manicurists, pedicurists and a masseuse. Up the central staircase, after climbing three stories, we saw the rooms; four to a floor, branched off like a cross. Three of the rooms had beds laden with quilts and pillows. They all had a small bathroom with towels and monogrammed bathrobes. Candles, incense burners and a small stove for heat made up the other creature comforts.

"This," I said to Jerry, after taking the tour, "Could prove to be very interesting!" I raised my eyebrows high twice and tapped an imaginary cigar in my right-hand mimicking Groucho Marx, to emphasize my statement. (I tend to put humor in whenever the chance presents itself.)

After dropping off my traveling bag in my room, I rushed downstairs and plopped myself into a comfortable barber chair and proceeded to treat myself to a neck massage, a haircut and a close shave. First, my skin was moistened by wrapping it in steaming hot towels. Then a generous amount of foamy white cream was added and expertly removed by a shiny, leather-honed, single-edge blade with a pearl handle. A manicure and pedicure were happening at the same time. I lay prone in the chair, surrounded by three women on stools, shaving, cleaning, filing, massaging, while gabbing and giggling to each other throughout it all.

An hour later, feeling totally pampered and refreshed, I slipped out of the chair, paid the tab (a thousand yen, which was less than ten dollars American) and joined Jerry, who was waiting to go to lunch.

"Don't think I've ever seen you more relaxed," Jerry said. "I made an appointment myself while I was waiting."

We lunched on the second floor of an open-air restaurant called Louie's overlooking the bustling metropolis. The owner, Bruce Lee, was half Caucasian and half Japanese. His father had been a career Navy man. His Japanese mother was the daughter of the original owner of the restaurant, who had since passed away. We ordered our first beer and with that he voluntarily told us "his story."

In 1936, his father had been stationed at Alameda Air Station outside of San Francisco when he courted Bruce's mother, Win Lau, who was attending the University of California, in Berkley as a foreign exchange student. They met at the USO club where Win Lau was a hostess. They fell in love, married and Bruce was born in 1937, four years before the United States entered the war with Germany and Japan.

His father, unfortunately, turned out to be an alcoholic and wife beater, and his mother soon filed for a divorce through the military courts. They shipped his father off when the US entered the war. Bruce and his mother, being of

Japanese descent, were placed in an internment camp in Tule Lake, California, south of San Francisco. They were imprisoned there behind high wire fences until the atomic bombs were dropped on Hiroshima and Nagasaki, ending the war on Victory over Japan (V-J) Day.

After the war, Win Lau and her son were taken under protective custody. Hidden behind a gated, walled retreat high in the Sierras, she worked as a maid, nanny and laundress for a wealthy shipping magnate who had literally "adopted" her and her son. During this period, Bruce was tutored along with their children, receiving a special education.

In 1950, mother and son returned to Japan, receiving free passage to Yokohama aboard one of the freighters that the shipping magnate owned, along with $12,000 U.S. dollars, equal then to 4,320,000 Japanese yen. They rejoined Win Lau's families in Yokohama and with her stateside fortune, bought the building her father's restaurant was in and helped in establishing its reputation and popularity. In 1957 when her parents died, she and twenty-year-old Bruce took over the operations.

Jerry and I spent more than three and a half hours listening to Bruce's story, during which he introduced us to his special sake, never letting our small white porcelain cups go empty. A special camaraderie formed between us within a short time, especially when the boxing matches showed up on the black and white TV suspended above the bar at which we sat. Bruce and I discovered we both loved the sport.

About 5 p.m. the bar started to fill up. The fleet was in Yokohama with more and more sailors in dress blues roaming the streets below. Soon two sailors entered the restaurant and mounted the stools to my right.

"Hey, turn up the fights!" the one closest to me yelled at Bruce. Bruce accommodated the well-built, boisterous, tough speaking, demanding "swabbie."

"You sons-a-bitches ain't foolin' nobody with your fancy Hawaiian shirts on," he said, looking over at Jerry and me, poking his left elbow into my ribs, spilling the cup of sake I had just raised to my lips.

"Shit, man, why'd you do that?" I questioned.

Immediately Bruce wiped up the mess on the bar and quickly refilled both my agitator's white cylinder cup and mine. "Dino, I want you to meet Rolf Geartone, one of the roughest little son-of-a-guns you'll ever meet, pound for pound, Bruce told me. "And don't touch his buttons."

"Pleased to meetcha, ya motherf–ker!" Rolf growled extending his hand over to me for a shake, his sparkling blue eyes filled with amusement and friendliness. I caught the warmth and sincerity expressed in Rolf's eyes and immediately forgave him for the poke in the side. Rolf's hand slammed into mine and, when I felt his iron grip squeezing my hand, I was quickly reminded of Bruce's informative warning seconds before.

"We're here for the West Pac fleet boxing championships to be held at the Yokohama Sports arena tomorrow night. I'm one of the boxing trainers - used to rumble in the ring myself - wasn't no sons-a-bitches who could beat me. Always got my shot off first. Anyways, we got six good fighters on the cards, and you guys are invited to come on over. Be our guests."

"We could do that. We don't leave until Monday morning." Jerry chimed in.

"We'll get you right next to the ring, close to the action, my treat." Rolf offered. "Or maybe you could help, run water buckets or some f–king thing."

"Out of sight!" I exclaimed, excited to be going to a live boxing match. We made arrangements and promised to link up Friday night for the fights. We then departed Louie's, playfully sliding down the center stair railing, into the busy street. The sunlight of day was now replaced by bright sporadically moving, flashing, blinking neon lights.

The streets were now alive with completely different types of people. The women in traditional dress had been replaced with mini-skirted, leather-booted, high-heeled, and heavily made-up prostitutes. The business suits had morphed into flashy Zoot suits of the thirties on the backs of men with shiny shoes, slicked back hair and cigarettes hanging from their lips as they hawked watches, TVs, transistor radios, jazz records, and lots of unmentionables. A carnival atmosphere hung in the air, temptation at every step, one noise replaced by another - a controlled chaos. We roamed around for a while but soon tired of the constant action and noise, so we strolled back to the hotel for a good night's sleep. But that didn't happen.

Arriving back at the Blue Moon was a welcome relief. The atmosphere was quiet, lights were low, nice music was playing and the B-girls were lounging, waiting for customers. Momma-san was leaning one elbow on the bar, chin in her hand. They all seemed to come alive when Jerry and I walked into the lobby-bar, as if someone had pushed a hidden button.

Momma-san clapped her hands and the girls surrounded us with gentle tugs, soft cooing, and red lipstick smiles. They enticed us into a large semi-circular burgundy colored leather-cushioned booth. Two girls flanked each of us on the right and left sides. Promises were whispered while darting tongues light-ly touched our necks and ears.

"Sailor boy, very handsome, can make Nancy Kwan very happy," the girl on my left said. I wondered what movie she picked up that name from? It sound-ed very familiar, and it looked as if she had picked me, rather than me making the choice.

Jerry and I stopped by the bar to relay our intentions to the Momma-san. It was traditional and polite to receive her approval of our choice and discuss the amount of yen we would be required to pay for their services. Jerry and I went to the room we were sharing to undress and drape ourselves with the oriental silk robes they provided for us, then on to the hot tub room where we would be shampooed, scrubbed, and pampered.

The two grinning girls were waiting, each dressed in short white deeply V-necked cotton robes, their arms and legs barely covered and cinched at the waist. They had posed themselves on the wooden deck that surrounded the sunken round redwood tub and had buckets filled with soaps, oils, and brush-es. They helped Jerry and me to disrobe and invited us to enter the tub.

"Jeez," Jerry screamed as his right foot first tested the water on the surface of the three-foot deep tub. "It's scalding! I can't get in there!"

"Must be hot to purify body and spirit," my voluptuous attendant, Nancy Kwan whispered softly. She then bent over and poured warm water over my body from a large pre-filled wooden bucket. "This will help you to accept hot water."

I plunged in, splashing everyone as water washed over the sides. My scream was shut off as my head disappeared momentarily beneath the surface. I was back out in an instant, my body reddened by the immersion. My breath had been taken away and my eyes had widened. I noticed a hose on the wall and a cold spigot. I immediately spun the handle on the faucet, grabbed the hose as it straightened out with pressure and doused myself frantically, then shoved its spurting end into the tub.

"Crazy American!" Nancy Kwan exclaimed, not expecting my quick action.

"I'm not going to toast my family jewels in a hundred and twenty-degree wa-ter," I answered her in the same tone of voice.

After a minute, I retested the water temperature. Satisfied, I returned the hose to the wall, turned off the spigot, and slipped back into the tub sighing, "Whew, that's a lot better. Okay, girls, purify my body. My spirit has soared."

They laughed and giggled and started to soap me down as Jerry slipped cautiously into the now bearable 102-degree water. "Thanks, Dino, quick thinking," he whispered with a sigh of relief.

We ordered up a couple of tall Asahi beers and the fun began. After a bit of fooling around with the now-naked ladies, we hopped out of the tub and raced to our room, leaving the bathhouse a complete shamble.

We hurriedly pushed the two small beds together, making one larger play-pen, where a frolicking wrestling match with slight sexual undertones took place.

But even at twenty years old, you can only laugh and play so much when two sweethearts are paying special attention to the two of you! We had never experienced anything like this in our lives!

Later, completely spent, I passed out, a slight smile creasing my face as the action of the last few hours replayed itself over and over as I slipped deeper and deeper into the abyss.

It was a little after noon when my laundered and ironed clothes were delivered to my room. I dressed, luxuriating in their freshness and immediately felt revived. Right after, Jerry and I left to play the tourist scene, grab some chow and head off to the fights. ∼

CHAPTER 20: RUMBLE-YOKOHAMA STYLE

We arrived early and looked around. We could see the arena across a large courtyard. People in all types of dress, mixed with uniformed men from the fleet, were mingling together. Others were in long lines at the ticket windows. The flags of our two nations snapped in the wind above six double swinging glass entry doors. The air held an exciting festive aura. Rolf had instructed us to follow the fence line that bordered the back perimeter of the arena and look for a gate where the fighters from the fleet would be arriving by bus. Parked in back, buses and staff cars from the Army, Marines, and Air Force were lined up, their guards standing next to them at parade rest.

Two Marines were swinging the heavy iron back entry gates open for two dark midnight blue Cadillacs with the Navy insignia on the sides of the front doors. A four-star Admirals' flag adorned the two flying lady art deco hood ornaments.

We stood back as the limos spilled their contents on to the blacktop. Everyone in the area snapped to attention and saluted. Nine high ranking officers got out and to my amazement there was Capt. Jones, our flight commander, and Admiral "T-Bone" Haggard, our distinguished passenger and his aide.

"At ease," the Admiral said softly after returning our salutes. They turned and disappeared through the arena's rear entry steel doors. We dropped our salutes just as the Navy buses pulled in with our fighters and their trainers. I picked out Rolf's smiling face sitting in the first seat of the first of two buses. He waved at us.

The bus's air brakes whooshed and groaned as they came to a stop. The exit doors, tightly rubber sealed, sucked fresh air into their interiors as the driver of each bus pulled the long-handled arm that operated them up. Rolf was first off the lead bus.

"Hey, glad you guys could make it! Let's get our asses into the locker rooms. We've got some fists to wrap!" Rolf said.

We entered the steel doors. Walking down the tunnel-like hallway, our footsteps and voices bounced off the walls as we proceeded down to a series of locker rooms. Rolf entered the first door on the right with a sign above it saying, "WELCOME 7TH FLEET BOXERS - NAVY vs. MARINES."

Once inside, he gathered us around in a small circle and began his speech. "Okay, we'll be fighting the Jarheads (Marines) tonight. They found out we had a couple of professionals and want to give us a go for whatever - shoestrings, case of whiskey, or just plain satisfaction. Our boys have been working out hard, using the medicine ball, speed bag, heavy bag and sparring with each other. We've voted for a 22-foot ring to make for a more rapid fight. It's a good ring size for anyone who likes to run away. Believe me, that won't be our guys. We also decided on two glove sizes: 12 ounce for the amateurs and, for the pros, the 6-ounce gloves that have less padding and little more leather. Our pros are real fighting men and they don't need to be hiding behind two 'puff balls.' And when they hit their opponents, we want the punches to hurt a little bit, have some effect, if you catch my drift." Rolf threw a couple jabs and an upper cut into the air to demonstrate his meaning. He went on and on. This man was never lost for words.

"Now we got six bouts on the card tonight, four pros and two amateurs. The amateurs will go first and then we'll follow with our pros - okay - let's go, the guys are in the next locker room."

The adjoining room was much like a small gym. A couple of the fighters were shadow boxing, some were getting rubdowns and others were having their hands wrapped with tape.

"Yo, men, listen up!" Rolf yelled as we entered the room. "First, I want ya to meet a couple of flight jockeys that are going to help out tonight. This here's Don, and his partner Jerry. They're here with the VR-21 transport squadron, so be nice to them. They could be your ride home one day."

Rolf continued, "Now remember what I taught you sons-a-bitches. Work in a shell; keep your left arm placed across your face just below the eyes and your right across your mid-section around the solar plexus. This'll put you in the clinch mode of fighting. It'll keep you close in and you can ward off any jabs with your forearms and react with hooks, alternating right then left. Stay in close, don't back off, be the aggressor, and throw the weight of your body into each punch, come from the ground whenever you can, using the power in your legs."

He called for the first amateur to fight. "Okay, Ive, you're first up. Follow behind me. Seconds, come behind Ive, and you two guys," he said pointing to us, "Grab the buckets, water bottles, towels and liniment and bring up the rear." We went through the door and out into the hallway.

"Stay tight and chant 'Navy! Navy! Navy! Navy!!!'" Rolf prompted.

As soon as we hit the main arena with its bright lights and the noise of the crowd, our moods became aggressive. We stepped up our strides to a bouncing shuffle screaming loudly, "Navy! Navy! Navy!!!" The cries were picked up by our supporters, while on the other side we could hear, "Marines! Marines!!!" echoing against our chants.

Our fighter entered the ring. The ring announcer called for silence and asked that all stand while the national anthems of the United States and Japan were played over a loudspeaker. Flags were lowered from the high ceiling above, heads were held high, silence reigned for a few moments, and then a loud applause and cheers arose from the spectators after the ceremony introductions.

Next, the referee and the fighters were introduced. Boos and cheers were exchanged between the Navy and Marine constituents. The fighters were brought together into the center of the ring, given their instructions, told to shake hands, return to their corners and come out fighting at the sound of the bell.

Jerry and I sat on the wooden steps that led up to the ring, our chests at mat level. We didn't get a chance to be of any help during the first two fights since both our amateur fighters were knocked on their butts in the first round.

We suspected that Marines had lied their asses off and substituted pros rather than amateurs, and they proceeded to work our Navy boys over, decking them within minutes of the opening bell. Both Irv and Bing, the two that took the beatings, were starry-eyed and bleeding after their matches. They apologized to Rolf as they were helped out of the ring and led back one at a time to the locker room.

There was a break before the first of the pro-fights, and Rolf gave his pep talk. "Don't worry, guys. Your pride's hurt more than anything else. You got screwed, blued and tattooed, but we'll get even with them sons-a-bitches. The next fights are for you. Their underhandedness raised the hair on the back of our necks, so we'll get some f–kin' revenge for you, we'll whip their asses," Rolf said, red-faced and raging, spit flying out of his mouth.

"Red, George, Hunter, Rocky, it's up to youse guys to go out there and show them jarheads that we can swab the deck with them. Now get over here and let's stack hands and gloves together and go give 'em hell!"

The big boys followed Rolf's orders and joined forces. They stacked their hands and gloves one on top of another, transferring their energy to each other and vowing to win. The locker room door opened and a head poked in, "Five minutes," its voice said.

"OK, Red, you're up." Rolf said, as he waved his hand for all of us to follow him back out to the arena. Jerry and I flanked our fighter and swinging our shoulders, cock-walked back to the ring chanting "Navy! Navy! Navy!" as we went.

The fever had risen; you could feel the energy streaming through the crowd. Rolf parted the ropes and Red slid through into the off-white canvas. His opponent was already in his corner and appeared to be overconfident, assuming his fight was also going to be easy, taking the past two wins as a sign of weakness on the opposing side.

Heavy bets were quietly being made. Gambling was frowned upon by the military, but you could see subtle little signs being passed amongst the crowd. The bell rang and the first round began. Red used the strategy that Rolf had taught him, and he was able to use his right hook efficiently. The match was in its sixth round when his opponent, apparently tired and frustrated with not being able to connect any good punches, dropped his hands too low, exposing his face and was cold-cocked in the head. He took the eight count, tried to rise but fell back after only reaching his knees. One down, three to go!

The "Tank" was next. "Go get 'em, George," we all said, now somewhat reassured. Get 'em, he did. When the bell sounded, Tank ran across the ring and floored his opponent before he could get more than two steps away from his stool. He hit him with a classic "One Two," a powerful right cross followed by a left undercut that came up from the floor. The Marine never knew what hit him. The Navy side of the arena went wild, the crowd rose on their feet, some standing on their chairs, and a loud cheer of "Tank! Tank!" filled the air. A beaming smile lit his face as Rolf rushed into the ring, grasping him around the waist, lifting him into the air, and spinning him in a circle, his hands held high in the air signifying victory.

"God damn, did you see that? God damn, it was perfect. God damn," Rolf kept repeating, as he escorted George out of the ring completely beside himself. "Did youse guys see that?"

"We saw it, Rolf, we saw it," Jerry and I answered, equally excited.

"How the hell did you think we could have missed it?" I echoed, my heart racing.

The Admiral came over, adding his congratulations, patting the sweating fighter on his back. Tank was a hero. The next fight of the heavyweights went the full distance and our fighter won on a decision. The Marines had been put in their place.

Next came the main event. The tone turned very serious. We were one up, three out of five, and the big Kahunas were up: Rocky Tipazio and Hank Magaluski - well - cutting to the chase without a blow by blow commentary, in the sixth round after a good battle, Marine Magaluski finally decked our Rocky. Damn!!

It was one hell of an exciting evening, blood and all, and it turned out even, three for three. I cherished that night and for years to come, it would re-enter my mind almost every time I watched the fights on television.

We thanked Rolf for the great show and the opportunity to share in the sporting event. We exchanged addresses and promised to get in touch sometime in the near future, and then we grabbed a cab and headed back to the hotel exhausted. Little did I know that many years later, I would live down the road from him in the little town of Bellevue, Idaho. Rolf is 91 years old now and is still a rough S.O.B. ~

CHAPTER 21: ROUND THE HORN - HOME

The next day we woke mid-morning, packed our bags, checked out of the Blue Moon, grabbed a cab, and headed back to Atsugi to catch the bus to the base and some sanity. Arriving there, we changed into blue dungarees, the working uniform, and went out to the flight line to muster in. The Chief and his second, Dennis, were there, both with their arms folded and questioning looks on their faces. Neatly piled under the plane's shadow was a conglomeration of teak furniture, jade and ebony statues, transistor radios, record players, motorcycle helmets, silk kimonos, etc., etc., etc.

"Where the hell are we going to put all this shit?" The Chief questioned as we approached.

"Looks like the higher ups went a little wild in their gedonk shopping," I said. "We got a job on our hands. Let me get the orderlies and my slide rule. We might have to reconfigure the accommodations or leave some behind for the next flight going back to Barbers Point."

"Yeah, and remember we still have some goodies to pick up in Kodiak and Point Mugu." added Dennis.

"But most of that will go in the belly, right?" I asked.

"Right," the Chief confirmed.

Kenny, Mick and I spent most of the afternoon computing on paper, with the aid of the weight and balance slide rule, where the heck to put everything. After selecting priority items that no one wanted to leave behind, we stuffed them in every available nook and cranny. Figuring in the full fuel load needed to reach Kodiak, Alaska, we decided that some of the excess baggage - mostly large, cumbersome items - would be left behind for the follow-up flight. I was sure we'd hear about this when we returned to the squadron back on Oahu.

We were scheduled to take off at zero eight hundred the next morning, so the crew worked feverishly to have everything ready for the Admiral and his entourage. The next morning after a quick breakfast of steak and eggs we mustered at the nose wheel of the R6D to greet our well-rested passengers. This was the 23rd day of the tour and we were on the down side to a full circle. We would fly all day, heading northeast to the Aleutian Islands that made up the Alaskan peninsula and straight into Kodiak, the southernmost islands in the Gulf of Alaska.

The bus squealed to a stop in front of the steel four-wheeled ramp pressed up against the shiny fuselage, so close that when the officers stepped off the bus they had to take two only steps on the blacktop before ascending it.

Our Capt. Jones was the last to get off. He smiled and saluted us saying, "Party's over, guys. Load up, secure the doors, and let's fire this puppy up and head for home."

"Yes sir," we answered in unison, following him up into the silver tube.

I took up the rear, and when I stepped off the ramp into the fuselage, I turned and signaled to the ground crew to remove the ramp.

I closed the hatch, secured it with a red flag and walked to the cockpit, "Hatch secured and ready for takeoff, Sir."

"Roger that," came the reply.

The reciprocal engines one by one, in quick succession roared to life, each farting out a puff of bluish gray smoke upon contact.

"Checking one and two - OK - check three and four," said Capt. Jones.

"Three and four, OK," co-pilot Comdr. Sullivan answered.

"Check," he answered, giving the thumbs up sign to the ground crew to "pull chocks." He waited until the fire truck backed further away and then ordered, "Brakes off, up the revs, prepare to taxi to takeoff position."

"Roger that," the co-pilot responded.

At the far end of the runway, its engines at full throttle, 427 was soon airborne.

The stewards went to work immediately serving coffee and donuts to the inspection team. The flight across the ocean was a long leg; it seemed to drone on for hours. A more relaxed atmosphere now engulfed all of us after a week of R&R.

Observing that Jerry and I had assisted at the fights made the Admiral aware that we shared a similar interest. During the flight, he and I got into some interesting conversations. Though our age difference was more like father and son, some of the stories we exchanged during our moments of privacy were bonding. I knew that I had in "T-Bone" Haggard, a person who would come to my defense if ever that need arose. I also felt that Capt. Jones had picked up on this connection, etching within his brain a note that I was indeed an asset to his crew.

Over the years I realized that this charisma was one of my strengths. My personality has enabled me to mix with all kinds of people, and I find that I'm mostly at home wherever I may be in my travels.

Hours later, as the miles clicked by, I was sitting in my seat back by the galley, daydreaming with a cup of coffee in my hand just gazing out the window. I suddenly spotted the first island on the southernmost tip of the peninsula that formed the chain of the Aleutian Islands, which looked like a drop of black oil floating in the shiny silver blue ocean below. We were flying through broken clouds and the image would appear for a moment then disappear, then reappear, growing larger with each sighting, alerting me to the fact that we were getting closer to our destination.

A short time later, Capt. Jones pulled back on the throttles, the pitch changed, softening the drone of the engines, and we began our descent. The sun was in its final phase, elongating the mountain shadows on the fjord-like bay's water as the plane approached a lighted airstrip that seemed to beckon us with the end of its finger: Welcome to Kodiak!

Upon landing, the engine propellers were immediately reversed for braking. Number 427 slowly swung around as we reached the end of the short runway and taxied back to a makeshift terminal. The plane rocked back and forth when Capt. Jones hit the brakes and we came to a halt. Waiting for the last whisper of the propellers to disappear, I then heard the soft bumper ends of a sky ramp hit the exit side of the plane. I immediately removed the red flag that I had placed on the hatch, slid the heavy handle up and swung it wide open, welcoming in the fresh sea air. It was dark and silent. No hoopla greeted us. This was only an overnighter; a gas and grocery stop - no inspection here. A rattletrap of a bus picked up the officers to take them to their night's lodging and dinner.

"Okay, guys, lock her up for the night. Meet you at the enlisted barracks that's right next to the chow hall where you can see the lights on up there on that hill," the Chief said pointing into the darkness. It would take only about five minutes for us to do a quick cleanup. The rest of the crew scurried on ahead with the Chief. The bus came back and picked us up. We were famished, worn down and frazzled, and could only think of filling our bellies and getting some much-needed rest after the long flight. After a dinner of fresh salmon steaks, potatoes, green peas, fresh corn bread and honey, (love that Navy chow,) we went straight to our bunks.

"Nothin' like hitting the sack with a full stomach to lull you to sleep," I said as I slipped between the clean sheets of the already made-up bunks, fluffing up my pillow.

The next morning dawn broke noisy. Seagulls were feeding on a run of some unknown small fish out in the bay, and the cries of a pair of bald eagles could be heard circling above looking for bigger pickings. The daylight also revealed the smallness of the remote base. We were truly out in the boondocks.

After some more gedonk squeezing in the belly of the aircraft, Kenny, Mick and I made enough room for whatever was coming. It was a jigsaw puzzle, but we refitted everything and gained about ten cubic feet or so.

"Think that'll be enough?" Kenny asked me when he inspected the void.

"Got to be, I was just informed by the Chief that they're bringing a couple hundred pounds of King Crab legs and some boxes of silver salmon. They're all frozen so we won't need any ice for them, but when we pick up the milk from the PX in Alameda, we'll have to put the cases of milk on the bottom, then bagged ice, then repack the crab legs and salmon on top, and wrap it all in oilcloth." I sighed. "Our weight is going to be way over the limit. We'll have to talk to the Captain and get him to leave behind some more of the stuff these guys bought in Kowloon and Yokohama, or else we'll burn our gas load off before we reach Alameda," I continued.

"No problem, Dino," Jerry said, overhearing my concern. "Just received word up in the radio shack that we got another plane sitting in Alameda, deadheading (no cargo, no passengers) back to Barbers Point, so we can shift some of the load."

"Super, that solves it, makes it simple, and it'll give me a little more time to spend with Gina," I said, relieved.

"Now who the hell is Gina?" Jerry asked. "Another one of your conquests?"

"Hey Jer, you know the sailor's motto, 'a girl in every port'. I met Gina on the last trip I had to Alameda. Met her at the enlisted men's club. Her dad's a Warrant Officer. They live on base. She's quite the babe. Drives a new 1960 red Thunderbird convertible, you know the one that's shaped like a cigar. Her dad gave it to her for her eighteenth birthday.

"You're too much, you son-of-a-gun, you never let any grass grow under your feet, do you?" Jerry said with a smile. "She got a girlfriend?" he asked hopefully.

"Sorry Jer, no double dating with this pumpkin! Ve vant to be alone!" I said, mimicking a German accent.

Our conversation came to a halt when a faded, flat yellow, electric flight line shuttle cart pulled up, carrying a silver aluminum refrigerated case, sitting on the flatbed behind the driver.

"Hey guys, here's the good stuff, compliments of the local fishing and crabbing fleet. We trade off diesel fuel, got a surplus of it - works out great," the delivery boy said. He hopped out of his seat, popped open the lid of the cooler exposing its contents, and 'Voile!' - boxes of fresh edible Alaskan sea treasures in sealed boxes.

"Whoa-ho, I think we might be running a little black market here," I whispered to the guys standing around him.

"Only if we were exchanging hard cash, Dino. This is more like receiving a present," Jerry said.

"Yeah sure, we're only the couriers, but you can bet someone on the other end is going to have his palms greased with a little green. Well, let's pack it tight and quick cause here comes the bus with the live load." I replied.

We took off around 0900, the plane straining for liftoff with its increased weight, heading down the coast back to civilization. This time, I'd be entering the San Francisco area flying over the Golden Gate Bridge, rather than sailing under it on the USS Kearsarge.

About two hours out from Alameda Air Station, I reached over the radio-man's shoulder and handed him a phone number.

"Hey Rudy," I whispered, "Call the station's communications center and have them call this number, ask for Gina, and give her our ETA."

"Never one to waste a minute. Right, Dino?" Rudy said, smiling, and I went to pack up my civvies for the fun three days awaiting me in the Bay Area.

Approaching the city at dusk, I was happy to see warm lights after thousands of miles of dark-blue ocean. The Golden Gate Bridge, its structure softly lit in light amber, seemed to be suspended in the air with its reversed image reflected in the dark silver mirror-like water below. As we passed over, I went forward to watch the approach. Standing behind Jerry, on duty at the radio desk, and peering into the cockpit, I had a bird's eye view over the instrument panel through the V-shaped windows. On the left, Alcatraz Island appeared with its forbidding empty dark prison buildings, contrasting sharply with the city's brilliant display of illumination in the distance.

Up ahead across the bay, I could see the landing strip lit up at Alameda Air Station. Off to the left, the Bay Bridge, connecting San Francisco with Alameda and the city of Oakland, duplicated a similar image against the night sky, its lights an outstretched pearl necklace between the two shores.

Once over the breakwater, the plane feathered back its engines and drifted silently down until wheel contact with the runway, the roar of the reversed engines breaking the plane's speed, bringing this leg of the trip to an end.

"San Francisco open up them pearly gates," I sang silently to myself.

We taxied up to the terminal, the ground crew on duty directing the pilot with lighted wands indicating where to park the plane for unloading. As the plane swung around, placing its port side with the exit door facing the main terminal, I could see a red convertible with its lights out, waiting near the tarmac.

Its top was down on the warm June night, and sitting on the top of the driver's seat leaning forward, her arms on top of the windshield, was a striking honey blonde - Gina! My heart started to race, but I had some business to take care of first, so I forced myself to remain cool and nonchalant. She'd understand, being a Navy brat.

I opened the door once again to the smell of salt air, although a bit more humid and less pure than Alaska. The ramp approached, pushed by two dungaree-clad sailors, the duty officer following close behind, ready to greet the Admiral and his tour. He rushed up the stairs as soon as the ramp made contact with the side of the plane. I stepped aside to allow him entrance.

"Welcome to Alameda Air Station, gentlemen," he greeted, snapping to attention and saluting the Admiral who had just released his seat belt and stood up. He led the way down the ramp and into the terminal. The Admiral and his entourage followed, ducking their heads through the exit, briefcases in hand.

"Tell Capt. Jones it was a good flight and nice landing," the Admiral said, passing by me on the way out.

The Captain, Commander Sullivan, Chief Segona, Dennis, Jerry, and Rudy came out of the cockpit area one by one. I comically bowed low, Japanese style, and waved my hand towards the open portal.

"Right this way, sir, the Admiral wishes for me to extend his pleasure and satisfaction for a good flight and marvelous landing," I said to the Captain.

"Thank you, Yeager, you've been an attentive and informative orderly," he answered, swinging onto the top step of the ramp. Turning around to the orderlies, I said, "You'd better follow those guys and get a ride to the enlisted quarters. I'll lock up and we'll tackle the cleanup in the morning."

"Move the ramp and secure the aircraft," I told the ground crew.

Gina, seeing that I'd finished my duties, hopped out of the T-bird, ran up to me and, leaping in the air, wrapped her short-skirted legs around my waist, her arms around my neck, and planted a big wet one on me.

"Dino, my fly boy," she said, her eyes sparkling.

"My Gina Lola-bridge-a-da," I said, squeezing her tightly and swinging her around in a circle. Gina babbled as we walked to the parked car. "I was so glad to get your letter last month. I've been hoping you'd be on schedule. Mom and Dad are down in Monterey for a week, and we've got the house to ourselves! Isn't that great? Let's hurry home. I've got your favorite dish in the oven - roasted chicken." (Now here's a woman who knows the way to a man's heart - through his stomach!)

I opened the door for her and she slid over the center console and into the passenger seat.

"You drive," she said.

Sometimes it's hard to tell what I love more, women or cars. Luckily, this time I had both. I smiled and turned the engine over, the sound of power rumbled out its rear dual exhausts. I shifted to low range and hit the gas. The T-bird squatted down and raced forward. The rear wheels immediately let out a small squeak as they bit the pavement.

"Better slow down, Dino, we're on base, not the freeway," Gina warned.

"I know, I know, just wanted to get some of my 'ya-yas' out."

"Save your 'ya-yas' for me." She answered as she scooted over and put her arm around me. The radio was tuned to 104.5 KFOG, and the top forty countdowns were at the No. seven hit, "Mr. Lucky." It was singing my song!

The tiny cottage she lived in with her parents was located across from a small waterfront park. From across the bay, the city's lights reflected all the way over to our shoreline. After dinner and a bottle of Dad's wine, we walked hand in hand along the green belt bordering the water, reminiscing about our last encounter and the time that had passed in between.

Gina smelled of Jungle Gardenia, my favorite perfume besides White Shoulders. We kissed. Her lips tasted of sweet milkweed. That night we fell asleep in each other's arms, wrapped in fresh yellow daffodil printed sheets, in an antique four poster bed. Outside, the sound of distant foghorns echoed in our subconscious.

Three days later we transferred the bulk of 427's contents to the R6D that was deadheading back to Barbers Point, lightening our load. The cases of milk bound for Guam and the crab legs and salmon for Oahu were restacked and packed with ice. I was once again saying good-bye to Gina, promising to grab an Alameda turnaround as soon as one went up on the flight board back at VR-21.

I'd been gone from my home and my beach for thirty long days. So far, we had logged over 22,000 air miles, with another two thousand plus to go. For a twenty-year-old, it had been the experience of a lifetime, one that would be etched within my brain forever. As the plane lifted into the sky, I could see fishing boats far below heading out to sea, leaving pencil etched white lines behind them. We were on our last leg, on our way HOME! ~

Chapter 22: Just A Gigolo

On June 17th just after midnight, we ended our journey as our wheels touched ground back on home turf. A crew of seven from Aero-Equipment met to relieve us of our aircraft. The other plane that had deadheaded from Alameda with most of our load beat us in by two hours and was already in the hangar, its contents spread out on the deck on display, waiting to be claimed. # 427 would join it and soon undergo a thorough inspection after its long but trouble-free flight.

I went to the barracks and slept well the rest of the night. The next morning I reported to Chief Harris at Aero-Equipment, turning in my performance reports on Ken Logan and Mick Farr. I went over a checklist, making sure all the gear we'd left with was returned and accounted for. Then I went to the hangar and checked on #427. Its executive mahogany interior and posh leather seats had already been removed, the windows stripped of their fancy curtains, and the special steward's galley had been shipped off to the commissary for cleaning and storage.

On the outside, the two-piece aluminum cowlings that surrounded the front section of each engine had been removed, exposing the circular cylinder piston-driven engines, badly in need of some serious cleaning. Three giant jacks, one under each wing, the third under the tail, were now supporting the plane. Its wheels had been removed for tire changes, and the brake facings were off ready to receive new backing plates.

The Admirals' Inspection flight and shopping tour was now history - and what a trip it was!

I went into the air office to check the flight board. Steve, my roommate in Waikiki, was on duty, sporting new third-class stripes on his sleeves.

"Yo, Dino, glad you're back. We all missed you at the beach," he greeted.

We clasped hands over the counter. "What are you doing here, Steve-o?" I asked.

"Hey, see these?" he said, pointing to the eagle patch with a single stripe chevron. "Made rank, third class petty officer, and now I'm the new flight coordinator."

"Out of sight," I replied, knowing that now I had another 'in' to getting preferred flights.

"In fact, gotcha on the board already, an Alameda turn-around. You'll have two days there before you're bumped back to here." Steve said, turning and pointing to the flight board with a long rubber tipped hickory stick.

"Really? How lucky can one get? Gina will be surprised to see me again so soon. So, let's see - let me add this up - been gone thirty days, that's ten days crew's rest, takes me to the 26th of June, then eleven days of duty on base, then one day's crew's rest before takeoff on the 7th of July. Great duty, don't you think?"

"Shit, you got it made, no wonder you don't want to go up in rate," Steve commented.

"In my case, it's just better for me to hang in there as an airman," I answered.

"So I'll see you later at the pad. I'm off at six tonight, and - Oh - by the way - the girls next door really missed you this last month," Steve said.

"Well, speaking of girls, I met four stewardesses' in Guam that have a huge house up in Makiki Heights. They say they have a progressive party going on all the time. Got their phone number right here," I said smiling and patting my back-billfold pocket.

"You know, I've heard about those parties, new chicks all the time," Steve said, interested.

"Well, we're in now, partner. Catcha' later, gotta hit the beach."

My '50 Mercury convertible needed washing badly, especially the hood, trunk and canvas top, which had accumulated a splattering of sea gull droppings, during the thirty days that it had sat inactive. I opened the driver's door and was greeted by a musty smell. I rolled all the windows down quickly to air it out. Hopping in, I started it up and drove it over to the wash rack at the motor pool. It took about two hours to scrub it down, using Bon-Ami scouring powder from top to bottom. The body was only primed, so it didn't bother the finish, and the top and the wide sun-yellowed, whitewalls came out gleaming white. I wiped the car down, put the top down, snapped on its burgundy colored leather cover, hopped in, got a pair of sunglasses out of the glove compartment, adjusted the rear view mirror, and headed off base onto Nimitz Highway, into Honolulu and Waikiki beach.

Purple and white bougainvillea spread up both sides and over the arched entryway to the small duplex on Royal Hawaiian Avenue, welcoming me home with a rich perfumed fragrance as I unlocked the door. I went to the back bedroom to change clothes, get my beach towel, suntan lotion and swim suit. I could hear music coming through the thin wall that separated the two apartments.

The girls next door, Shara and Constance, were from San Jose, Calif. They were spending their summer here attending the University of Hawaii. There was no romantic involvement with either of the girls, but they were my good friends. We shared lunches and dinners together and spent time on the beach.

I knocked my knuckles on the wall, and called out, "Hey, it's me, Dino. Heard you missed me. Can I come over for a snack?" I said sweetly - and that was a yes.

About an hour after a leisurely lunch, Connie and I headed to the beach. She wanted to try to surf so I signed in at the Ala Wai Canoe Club and checked out a 9'10" balsa surfboard that we could go out tandem on.

I started with instructions on the beach, showing her the proper stance and how to balance the board. We entered the water, and I held the board as Connie lay face down on it and practiced paddling movements. After she felt comfortable with the board, I joined her on it. Getting past the shore break was a little difficult, and we were thrown backwards into the water several times before the timing was right and we made it out to the lineup. Beyond the break we turned the board toward shore, sat up and observed the other surfers catching rides. I pointed out the better surfers and their techniques, noting their placement and timing.

"Ready to try, Connie? Looks like a nice set forming."

"Lead on, cowboy, catch me a ride," she said, tossing her long hair around as she took the prone position on the board. I knelt behind her, hunching low as I paddled into the oncoming set, reading the wave.

"Here we go, paddle like hell," I said, dropping down behind her, my chest resting on her hard buttocks. The board surged ahead gaining momentum, propelled by the force of the approaching wave, but it passed below us. My timing was a little late.

"Missed that one, but a good try, Connie. It felt good, synchronized. We'll catch the next one." I said encouragingly. We were now in good position and I could see and feel the next wave starting to crest.

"Here we go," I said. I'm sure Connie could feel the force of my arms moving fast behind her, as she paddled furiously to my urging. The board surged forward. This time, its nose extended higher than the surface water, and I came quickly to my knees, then into the standing position.

"I'm up. Come to your knees and stand up," I yelled. Connie moved her left knee under her body between her hands near her waist, her right knee following instantly, moving forward as she released her hands on the side of the board and stood up. She did it fast, and I couldn't believe how smooth it looked.

"You made it, ride it out, and I'm off," I said adjusting the balance and dropped smoothly off to the downside. Connie felt a little extra push and a slight waiver in the board as I left, but with two quick steps of her own, using her outstretched arms for balance, she was in a better position and felt the rails of the board skimming the wave as she guided it along its breaking force. Later she told me that a thrill ran through her stomach continuing up to her heart as she watched the shoreline draw closer, riding out the wave and dropping off into the shallow water.

"YAHOO!" She yelled, raising her arms above her head in jubilance. She immediately turned the big, but light board around, remounted it and headed back out, paddling with renewed energy towards me. I was part way in, waving my arms back and forth to help her locate me.

"You looked great!" I shouted.

"I loved it. I'm hooked but don't call me a Gidget, please," she replied. We spent the rest of the afternoon sharing successes with failures, never quite achieving the quality of that first ride again but gaining more experience. After our session, lying on the beach in front of the Princess Kaiulani Hotel, I told Connie about my trip and meeting the stewardesses in Guam.

"What a coincidence," she said. "Shari and I were up there at a party last week. It started at the Reef Hotel on Thursday night with a group in from Los Angeles and moved up to the mansion on Friday afternoon for a pool party. It's probably still going on in some shape or form. I think there are about eight girls that live there from three different airlines. There's always people coming and going - an open house - so to speak."

"It really is a small town, isn't it? I love Oahu during the summer with so much going on. I especially like watching the girls getting ready for the 'Best Tan Contest' that Coppertone sponsors." I said.

"I know, isn't it a riot?" Connie agreed.

"Yeah, first they start off with a one piece, then after a week or so they switch to a two-piece exposing their midriff, which they immediately burn, their bodies now sporting one shade of red and one of reddish brown. The real brave ones, trying to compete with the local "wahinis" in their bikinis, switch to skimpier bikinis, revealing more skin to blister and peel under the tropical sun, now showing three progressions of color toning, and then they wonder how you can tell how long they've been here." We laughed.

Later, back at the pad, I caught a quick shower to wash off the salt residue that had dried on my skin. I wrapped a towel around my waist, allowing my body to drip dry in the comfortable 82-degree temperature. I picked up the phone and called the stewardess, Annie Williams. She was on a Continental flight to Australia, but I was invited to come on up by Peggy and Linda, two of the girls I'd met in Guam with Annie. I hung up the phone and heard the rumble of the dual exhausts of Steve's '50 Mercury convertible. He'd just pulled up out in front and he loved rapping his engine a couple of times to announce his arrival before turning the key off. We had identical street machines - both were 1950 Mercury convertibles. They mimicked each other, both in gray primer, white tops, white wall tires and baby moon hubcaps. We'd built them together at the base's hobby garage. We loved the looks we'd get when we cruised the Ala Moana Boulevard in Waikiki Beach together, one behind the other.

I slipped my flip-flops on my feet and strolled out to the curb to meet Steve and tell him about my day and the upcoming party. Connie and Shari were sitting on their lanai with four glasses and a pitcher full of Mai Tai's waiting to be consumed. Together, we strolled over to join our neighbors.

"I just love those two cars together," Shari said, nodding her head towards the street. "They look like a couple of baby whales with wheels attached."

"Never thought of it that way. Must be that implanted maternal thing a woman has," Steve said, as he grabbed the pitcher and filled everyone's glass. During the following conservations, I invited them to come to the party at the stews' place, but they already had previous dates. Good for them!

"Well, it looks like you're on your own, Dino," Steve said, "But make sure you give us a full report tomorrow."

The cocktail hour ended and we parted, each to pursue our own interests. I hung out for a while, resting on the couch, reading, and practicing music on my baritone ukulele. Around nine, I washed my face and shaved, refreshing myself. I put on a pair of white shorts and hung a nice Hawaiian shirt on my shoulders. I brushed my teeth, slapped on some 'Sail' after-shave lotion, slipped on my flip-flops, headed out to my convertible and hopped in.

I felt good, like something new and exciting was about to happen - a premonition? I turned the key and brought the V8 engine to life, shifted into first gear, did a quick U-turn on Royal Hawaiian Avenue and headed towards the hills and the mansion in Makiki Heights. I connected with the NaPali two-lane highway that would take me into the highlands. I followed the directions on the note

I got from Annie in Guam and exited onto Waipahu Road. I weaved around the curves that took me ever higher into the NaPali cliffs. Behind me, below in the flats, the lights of Waikiki appeared as small twinkling colored jewels. Near the top, I came to an unguarded gated community. The square red brick columns on both sides of the entry each held up a seven-foot long, ten-foot high curved ornamental gate opened to homeowners and visitors. I passed through the massive gates, under the curved iron archway connecting the two columns that displayed a scrolled sign in steel letters, reading, MAKIKI HEIGHTS.

"No wonder these parties go on forever. Who'd want to leave this sanctuary?" I thought to myself.

I passed a large white Southern colonial house on my right with a sweeping manicured lawn that led up to its massive porch and columned entryway. A posted, black and gold enamel sign hung on a white post near the road, a small light above it identifying its occupants, W.F. Quinn. I knew that the first governor of Hawaii, W.F. Quinn, had recently been elected to office when Hawaii was admitted to the Union, becoming the 50th state in the United States of America.

"Ummmm, nice neighborhood," I said to myself, "even the gov' lives here." I came to a big cul-de-sac ending the road. Its perimeter was bordered on the south side by a three-foot high volcanic rock wall, preventing wrongful entry into the deep canyon below. Cars were parked in a semi-circle around its edge. I pulled up in front of a snazzy, red Porsche coupe and shut off my engine. I could hear soft music drifting down from the estate above, mixed with voices and an occasional burst of laughter.

I walked back and soon found a cement staircase that lead up to the party. I'd climbed about fifty steps when I came to a landing with a small, roofed, three-sided building, painted yellow and green, a rest bench inside it. A silver and black aluminum sign hung above it, facetiously displaying, "Bus Stop."

Hidden within its shadow, a couple wrapped in each other's arms were involved in a heavy petting session, completely unaware of my passing presence. I smiled to myself and took the next fifty steps two at a time.

Reaching the top step, I found myself facing a large two-story mansion, its bank of four double French doors on the ground level opened to a large pool and patio area where about thirty people were mingling. Wow! (Scene changes from Gidget to Casino Royale.) I walked down a flagstone walkway leading to the patio, feeling confident that I would fit in with the diversified group of people I was about to meet. I nodded and smiled as I weaved through different groups. Some raised their glasses in greeting as I passed on into the great room of the mansion.

People were shaking it up on a shiny oak floor, immersed in their own version of the frug, the twist, the dirty boogie, the pony, the watusi, or mashed potatoes, all popular dances of our era. They were rockin'& rollin' to the sound of Jerry Lee Lewis's "Great Balls of Fire," which was blasting from two five-foot tall stereo reverb speakers placed opposite to each other in the far corners of the room.

I spotted my hostesses, Linda and Peggy, hovering over a large crystal bowl, both busy ladling out an orange cinnamon-colored liquid into guest's glasses. Joining the line to receive my allotment of "whoopee juice," I slowly moved to the front.

"Fresh glass, please." I asked.

"Oh, look!" Linda said enthusiastically to Peggy. "It's that guy we met in Guam, Dino!"

"Be careful of this stuff, Dino, it'll get to you," Peggy said, handing it to me.

"Save us a dance," Linda called out to me as I stepped away from the makeshift bar.

Waving my glass in thanks, I roamed through the house on a self-guided tour, checking out the chef's kitchen and an adjoining breakfast nook area with its attached bird aviary. I passed into a formal sitting room next to a well-stocked library, and then went into the main foyer, which was lit by a chandelier and had a grand staircase leading up to the second floor. On the staircase, sitting alone was a beautiful woman, whom I think was a bit older than the rest of us. Long, wavy, strawberry blonde hair hung over her deeply bronzed tanned shoulders. Embossed on her loose fitting, updated Japanese sarong style dress, a giant fire breathing dragon crawled up one leg and crossed her body at the waist. Its head and extended clawed front feet caressed her ample bosom on the opposite side.

"Nice dress," I commented.

"Well, thank you," she said. "It's one of my favorites."

"And, if I might be ever so bold, what's in it is even nicer," I continued.

"Coming from a handsome young gentleman such as yourself, I accept the compliment. And your name is?" she asked.

"Don Yeager, but friends call me Dino".

"I'm Wanda Wheatherby - and I," she said, with a soft suggestive voice, "could be your friend."

I walked over, took the tips of her fingers into mine, bent at the waist and kissed her hand, which was adorned with a three-carat diamond ring.

"Oh, how gallant," she said.

I liked her. I heard the tempo of the music change in the great room - Johnny Mathis was singing "Misty." I asked her to dance.

"I love Johnny Mathis," she said in answer, accepting my hand as I lifted her off the stairs into a standing position.

Her dress fell onto her curvy body as she rose, revealing a much taller and more perfectly formed woman than I had expected. Entering the great room, I spun her once onto the dance floor, coming together as she circled into my arms, our bodies molding perfectly together.

"Nice fit," I whispered into her ear.

"Maybe too nice," she answered, pulling me in even closer, her lips and cheek brushing my neck as she buried her head into the curve of my shoulder. That dance sealed our union. The rest of the evening we only had eyes for each other. I did dance with both Linda and Peggy, my hostesses. They introduced me around, but I always seemed to end up next to Wanda. Around midnight, I made her a proposal.

"Do you have a ride home?" I asked.

"As a matter of fact, I don't. I took a cab here and I'm ready to leave. Are you asking me?" she answered.

"Well, if you don't mind riding in a low-slung street machine, yes."

"Is that some kind of hot rod?" she asked.

"A mild version. This is a custom 1950 Mercury convertible. It's sort of sporty."

"Sounds like fun, I could use a little more fun in my life." She smiled and slipped her arm into mine. "Let's just disappear."

We did, and during the ride back to Waikiki, Wanda opened up to me. She had been married for nineteen years to the same man ever since she was twenty. They had no children and were experiencing some marital problems, so they had decided to separate for a year. They had a successful business in Santa Barbara that provided for them very well. She was traveling throughout the tropics, starting with Oahu, then on to Tahiti and Fiji, ending up in Sydney, Australia. Her husband was traveling the other way, to New York, and then on to London, Paris and the Mediterranean, then to Australia where they would meet and decide on their future together.

Wanda had decided on her sabbatical to "live it up." She had leased the penthouse apartment on the top of the Sheraton Hotel, a recently built high-rise across from Waikiki Beach, where she would reside for the next month. Then, when she felt the time was right, she was going to board a friend's yacht, a fifty-four footer that was soon to arrive in Honolulu and would eventually continue to Australia via the South Sea Islands.

Nearing the hotel, we decided to meet in the morning and spend some beach time together. I dropped her off at the front entrance and watched as she entered the brightly lit lobby. Her swaying hips disappeared from view but not from my mind. I drove around the block and headed home, only one-half mile away. It was very quiet on Royal Hawaiian Avenue. I parked the Mercury and remained in it, going over the events of the day and evening. Exhausted, I fell asleep at the wheel.

I was shaken out of my stupor around six the next morning. I blinked my eyes, finally focusing on Steve's face.

"Have a rough night, buddy?" Steve asked. "Looks like you couldn't even make it to your own bed."

"Wow, I must have passed out! Wasn't drunk though, just beat, and, oh my God, wait till I tell you of the wonderful woman I met last night!" I commented through a yawning mouth.

"Well, why don't you go take a shower to wake up, then we'll grab some breakfast down at the Reef," Steve suggested.

"Sounds like a plan." I said crawling out of the car and shuffling my way up to the duplex's door. At breakfast we exchanged gossip, going back over the month I'd been on the road up to the present, including the events of the night before. Soon Steve left and I remained to relax a little longer. I scanned the morning paper, had a second cup of coffee, paid the bill and headed back to the pad to call my new friend, Wanda, and get my beach gear.

10:00a.m. I dialed the phone and finally reached her. A soft sleepy voice answered on the other end, "Hello."

"Good morning, Wanda, this is Dino, your last night's chauffeur, remember? Hope I didn't wake you."

"You didn't. I'm just being decadent, lying here reading. Looks like a beautiful day out there. I'd better get a move on."

"They say the best time to sunbathe is between eleven in the morning and two in the afternoon." I said. She agreed to meet me in an hour. I strolled out of the house whistling, a large beach towel wrapped around my neck, small blue and white Pam Am flight bag in my hand stuffed with Coppertone #4 suntan lotion, a pair of binoculars, an extra pair of shorts, a T-shirt and a copy of James Michener's fat book, Hawaii, which I predicted I wouldn't read a page of that day.

I entered the lobby just as Wanda was exiting the elevator. She wore a form fitting, bright silver, Jantzen one-piece bathing suit. Above her hips a brightly colored sarong was tied emphasizing her trim waistline. Her feet were slipped into a pair of open toed, two-inch high platform togs, adding form to her already shapely legs. On her head, tipped at an angle, was a large brimmed, silver white, straw beach hat. Under it, her eyes were hidden behind aviator-style, silver-mirrored reflecting, sunglasses giving her a mysterious allure.

Oooh, Mrs. Robinson, and here I come. (I was living The Graduate before it was even produced.) In her right hand, she held a long-poled beach umbrella, and in her left, a large straw beach bag matching her hat, with large, soft cotton, peach-colored, beach towel spilling over its edge. She walked towards me, her movements not unlike a model on the runway, smooth and fluid, expressing beauty, maturity, and sophistication. Admiring eyes followed her every move. I felt proud as I held the door open for her to pass through, saying to her as she did, "Perfect timing, and you look great!"

"Well, thank you, Dino. I feel great!" She said with a beaming smile.

We walked across the street to the beach side. Strolling along the sidewalk, we passed the covered sitting areas where the local men were playing games of checkers and chess, passing away the time of day. We stopped for a moment for a cool drink to take with us on the beach, and then took the vine-covered beach walk that bordered the Princess Kaiulani to the beach. Reaching the arbor at the end, we slipped off our footgear and stepped into the soft, warm, beige white sand of Waikiki Beach.

"Do you have a favorite spot?" I asked.

"No, you pick."

As we walked towards my favorite people-watching spot, I was greeted with a wave of the hand or a spoken "Good morning," or "Yo, Dino, how's it going?"

"You seem to know everyone on the beach." Wanda commented.

"Well, it's been my beach for the last two years, and you kind of get to know everyone. A lot have their favorite spots, which they claim early in the morning every day. Then some disappear for months at a time, going away to the mainland, only to reappear in the same spot later. Others spend every waking hour from sunup to sunset rooted in their claimed spot, day after day, seldom changing their position. They're really true beach bums, deeply tanned and slightly wrinkled like worn leather. It was that way at the beach near The Pike, back in Long Beach, Calif., too." I explained.

"I know. We have our regulars at Santa Barbara, also," Wanda added.

"Speaking of favorite spots, here's mine." I said putting my bag down against the concrete jetty that extended out into the water in front of the Reef Hotel.

"Automatic back rest?" Wanda commented.

"And wind break," I added. For the next four hours we entertained each other, playing in the surf, walking the beach, and talking to friends of mine. We lunched at Duke's on the beach, and then went to play volleyball at the Army's beach resort, Fort DeRussy (where all service men were welcome,) and finished off with a drink at the underwater bar beneath the pool at the Reef Hotel. It was a great spot to be entertained, watching the water nymphs performing their synchronized moves right in front of us through a large curved window in back of the bar that ran its full length. Very cool!

Arriving back at the Sheraton around five o'clock, Wanda thanked me for the wonderful day and asked me if I would come back to the lobby around eight and check in with the concierge. He would allow me entrance to the elevator to the penthouse. She also asked me not to eat and not to dress up, just come casual.

I shrugged my shoulders, thinking this was a kind of a strange request but, oh well, it looked like she wanted to run the show. Back home, I showered, applied a moisturizing cream and rested, allowing the heat of the day's sun to emit from my body. I cooled off outside on the lanai, enjoying the evening breeze coming off the Alawai Canal a half block away. At seven-forty, I put on one of my Aloha shirts, a pair of shorts, and my flip-flops. I combed my hair into a style, stuffed my billfold into my back pocket, slipped on my watch and headed back to the Sheraton - for - whatever?

When I arrived in the lobby, the concierge, a sharply dressed man, came through the office door behind the main desk.

"Ahhhh, Mr. Yeager - Dino, isn't it? I've been waiting for you, if you'll please follow me." He indicated the way with a sweep of his hand and started to walk a carpeted hallway towards the elegant retail stores on the main floor of the hotel. Part way down he stopped at the entrance to an expensive appearing men's store.

"Ms. Wheatherby has chosen a stunning wardrobe for you. She has exquisite taste and wishes for you to choose from her selections whatever pleases you," he said with a smile, entering the store.

I was flabbergasted. All of a sudden, I understood what she meant, when she asked me to dress casual when I came to pick her up. She wanted me to appear well dressed and affluent if I was to escort her around the dining rooms and nightclubs of Waikiki. No problem there, I can dig it.

"Oh, by the way, she said, "Not to hurry. Dinner reservations are not until nine-thirty," the concierge continued on, as he started to lay out the pre-selected garments. I looked over the array of slacks, shirts, shorts, shoes, light sport coats and accessories displayed on the tables in front of me.

"So this is what it's like to have an unlimited bank account," I thought. I selected a pair of pale blue silk slacks, a beautiful light white cotton "buccaneer" shirt with full billowing sleeves, a slim tan belt and a matching pair of tasseled loafers. I adjourned to a changing room, stripped off my casual beach outfit and slipped into luxury. I was styling and loving it.

Everything fit perfectly, even the shoes. "How did she know?" I wondered. "Probably the same size as her husband of nineteen years." I folded my old clothes, placed the flip-flops in-between and stepped out of the enclosure.

"You look quite dashing. I'm sure madam will be pleased. Should I ring her and tell her you are ready and on the way up?" he asked.

"Please do."

He went behind the cash register, picked up a house phone and dialed the penthouse house code number. I heard him say, "Mr. Yeager is ready, madam. Shall I send him up?" (A short pause.) "Yes, he liked them all. (Another short pause.) "Yes, madam, I'll give him the key that allows the elevator to reach the penthouse. Very well, madam, and the Sheraton thanks you, also. Good evening." He hung up.

"I take it that you're a very lucky young man," he said smiling, handing me a gold passkey. "Insert this into the penthouse slot, turn it towards the right, and it will allow the elevator to proceed to the top floor."

"Thank you, and yes, tonight I feel very lucky!" I said, twirling the key around my index finger as I left the lobby and strutted down the hallway to the elevator. I followed instructions and soon the white light above the initials PH lit up, a small bell chimed, and the double doors slid open revealing Wanda standing there in a huge off-white room, holding a bottle of Champagne and two glasses.

"Welcome, handsome! They fit—great! I thought maybe you were a perfect forty-two regular, and I was right!" She said with a smile, handing me the emerald green, gold embossed bottle. "Would you do the honors, please?"

"Wanda, I'm speechless! I really don't know what to say, other than thank you," I said, taking the bottle from her outstretched hand.

"I'm sure you'll make it up to me in some manner or another," she said with a suggestive wink.

I popped the cork, it hit the ceiling, we laughed and I poured. We clicked the crystal vessels together. Wanda made a toast. "To us and a great time together," she said.

"Touché!" I replied as we crossed arms and raised the glasses to our lips. The bubbles tickled our noses as the smooth light liquid slid down our throats. We walked to the couch facing the open sliding glass door that led out to the lanai, overlooking the ocean. She pulled her floor-length black sequined sheath dress up, exposing her legs to the upper thigh through the slit in its side. She placed the bottle of champagne and her glass on the side table next to the couch.

"Before we go any further," she said, "I think we should have another glass or two of the bubbly. Then I'll call a cab to take us to dinner. I've made reservations for us at the Hilton Hawaiian Village for the late dinner show featuring Alfred Apaka."

She smiled, kissed my lips softly and turned towards the phone on the side table and dialed for a cab. She excused herself and disappeared into the bedroom. I sat alone on the couch for a few minutes, a huge Cheshire cat grin spread across my face. OMG! I sipped my champagne and took in the surroundings, not quite believing what I'd fallen into. Wanda reappeared, a gold-flecked black cotton shawl gracing her shoulders and a matching evening handbag. The phone rang, letting us know the taxi had arrived.

"One other thing," she said, reaching into her small bag. "Here's two one-hundred-dollar bills to allow you to pay for everything tonight and to tip well. If there are a few pennies left after the evening - just keep them in your pocket."

Surprised once again, I slipped the two crisp bills into my billfold. "I don't know what to say."

"Don't say anything. Just enjoy the ride, Donald. I'm going to use your proper name, and we'll let your peers call you Dino, okay?" I liked that, being proper and all.

As we rode the elevator down to the lobby, a song made popular by the singer

Louis Prima stuck in my mind. "I'm just a gigolo, and everywhere I go, people smile at me." I giggled quietly within.

That night we dined, drank, sang, and danced the night away.

Our friendship blossomed and I spent most of the summer keeping her happy. It was indeed my pleasure.

Near the end, she tried to entice me to sail away with her on the yacht to Tahiti. I was tempted, but the thought of another court martial for going AWOL made me shudder. I reluctantly declined her tempting offer. I did, however, see her off. I waved good-bye from the dock as she motored out of the Honolulu marina on the yacht of her friend, Samuel, who had arrived from Santa Barbara a few days earlier. She stood on the aft deck, her strawberry blonde hair whipping in the wind, with a forlorn look on her face. She smiled and threw one last kiss to me across the water in remembrance. Scrolled on the fantail of the departing yacht was the name, "RIDE'N FREE." I turned and walked slowly away thinking - wow, now this one is for the books. ~

CHAPTER 23: BACK TO JAPAN

Overwhelmed with infatuation, it took me a long time to get over Wanda. I often daydreamed, imagining myself sailing the open ocean with my arms around her, exchanging smiles while we watched the sunset blast the sky with fire-like colors, as we traveled to an uninhabited tropical island in the South Pacific. She had introduced me to a lifestyle that I could get used to. And later in my life, though I never searched for it, I readily accepted it when it presented itself to me.

One of the ways to forget an old love is to replace it with a new one. I found it in a bathtub-shaped '29 Model A Phaeton, four-door convertible. It was a real Waikiki beach buggy, painted eggshell white with a Navy-blue canvas top. It ran on red spoke wheels, sporting 16-inch white wall tires. The Mercury was still my main mode of transportation, primarily for travel back and forth from Barbers Point when I had duty. But back in Waikiki, the Model A took precedence.

The A was very popular at the Kau-Kau drive-in. The girls working there often kept the front center parking spot in the semi-circular, open-aired restaurant, reserved for it. I would announce our arrival by honking its ooh-ga, ooh-ga horn, pull up to the center front section, and shut off its four-cylinder engine.

Since its timing was slightly off, it would backfire like a held back fart, surprising the "bejesus" out of some unsuspecting patrons. It would immediately follow up with a stream of steam whistling out of its brass radiator, adding some comic relief. We always got a laugh out of the A's peculiarities. Then one or two of the car hop girls would rush up to the front of the car and pretend to cool it off by pouring a glass of water over its hood ornament, fan it with their hands, and blowing on it with pursed lips. The girls reveled in being a part of a fun.

I flew off on another trip to Japan, which turned out to be a routine "milk run." The plane, #426, sister ship to #427, flew stripped of seats, replaced with silver aluminum milk cans and four "bird cages," all covered with cargo nets and tightly strapped down.

Birdcages were confidential tracking devices the Navy used for surveillance of enemy submarine movements and locating missile sites. Highly sensitive, each was mounted within a protective steel cage with rounded outside corners. They hung suspended on spring-loaded cables, encased in thick foam and covered in a fire protective material. I had never actually seen one in the flesh before, so they were a mystery to me.

We stopped in Guam to refuel and deliver the milk. We stayed overnight and took off early the next morning before sunrise - to Japan.

Dark cloudy skies and pelting rain driven by high winds greeted us when we arrived in Atsugi. Two canvas-covered military police jeeps met the plane, both occupied by a driver and three heavily armed marines carrying semi-automatic weapons dressed in combat gear. A large black unmarked van followed and pulled up directly under the cargo door ready to receive the birdcages.

The plane captain, Lt. Cmd. Blakesly, met the receiving officer at the opened hatch just as he rushed up the conveyor belt ramp that had been pushed up to the plane to transfer the load. They saluted each other, exchanged paperwork, and within minutes we were relieved of our load and the responsibility that went along with it.

A VR-21 relief crew, waiting for the aircraft, met us after the area was cleared and took over command of #426. It was refitted with a long row of triple seats from the Aero-Equipment division for the return trip. Their mission was to fly to Okinawa where they would pick up a load of Marines and transport them back to Barbers Point, where buses from Kaneohe Marine base would pick them up. My group and I would take crew's rest for twenty-six hours when we in turn would be bumped out.

A heavy rain and dreary weather kept us on base. So we spent our time resting, reading books, playing pool, ping pong, watching the boob tube and filling our stomachs. It was during this off time that I decided I needed to take a break from flight duty and from the "Rock," our nickname for the island of Oahu. Even paradise can become boring after a while. In my case, however, it wasn't boredom I was trying to escape. I just needed a change, and I needed to get back to my family in Minnesota. I had thirty days annual leave coming to me and I would put in for it when I got back.

Our turn around flight, #517, arrived from Edwards Air Force Base, home based in the Philippines, carrying twenty-two military dependents on their way home to the States. We were to take on seven more from here and fly them as far as Hawaii for their R&R. The civilians were fed and had time to stretch their legs while we did the crew switch, refueled the plane, added fresh water, coffee and box lunches.

Three hours later, we took off for Wake Island where we would refuel and then continue to Barbers Point. Military ground transportation would take them to Pearl Harbor where they, the dependents, would be processed out of the South Pacific.

Normally MATS (Military Air Transport), a division of the Air Force, would handle a situation like this, but at times the Navy shared the duties of other branches of the service.

I enjoyed caring for and entertaining the homeward bounds. In a way, it strengthened my desire to return to the mainland, back to St. Paul, Minnesota where it had all begun. It was a pleasant flight, the first hours spent in idle chit-chat with a few different individuals. "Where you from?" "Where you going?" "Did you like living in the Philippines?" "Are you glad to be going home?" etc. etc. etc. After I served the box lunches, the drone of the engines put most of them to sleep.

We put down on Wake Island a little after midnight for a quick refueling. The landing, along with the roar of the reversed engines for braking, woke a few who muttered in their sleep, then drifted back to dreamland. Nobody left the plane except the first mechanic to help with the refueling and to sign the AV (aviation) gas chit handed to him. The fuel trucks disconnected their static lines, rolled up the long hoses and left, their red and orange lights disappearing into the darkness. Our mechanic came back on board, I secured the hatch, and the plane resumed its journey home.

Many hours later, the wheels of the R6D touched down on Barber Point's oceanside runway. Each wheel gave off a small puff of blue-white smoke when it came in contact with the blacktopped surface. Taxiing up to the VR-21 section of the tarmac, I could see two gray Navy buses waiting for our departing passengers, each labeled with the blue lettering - PEARL HARBOR NAVAL STATION - on their sides.

"Your buses are here," I announced to the passengers. "Thank you for flying with us. We hope you had a comfortable flight and have a safe trip the rest of the way home." I opened the hatch and waited for the ramp to be secured in place. I watched as each one took their first step on to it while thinking about flying home myself.

I secured the plane, loaded up the aero equipment electric flatbed that met us with my flight gear and returned it to the Quonset hut for inspection. I immediately requested a thirty days military leave, which was granted. The Yeoman on duty was instructed to draw up my papers. I ran to flight quarters to tell Steve to take me off the board for the next thirty days.

As I entered the office, Steve greeted me. He put aside the morning paper he was reading, took his feet off of the desk and swung his swivel chair around.

"Yo, Dino, you're back."

"Yeah, but not for long. I'm going home on leave."

"How are you going to get there? We don't have any trips going to Alameda for two weeks."

"Check out Hickam Air Force base for me and see if the fly boys have got anything going anywhere, maybe I could hitch a ride. Meanwhile, I'm going to walk my papers through so they clear faster. Be back in an hour or so, okay?'

"I'll get on the horn right away and see what I can dig up for you," Steve said, picking up the phone. It was near the end of the day and getting close to dinner time when I returned to the office waving my approved leave papers above my head.

"Got em'," I said, "Did you come up with anything?"

"As a matter of fact, you're in luck," Steve answered. "Hickam has a C-130 that flies to Nellis Air Force base outside of Las Vegas, Nevada, early tomorrow morning at 0700. They got three jump seats available, ya want one?"

"Yeah, pencil me in, and do you think you could run me over to the airbase at Hickam early in the morning on your way to Waikiki?"

"You got it, bud. You're on your way home!" Steve said, smiling. ~

CHAPTER 24: HITCHHIKING

We arrived on the tarmac of Hickam Air Force Base just as the giant C-130 was belching out its first puff of blue-gray smoke from engine number one. Sitting inches from the ground, a thin line of light separating its belly from the blacktop, it looked exactly like a very large beached whale. The small slanted cockpit windows and the yellow pointed nose cone directly below them that held the radar sensor gave it a comical, friendly look. You could have painted a smiley face on it. I entered through the yawning cargo door that took up the whole rear of the aircraft. Two military jeeps followed me up the giant ramp. I was directed to the hanging canvas seats that lined the bulkhead on the right side of the aircraft and handed a pair of padded foam ear protectors. The jeeps were secured to the deck with steel tie downs. The rear hatch rose from the ground, the hydraulic system smoothly securing the cavernous tube within itself.

The remaining three engines fired up. The noise was deafening, and the plane shook like it had the heebie-jeebies. The crew chief smiled and mouthed, "Welcome aboard," as he passed me on his way to the cockpit. The engine's vibrations were felt throughout the aircraft as the "Guppy" (the C-130's nickname) roared down the runway, and then gently lifted into the "wild blue yonder."

The trip across the Pacific was a total bore, drone-drone-drone, noisy beyond belief. I instantly became highly appreciative of VR-21's R6D planes, and their relative quietness. I slept most of the way since conversation was held to a minimum, as each word had to be yelled to be heard. As we approached the coastline off San Diego, I was invited to climb up into the cockpit and enjoy the view. It was truly magnificent. We were flying through wind-stretched stratospheric clouds that offered a spectrum of colors reflected off the moisture droplets that were contained within them. It was like being in a kaleidoscope's chamber. Colors flashed from flat gray to brilliant white, with blues, reds, purples, and oranges appearing and disappearing as we broke through different layers. I watched in awed silence until the last ray of day's light disappeared. Soon, the blinking lights on tips of the wings became more visible in the night's darkness. I returned to my harness seat.

San Diego passed by in the distance unnoticed, as we flew slightly south of the city skirting commercial air traffic. As we closed the distance to Nellis Air Force base, a small dot of light appeared far off in the distance, not unlike the first star of night in an upside-down black sky.

"Las Vegas," the pilot exclaimed, as if in answer to the silent question that was lurking in the back of my mind. As we approached, the lights grew in number. They bounced and flashed like a man-made centipede seemingly crawling along the dark landscape but going nowhere. The throttles were pulled back on engines two and four, fuel richness adjusted, flaps down, and for the first time in over ten hours, the C-130's roar dissipated as it floated alongside a strip of blue and red lights of Nellis' runways on the northeast side of the city.

The touchdown was smooth for such a monster of an aircraft. We taxied down the runway following the yellow line to the operations flight office holding area. Engines one and three were shut down first, followed by the idling two and four. All the electronic devices were switched off leaving us with only the battery power. It was now surprisingly silent, compared to the loud roar of the engines that I had tolerated all day long. In comparison, the soft hum of the hydraulics dropping the huge tail cargo door was music to my ears. I unbuckled my harness, grabbed my luggage and walked down the ramp out of the plane into the warm desert air. I took a long deep breath, a welcome relief from the stale, recycled, pressurized air that I had been inhaling. The propellers were whispering as they grabbed their last bit of air, and then there was only silence. How delightful.

"Ahhhhhh, the first leg of my journey over," I thought. I was finally free of the island "rock" syndrome. It was the summer of 1961.

The two mechanics on the flight crew informed me that there was lodging for the night available for me at their barracks. The older of the two, George, offered to take me out to the highway in the morning, where I would begin my "thumb trek" across Middle America.

In the fifties and sixties, hitchhiking was a fairly easy and reliable mode of transportation. People were curious, rather than suspicious, of a person standing on the side of the road with his thumb held high. If you were in a military uniform, it was even easier, as patriotism was at an all-time high.

The next morning dawned bright and blue. After a complimentary breakfast of steak and eggs, George took me off base and dropped me off on the highway north of Las Vegas heading north-east to Salt Lake City, Utah. I placed my shiny tin suitcase on the roadside, took a deep breath and waited for the first Good Samaritan to come along.

Seven cars whizzed by, my gaze and right hand following them as they appeared and disappeared, moving on down the road. There was a lull for a few minutes. Then I spotted another automobile approaching. I took a step out into its path, beckoning strongly with my thumb, my intentions extremely obvious. A white Cadillac hit its brakes, the nose dropping sharply, until it stopped within inches of the shiny suitcase.

"Going as far as Salt Lake," the driver said, leaning across the front seat and looking at me through the open passenger window.

"Great." I replied, opening the door and sliding into the "shotgun" position.

"Smart thinking," he said, "Placing that shiny suitcase next to you. It flashed me down before I really even seen you."

"One of my buddies said it would work, so I thought I'd give it a try."

"I'm Luther Ashley," he said, introducing himself.

"Don Yeager," I replied, offering my right hand for a shake.

"Where you headed?"

"Home, to St. Paul, Minnesota, to visit my family. I'm currently stationed in Hawaii."

"Good duty?"

"Not bad. I have a great job, and I live off base, two blocks off Waikiki Beach."

"Whoa," he said, looking at me, his eyebrows lifting, "Sounds like good duty to me." His eyes returned to the road and we drove on.

Luther turned out to be a Mormon missionary. He was a small man; around five foot four and weighed only about 140 pounds. He sat on a pillow while he drove. His blue eyes barely met the top of the steering wheel. His stature didn't fit the behemoth Cadillac, but his mind made up for it. During the ride he related stories to me of his missionary ventures to different Third World countries that included the headhunters deep in the interior of New Guinea. I listened as he elaborated on the prophecies of Joseph Smith and the Church of Latter Day Saints. Seven and a half hours and five hundred and seventeen miles later, I parted company with Luther.

"Well, that was interesting." I spoke out loud to myself as Luther sped away. "I wonder what's next in store for me."

I turned east and walked up the eastbound highway looking for a good spot to hang out until someone stopped to pick me up. It was late Saturday afternoon, around 5 o'clock, approaching the cocktail hour. I'd covered over 500 miles and had another 450 to go before Cheyenne, Wyo., my next destination. The traffic was slight, most people traveling earlier in the morning on the weekend. A few semi-trucks heading for Middle America whizzed by me, the after draft slapping my bellbottoms against my legs. I kept my white canvas sailor hat down tight on my head so I wouldn't have to chase after it when they passed by. A couple of families waved and smiled but failed to offer a lift. I waved and smiled back. Finally, a lone traveler in a Buick sky cruiser, station wagon picked me up.

"Going as far as Laramie," he said.

"Great, close enough." I said as I threw my luggage bag in the huge empty space behind the front seat.

"Name's Don Yeager."

"Tim Ryan." The curly red headed man behind the wheel answered and in the same breath he shifted into drive and continued on.

"Looks like you're on leave. Going home?"

I gave him the usual details. After a short while, conversation lulled, and I catnapped till we reached Green River where we stopped for a mid-afternoon lunch. Tim had a red and white cooler in the back with some sandwich fixings, which were simple, white, on white, on white; Wonder Bread, mayonnaise, and sliced turkey breast. It still hit the spot. I took a few photos of the surrounding scenery and we sped off after about a fifteen-minute break.

It was getting near sunset when Tim dropped me off at a mileage sign that read, Cheyenne 45 miles.

"Here's where I turn off. Sorry I'm not going any further," he said, yawning out the last few words. "You shouldn't have a problem though. It's Saturday night and there's a rodeo in Cheyenne.

"Okay, great. Thanks for the ride, and adios amigo," I said as I hopped out of the station wagon.

The vacuum cleaner exhaust sound of the station wagon slowly dissipated leaving me in a quite empty space. I glanced both left and right, observing only the white pencil line in the middle of the blacktop highway disappearing into the horizon.

"Oh, well," I sighed out loud to myself, "Someone else will come along."

To kill time, I entertained myself playing with my white canvas sailor hat, flipping it into the air and catching it on my index finger. Reshaping the brim with both hands, I'd repeat the process. Dusk was approaching and the colors blasting across the horizon in the vast barrenness of the prairie reminded me of the spectacular sunsets I often viewed in Hawaii, minus the water reflection.

Here, I didn't experience the red ball of fire disappearing inch by inch into the ocean's horizon. Instead, this particular evening, I was greeted by a somewhat dismal grayish-blue darkness, pitch black along its edges.

Suddenly, way out in the distance, I noticed a fast-moving trail of dust rising up in the air, moving along a hidden dirt road far out in the deserted countryside. It was moving in a direction that would intersect with the highway. It disappeared for a moment and then was replaced by two small dots of light heading towards me.

I placed my tin suitcase out in the road, aiming it so the lights of the approaching vehicle would hopefully reflect off it and I stood back. I watched as the headlights grew as they rapidly approached. The vehicle was traveling at a high rate of speed and zoomed right by me. I frantically waved my white hat in the air. I knew he could see me. It wasn't that dark yet. Then I heard the squeal of braking tires, the rubber scarring the road as the tires bit the asphalt. I saw the backup lights flash on as the transmission was rammed into reverse. Excited, I ran to meet it, the sound of an over-revved engine and a whining rear-end breaking the stillness of the night. Little did I know that my lucky streak was in for a slight downward turn.

A rusty four-door Chevrolet stopped. As I peered in the window and observed the occupants in its dimly lit interior, I immediately had second thoughts. But hey, here I was stuck out in the middle of nowhere with fast approaching darkness and no traffic. I was committed. The backdoor pushed open and a large guy crawled out and motioned me into the backseat as he grabbed my suitcase and threw it into the unlocked trunk. He got back into the car squeezing me between himself and the man on my left.

There were four of them and they all reeked of sweat, smoke and liquor.

"Hey, amigo, you one strange dude to find way out here. Didja lose your boat?" the driver joked in broken English. He glanced at me through the rearview mirror; a bright gold tooth lit up by the dash lights reflected a sinister smile.

"I know, I kind of got dropped off in no-man's land, didn't I?" I replied with a weak, sickening laugh.

"Well, now we got the sono-bitch, what we gonna do wit 'im?" The rough-looking, short one, riding shotgun said, slurring his words.

"What do you mean, whatcha gonna do with me? You guys are kidding me, right? Maybe you'd just better drop me off," I said hopefully, my heart racing a thousand miles an hour.

"No f–king way, amigo, you're along for the ride," the driver said. "Ain't that right, José?" He glanced to his right.

"Si, Ricardo, dis da only way he be dropped off." He opened the glove box and removed a Western .45 cal. six-shooter. He turned and pointed it at me pretending to fire off a round, with a click of his tongue.

My insides squirmed and I started to sweat. "You guys are really only kidding, right?" I repeated, but not with much conviction.

"Maybe you think we kiddin' but maybe we mean business," the tall one, who had shoved me into the car, said in a deep, slightly pissed-off sounding voice. They all laughed wickedly and passed around a bottle of Jack Daniels.

"Better maybe you join the party," Ricardo said, passing back a pack of Camel straights, offering me one.

"Guess maybe I'd better." I said, taking a slug of whiskey, lightening up a little. I felt a little better - very little - but better.

"You be pussy, we treat you like pussy, you be man, we treat you like man." Ricardo continued.

"Well, I'm no pussy, but you've put the fear of God in me," I said.

They all laughed again, this time a little more playful and I forced a smile out.

We arrived in Cheyenne around 9 p.m. and pulled into the dusty, potholed, dirt parking lot of a cheap motel on the strip. Except for Ricardo, and me faking my inebriation, the other three were pretty plowed under from downing a bottle of whiskey and half a case of beer. They parked the Chevy in the rear of the motel and Ricardo went to the front desk to check in. José and the other two pulled me out of the car and held my arm. Ricardo came around the corner, room keys jingling in his hand. He went to the trunk, got their gear and my suitcase out of it, walked over to the motel, opened two adjoining doors, and we split up, Ricardo and José in one, me and the two bullies from the back seat in the other. DAMN!

I was scared shitless. I felt that there was something amiss here and was afraid that I was about to become a victim of some sort of foul play. I played along, slurring my words and peering through half-closed eyelids. The door opened and Ricardo and José came in from next door.

"How is he?" Ricardo asked the tall one.

"Pretty smashed, don't look like he's a goin' anywhere soon," he answered.

"Leave him here. Those two might start to get along better, now that he's f - ked up." Ricardo said, turning and exiting the room convinced that I wasn't going anywhere. The three of them left.

I heard the car start up and drive off. I started to undress, stumbling around as I slipped off my uniform. I pretended to be drunk and watched my guard out of the corner of my eye. I put the tin suitcase on one of the beds and unconsciously folded my uniform neatly. My mind was racing and my heart was beating like a bass drum. My adrenaline was peaking, but my power, strengthened by fear, was racing to my arms and fists. I sensed a movement behind me, then felt a hand squeeze my buttocks! I screamed out loud - ECHAAAAAH! The Mexican shrunk back, surprised at my outburst, his eyes opened wide. At the same instant, I exploded and went into action. I grabbed the handle of the tin suitcase in both of my hands and swung it up from the bed in an arc that connected with the left side of my assailant's head. Stunned, he hit the deck hard with his head and was out like a light. Thank God.

I picked up the suitcase and my sprawled uniform from the floor, threw them on the bed, opened the tin container, grabbed a pair of Levis and a t-shirt out of it, stuffed my uniform in their place, slammed it shut, hurriedly slipped on my shoes, and raced out of the door into the darkness. On the way to the street, I saw a cardboard box about the size of the suitcase next to the dumpster.

"Perfect." I thought, knowing that when the others returned, they would come looking for me and they would probably spot the suitcase right off the bat. I dumped my clothes into the box, threw the suitcase into the dumpster, and sped out of the motel parking lot. I ran two blocks past the main street where we'd entered Cheyenne, then turned east and headed further into the city. I was tired, hungry, and thirsty, but I rushed on, realizing that I had to make tracks fast and gain some distance.

I continued down the side street for what felt like a long time, trying to gain as much distance that I could from the motel. I felt relatively safe now that I was disguised in my civilian clothes, carrying a box of clothing like a drifter, and I detected no sign of pursuit. I went a few more blocks, and then decided to take a chance and get back onto the main drag and try to hitch a ride out of town.

I hid in the shadow of a building on the corner and observed the traffic for a moment before I got the nerve to venture out and expose myself. My heart was beating rapidly, and I had a bad case of the dry mouth. I crossed the sidewalk and stepped off the curb into the street and raised my thumb into the air, a pleading expression pasted on my face. This was turning out to be like a road movie from hell.

"Someone, please stop. Someone, please stop. Someone, please stop," I repeated over and over at each vehicle that approached me. Finally, after what seemed like an eternity but was in reality only minutes, a brown and white, two-toned, Pontiac station wagon honked its horn at me and pulled over to the curb. I stepped back onto the sidewalk and ran to meet my saving grace.

Slightly winded, I reached the car and bent down on one knee to get my face level with the occupants and peered into the interior. A grossly fat arm was slung out over the passenger's door window. It was attached to an enormously obese woman sitting inside. She must have tipped the scales at around 350 pounds. She had scraggly, unkempt, windblown hair, sweat running off her forehead and moisture on her thinly mustached upper lip. A plain blue and white flowered sack-like house dress draped her form. Next to her, a skinny man with a blue and white striped railroad hat on his head and matching coveralls sat behind the wheel.

"Where ya going, Sonny?" The fat lady asked.

"Home to Minnesota, ma'am."

"Are you a good driver?"

"Yes, ma'am."

"Well, you'd better hop in. My old man's getting pretty tired and we need to be in Sioux Falls, Iowa, by noon tomorrow." I opened the door behind her and crawled into a cluttered rear seat.

"And don't call me ma'am. My name's Dorothy, and this here's Elmer, my hubby."

"Yes, ma'am, I mean Dorothy. I'm Don, pleased to meet you."

"Drive on, Elmer, we gottcha' a relief."

"Yes, Mother," he replied.

"Oh my - one of those - hen pecked," I thought.

Tucking myself down in the seat, I finally allowed myself a sigh of relief. I turned around and peeked out the back window to make sure I'd made a clean getaway and there wasn't a rusty old Chevrolet behind us with four shadowy figures in it. Satisfied, I whispered a prayer, "Thank you Lord, thank you." The city lights disappeared and soon we were out on the prairie again. Skinny Elmer drove slowly, around fifty miles an hour, fifteen miles under the legal speed limit. It made me nervous and anxious. I wanted to tell him to get his ass in gear but thought better of it. At least we were moving forward. The night was hot and humid, so all the windows were rolled down. I sat behind Dorothy and the sweat wetting her underarm fanned back into my nostrils. I rearranged the seat and moved over to the other side only to be blasted in the face from the spray of Elmer's juicy chewing tobacco spit that he weakly squirted out of the side of his mouth.

"This is too much," I thought. "Next time I'll fly." But I wanted the adventure, and this time I was getting a plateful.

Exhausted I finally fell asleep, hungry, but safe for now. But, shit, that didn't last long, either, and next thing I knew I was rudely awakened by a surprisingly sharp jolt, a series of bouncing back and forth and then a sudden stop. Wouldn't you know - Elmer had fallen asleep at the wheel! Fortunately, we were out in the plains and the terrain was so flat there was no embankment to cause a roll over.

"Ah, maybe we should change places?" I joked to Elmer.

"I think it's one hell of a good idea," Dorothy yelled, "Elmer, you get your skinny ass in the back seat and let that young man take over!"

"Yes, Mother," he answered sheepishly. "I must've drifted off."

"Ain't no must've 'bout it, now move. Donny boy, you take over and get us home safely, ya hear?"

"Yes, ma'am, and don't call me Donny!"

"And don't call me ma'am!"

"Yes, ma'am."

We both chuckled and I took over the wheel, happy to be in charge and to have a window to myself. I put the Pontiac wagon in gear, pulled back onto the highway, pointed that Indian Chief hood ornament straight down the road and kicked it up to around sixty-five miles an hour. The fresh air felt good and soon I got snores and grunts from the sleeping couple, so I adjusted myself comfortably behind the wheel and settled in to greet the dawn and the morning sunrise.

We arrived in Sioux Falls a little after noon the next day. I was still miles from my house on Lafond Street in St. Paul, but I was making fairly good progress. Elmer and Dorothy bought me lunch, thanked me for my help, and then dropped me off on highway 90 heading north towards my destination. They were really nice folks, but I was glad to be out of that Pontiac.

I had lifted a felt pen from the restaurant where we had lunched and proceeded to write St. Paul on the side of the cardboard box that held my clothes. Also, in the restaurant's bathroom, I had changed back into my dress white uniform.

It was only a matter of minutes before a white 1956 Lincoln Continental four-door hard-top convertible driven by a man with a pretty blonde sitting next to him pulled up to me and said, "Hop in, sailor boy, we're heading your way."

I slipped into the cream-colored leather back seat. I shut the door and he put the pedal to the metal. "Now, this is more like it," I thought.

The three of us had made small talk for about an hour when the driver, a suited-up used car salesman by the name of Benny, pulled over to a liquor store on the side of the road. He went inside and came out with a brown paper bag. He hopped back behind the wheel and we sped off.

"Whatcha got in the bag, honey?" Asked the blonde.

"Some joy juice for you and me, baby. We ain't runnin' away from my old lady and your old man and not goin' to have us some fun now, are we?"

"No, honey, we're going to have us a party!" she said, sliding over next to him, putting her arms around him and nibbling on his right ear. She turned and winked at me. "That's if the good ole' sailor boy don't mind."

"Hey, I don't mind. In fact, you guys can have the back seat and I'll drive if you want."

"Whatcha think, Benny? We got us our own chauffeur. Let's go mess around in the back seat. We've never done it there before. Besides, I'm tired of those sleazy motel rooms."

Benny took a slug out of one of the pints of Southern Comfort that he'd just bought and pulled over to the shoulder of the road. He slid out of the front seat and she followed. I hopped out of the back, ran around and opened the opposite rear door for them. They were both laughing as he slapped her on the behind. They literally crawled onto the soft glove leather cushioned back seat. I smiled, shut the door and got behind the wheel. Now, I really was a chauffeur. I giggled to myself - this was turning out to be rather interesting.

"Drive on, James!" Benny laughingly ordered from the back seat.

I checked the side and rear-view mirrors and, seeing no approaching traffic, pulled back on to highway 90 and headed on down the road.

Benny and the blonde played games in the back of the car while getting more inebriated, drinking straight out of the bottle. I had a hard time keeping my eyes on the road as I snuck peeks in the rearview mirror, watching the antics of those two who seemed to be completely unaware that there was someone else with them in the car.

They were feverishly going at it, completely ignoring my existence. I was so engrossed with the exhibition that I hadn't noticed I was kicking butt on down the road at close to eighty miles an hour.

The action in the back seat got wilder and I was getting a little distracted, trying to watch the show. My eyes left the road, the car started swaying, and we ran off the road. Then I over corrected trying to yank the wheels back onto the highway - then it happened - the right front tire blew. BAM! It sounded like a shotgun blast.

"Shit, hold on!" I yelled as the car started to skid sideways. The brakes locked up and the tires started smoking. We bounced back onto the highway, the tires screeching, laying wide tracks of rubber on the asphalt as I tried to correct the slide. In an instant, I was looking back the way we had come. Benny and the blonde were thrown on the floor, and then, bang - all of a sudden it was over.

"What the f - - k happened?" Benny screamed from the back seat as he righted his half-naked body back up into the seat.

"Blew a tire." I said.

"Hell of a thrill!!!!" the blonde drunkenly laughed.

"Thought I'd died and gone out into space. Made my ears ring," Benny laughed.

My heart finally slowed down and I joined in the laughter. "Guess I took you two on a good ride."

"You sure did, boy, you sure did." Benny said as he retrieved the bottle of Southern Comfort from the floor, uncapped it and passed it over to me. "Here, have a hit." This time I joined in, taking a big swig and emptying the bottle. Benny lit up a Camel straight and took a deep drag, then blew the smoke out strongly, as if in relief.

"You know, buddy?" he said, looking at me. "After you put on the spare, I think this is where you get off."

"Yeah, guess I kind of blew that one," I replied, "And I don't blame ya for firing me. But you got to admit, you sure got your kicks on Route 66, (pun intended.) Thanks for the ride."

I stood on the side of the road, chuckling to myself. "What a crazy world." I thought.

This time, I hadn't even put out my thumb when a baby blue 50 Ford "Shoebox" (so named because of its square shape) pulled up along the shoulder of the road. A young girl about sixteen years old leaned halfway out the passenger side window and yelled out to me, "Hey Sailor, need a ride?"

"Oh, oh, here we go again." I thought.

"Love one!" I answered as I picked up the cardboard box and cradled it in my arms. It was a two-door club coupe and I had to squeeze in behind the front seat as the girl leaned the back of it forward.

"Ever hear of suitcases?" the girl sarcastically asked.

"Believe me, it's a long story," I answered.

"Sailor boys always got some stories to tell," she said raising her eyebrows up and grinning wide, her brown eyes shooting flirtatious arrows in my direction.

"Oh my," I thought.

"This here's my mom, Julie," she swung her head towards the lady behind the wheel. Then, whipping it back towards me, she continued enthusiastically, "and I'm Crystal, what's yours?"

"Don, or Dino, which is my beach name. I answer to both."

Her mother turned and said, "You'll have to excuse Crystal for her over exuberance, but she's been bored to tears, and when she saw you standing on the side of the road looking lost, she begged me to stop and pick you up." She shifted the Ford into low gear, glanced into her side mirror to check traffic and we were back on the road.

"How far are you going?" She asked in her next breath.

"All the way to St. Paul, and you?"

"Actually, we're going into Minneapolis, so when we get close to where you want off, just let me know."

"Hey this is great. I may even get home in time for my mom's fried chicken dinner."

"Well, it is Sunday and we're not that far away. We should be there sometime late afternoon," Julie replied.

During the next few hours, Crystal took every opportunity to secretly flirt with me. She would close her eyes and then slowly open them and gaz at me dreamily. Oh, you could see, she loved teasing me. I chuckled under my breath and let her play her little game. I was amused.

We headed into the Twin Cities on Highway 35, bringing us nearer the Mississippi River and University Avenue.

"I can hop out on the Avenue and grab a bus into St. Paul, and you ladies could continue into Minneapolis," I suggested.

"That'll work for us." Julie said.

I got out of the Ford, and then turned around to retrieve my box from the back seat. As I was backing out with it in my arms, I got a surprise. Crystal grabbed my head in her two hands and placed her lips on mine. Her mother coughed, interrupting the innocent intimacy. "Crystal," she commanded, "Enough already!"

With that we waved good-bye. I crossed the street to catch the bus down to Dale Street where I could transfer to another bus that would take me to Lafond Street and I'd be within half of a block of my house. The bus went by Porky's Drive-In, where my hot rod buddies from the Devils' Deputies and I used to hang out, past Montgomery Wards, where my mother used to take us kids shopping on Saturdays, past Brown and Bigelows Printing, where my Dad worked, past the roller skating rink, the Minnesota Twins baseball field, and the Faust theater. All of these were bringing back memories of my childhood and high school years. It was getting on to almost four years since I had a liberty here, except for the one I had right out of boot camp, and that didn't count.

But, meanwhile, I had traveled extensively, mixing with different peoples and cultures of the world, experiencing numerous firsts, while escaping death and bodily harm that had befallen some of my mates. I'd grown up fast in the Navy and I felt worldly now, compared to my Frog Town upbringing.

I hopped off the bus at Dale and Lafond and walked down the street to my house. Folks were just getting out of afternoon Bingo from our church. Cars and pedestrians were moving down the street, some honked at me in recognition, others stopped to greet me. I felt special and important as I rushed up the green painted stairs to the front porch of my parent's home. They were both sitting on a wooden swing seat suspended from the ceiling watching the Sunday promenade. When my father saw me approaching, he leaped up to greet me. Surprised, my mother almost tipped over backwards on her rocker onto the porch floor.

"Hey, boy! Where the hell you come from? This is sure a surprise!"

"It's how I wanted it to be, Dad." I said as we hugged each other.

Mother Rose yelled at me in her usual manner, "You could give your poor mother a heart attack showing up unexpectedly," as she hugged and kissed me. "And I noticed you showed up in time for Sunday dinner."

"You don't think I'd miss a tradition, do you?"

"Not if I know my son," she said. "Go get your brother and sisters. They're playing in the back yard, and we'll sit down to a nice family meal."

"Fried chicken, I hope." I said.

"Nope, but one of your favorites: Pot roast, mashed potatoes and gravy, baby peas and homemade apple pie," Dad answered.

"Great! I just traveled steady for three days and nights and almost six thousand miles, even crossed an ocean to get here for Sunday dinner. I'll get the kids."

I went to the backyard to call my siblings, Dennis, Marilyn and Joyce.

"Hey, kids, Sunday dinner time." I called.

"Donny, Donny." They yelled at the top of their lungs when they saw me, rushing to crawl on me and hug me. I fell to the ground and we all started wrestling, tickling and pinching each other in good fun.

"All right, kids, up off the ground, go wash your hands and let's eat dinner. Your father's hungry," Mom yelled out of the kitchen window.

We all raced into the house and lined up at the sink in the one bathroom we all shared and hurriedly washed our hands and then took our prospective places at the table. Dad led the blessing and we all responded with "Amen." I was glad to be home.

I spent the next week visiting relatives, school buddies and a few old girlfriends, relating to them my latest adventures and experiences. Most, having led sheltered lives at home, couldn't believe some of my stories. "You're kidding; you can't be serious, you're pulling my leg and no shit," were some of the comments received.

But after a week I got bored with the humdrum daily life routine that everyone seemed to have settled into. Having a more adventurous spirit, I felt it was time for me to go. I longed for my beaches in Hawaii, my Mercury convertible and getting together with my latest girlfriend, Ann, who waitressed at the Kau-Kau drive.

I made a long-distance phone call to Steve, my flight coordinator, roommate and friend, and he hooked me up to a VR-21 flight leaving Alameda Air Station out of San Francisco the following week. I had him manifest me in for a seat back to the islands. He did. Then I called Gina in Alameda. Things were working out so well - again.

I booked a commercial flight on American Airlines out of Minneapolis for $75 one-way, a special service rate, said my good-byes and left. I'd spend my last few days of liberty with Gina in Sausalito and San Francisco, then have her drop me off at Alameda bass operations, and off I'd go.

I would not return to my hometown for the next fifteen years. Instead my family, except for my sister Marilyn, would soon relocate to California to be near me. ~

Chapter 25: One Day, One Night

I arrived back on Oahu aboard plane #453 of VR-21's fleet. It was August, a month before my twenty-first birthday. I'd been in the Navy almost four full years, stationed at Barbers Point for most of that time. I had gained weight and my body had filled out to be far more muscular, due mostly to my weight-training program, swimming, body and board surfing, the Navy's bountiful food and, oh yes, beer–the source of lots of carbohydrates.

I checked the flight board and noticed that I was scheduled to fly out to Japan in three days, giving me just enough time to catch up on what I might have missed while on leave and pick up where I'd left off with Ann, the waitress I had been seeing since Wanda left.

I hopped into the Mercury and headed to Waikiki. Half way out the gate, I remembered that Ann had mentioned that she could use a new mattress, as the one she was sleeping on at her family's homestead was rather worn out. I hit the brakes and did a U-turn back onto the base.

"Forgot something," I told the Marine on duty. Back to my old tricks, I went down to the supply depot, drove around the back so as not to be observed in the act of commandeering Navy goods and parked between two large dumpsters. My Mexican, buddy Sanchez owed me a favor and I figured this was as good a time as any to collect. I walked into the large warehouse and caught him just leaving for the chow hall for lunch with the rest of the crew.

"Hey Amigo, hold up for a minute, would you?" I yelled.

He waved for his crew to go on without him and walked back to meet me. "What'cha need, good buddy?" He asked.

I lowered my voice to a whisper. "Well, I have this new babe that I'm trying to make points with and she could use a new mattress. Looks like I came at the right time. I'm glad you're here."

"Yeah, well, we did get some re-issues in. They're rolled up and still have a plastic covering over them. I could probably let you have one of them, no problem. How are you going to get it out of here?"

"I got the Mercury, and it's got one hell of a big trunk. I'm sure we could stuff it in there.

"Okay, let's get one quick and see if it'll fit. If it does, remember you didn't get it from me, got that?"

"Got it," I assured him.

We grabbed the mattress, took it outside, opened the trunk and jammed it in. It barely fit. Sanchez had to sit on the turtle back shaped trunk, adding his weight to force its closure while I locked it. DONE!

I hopped in the driver's seat and winked at Sanchez, who returned with the gesture of holding his index finger to his lips. "Not a word," I whispered, as I brought the V-8 to life and slowly drove away.

My heart began to beat stronger as I neared the gate but returned to its normal pace as the guard waved me through. It was another beautiful day in paradise. I cruised on down the two-lane highway, which was bordered by sugar cane fields on both sides. I smiled to myself, planning my next two days off. First, I'd go to my apartment, grab my beach gear, drop by the Alawai Canoe Club, grab a 10-foot balsa surfboard and catch some waves. After, I'd grab some sun, slam down a couple of beers, go to the Kau Kau Drive-In, park in Ann's section near the back, consume a couple of double cheeseburgers and a Coke and show her my surprise hidden in the trunk.

Everything went according to plan. Steve decided to come with me. We got to the Kau Kau Drive- in just as a yellow and black Nash Metropolitan was vacating a spot in the back row. I pulled up close to him so that I could back into the spot. I shut down the engine and turned on the parking lights, indicating that we were ready to order.

The girls waved to us from the pickup station. Ann was waiting for an order to come up. She held up one finger to let us know she'd be but a moment. I shut off the lights and watched as Ann lifted her tray into the air and sashayed her cute little shape towards us, delivering her order along the way.

"Hi, babe, where's the A?" she asked, leaning over and giving me a small peck on the lips.

"Sittin' curbside back at the place. Couldn't carry the surprise I got for you in it. But, hey, check this out." Excited, I leaped over the closed door of the convertible and ran around to the rear of the car. Ann followed with a curious look on her face.

"Close your eyes," I said as we stood in front of the trunk.

Reaching down, I unlocked the lid and slowly lifted it, exposing the mattress.

"Oh, baby!" she exclaimed with glee. "Can we initiate it tonight?"

"Where?" I asked.

"You can follow me up to Kalihi."

"What about your other boyfriend, Buzz?"

"No problem, he's at sea."

"And what about your family?"

"Most of my pay from here goes to support them so they never question my actions. I'm sort of in control, so again no problem. Besides, they'll like you," she answered with a twinkle in her eye. "Let me get your order. It's on me."

We ordered two cheeseburgers, large fries, and chocolate malts, turned on the radio and listened to some rock n' roll. While we waited, we engaged in idle conversation, about my venturing into unknown territory up in the Palolo Valley.

Our orders came and we filled our bellies. Afterwards, I made arrangements to rendezvous with Ann later that night. We would meet at the base of the foothills, where the two-lane Pali highway began.

To kill time in between, we cruised downtown to Honolulu's infamous Hotel Street to check out the action. It was a riotous area with a carnival atmosphere, reminiscent of the Pike in Long Beach and the North Beach area in San Francisco. There were strip clubs up and down both sides of the streets, all crammed into a three-city block area.

Prostitutes, transvestites, and scam artists roamed outside the clubs luring in the uniformed Navy, Marine, Army and Air Force personnel who were looking for a good time. Being locals, we liked to slum around there once in a while. It was fun. There was always a lot of action going on. The Shore Patrol canvassed the area, along with some of the local police. They were always hauling someone away in the paddy wagon: a disgruntled whore who didn't get paid for her service or an upset John who just got robbed of all his cash. The other side of the tracks, from the famed Waikiki Beach area, was a cesspool.

My lowered Mercury rolled ever so slowly up and down the strip. We made U-turns at the Alawai Canal Bridge on the south end and at the taxi garage to the north. Every pass we made past CHIROS NIGHT CLUB, there were two sexy looking Samoan babes leaning up against its walls. Their long, flowing hair was adorned with flowers over their right ears, meaning they were available. Both wore colorful sarongs wrapped around their waists, showing more than ample leg through the thigh-high split on the side. Their makeup was flawless, enhancing their good looks. As we drove by, the girls called out to us in sweet sexy voices laced with suggestive remarks. Their enhanced body movements enticed us to stop and pick them up.

After the third pass, I looked over to Steve and said, "What do think, Steve-o?"

"They look like a couple of transvestites to me. You know what the custom is in some of those Samoan families. There's always a boy who takes on a woman's role. I think they call them Mahos."

"You know I think you're right, we very well could get in serious trouble." We waved and yelled out "Aloha!" and sped down the street.

I dropped Steve off at home and went to pick up Ann so we could bring the mattress to her place. Staying with her in the house she shared with her family made me uncomfortable. When I awoke the next morning, I felt compelled to leave quickly. That, plus the - almost incident - of the two transvestites the night before made me take a long look at how I was living my life.

After breakfast back at the duplex, I took a long "thinking" shower, starting off with a few deep breaths. I contemplated the future, wondering what was going to happen in the next few months as I neared my discharge from the Navy. ~

CHAPTER 26: COUNTDOWN

There were times I could change my physical outer appearance, like a chameleon changes his within the surrounding environment.

Back at base, I stepped into my cubicle and once again transformed myself from beach bum to sailor. I dressed in my crisp starched tailored work blue bell bottoms and one of my form fitting short sleeved shirts. I slipped a black canvas belt through the loops of the pants and hooked it up in front with a shiny brass buckle with crossed anchors on it. I sat down on the lower bunk and laced up a pair of black, spit-shined polished work boots on my feet, then "baseball" rolled the visor on my blue working cap, tucked my longish, sun-bleached, light ash brown hair into its cavity and slipped it down onto my head.

Back on the tarmac, the first face I ran into was that off Chief Segona.

"Well if it isn't 'Hollywood'!! Come to put in a couple hours?" He said sarcastically, with a smile and a chuckle.

"Yes, sir, I'm at your command!" I beamed back, snapping to attention and respectfully saluting him, although as a non-commissioned officer, it wasn't necessary.

The chief nonchalantly returned the salute and said, "Oh, by the way, that second class mechanic over in the VP squadron wants to talk to you about trading your Mercury for a '40 Ford he owns."

"You mean the plum-colored one with the Buick engine in it?"

"Yeah, that's the one. He just lowered the front end two inches. Looks real good."

"Hey, thanks Chief, you know, I've got a passion for '40 Fords, this would be my fourth '40."

"But, could you part with the lead sled?" he asked.

"I never thought I could. But lately the Mercury and me have been getting to be a little too well known with the local cops around Honolulu. This might be just the time for a trade."

Two days later, I was tooling around in the plum-colored coupe and the Mercury was history. I got my sailor friend, "Bogie," to pinstripe it. We named it the Casual Coupe and painted a pear shaped character with big flat feet named Scooby-Doo on the face of the glove box. I also had two interchangeable shifting forks for the '39 Mercury floor transmission. You simply put it in neutral, unscrewed it, lifted it up and out and replaced it with the other. One was a number 8 pool ball-topped short shifter; the other curved high up above the dash and was topped with a Van Dyke-inspired eyeball. Too much fun! Couldn't leave a new rig alone until I made some sort of change.

For the next few months, I avoided the Waikiki area. I gave up my apartment. Shari and Constance threw me a "moving out" party. Constance invited me to her wedding in San Jose, Calif., on November 24h, two days after I was to be discharged from the Navy in San Francisco. It would be perfect timing. I sold my interest in the "A" to Steve and left the Royal Hawaiian Avenue digs for the North Shore in my new, plum-colored '40 Ford.

I started hanging out exclusively on the North Shore, frequenting the surfing beaches. It was at Makaha that I met a local Hawaiian girl, Lalina Pohoe. Her family had a simple weekend beach house at the end of the paved road made out of recycled lumber, bamboo poles and palm branches. During those visits, I'd slip into a native mode. I spoke Pidgin English with them and enjoyed the laid-back easy style. Life was good again - as change is good. I busied myself romancing Lalina and flying quick trips out of Barbers Point. I stayed out of trouble while casually enjoying my last few months on the island. I was growing up - some.

On the first of November I shipped the '40 Ford to Oakland aboard an ocean carrier so it would be waiting for me on the dock when I got there. Ten days later, I packed my civvies into a cardboard box except for one change of clothing, which I put into a small overnight bag - just in case. I organized my duffel bag according to Navy regulations, with my uniform and all that had been issued to me four years before. I draped myself in my dress blues and caught the bus to

Pearl Harbor where I'd be issued my discharge orders and given transportation.

The processing took a few hours of standing in line for this, standing in line for that. My orders were stamped by an unsmiling yeoman, doing his boring job of giving men their road to freedom while he was stuck in his steel chair behind a steel desk.

The last yeoman in the line of desks, the WXYZ check out, was a quite striking looking WAC who, with a smile and a "Good luck Sailor," handed me my orders and commercial tickets on World Airlines to San Francisco. Later, after we arrived at the San Francisco International Airport, a bus would meet those of us being discharged and transfer us to Treasure Island Navy Station where we would be mustered out.

Arriving at the Honolulu airport, I checked in, was issued my boarding pass and told that I'd be departing at gate 5. My heart was racing for two reasons: I was heading into a new chapter in my life and I was leaving a part of myself behind in a paradise that I had grown to love. I let out a deep sigh, sad at the thought of leaving. But flying on a commercial airline instead of military aircraft seemed to ease the pain of my departure. It made it feel real.

I walked up the ramp into the plane and immediately recognized the stewardesses, Vivian and Marty, two "party animals" I'd met at the mansion in the Heights. Our eyes met and they motioned me back to a seat by the galley where, after we were airborne, I was treated like a celebrity the whole flight. I liked the way civilian life was about to begin.

At the San Francisco airport the 'stews' decided to continue our party and give me a farewell I wouldn't forget. Okay, I'm game, always ready for an invitation. I had twenty-four hours before I had to report in at Treasure Island and the girls also had a twenty-four-hour crew's rest before their next flight. "Bingo!" They enticed me to layover with them at their digs in Sausalito.

I went to the USO complex that the airport provided for servicemen and changed out of my uniform while the girls went to pick up their car. I went outside and passed by the shuttle bus as if it didn't exist. I whispered to myself, "Catch you later." I heard a horn honk, and I saw two smiling faces in a yellow '61 Ford convertible.

"Throw that bag in the back seat and hop up here in front with us," Vivian said, opening the passenger door and sliding out to let me sit in the middle between them.

"Wow!" I thought. "Another stroke of luck. How long can this go on?"

Marty pulled out into traffic and we were on our way. On this gorgeous day I marveled at the sights as we drove through the city past Golden Gate Park and onto the famous Golden Gate Bridge that arched over the entrance to the bay. Gazing down at the water below, I reflected about when I had first visited San Francisco almost three years ago, standing at attention on the flight deck of the USS Kearsarge. Now I felt different, elated but more relaxed and confident. Passing over its span, wind blowing my hair, salt air in my nostrils, I knew I'd gone full circle. Soon I'd be out of the service. A whole new world out there waited for me. Today seemed to be the start.

The bay's water sparkled, shimmering from the reflecting sun as we wound our way down the curved road that led into the small town of Sausalito across the bay. On our left, small homes and apartments loomed out of the trees, cantilevered out from the steep hillsides that shot up from the roadside. On the right, waves lapped at the sea wall as we cruised along, the breeze from the bay filling our nostrils with a refreshing moist, nautical scent.

Marty turned off the main street and started to climb a narrow one-lane road that meandered precariously along a steep drop-off opposite the waterside. The views were awesome. High up at the end of the road she pulled the convertible into a vine-covered carport that sat on the edge of the side of a hill. A swinging, thick rope bridge with wooden planks reached out on one end, connecting the carport with a small cottage built on stanchions embedded in concrete far below in the earth, a hidden haven hanging out in space amongst the trees. "Very cool!!" I commented.

"Yes, and we love it here, and nobody bothers us. It's where we recover our sanity after flying. Grab a beer out of the fridge while we change. Then we'll walk down into town for some dinner." Vivian said in so many words, and then they both disappeared into the same bedroom.

Grabbing a Budweiser, I went out on the deck. Listening to a sound coming from the small bathroom window that looked out on the deck, I could hear a shower running and their voices conversing and laughing together. I overheard bits and pieces and it sounded like they were planning something, but over the noise of the shower I couldn't quite pick up on what it might be. I went back into the living room and sat down in a black leather wing chair. Soon Marty came out, smiled at me and went to a small wet bar next to the open sliding glass door leading out to the deck and offered me a gin and tonic.

"It'll mellow us out a little before we go to dinner," she said, as she handed me a bucket glass full to the brim. "Cheers," she said, adding a wink of her eye and we clicked glasses. I knew it meant something good.

Vivian came out of the bedroom to join us, singing, "La-dee-dah, La-de dah." She had completely transformed. Her hair was all let down and ruffled with natural curl cascading softly around her shoulders and a small clump of daisies pinned above her left ear. A floor length tie-dyed, pleated peasant skirt hid her sandaled feet. Her wrists and arms were ringed with countless bracelets. Around her neck were beads, crystals and miniature Tibetan bells, which jingled softly as she walked towards us.

"Wow, a princess!" I breathed out.

"Yeah, she's a true bohemian at heart." Marty commented.

As she drew near, I could smell the pungent odor of Patchouli oil, the scent favored by the New Age marijuana users. Brushing her lips past my cheek, she whispered in my ear, "Thank you, for the compliment."

I felt very lucky to be with these two special ladies. Things were looking better every minute. I smiled, but remained cool and passive, just letting the good times roll.

We finished our cocktails and headed out the door and down the road. We had walked about one hundred yards when we came upon an inconspicuous wooden staircase that dropped down through the forested hillside.

"We'll use the secret stairs to get down to the middle of town," Vivian said. "There's a number of them throughout these woods. The locals are pretty much the only ones who know about them. They were built back in the forties by neighbors who wanted to visit one another and needed a quick way to get into town without driving. Lots of them are overgrown, rotting, and no longer in use, but we use this one all the time."

I was surprised and amazed at the amount of work, lumber, and cement that went into creating these descending pathways. Even more surprising was how they linked together with others. We came out in the middle of town, directly across from the park that bordered the bay.

"Wow," I said, "That was a trip. You could get lost in that labyrinth if you didn't know where you were going."

"All you have to remember is to go left, and down, at every turn, and then reverse on the way back up," said Marty, smiling and spinning around in a circle, her arms held out wide.

The three of us tripped on down the street till we came to Zacks and the

Boathouse, two restaurants on the waterfront that bordered each other.

"Let's eat oysters at Zacks, then go listen to the blues at the Boathouse after." Vivian suggested.

The rest of the late afternoon and on into the evening was a marathon of cocktails consumption, oyster shucking, laughter, dancing and lots of suggestive physical contact. Near midnight Marty suggested we call a cab instead of making the climb back up the stairs in the dark. We'd forgotten to bring a flashlight to guide us back, plus we were slightly inebriated.

Back at the pad, the girls made up a bed for me on the couch and said goodnight. I was a little taken back, somehow expecting more. Left alone, I took off my clothes and slipped between the sheets.

"Guess I was wrong," I thought. I fluffed up the pillow and turned on my side. I lay there, the events of the day running through my head. I considered getting up and sneaking into one of their bedrooms, but which one? As the thought lingered, I saw in my subconscious mind both Vivian and Marty naked as I fantasized how they might look. I imagined one of them gliding through the door floating on air towards me, her feet barely touching the floor. I felt that my thoughts must have been transferred through space as I felt a warm body silently slip in with me. I turned and took the apparition into my arms. The aroma of Patchouli made me realize I wasn't dreaming...or was I?

I awoke the next morning to the smell of bacon, eggs, toast and coffee. The girls were draped in loose fitting, lavender cotton robes, both busying themselves in the preparation of feeding their shared lover of the night before.

"Morning." I said.

"And a good morning to you," they replied in unison. "Did you sleep well?"

"Like a baby."

"There's a fresh towel in the bathroom for you if you want to take a shower," Vivian said, pointing the spatula she held in her hand towards the door.

"Thank you," I replied.

I showered and shaved, my mind slightly in a fog. I breathed in deep the musty smell of the foliage that grew on the hill outside through the small opened window in the shower. Refreshed, I got out and dried myself. Suddenly a light bulb went off in my mind and brought me back to reality.

"Shit! I have to report in by noon today," I whispered to myself.

I opened the door a crack and called out, "I need my uniform and have to be on base by noon today!"

"Don't get excited. One of us will get you there," Marty said, while sliding my big duffel bag through the partially opened door.

"Thank you." I pulled out my blues, unrolled them, slipped into them and rejoined the service. A large plate of food greeted me when I emerged from the bathroom. The girls had changed into tank tops and short-shorts. They both looked great.

"Eat up and we'll flip a coin to see who drives you over to Treasure Island," Vivian said. She pulled a quarter out of a jar on the counter. Marty won. We made small talk as we ate. When we finished, Vivian took the plates, placed them in the kitchen sink and very nonchalantly said, "It's been real, Dino. After you get out of the service and back in the real world, give us a call when you're in the area." She leaned over and gave me a kiss on the cheek, whispering for the third time, "Thank you."

"Guess we'd better be going," said Marty. We busied ourselves during the hour ride to the base, joking about the events of the previous day, but nothing was ever mentioned about the secret encounters. I realized when she dropped me off at the gate and leaned across the front seat to shake my hand (no kiss here) that I would probably never see either one of them ever again. I was a passing in the night, something that had just happened to happen.

For the next nine days I just hung out by myself. I pulled small duties while going through the discharge process and got my head together as I had a lot to think about to prepare me for the rest of my life.

On November 24, 1961, I thankfully received my Honorable Discharge. Later, I would frame it and hang it on a wall. It is still with me - even to this day. It really was a miracle that I had achieved this goal, considering my blatant disregard for a life of regulations. I had literally squeaked through the last four years. The reward? I grew up, becoming more mature and a little bit wiser in the ways of life.

The Navy gave me a thousand-dollar check, my discharge pay, so all together; I had about three thousand dollars. With a plan in mind, this would pay my first and last month's rent and cleaning deposit, furnish an apartment, and start me off in college. I was on my way.

The ship carrying the '40 Ford arrived at a wharf in Oakland. I grabbed a series of buses that took over half of the day to reach my destination. After receiving the keys from the dock master, I was soon behind the wheel. It turned over slowly, the battery a little weak, but caught spark on its third revolution as

I pumped the gas pedal hard. It roared to life like a sleeping lion speaking to me, and I rapped its pipes in celebration.

Next, I called Constance to check on the particulars of her wedding. It was going to be held that Saturday at an old sea captain's estate located far up into Los Gatos foothills outside San Jose.

I took some time to check out the city college, following up on some job opportunities, and looking for a place to live. I found a two-bedroom apartment on Delaney Street in San Jose, about four blocks from the city college. The apartment was in a great location, had a carport and a small swimming pool. Unfurnished, I'd have to start from scratch, one piece at a time depending on how the funds stretched.

At that time city colleges in California were free - all I had to pay for were my books and tools. I enrolled in the drafting classes and made mechanical engineering my major. ~

CHAPTER 27: SAN JOSE DAYS

Now that I was settled in San Jose, I could attend my Waikiki next-door neighbor Connie's wedding, which I had been invited to while on the island. I washed and shined the Forty, then dressed in my best. Luckily, this was California, and my Hawaiian dress shirt would fit in perfectly at the wedding. I left my empty shell of an apartment, drove up Saratoga Avenue for a ways, and then turned left towards the foothills, following Connie's directions. I felt free and wonderful, excited about who - and where - I was in this present time.

It took about twenty minutes to get to the little town of Los Gatos, which was nestled in the foothills of the Santa Cruz Mountains. I powered the '40 Ford coupe up the twisting, narrow, rural Hilltop Road until I spotted a gateway decorated with pink and white streamers. Two massive stone pillars cast into roaring lions, heads twisted with one paw raised, guarded the entrance to the sea captain's old estate. I rolled into the large outer courtyard paved with multi-colored handmade bricks and parked alongside a pink Mustang convertible, thinking as I did, "I bet a pretty blonde drives that one."

A large double arch entry door yawned open, a trusting invitation to all who approached it. I passed through, entering a semi-circled half-domed foyer. My footsteps echoed in it and led me to a far wall of emerald green glass. Another arched door, part of the wall, entered the garden. I walked down flagstone steps, bringing me once again outside on a natural plateau that tiered out over the edge of a fifty-foot drop. Below, sunken into its own cavity, was an Olympic-sized swimming pool reflecting the blue sky off its surface. A two-passenger, generator-powered tram, cranking itself up and down on mini steel rails, carried guests to and from the poolside patio below.

I'd arrived a little late. The nuptials had already been performed, the reception line had diminished, hands had been shaken and the bride kissed, and the party was now in full swing. I scanned the scene and spotted Connie standing next to a tall rugged-looking gentleman dressed in a tuxedo, sporting a rather large head of black curly hair styled in an afro. As I approached them, she rushed to greet me, beaming a large smile.

"Dino," she said, "How good of you to come - come meet my husband Cary."

I raised the champagne glass that had appeared in my hand as a silver tray filled with shining crystal glasses floated by me. Cary raised the glass he held and said, "Heard a lot about you, make yourself at home and wander about. When we get a free moment, we'll introduce you around."

Momentarily alone, I stood there entranced by the sweet music of happiness that only a marriage filled with love can bring. I breathed deep and bathed in the warm sun, taking in the beauty stretched out before my eyes. The Santa Clara Valley below was filled with orchards of peach, plum, cherry and mango trees. There were also fields of strawberries, artichokes, sweet corn, sugar beets and yams. The squared-up fields were bordered by narrow dirt roads meandering around. Quite impressive, but with time most of it would sadly disappear when rural suburbs would eat up the land, destroying the beauty.

Lake Visona, four miles away, was spotted with small dots of white sails waving like flags on its deep blue windy surface. I gazed at the one dark strip running up the valley's gut - Highway 17 - a four-lane autobahn, notorious for the high-speed crashes on its winding curves that carved through the mountains leading up and over to the beach at Santa Cruz. Therefore, it was named "Blood Alley." My eyes followed its path to the northeast. Way out in the distance I spotted two huge silver metal domes. The afternoon sun bouncing off of them was enhanced by the reflection of the water of the wetlands of Milpitas behind them. I was dreamily taking it all in when a soft arm bumped me. A sweet-sounding voice and the aroma of Jungle Gardenia perfume brought me back to focus.

"Oh, excuse me, now I've gone and done it, spilled my champagne and yours, too. Guess we'll just have to get us another one," she said, smiling and shrugging her shoulders, her arms raised to the sky, an empty glass hung upside down from her outstretched hand. She was good-looking and well dressed. Her hands were exquisite, like the models you see on TV in the Jergens hand cream commercial. On her slender fingers, long nails were painted a soft rose-pink color, enhancing their length. She batted her eyelids playfully.

"Hi, I'm Nicki, Connie's little sister," she said. "And you're Dino."

"How'd you know that?" I asked, amazed.

"Connie told me about you. She said you're her friend from Hawaii and probably would like to be entertained. Come on, let's go get these glasses refilled." She grabbed my arm and led me off.

"Wow!" I thought. "Here we go again!" She turned out to be quite nice, highly educated and very sophisticated.

As the afternoon wore on, she kindly showed me around and introduced me to her friends and family as if she'd known me forever. She told me their father was a big wig at Lockheed and pointed it out in the distance next to the two large domes I had noticed before.

"What are those?" I asked.

"Those are giant hangars built during World War II to hold dirigibles, large helium-filled airships used for spying. The hangars are so massive they actually create their own weather inside, like fog and mist. Sometimes, it even rains."

"You're kidding."

"Nope, and that's Lockheed Missiles and Space before it on the right. They're both behind the little town of Sunnyvale - that you can barely see - way out there in the boondocks. You can reach them on Highway 101." Oh, by the way, they're hiring if you're job hunting, I'll give you my father's name. Better yet, I'll call him and have him put your name on the list for an interview, if you want."

"Hey, that would be great, seeing as how I am unemployed at the moment."

We spent the afternoon till dusk together. I got her phone number and more information on Lockheed. We left at the same time but in different wheels - me in my plum forty and she in her pink Mustang convertible - I knew it!

Arriving back at my empty apartment, I pulled the front seat out of the car and slept on it on the floor, vowing to go furniture shopping as soon as possible. But first on the list was getting a job!

The next day I headed out to the Lockheed Missiles and Space facility. The plant was truly out in the boondocks, and it was completely surrounded with eight-foot tall cyclone fencing topped with wound barbed wire. There was a guardhouse and you were required to show your ID if you worked there or you'd damn well better have an appointment or be on the guest list. Security was military tight.

"Don Yeager, hmmmmm," the blue uniformed guard pondered as his finger ran down a list on a paper that was clipped to a board hung on the wall. "Oh yes, here you are, employment office, first building on the right, middle door." Then he reached over and clipped a VISITOR badge on my shirt collar. I thanked him and, like a person with a purpose, quickly walked to my appointment. The interview couldn't have lasted fifteen minutes; it was as if they had been waiting for me. And with my Navy background and experience, I cinched myself a position at Lockheed. I would start the next day - on the ground floor - as a stock clerk.

The money wasn't bad and the benefits were terrific. After a week of working, I discovered that one could advance fast through the ranks as soon as one gathered a little seniority. I got assigned to the new Agena D program that designed the power booster for the space rockets and, after a short three months, I was upgraded to dispatcher. Excited, I called Nicki and thanked her, knowing that it was through her father's clout that I got out of the stock room so soon.

That night I rang up my brother, Dennis, who was attending St. Thomas Boys College back in St. Paul and still living at home. I knew my brother's dream was to attend either Santa Clara or Stanford University here in California. I told him about the mild climate, my apartment and my new job at Lockheed. I added that I had an "in" and felt I could get him on the payroll, also. Dennis seemed excited and receptive, but he needed to finish up the semester and it would take him some time to get his college transcripts together. I told him not to worry. When he showed up, I would help him get established and I left it at that.

I started dating Nicki, naturally. She introduced me to the nightclubs, dinner houses and the varied nightlife in the area. There were cocktail lounges with piano bars, topless dancer bars, biker bars, dance halls, pizza parlors with rock and roll music, clubs that featured big name entertainment like the Doobie Brothers, Lee Michaels and Frosty, Lydia Pence of Cold Blood, Big Brother and the Holding Company, Jefferson Airplane and on and on and on. It was a happening era - the 60's. We went to cowboy bars; swing bars, Latin music bars and even bowling alleys had lounges with music. Dance contests were all the rage - the twist, the cha-cha, tango, the swing and ballroom dancing. Big money prizes and free food drew standing-room-only crowds. Some contests took two to three months to eliminate all the contestants and finally pick a winning couple. What a feast of entertainment there was. Sometimes there was so much going on that it was hard to choose.

One of my favorite hangouts was Rico's Pizza on Campbell Avenue in the San Jose State College area. It was there that I encountered a guy named Lenny Holmes. He was sitting at a table with a petite dark Italian-looking girl when Nicki and I walked to catch the nine o'clock show of a popular local singer. The place was jam packed, but there were two seats at Lenny's table that looked as if he was saving them for someone.

"Good, you saved us seats," I said as I pulled one of the tipped chairs away from the table to allow Nicki to sit down. He immediately shot up from his seat in protest.

"Beg your pardon," he said. "Those seats are taken."

"They are now!" I boldly stated and sat down. "Tell you what, if your friends show up, we'll get up, okay?" Nicki, on cue, quickly flirted with Lenny, who resembled a big football linebacker. Momentarily calmed, he smiled, sat down and said, "Well you got guts, I like that, here have a beer," and he shoved two big beer mugs in front of our faces and poured them full from a large pitcher.

"Hey, thanks. Name's Don Yeager," I said introducing myself.

"Lenny Holmes, and this is Myra." He tipped his head towards the pretty girl on his left, took my hand and shook it.

"Nicki here," I indicated, using the same mannerism.

"Yeah, buddy, I was gonna bop you one across the head for your intrusion - until I saw her," Lenny commented. "Besides, I was getting tired of saving those damn seats and getting the evil eye from everyone in the joint."

"T'was meant to be," I smiled, and we clicked our mugs together in a mutual newfound friendship.

Lenny had just arrived in town from Medford, Ore., having freshly enrolled at San Jose State; he was still looking for a place to live. I liked the guy right away, so I mentioned that I had a two-bedroom place that I had just furnished and that a room was open. We became roommates, later; unfortunately, I would come to have some regrets.

Lenny drove a new '63 Chevy Impala, low to the ground with a big 409 cu. in. engine—a real screamer. He was a playboy with a silver spoon in his mouth.

He received a fat check every month from his father who owned and ran a large lumber operation in Oregon. You could tell that he controlled Myra, his girlfriend, who lived in a sorority house on campus, and he cheated on her, (I later would observe,) by hustling every skirt that would have him. He was always skipping classes to have an affair in the middle of the day. Many a time I would come home for lunch in between my classes at San Jose City College and find Lenny's bedroom door closed, knocking off a "nooner." He was also a prankster, a slob, rude and inconsiderate, proving to me that having money didn't necessarily include having good manners or class.

One night, I returned home late after working the swing shift at Lockheed and found the apartment in a complete shamble. Clothes strewn everywhere, beer bottles, potato chips, dirty plates of spaghetti still sitting on the coffee table, cigarette butts in loaded ashtrays and Lenny passed out on the couch with some babe in his arms.

Cursing like a trooper, I tried to arouse the two. They only mumbled drunkenly. I went to my bedroom, tired from a long day of attending classes plus putting in eight hours at Lockheed only to find my bed occupied. Angry because of the intrusion, I was about to rip the body from my bed when I suddenly realized it was my younger brother Dennis.

I shook him, "Hey, Denny, wake up."

He slowly came out of a tired, trance-like sleep.

"Oh, it's you, bro," he said rather thickly.

"Of course, it's me. Who else would you expect? Seeing as your ass is in my bed, nice to have you here, but what the hell went on here tonight?

"Your roommate wanted to party to help welcome me to California."

"Why didn't you call me at work to let me know that you'd arrived? I didn't even know you were coming."

"I wanted to surprise you."

"Well you sure the hell did, you skinny little sucker. Go sleep in Lenny's room, since he's passed out on the couch. We'll pick this back up in the morning," I said.

Little brother sheepishly left the room. Sighing, I undressed and slipped between the sheets, too tired to deal with the situation at one o'clock in the morning. I'd get things straightened out the next day. I think now was as good a time as any to rid myself of my roommate and replace him with a member of my family.

I slept fitfully that night and was awakened by the coffee pot being banged carelessly on top of the electric stove in the kitchen. I leapt out of bed, threw on a pair of shorts and stormed out of my bedroom. Lenny and his overnighter were sitting at the little bar I had decorated in beach style in remembrance of my days in Hawaii.

"Looks like you had a little bash last night, eh roomie?" I said, my tone of voice expressing disfavor.

"Yeah, might have gotten a little carried away. Lots of people kind of just showed up. But, hey, your brother dug it," He answered, unapologetically.

"Well, it looks like we're going to have to make some changes now that my brother has arrived on the scene."

"No worries, my grade point average is way down, and my Dad's putting a stop to the cash flow. He wants me back in Medford. I guess I'll be giving the University of Oregon a go next semester. Can't say it hasn't been a real ball here, though, seeing that SJS was voted this year as the No. 1 party school in the nation by Playboy magazine. And, hey, I was here," Lenny replied, his "gotta-luv-ya" smile spread across his face.

"So you're out of here, anyway," I said, feeling relieved.

"Yeah, finals are next week. I'll cram, hope for the best and then head back home. Meanwhile, I'll try to make myself scarce. Come on, babe, let's go." He and the girl left, then Dennis appeared from around the corner. "Gee, bro, sorry about last night, but that guy is just crazed. I don't know him, so I just went along with it. Thanks for letting me sleep in, though. I needed it. I've been traveling for three days."

"How'd you get here, by bus?" I asked.

"You know Mom, scared of planes, wanted me to take the Greyhound Express. It wasn't so bad, I got to see some great country and besides, I wanted to surprise you."

"Well, you sure did. But look at you - you're skinny as a rail. We've got to get some meat on those bones." I grabbed him and gave him a hug. "Welcome to California, you're going to love it."

The next two weeks were busy for us. Being a few years older and many years wiser, I took charge and got him settled in. Lockheed took him on so he had a job providing an income. Next, we bought him a set of wheels, a two-toned, red and white, 1956 Oldsmobile Holiday, two-door hardtop convertible. He was tickled pink. It was his first car, and he was in California! Yahoo!

I decided it was time to get out of my hot rod stage, so I sold the 40 Ford and bought a nice clean 1957 Chevrolet 2 door. Clean and simple it was - painted lime green - with a small V/8, no frills, just a good commuter car that was good on gas.

Well, now, we both had car payments, insurance, rent, food and whatever money was needed for a comfortable, young bachelor's life-style. So, I needed to buckle down. I took on all the extra work I could get at Lockheed, working Saturdays and sometimes Sundays. My dedication helped me to advance faster up the ladder. I moved up from stock clerk to dispatcher and then on up to the position of expediter, all before my first year was up. Being an expediter was a cool position. It gave me freedom to move about, allowing me to travel between buildings and to be allowed outside of the guarded gates during working hours. I found out that if I did my job of chasing parts for the Agena D boosters, moving them on to the Nirop division where they were coupled with the rockets, this would keep my supervisors happy with updated reports they could pass on to the day supervisors, the Lockheed big boys. I could disappear for short periods of times without getting in trouble, just like being back in the Navy again, where I had honed this particular skill quite well.

Nearby, outside the guarded gates and beyond the huge parking lot was a country roadhouse called the Brass Rail. Its drawing card included great food, strong cocktails, and fun rock n' roll till two o'clock in the morning. It became my new hangout. I ate dinner there most every night.

On Thursdays and Friday nights, after punching out from my swing shift at midnight, I would rush over to slam down a few Cuba Libres (rum and coke) and dance with the girls who showed up from the electronic plants that were continually sprouting up in support of Lockheed. This particular area would later become known as Silicon Valley.

The twist was the dance rage at the time, made famous by Chubby Checker. I was a "twisting fool" and had all the moves down. There wasn't a dance I couldn't do - I could swing dance, do the cha-cha, the rumba and, of course, a nice sensuous slow dance.

The band at the Rail was a group from Oakland called The Sonny James Trio, composed of guitar, drums and bass. They played the roadhouse on Thursday, Friday, and Saturday nights. Sonny, the lead singer and guitarist, had quite a following. He was big and jovial with great stage charisma, and he reminded me of B. B. King. The place was always packed with good-looking women and men of all ages and races. It was one happening place.

I was one of the regulars and became close friends with both the bartenders and the band. In fact, a lot of the regular patrons became a sort of family.

The head bartender, Bill Mendenhall, who was dark skinned, had curly black hair, and half-closed, smoky orange brown eyes accompanied by a pasted on smile, always drew a bevy of beautiful women at the barstools in front of the bar. He was also a scrapper, poised to settle, in a quick way, any disturbance that might arise. He wore a few scars, proudly, in evidence of his underlying roughness.

Dressed in tight black slacks, a freshly starched white shirt and designer tie, he would apply his trade with speed and efficiency while making you feel like you were the celebrity. His conversational talents were endless, and he made sure everyone at the bar was introduced to each other and made comfortable. He loved to get the patrons involved in small games of chance, like Ship, Captain, Crew or the game Horses, all played with the dice cups. He made loads of money in tips and spent them by hosting an open bar, after-hour party on every Saturday night at his house after we were swept out of the Brass Rail.

He owned a large sprawling, early California, Frank Lloyd Wright-inspired, one-level ranch-style home about a mile from the Rail in a suburb near Sunnyvale. It was furnished in "early nothing," but he had a full bar and a dynamic sound system - it was definitely a party house. The afterhours hounds, of which I was one, loved to continue on there until the early morning hours. The surrounding streets would fill up with cars, and the family from the bar would meander up the walk into the house where Bill's roommates would be behind the bar already pouring drinks. Ray Charles would be blasting from the record player singing, "What I Say," and the living room was crammed full with insane dancers till all hours of the morning.

It was one of those crazy nights that I met Maria Miller. She was a beautiful young woman of Mexican descent, an exotic beauty who could have portrayed a number of nationalities: French Polynesian, Asian, Caribbean, etc, etc, etc. Miller was her married name, as she was a recent divorcee. She worked as an electronics assembler, on the line at an electronics plant in Palo Alto. She was quiet and demure, giving off the feeling that she had an aura of a protective shell wrapped around her. Still, she was pleasant enough and had a wonderful laugh when amused.

I approached her with sincerity and respect. I'd felt the vibrations and sensed that she was a special person and would have to be handled with kid gloves. I

asked her to dance. She had great moves and felt light in my arms. We molded together perfectly. She smelled wonderful.

She had recently divorced a sailor boy from Wisconsin who left her with a
small baby girl named Catherine. She had married at eighteen, innocent and
naive to the world. Now she was struggling on her own, somewhat lost and
confused. My heart went out to her and I vowed that this was a woman I was
going to help all I could - not to be one of my conquests.

Maria lived in a small apartment in the slums of downtown San Jose on Vine
Avenue. She had no furniture except a bed to sleep on. One night after a date,
I spent the night with her - no sex - just warm, tender cuddling, just sleeping
with a sweet smell - simply wonderful!

Her little baby, Cathy, was asleep on the floor, wrapped in a small pink blanket. I told myself then that this woman deserved something better. So, in the
next week, I helped her move into an apartment across the street from where I
was living with my brother. I helped her get furniture, and she found a roommate - a young woman she worked with, and who also had a small child. That
year we all spent Thanksgiving together, like a family. Maria was a great cook
and I loved a home cooked meal. We became good friends, lifelong friends, in
fact. And in the future there'd be many adventures and interesting stories to
share when it came to our relationship. Between newfound friends and brother
Dennis, college, work and music, the next couple of years went by at a steady
pace, and then the unthinkable happened! ~

ROCK
&
ROLL!

BOOK THREE

CHAPTER 28: CHANGES

"KFOG interrupts their music to bring you this important message:"
NEWS FLASH!
FRIDAY, 22nd of NOVEMBER 1963
PRESIDENT KENNEDY SHOT IN DALLAS, TEXAS!

Our world as we knew it stopped for a moment, as everyone - stunned, listened in dead silence and disbelief.

The boomer generation's idol was felled from his throne. Camelot was nearing an end. This would be a moment that would be etched forever in our minds.

I was at San Jose City College, outside on a sunny day on campus, books in hand, eyes to the sky, when I listened to a sad voice softly delivering through the cone-shaped loudspeakers spaced among our halls the tragic three-word message, President Kennedy Shot!

Years later, perhaps LIFE magazine put it best: THREE SHOTS IN DALLAS STILL REVERBERATE IN IMAGES THAT ARE FOREVER BURNED IN MEMORY.

This was truly the beginning of the sixties with all the politics, passions and loves, the music of the time with its many messages, and the artists who performed them, the style of clothes we wore, and the hair many of us grew long, and the living in an increasing psychotropic world and getting through it while remembering those who didn't. The Beatles took America by storm, followed by The Rolling Stones and many, many more to come. Cassius Clay became the youngest man ever to win the heavyweight boxing title, and a giant step for mankind came with the first walk on the moon. Edwardian dress was in and bellbottoms flared at the bottom of most hippies' legs - and, of course, there was VIETNAM. From all of these things, kick-started with the assassination of President Kennedy and of those to follow; Bobby Kennedy, and Martin Luther King - a shrinking, changing, ever more ambiguous world would emerge. One that would never repeat itself ever again in history, the late sixties and early seventies would live in our minds forever as a truly free-spirited time.

Around 1964 my life changed, as well. I quit Lockheed and became a hairstylist. My brother Dennis graduated from San Jose State with a degree in engineering and a new career at IBM. Maria advanced to line supervisor, and the founder of the company noticed her beauty and charisma, pursued and won her.

I met a hairstylist, Jean Stokes, at the Corral, a country western bar in San Jose. She was with a girlfriend, Lydia, and a big Italian guy named Fred Merconni. I joined their table and after a few drinks, dances, and conversation, found out that they were also my neighbors.

I had just moved into a large singles complex in the city of Sunnyvale just off Highway 9. This busy and popular thruway easily accessed the spreading mass of new malls, huge complexes of apartments and home developments that were spreading across the Bay area like wildfire. Jean and Lydia lived only a few doors down from me. I started dating Jean, and occasionally we would double date with Fred and Lydia. The relationship introduced me to the world of hairstyling.

I was still working at Lockheed, but now as a technical illustrator. I always loved art - art of any kind. And here I was - back on the drawing board. I worked the day shift and got off work around five o'clock. After having dinner at the Brass Rail or at home, I would run down to the Town and Country Mall where Fred worked at his mother's hairstyling salon, "Hair by Ann." I became fascinated with the positive energy flow and the creativity of the stylists at the salon. It was a welcome step above the humdrum manufacturing atmosphere where I worked presently.

Fred Merconni was a big Italian boy, had a bright smile and a certain flair about him. His mother Ann Rentoro, a beautiful, bleached blonde, owned two salons. She lived in the suburb city of Saratoga, in a luxurious custom home in the foothills. She was a wonderful woman, very stylish, and well known in the community as a successful businessperson. She was also a great cook and good mother to Fred, and one who loved to entertain.

As I became friendlier with Fred and Ann and the stylists at her salons, I became infatuated with Ann and she with me, despite the 20-plus years difference in our ages. We had a mutual admiration - no more - no less. She would often invite me to come along with Fred to her home for dinner - and when she didn't want to cook she would treat us to an evening at one of her favorite restaurants or nightclubs. She drove a big Cadillac, two-toned, bright metallic gold with a white top. I sometimes would meet her at the salon or at her house when asked to chauffeur her around in her "boat," as she liked to refer to the Cadillac.

One night after a fabulous prime rib dinner at the Brave Bull, a restaurant across the street from her salon, sitting around a large table in posh burgundy colored leather chairs, while sipping an after-dinner brandy, she conveyed an offer to me.

"Don, sweetie, has Freddie told you that I'm going to open a beauty college?"

"Gosh, no, Ann, but it sure sounds like a good idea - you being a salon owner and all. Where and when?"

"I'm looking at a location north of here in the little town of Livermore. There are already two large schools here in San Jose, and I think I can tap the rural market as it grows. There are lots of kids out there graduating from high schools looking for a career to go into - do you think you'd be interested in a career change?"

"I don't know how I would fit it in, you know, with going to City College and working at Lockheed."

"Look, why don't I make you an offer you can't refuse. You're a talented young man and you know design and balance, being a technical illustrator. You know and understand coloring, which I can tell by the way you coordinate your clothing. You know how to treat people, and the ladies love you. I think you'd make a great hairstylist and, being a good friend of my boy Freddie here, I'll give you a full scholarship in my new school. How's that sound?

I was flabbergasted. "But how will I make a living?"

"Don't you worry about it, I have friends in high places and a few ideas that'll make it easy for you," she said confidently. "What do you say?"

"I say YES!" We raised our glasses in a toast and clinked our glasses in agreement. We'd work out the particulars later. Fred looked me in the eye and winked behind a large smile. He was happy that I had accepted his mother's invitation.

That Monday at work, I crawled up onto my stool, leaned my forearms on the drawing table and glanced up and down the long line of fellow illustrators busily bent over their prospective projects. "I feel like I'm just a number here," I thought. "Ann's right, I could be a good hairstylist and I bet I'd love it."

As I daydreamed, I tapped the eraser end of my pencil on the half-finished drawing in front of me. I decided then that I would put in my two weeks' notice at the end of the week. The timing would be perfect. The school was near completion, and Ann had found me some part-time work at the Saratoga golf course. I would finally be out from behind the desk, back into the sunshine and the light of the world, rather than feeling trapped in a windowless building and punching a clock.

I was brought out of my daze by a hand on my shoulder. "Hey Don, you got that schematic on the titanium EHR done yet?" My supervisor asked, with a slight hint of sarcasm in his voice.

"No, but I'm working on it."

"You know you got a deadline to meet."

"Yeah I know. I'll make it."

Oh boy, that was it, the straw that broke the camel's back! That Friday I gave my notice.

Somewhat irritated, my supervisor held my resignation in his hand. He turned red in the face and spat out with an air of arrogance, "You'll never make anything of yourself by quitting Lockheed, you know you're giving up a good job here."

He was just pissed off that he was losing one of his performers who made him look good up in the front office where his father was a bigwig.

The next two weeks were busy ones. I moved out of the apartment I had just moved into, which luckily, I had not signed a lease. In my search for a new location, I found a small three-bedroom home on the opposite end of town. It was perfect - two minutes to the freeway - then a direct shot to Livermore where I would be attending Beauty College.

I took over the master bedroom. Fred became my roommate and took the second. Rounding out the picture, a Greek friend of mine from Lockheed, Nick Remis, took over the third.

I had a substantial stash of money that I had been saving and on impulse - to celebrate - I went out and bought a bright canary yellow, 1957 classic Thunderbird and traded in the Chevy. It was a giant relief to me that I actually had the balls to quit a good-paying job and go out into the world into a new career. I was excited and ready. The T-bird was my reward.

Ann held a grand opening at Rentoro's College of Beauty with hors d'oeuvres and champagne served by four of her top stylists from her salons. They were dressed in white ruffled shirts and tight toreador pants, adding a certain touch of class. The event was well advertised and equally well received. I was introduced to the director, Lyda Santé, a very round, jolly, matronly looking woman and her recently hired cosmetology teacher, Sandra Williams. Sandra was exactly the opposite, small and demure, with auburn red hair and a load of freckles. I also met the other students who had enrolled for the 1600-hour course. There was a mixed bag of young girls and older women and one other guy, Percy, a few years younger than me, who turned out to be Lyda's nephew and very gay.

Sixteen hundred hours was the required number of hours of theory and practical work that one had to study and perform before becoming eligible to go to the State Board exam for a cosmetology operator's license.

Mornings were spent in the theory room, studying the equivalent of - or, at least it seemed like it - the first semester of nursing. It included the study of anatomy, skin, hair, blood, diseases and first-aid. After lunch, the afternoons were spent "on the floor." A station was assigned to each student. The more advanced future stylists were placed up front near the reception area where the clients and the supervisor, Miss Santé, could observe their talents.

Beauty schools offered lower prices to the community in order to give the students live heads to work on. The floor was where you learned how to shampoo, cut hair, give permanent waves, apply color, do roller sets and comb-outs and, most importantly, sell hair-styling products and one's talent.

School started at eight o'clock in the morning with theory taught by Lyda. I did well in theory. It was interesting to me and Lyda had a unique way of presenting it. Out on the floor it was a different story. I found out my hands were a little too large. My thumb was so huge it wouldn't fit into any of the regulation scissors. I solved that problem by having a metal shop heat and expand the opening in my shears. When I attempted to wrap my first permanent wave with those teeny, tiny little rods, I was in trouble. The wrapping papers would slip out or I'd put the rods in crooked or they were either wrapped too tight or too loose. It was frustrating and embarrassing.

"Don, you'll never make it as a hair stylist with those big mitts of yours. They're more like mechanic's hands." Lyda said to me one day. She proceeded to tear all those little rods in my wrap apart and made me start over. It took me almost four hours to successfully wrap my first perm.

That almost put me over the edge. I wanted to walk out and forget that "f-king prissy business." But I didn't. Later that night, expressing my frustration to Fred, he helped me out by showing me "the book wrap," an alternative to the frustrating "flat wrap." It was easier for my mitts to handle and gave me confidence to continue.

I decided to give it my best and show them that I could do it - and do it well. I had a plan. First, I wooed Sandra, the young teacher, into giving me special attention. My strategy had to be discreet and programmed very carefully. I asked to have my station changed, far away from Percy, out of the way of Miss Santé's eyes, and surrounded by other students whom I thought would be helpful to me. We did this one week when Lyda was away at a seminar. She was not happy with the change when she returned but didn't reprimand Sandra, as the floor was technically hers. I began to excel, and the local paper did a story on me, titled Rolling with the Punches. Completely appropriate, I thought.

The beauty world is a multi-billion-dollar business. There's a lot of money to be made out there. Many of the top stylists in the world are as famous as movie stars. Big shows are held in large arenas and in fancy hotels. We students were encouraged to attend these giant affairs, which would be packed with hairstylists of all ages, nationalities and color. Most of us dressed to the nines, and some of the costumes worn by the more flamboyant were both mind-boggling and amusing.

During the sixties, Edwardian and Renaissance clothing were in fashion, strongly influenced by the British invasion into our culture. The year was 1964 and the mop-topped Beatles had arrived. Rudi Gernreich introduced the topless bathing suit. Vidal Sassoon from Bond Street in London created the asymmetrical cut - the "A" line. The cut went wild when he introduced the style on Barbara Streisand coiffed for the movie Barefoot In The Park with Robert Redford. Soon stylists were getting more dramatic, and hair coloring was becoming outrageous, platinum blondes showing up everywhere.

It was an exciting time to be a hair designer. I was only on the ground floor but loving every minute of it. I attended every show I possibly could - learning from the best.

This in itself was a social revelation for me, introducing me to the elite and making for exciting times. I was introduced to the hierarchy of the profession and it slowly opened doors for me. I became a whiz at razor cutting and had certain flair in my movements when I was creating a new style. So, on stage I went.

My first competition was at San Jose City Hair Dressing Academy. Schools in the area competed against each other to show off their talents. The teachers prepared their best students to perform in front of other students from other schools in hopes of luring more students their way.

My attendance at the shows and my visits to Ann's salons improved my visionary concepts of design and instilled in me a confidence that zoomed me ahead. I felt I was a part of the professional world of hairstyling long before my graduation from Beauty College.

At one important inter-college haircutting contest, I had handpicked a gorgeous girl with a great mane of hair to be my model. I'd dressed nicely in a black suit, white shirt and a small bolo tie. My model, Julie, was also elegantly dressed with her makeup already applied, ready to complement the cut I was to create on her to frame her beautiful oval-shaped face.

Fred and Ann were present and seated in the front row of observers and judges. We soon took our places on stage. As I was ascending the stairs with my model, I heard Fred whisper to me, "Don't worry, do your best, like we taught you and you'll come out smiling." I glanced down at him, noticed his grin and wink of encouragement and silently mouthed back, "Thanks."

It was a thirty-minute-long contest. A wet cut competition. When the bell sounded, the crowds' murmurs dissipated and the air was replaced with soft sounds of scissors snipping, razors sliding, combs combing, and the shuffling feet of twenty students, all moving around our models' heads as we feverishly raced to finish our individual creations to perfection within the allotted time.

I was the first to lay down my tools and step off stage. I'd finished in less than the thirty minutes, but my design had been implanted within my brain. I'd practiced it often on customers and on some of the girls at the beauty school in Fremont. I felt confident that it was perfect. I sat down in a chair between Fred and Ann and received a smile of assurance and a squeeze of the hand.

One by one the other students left the stage. There was only one left when time ran out and the bell sounded. A hush hung over the crowd as the judges climbed the stairs to the platform, with combs in their hands to check the cuts. They stood over each model and combed through the hair, checking length, evenness, weight, movement and flow and how perfect the style fit each model. They returned to Julie three times and on the third time, the head judge took her hand and asked her to rise, declaring me the winner!

Fred and I leapt into the air yelling, "All right, all right." I ran up the stairs, kissed my model and accepted the trophy. I was on my way.

The news of my performance flew through the schools and salons and I, at least for the moment, was the celebrated one among the tight niche of young hairstylists in the Santa Clara Valley. I knew I'd have to keep on top of it to continue the fame. My next competition was an "Evening Fantasy" contest held at Harrah's Wagon Wheel Casino in South Lake Tahoe.

Lyda, the school director, was close friends with other former famous stylists - turned educators. Among those were the famous Salvatore from the Sacramento Valley and Leo Passage of Pivot Point out of Chicago. Lyda kind of liked me now and showed new interest in me. She began teaching me the "pivot point" method of styling hair. She showed me how to comb wet hair, laden with thick styling lotion, into moving curves that swirled around the head and connected with each other, using a strong Marcel finger combing method, a technique that went back to the 1800's when hair fashion and wig design were the highlight of aristocratic fashion in the royal courts of Europe.

After creating the design, she would then show me how to carve each curl out to create flow and volume. Using flat pin curls, moving into slightly larger, half-off-base curls connecting into upright barrel curls, she could create a look of a shell-shaped wave cresting off the crown of the head. Fantastic! She had the talent and was now passing some of her knowledge on to me. Thank you, Lyda.

One of my regular clients, Dotty, a buxom, bleached blonde in her early thirties, volunteered to be my model for the show in Tahoe. We had met at the Brass Rail dancing one evening and had become close. She loved having me do her hair and allowed me to experiment. I had previously razor cut my design into her hair, removing excess length and bulk. I touched up her roots by laying a fine line of blue-colored bleach on them, then colored the hair a sandy champagne blonde from L'Oreal (Lyda's favorite product line,) and tipped the ends to platinum blonde to accentuate the style after its final comb-out.

I practiced on her in the evenings after school. Afterwards, we would usually dine and dance together. Then I'd spend the night at her place instead of driving back to San Jose. She was seven years older than me, but I had discovered that I was easily attracted to older women, especially after the episode with Wanda in Hawaii. I responded to their fragrance, dress and their maturity. Most were fairly successful, had nicely furnished apartments or homes, could cook marvelous meals and were warm and sensual.

The contest in Lake Tahoe was at 11:00 am on a Saturday morning. We left Friday afternoon and drove four hours up over Emigrant Gap through the Sierras down to South Lake Tahoe. We got a room in a small motel a few blocks down from the Wagon Wheel. A light dinner followed and then we retired for the evening since the next day would be rather hectic.

After an early breakfast the next morning, I dressed in my suit and Dotty in her show dress. We buzzed up to Harrah's Wagon Wheel in the T-bird to prep for the contest.

When we arrived, I signed in and was directed to where the shampoo bowls and dryers were set up. Us students, being of the lower echelon, and our models, were squeezed into the hallway outside of a large meeting room where the contest was to be held. It was utter pandemonium with people trying to avoid bumping into each other and the dryers' creating an unbearable heat in the tight quarters. But after most of the models' heads were set and dried, things quieted down to a low roar.

Our contest was two-phased: first, the models were escorted out and ascended the platform and were seated in chairs in front of small stations fitted with mirrors. We remained in the wings while the judges scrutinized each set on its structure and finish. Then we were called on stage to perform our comb-outs.

Once in place, standing behind our models, the head judged announced the rules.

"Good morning, ladies and gentlemen. The judges have inspected the wonderful work that these up-and-coming young stylists have created and are assured that we all are going to see and enjoy some true fantasy designs come to life in the next few minutes. The stylists have fifteen minutes to finish their creations. We will call out the last five minutes," she said. She looked down at her watch. After a moment her eyes lifted, a smile crossed her face and she announced in a stronger voice, "You may begin."

It was like a bunch of wind-up toys had just been released. Rollers and pins were removed from the hair and placed in small boxes held by each of the models on their laps. The models could assist their stylists by handing them their combs, clips, brushes and hair spray as they were being worked on.

I pulled up my sleeves a little bit and went to work, brushing vigorously into the style. It literally popped into place. Satisfied with its flow, I backcombed the hair to tighten up its base. I then took a fine-tooth comb and linked the lines and their movements together. I sprayed Aqua Net hairspray, the cement of the time, on lightly as the coiffure took shape.

"Five minutes," the judge called out.

As I reached the top, I placed the side of my hand into the curve of the wave at the crown of the head and, with light movements of a fine wire pick, smoothed the ends of the hair over the top of my hand, ending up with a beautiful crest. Satisfied, I sprayed the whole head with another shot of Aqua Net, adjusted Dotty in the chair, replaced my tools in the small box in her lap, removed it and stepped back.

"One minute." I studied my creation and thought it looked great.

"Time. Stylists please step away from your models."

Silent, nervous smiles were passed around as we all took our seats and waited for the judging to begin. Breaths were held. It took a half hour before the first model was asked to stand and escorted off the platform, eliminated from the competition. She received a round of applause for the stylist's efforts. One by one they dropped by the wayside, each receiving more applause accompanied by small murmured groans of disappointment. Soon there were only three left. Dotty was one of them!

"Would the stylists of these three models please return to the platform," a judge asked.

A stylist from a San Francisco school took to the stage followed by a striking six-foot tall Tahitian redhead dressed in a green velvet gown. I, likewise, took the stage. We nervously stood next to our models in anticipation as the trophies were brought up.

The head judge spoke, "Ladies and gentlemen, the styles created by these young people were phenomenal. We applaud their talents and effort. They truly are all winners. These three, however, excelled and deserve the honors. First place goes to Kevin Gline. Step forward, please."

The San Francisco student leapt into the air with a beaming show of glee on his face. Hugging his model, he raised the trophy high and received a standing ovation.

"And second place, Don Yeager; let's hear it for this young man's talent," he spoke into the microphone.

My heart skipped a beat. Adrenaline shot up from my toes, leaving a trail of goosebumps following it on up to my brain, which immediately gave me a cold sweat. It passed by, however, when I placed my hand around the trophy.

The redhead got her third-place award. Then the six of us—three future stylists and our three models—hugged, giving each other smacking kisses as we congratulated each other. The crowd stood and continued to applaud. It was great!

That night there was one hell of a party - happy and crazy hairdressers know how to party. We celebrated at the Top of the Wheel, a round restaurant bar and dance hall on top of Harrah's Hotel. To add to the excitement of the evening, a cha-cha dance contest with a prize of $100 and two free night's stay at Harrah's was about to begin. I signed up.

I led Dotty out onto the highly polished floor and with some smooth well-practiced moves - damn, if didn't win that prize also. I was on a roll.

The next two days we played hooky from school and work, lounged in our complimentary hotel room high in the Sierra sky, made love, ate fabulously, spent the hundred-dollar winnings plus more, and with a pre-filled gas tank and near empty pockets, headed back to Livermore on Wednesday morning.

Back at school I was once again a celebrity. Reflected in my mirror, the two trophies shone brilliantly under the lights, displaying to those around that there was true talent at that station. Clients of the school requested me above all. I was booked solid and loved it.

Soon after, my 1600 hours were up. I'd prepped for the mini board at the school and passed it. A week later I was in San Francisco taking the real thing. Anxious but confident, I breezed through the theory in the morning and the practical in the afternoon. It was a long day - but in the end - I was a licensed hairstylist.

Ann Rentoro, the schools' owner, wanted me to come and work for her at her West Gate Mall Salon. I refused the offer, wanting to prove to myself that I could go out into the world and find my own niche. I thought I'd found it in a beautifully decorated salon called Lydia's House of Beauty (funny, similar name to my school supervisor) that catered to the upper class in the little town of Palo Alto, about fifteen miles north of San Jose.

Lydia was in her early forties, petite, blonde and beautiful. She had a wonderful way about her and had a good business head. Her clients were the frosting on the cake, and she treated them as such. She had an assistant who helped her in the duties of shampooing, wrapping permanent waves and mixing color formulas.

At first, I was sparsely booked so I spent my free time observing the different techniques of the other stylists. I watched how they treated each individual client, how they sold themselves and their talents and that particular charisma that made each one of them very special to their clientele in their own way. I learned how to operate on a movable stool mounted on six balled wheels, putting me at eye level with my clients. I felt it made them more comfortable with me, and I was able to sell them on new ideas easily.

There was a definite pecking order at the Palo Alto salon, and I was at the bottom of the list - the intruder - and the only male, new to the business and not homosexual, as most male operators were in those days. I felt the vibrations but cruised through each day picking up any information and styling hints that I thought would prove valuable to me in my career. I looked at it as a learning experience. After three months of earning next to nothing, I took Ann up on her offer, left Lydia's and joined the staff at Rentoro's Salon of West Gate.

I immediately felt welcome. Ann made a special effort to personally come to the salon herself and introduce me around as one of the first graduates of her Fremont school. She insisted that I was to be made part of the "family."

A strong influence of the San Jose Italian community became more apparent when I became more familiar with Ann, her business and family ties and the restaurants and clubs she frequented. Those Italians liked to stick together.

The salon was in a prime location and a large percentage of the customers were walk-ins. The receptionist, Geri, took an immediate liking to me and picked customers she thought would suit me. She was good at it, and soon my clientele grew with the repeating customers.

Two other male stylists in the salon, little Anthony and Al Rosa, were as different as night and day. Anthony was a sweet, accommodating, "Yes, ma'am, can I help you, ma'am," type of guy with a little swish in his short steps, he barely topped 5-foot-4. His smile was toothy - straight out of a Pepsodent toothpaste commercial - and he smiled brightly with his eyes. Anthony was the receptionist, Geri's, favorite "boy toy." He did her hair every week for gratis, never ever changing her style, which he designed and thought was fitting for her. They had each other hooked and she gave him the best customers. I loved to watch their daily interactions.

Al, on the other hand, was tall with black curly hair and dark eyes, very cocky, the stylist to the swingers, the GO-GO dancers at the Ore House topless bar, as well as some of the elite from the woman's bridge club of the Saratoga Golf Club.

The mixture of women stylists in the salon ranged from sweet and innocent to rough and tumble, tall and beautiful to short and pudgy. We all had to be in uniform. We men wore blue smocks over our white shirts, pressed black slacks (no jeans), and polished shoes. The women dressed in pink dress uniforms and low-heeled shoes. Everyone's hair had to be in a recent style and sport either a permanent wave or have coloring in it to help promote customer services. I chose a loose perm and, with my long, large sideburns connected to my curly head, I resembled the singer Tom Jones - My, my, my Delilah.

Back then haircuts were $4.50. Shampoos and sets were $4.00. Colors varied: virgin bleaches $45.00, touch ups $25.00, regular tints $15.00. Permanent waves started at $17.50 and went to $55.00, depending on the length of hair and its condition. High-styling French twists, some topped with barrel curls, chignons, fancy page boys and asymmetrical styles, were $7.50 to $15.00, again depending on the length of hair and its final creation. Those were the days - and of course - gasoline was only 31 cents a gallon then too.

Anthony, Al, and I along with Sandi, and Charmaine were the high stylists. The others were "bread and butter" stylists,' doing simple bobs and bubble hair-dos. The pay was 50% up to $300.00 weekly take-in and 60% for anything thereafter. It was always a race to see who could bring in the most. Those of us who worked the hardest and longest hours took home some pretty good paychecks, and our tip jars were always filled with the "green stuff."

Al Rosa was the top high stylist. With his artistic flair, he could create some of the most amazing arrangement of curls on top of a head. We called them barrel curls and the name stuck. He did beautiful French twists, nice and tight with a slight movement to either side up from the nape of the neck.

Anthony was a kick to watch as he stood on a stool, his small hands reaching high trying to match Al's work. He was intense, and little beads of sweat dotted his upper lip and forehead. But that sweet smile of his never left his face, especially when he finished a style, stood back and filled the air with Aqua-Net hair spray, blessing his creation. "Thank you, Madame." His tip jar grew greener.

Sandi, Charmaine and I were the copycats. We learned from the experts and slowly developed our own techniques to create similar, but slightly different styles that carried our label. The others just seemed to plod along, happy with just having a job at Rentoros.

It was a fun place to work and everyone respected each other, helping one another in times of indecision or duress, or congratulating one when they completed a good job of coloring, a beautiful perfectly structured curled perm or a style with a special flair. This camaraderie impressed the customers and made them feel special, which brought them back every week. Everyone in the salon greeted the regulars as family, for they were the gold of the salon.

I worked at Ann's for about a year before things started to deteriorate. Geri was caught fleecing the till, stuffing some cash into her pocket book. This totally devastated Ann, who hated having the wool pulled over her eyes, especially by one she had placed so much trust in. Al Rosa left for a bigger, newer fancier salon called The Headliners, and jealousy began developing within the ranks.

One day Sandi said to me, "Don, why don't you open your own salon? Some of us girls like the way you handle yourself around customers and your fellow workers. We'd be willing to follow you."

I was surprised at the offer, but it implanted an idea in my mind, and I started checking the "business for sale" ads in the San Jose Mercury News. It didn't take long. I found a salon located six blocks down from the Mall on the same street, Saratoga Avenue. It was called "Bella Donna Beauty Salon." I contacted the owners and negotiated a deal. The purchase price was seven thousand dollars - a lot for what was included, but it had location, location, and location. I called my parents for a loan. They didn't have it to lend but said they would talk to Mom's brother Ignatius, who was making good money on the professional bowling circuit. Igs came up with the money. I gave my two weeks' notice, gathered up my customers, took three girls with me and became a businessman at the age of twenty-four.

For the next month, after putting in ten hours a day doing hair, the girls and I would spend the evenings and Sundays painting and installing new equipment, hairstyling stations and new flooring. Soon a bright blue awning hung over the picture window that faced the street with a new name scrolled in red letters - HAIR DESIGNS by MR. DON.

The salon became a success and soon the money started rolling in. Wigs were big back then and supplies, especially hair spray, sold well. Combining long hours and hard work, I paid the loan off in a year. I got into a fancy new apartment complex called the Richfield Albany House and bought myself a Jaguar XKE coupe, a '37 Cadillac, and a BSA 650cc motorcycle. Now, for the first time in my life, I was really on a roll and life was getting real interesting and sweet!

For the next few years I worked on my image, going with the flow of the times and dressing in a flamboyant style - it was the 60's after all. My bell bottoms flared out and my shirts were tailored to form fit. Accessories of large leather belts, fancy boots, long fringed vests and turquoise and silver jewelry completed my ensemble. I wore my hair full, covering my ears to the lobes and slightly longer than collar length. I bounced back and forth between wearing long chopper sideburns, a Van-dyke five-point goatee, and going clean-shaven. One never knew what I was going to look like from one month to the next. My philosophy was - and still is - a change of face - a change of pace.

With my newfound but hard-earned riches, my self-confidence soared; I developed a new happiness, and I needed a way to express it. I found it by digging into the roots of music. I bought a Jazz Fender bass guitar. I'd always had a natural rhythm and a good ear for what sounded good together. I taught myself some walking blues progressions while listening to The Paul Butterfield Blues Band, John Lee Hooker, Sonny Boy Williams and other blues artists. After a week or so of thumping away on those four fat strings, I found myself picking up on the harmonica riffs those guys played. It reminded me of that time I had experienced another blues harp player who had impressed me - Rambling Rudy - the hobo who had blown out a few riffs for Chuckie and me that night underneath the Dale Street bridge alongside the railroad tracks back in St. Paul. "Easily carried," I remembered him saying, when he held up the small shiny instrument between his thumb and forefinger for us to view.

Suddenly, a light bulb went off in my head. Hey! I want to do that! So off I went to find myself a good blues harp harmonica teacher. I started my quest by putting the word out in the local nightclubs where I hung out. After talking to a few musicians I'd become friends with, I came up with a lead - an old hillbilly from Georgia who had moved into a little shack out in Milpitas. I'd heard he'd been jamming with some men at a roadhouse out in the boonies, called The Hideaway. I gathered up a couple of buddies one night and we cruised out to the joint.

When we pulled up to the nondescript bar with pulsating beer signs in its windows, it reminded me of my early Navy days hanging out with Petty Officer "Skirts" when we hit the Cotton Club in Little Rock, Ark., back in 1957. Driving up to the front door, I shut off the engine. In the stillness, crickets were sounding off in the marsh behind the bar, and a loon was crying in the night. From within, the sound of some good ole' deep down funky blues wafted their way out of the open door and out into the night. It was kind of cool.

We took in the show, danced with some babes, and slammed down a couple shots of Jack Daniels, chasing them with a few beers. At the break, I went and introduced myself to the partially toothless, blues harmonica player.

"Yo, brother, mind if I talk to you a minute?" I said.

"Yes, sure, sonny, how can this ole' fart help ya?" He replied in a slow Southern drawl. He was sitting in a corner on an old rickety stool, his legs crossed showing a pair of white socks stuck in a scruffy pair of wing tips. His pants were about three inches too short for him and were held up with a pair of tattered old railroad suspenders with smoking steam engines running up and down the length of them.

"I love your blues riffs on the mouth harp," I said, "and I'm wondering if I could talk you into giving me a lesson or two."

"Sure nuff, more than happy to teach anyone the blues, that's wantin' to learn," he answered, his attention drawn to the package of RED TOP tobacco he held in his lap and the paper he was hand rolling a cigarette with. He licked it, sealed it, lit it up and took a deep draw. We sat and jawed till it was time for the next set, during which he scratched out a rough map to where I could meet him for my first lesson. We shook hands and he returned to the stage.

The boys and I closed down the bar that night, dancing, drinking, shucking and jiving with the regulars. And all the while, I kept my eyes and ears open to that good ole' boy, Latham, blowing on his blues harp harmonica. He was so good he could have become a legend, right place, right time, and I couldn't wait for my first lesson.

Tuesday I booked out of the salon early and drove out into the flat marshland of Milpitas. I followed the map, coming across a makeshift squatter's shack far out at the end of a road that dead-ended at a levee. Latham was sitting on a weathered wooden orange crate playing his harmonica. I stopped suddenly, my wheels locked, sending a cloud of dust over him.

"Jeez, I'm sorry, Latham, didn't expect you'd be right on the side of the road," I said apologetically.

"Now, no need to fuss, son. Pretty fancy car you got there. Whatcha call it?"

"It's a Jaguar."

"Rattle your teeth, did it? Dis road more fer trucks. Well, sit yer ass on down, I've been warmin' up fer ya."

I pulled up another orange crate close to him and took out my recently purchased blues harp in the key of A. For the next hour and a half he taught me how to cup it in my hands to send out different sounds, how to place my tongue on the reeds to bend a note and the basic scale. Then he sent me home to practice.

A month later, my lips and tongue toughened from hours of practice, I knew the scale forwards and backwards and I could bend a note on each draw. Latham then taught me my first song, per my request - John Mayall's "Room to Move," which I play to this day. From this experience would come many hours of pleasure, placing me in front of the microphone on stage with well-known bands in front of hundreds of people in all kinds of cities all over the country. Thank you, Latham.

My apartment complex was great. The apartments were built in a large square with a kidney-shaped swimming pool in the center. During the weekdays there was little activity around it, as everyone was away at work. But after four in the afternoon and on weekends, the poolside came alive with sunbathers and swimmers. It was quite the social center - the sixties single scene. A month after I moved into apartment # 1, a young married couple, Rich and Joy Lane, moved into # 7 upstairs. We met poolside and, after a week or so, became friends.

Joy had a single, 21-year-old younger sister Lynn, who visited almost every night for a dip in the pool. She had a beautiful bronze-colored, slim body with small perky breasts. Joy introduced us, we became friends and I became part of the family. I started spending two or three nights a week up at their apartment barbecuing on the back deck, drinking wine, and getting to know them.

One night Lynn brought home a bag of marijuana that she'd scored. We had all known it was out there but had never tried it. She'd brought some Zigzag papers, and we all sat around the kitchen table and rolled and smoked joints.

Rich, at the time, worked for a Ford agency in the parts department. One night, slightly stoned from the weed, he noticed I was rolling the joints on trade paper from his work that had the headlines, "KEEP THEM ROLLING." We nearly died laughing when we saw that. From that night forward, Rich and I became lifelong friends and later he would become the best man at my wedding.

Rich was a car lover like me. At the time he owned a red and white '62 Corvette. I drove a '64 Buick Riviera and had also recently acquired an Austin Mini-Cooper. On Saturdays we would get out the water hoses and buckets and wash our machines together. On the first Sunday of every month, we would drive to the fairgrounds in Pleasanton and race our sports cars through obstacle courses lined with orange pylons for the fastest time. Gymkhanas, they were called. Rich, being the better driver, always beat my time, but I did "one up" him. I flew solo in an airplane.

I loved the flying I did when I was in the Navy and I missed the thrill of being up in the air so I decided to take flying lessons. Reid Hillview was a small airport off Highway 101 south of San Jose, used primarily by private aircraft. I attended ground school for the required hours and, after becoming familiar with the basics of flying, my instructor Bob Lowe took me out to a blue and white Cessna 182. We pre-flighted the aircraft, strapped ourselves in, turned over the engine, contacted the flight tower and taxied out to the runway. I was excited. "Let's give it a try," Bob said. I pushed the throttle forward, played with the foot controls to hold a straight line and at his command, pulled back on the yoke and we lifted off. What a thrill! I was back in the air.

The next few weeks I filled my flight log with more hours, feeling more comfortable with handling the aircraft. On Dec. 9, 1969, I flew a cross-country leg. Droning across the golden hills, we noticed the highway below us was jammed with cars for as far as the eye could see.

"Wonder what the hell's going on below us?" Bob asked.

"Let's drop down and check it out." I banked left, losing altitude, bringing us closer to the scene.

"I know what's happening," I said. "This summer we went to a Creedence Clearwater concert at Altamont Raceway, and I saw a poster announcing a Stones' concert coming there this December. I'll bet that's what's going on."

Bob took over the controls and we flew over the crowd, who were parking their cars on both sides of the road, miles from the raceway. We had a terrific, bird's eye view of the action. When we buzzed the grandstand and stage below us, there were thousands of ant-like people milling about. It was very colorful.

"Yup, looks like a happening. Wish I could parachute in. That would be a trip, wouldn't it?"

"You'd have to be pretty good to land right on that stage 'cause I don't see an inch of ground down there that's not already filled by humanity," Bob commented.

He pulled back on the yoke and applied power, climbing up and away. Little did I know that we were flying away from a rock concert that would go down in rock and roll history.

The next morning I picked up San Jose Mercury News and read the headlines, "RIOT AT ALTAMONT, HELL'S ANGELS KILL ONE AT ROLLING STONES CONCERT."

Below that, a small blip mentioned the birth of a baby. A balance, I thought - one in, one out.

The world was getting crazier, and it was the one concert I didn't mind missing, but the memory of that scene viewed from the air would be forever embedded within my brain.

The "pill" had recently been introduced and was now accepted as the way to go for birth control. Practically every young woman had a thirty-day package in her medicine cabinet or purse. Joy and Lynn were ecstatic when they received their first pink plastic dispenser with the numbered little white pills showing through. They were anxious to see if they worked. The sexual revolution had begun and, all of a sudden, sexual bonds were uplifted, and everyone was doing it with everyone, well,l not everyone. Make love, not war, was the motto.

Along with free love came the free V.D. clinics. The first opened in the Haight Ashbury area in San Francisco, followed by one in San Jose. They were pretty casual - you went in - got shot in the butt with a hypodermic needle filled with penicillin, told to lay off having sex for two weeks and were sent on your way. The transmitted diseases in those days were simple and more curable.

Those days were free, easy fun times and actually quite innocent compared to other times in history. There was no depression, little crime and technology was at a birthing stage.

For the generation of the sixties, freedom of speech took on a whole new meaning. We were not the first protest, but the first to do it en masse, within and outside our country. Whether the cause was the Vietnam War, drug freedom, long hair, nudity, Gay Rights, or political activists, we wanted to be heard. We wanted to change the world. There's a saying that came out of those times, "If you can remember the sixties, you weren't there." Moving on to the seventies, all the big issues seemed to come to a head - black power, women's lib, the sexual revolution, the "drop out" youth culture, and the war in Vietnam. ~

CHAPTER 29: BEHIND THE CHAIR

Every day was a learning experience in the hairstyling world. I started doing stage work, teaching to my audiences what I had learned from the masters. For a year I represented and sold color products for Helene Curtis, performing on stage doing razor cuts and creating artistic patterns of color on pre-bleached heads of hair. I called my technique, Echo Coloring, the colors blending from deep browns and/or burgundy reds, starting at the nape of the neck and moving up through the spectrum following the style line, getting lighter until they topped the crown with a bright platinum blonde. They were really quite striking when done properly. Clients, traveling from as far away as San Francisco to the north and Monterey and Carmel to the south, would frequent my salon to get highlighted in this fashion. The San Jose Mercury News published an article on my styling, popularizing the salon and me. The phone wouldn't stop ringing. We had to raise our prices. As Lydia had told me: Once you're so booked you can't handle them all, raise your prices and you'll automatically lose 10% of the clients. Advice well taken, but sometimes you didn't lose anybody! Good!

A year later at one of the shows, a scouting agent for Pivot Point noticed me.

Pivot Point was an up-and-coming schooling technique using cone shaped rollers to create styles with more defined movement and volume. I only knew a few of the basics of the system that I had learned from my supervisor, Lyda, in Beauty College. It was a fascinating concept and I wanted to learn more about it.

After accepting their invitation to become a Pivot Point expert, I was flown to Chicago to spend two weeks with its founder, the famous Leo Passage, to study the fine points of his system.

I was put up in a high-rise apartment on Lake Shore Drive overlooking the great Lake Michigan. I was treated somewhat like a celebrity, opening the door for me into the entertainment end of the business. There always has been a little bit of Hollywood coating my outer surface. I loved to perform, and it was evident to those who knew me well. It was here that I met a man who would later become a legend in the beauty world, Paul Mitchell, whom I would perform with one day on stage.

Chicago turned out to be too hot and humid for me, somewhat like St. Paul where I had grown up. I had become spoiled, having experienced the joys of almost perfect weather in California and Hawaii. It was one of the many reasons that made me pass up the opportunity offered to me.

Grace, the director, wanted me to join the team of Pivot Point experts. I would be required to travel to the schools teaching their system and do daily reports on how they were complying with Pivot Point's policies. I'd be living out of a suitcase, going from city to city, hotel to hotel, required to report on paper my observations, each and every day. I loved to travel - but on my own schedule - when and where I chose to go. I hated hotel rooms and eating at fast food restaurants, so I declined the offer. I knew then and there that I'd be much happier behind the chair, being my own boss.

Being a hairstylist in this era went right along with the times. The rock musical Hair was playing at the Geary Theater in San Francisco. It was another wild, exciting trip to be involved in the hippie world and the culture shock that was rocking the nation. I was close-up and hands on, actually right in the middle of it. It introduced me to the Haight Ashbury district, to the flower children and to the somewhat innocent but devious world of heroin, uppers, downers and again, the smoke of choice, marijuana. I stayed away from everything except for the "Mary Jane."

Marijuana became as social as a gin and tonic at a cocktail party. One evening, I attended a party held at home in Hillsboro, an exclusive community south of San Francisco. It was situated high up in the hills in a gated community completely surrounded by giant eucalyptus trees.

That evening, after punching in the secret code I'd been given, the giant iron gates swung open, and I drove my white Jaguar XKE up the long driveway to the grand entrance. The lady accompanying me that evening was a striking tall blonde named Mona. She was thirty-five years old, eight years older than my twenty-seven. She, vice-president of the Merchants Bank in Los Gatos, and was the epitome of sophistication. I'd been involved with her secretly at her request for about three months. I rather liked the intrigue. She was dressed in a skin-tight green lame dress that she looked poured into. Her curves moved fluidly within it with each step. I parked the car and helped her out of the passenger side. She reached out and wrapped her arm around mine, and we walked across a wooden bridge, her three-inch high heels echoing each step as we approached the entry. The door opened as we came within a few steps of it. A tuxedoed attendant, his white gloved hand on the curved, iron handle, bowed as we entered.

A crystal chandelier hung high above our heads, illuminating the marble foyer. There were antique black walnut tables on both sides. Sitting in the middle of each one was a large silver tray piled high with perfectly machine - rolled joints. I helped myself to a few and dropped them inside my suit pocket.

We stepped down three stairs into a large rotunda. Strobe lights were flashing to the beat of the soundtrack of the rock musical Hair, which we were there to celebrate.

"Let the sun shine, Let the sunshine in, the sun shine in." People were swaying, singing, smiling, smoking, drinking, hugging and kissing, all in celebration of a wonderful happening. We melted into the crowd.

The party lasted till dawn and at seven o'clock the next morning, those of us who had hung on were treated to a wonderful breakfast of champagne and orange juice mimosas, fresh fruit, and eggs Benedict, served up at poolside in the bright morning sun. It was truly decadent.

It was not unusual for me to stay up for 24-hour periods during my twenties, surviving on a catnap here and there. At that age, in those times, we were wild and crazy with plenty of energy to burn. After eating, Mona strolled over to a white, wicker lounge shaped like a large baby bassinet and fell asleep.

Moments later a beautiful woman sat down opposite me. She was dressed in a pink leather ensemble consisting of a short skirt and a halter top with fringe that supported her tanned breasts. Her eyes were dark and deep. She wore false eyelashes heavily loaded with black, silver and gold sparkles. Her hair was ratted up and out like a peacock's crown. I had noticed before that she had had her eyes on me.

I said, "I enjoyed watching you dance last night. You have some great moves."

"I love to move like the animals, be it a snake, a prancing horse, or a stalking panther," she answered.

"You look familiar. Have we ever met before?" I asked.

"No, but we're in the same profession, and I've watched you perform on stage."

"Oh, really, where?

"Believe it or not, it was at a student competition in downtown San Jose several years ago. I believe you won first place."

"Did I compete against you?"

"Oh no. If you had, I might have won," she answered confidently.

Out of the corner of my eye, I saw Mona stretching. She got up and came our way. I knew I had only moments to wrap this up. Mona was notoriously jealous and possessive and apt to cause a scene, which I had learned to avoid at all costs.

"I like your moxie." I said. "What's your name?"

"Dana Facino. I work at the Neiman Marcus salon in the Greenbrier shopping center." She smiled, and seeing Mona approaching, whispered, "Stop by and see me sometime." With that, she got up and left.

I felt Mona's hands touch my shoulders from behind. "Good morning, my darling man," she said. "Who was the babe?"

I reached across my chest, touched her hand, and tipped my head back, looked her in the eyes and smiled, "Don't know, never caught her name."

I knew she didn't believe me, but we left it at that. Meanwhile, the gears in my head were clicking as my mind raced into the future. ~

CHAPTER 30: EUROPE

Months later on a Saturday night, sitting back in my black leather wing chair as I watched the fights on television, the phone rang.

"Don? Is that you?" the voice on the other end inquired.

"Maria?" I answered, sure it was her voice.

"Yes, it's me."

"Where are you calling from? I hear a slight ring on the line."

"Munich, Germany. My life has changed so much in the last few years, I just had to share it with someone, and you popped into my mind. How are you?" Her voice raced with excitement.

"Just great, I'm a hairstylist now, own my own business, driving an XKE - and you?" I asked, knowing that she was dying to tell me something.

"Well, I'm working in the foreign headquarters of the electronics company. John, the founder brought me and my daughter Cathy over here from Sunnyvale."

"Yeah, we kind of lost touch there for a while after I quit Lockheed, didn't we," I said.

"I know," she agreed. "Seems like we took different paths - but look - I want you to come visit me in Portugal, if you can."

"You what?" I exclaimed.

"I want you to come visit me in Portugal," she repeated, emphasizing each word. "Let me explain. John wants me to marry him, but he's still married—sooooo - meanwhile, I'm involved with a count who has a castle in Portugal. Last week, he flew Cathy and me in his private jet down to Lisbon for the weekend. We were met by a chauffeur-driven Mercedes limousine and taken to his castle high on a cliff overlooking the ocean. It was fantastic. I'd like to share some of my newfound fortune with you, if you're interested."

"Interested? Intrigued is more like it. I'll start working on it tomorrow." I said.

"Let me give you my address in Munich and my home and work phone numbers."

I wrote down the information, we said our good-byes and hung up. I poured another glass of wine, re-lit my pipe, settled back in my chair and giggled to myself. "All right, an invitation to Europe, how exciting." It would take a lot of planning and preparation, but I was eager to go for it.

The next day I informed the girls at the salon of my desire and appointed Sandy Wyman, my most trusted stylist, as manager, giving her a 10 percent raise in her commission. Next, I checked into purchasing a Volkswagen camper van to use for traveling while over there, and then I went to see Dana at Neiman Marcus.

I walked into the foyer of the salon and asked the receptionist if I might speak to Dana Fabio. She picked up a small microphone on her desk and paged Dana. "Dana, you have a visitor," she said in a sweet, singsong way. A moment later a smiling, sparkling-eyed beauty dressed in black leather and lace, hair piled high on top of her head, pierced by two large Chinese chopsticks painted bright red enamel emerged from behind a partition, comb and brush, the tools of her trade, still in her hand.

"Don!" She exclaimed. "I was wondering if I was ever going to see you again."

"Well, you've been on my mind ever since that night of the big party."

"Well, what are you up to that finally brought you by?"

"I'm planning a trip to Europe for a couple of months. I've a friend who's invited me to come visit her there, and while I'm in Europe I thought I'd grab a race or two of the Gran Prix racing circuit."

"Oh, I love racing. You know I have a 280 SL Mercedes convertible. You wouldn't want a traveling companion, would you?" She asked out of the blue.

"Are you kidding? I'd love to have a traveling companion. Let's have dinner tonight and we'll talk more about it. She came forward, hugged me, gave me a warm kiss on the cheek, turned, hiked up her skirt unto her hips and sashayed her way back to her station and her client. What a clown!

I walked out of the salon, not believing my good fortune. I thought "I might be going to Europe with an awesome beauty who has a fantastic outgoing personality. This is going to be one hell of an adventure!"

During the next six weeks, we were inseparable, spending every available moment getting to know one another, planning our trip, ordering up the VW, getting our passports and acquiring various connections to make our trip more interesting. We planned on being gone for a month or so - a trip of a lifetime.

One of my clients, who was a total believer in past life experiences, asked me to watch out for signs that felt familiar to me, indicating that I might have been there before in another life. She believed that because of my family's European ancestry, I might be returning to the Fatherland for a reason. Also, earlier that year I picked up on another possible connection. My weekly Friday morning client, Mrs. Jones, was entertaining a distant relative at her home in the Monte Serrano foothills. Her great aunt, one Madame Chantal Larue, was visiting her and her family for a week while on holiday from Paris.

During her stay, I was fortunate to meet and be of service to her. I styled her hair twice in one week, pampering her small skull with my strong hands. During one of her shampoos, undoubtedly the longest, sensuous shampoo I'd ever given up until that point, she fell in love with my hands and in the state of relaxed ecstasy invited me to spend an evening with her in Gay Paree.

"Donald dear," she whispered ever so softly in her drawling French accent,

"Do bring these lovely strong hands of yours to Paris and I'll treat you to a most marvelous evening of madness in the city that never sleeps." I accepted the invitation, gathered her information, smiled and thanked her.

On April 20th, 1970, Dana and I flew Icelandic Airlines over the Pole to Luxembourg, along with about fifty other seemingly "hip" travelers. Most of us carried the preferred suitcase of the times, bedroll and backpack. We were dressed in flowered jeans, fringed leathers, t-shirts, and other fun traveling clothes all accented with jewelry and "love" beads. We were seen as American hippies to some Europeans, mostly for our strange dress, and free and easy going spirit.

We landed in Iceland for a short stopover before continuing to Brussels. It was fourteen degrees, dark and dismal and the land was flat and uninviting. Of course, we were only at the airport, which tells little of any city or town.

Arriving in Brussels, we were met by the automobile broker through whom I had purchased the VW camper van. As the other passengers loaded into waiting taxis and buses, we slipped into the luxurious back seat of a Mercedes sedan and were whisked off to the heart of Luxembourg to pick up my purchase.

During the ride, our driver filled us in with the history of his beloved city. It was over a thousand years old, one of Europe's most important fortresses back in the Middle Ages. Ringed by three protective walls and eighteen forts, which were linked by twenty-one kilometers of tunnels and casements, most being carved from solid rock. This underground labyrinth of connecting passages and shelters that to this day still exists is a major attraction. We promised ourselves that we would try to wander the maze before we left the city.

Upon arrival, we were welcomed princely and ushered into a lush executive office where I signed all the necessary papers, obtained my foreign insurance policy from the Automobile Club du Grande-Duché de Luxembourg and the keys to my new Volkswagen pop top camper.

We were escorted to a small bed and breakfast hotel, compliments of the agency, where we consumed a wonderful dinner. We retired to a small cozy room high up in a converted bell belfry, which had a window looking out at the 16th-century Grand Ducal Palace. All lit up, it added to the allure of the evening, its facade flashing out of the blackness of the night. That evening we enjoyed the luxury of goose down feather beds, so deep and soft that we literally disappeared into them. We felt safe, secure and very, very lucky our first night on foreign soil. Ahhh, Europe. The next few months would be a new play in my life, as the entire world is a stage, and all of us actors in our own right.

In the morning after a wonderful breakfast of German sausages, crepes and scrambled eggs, topped off with a diminutive cup of dark, rich, aromatic coffee, we ventured out into the quaint hamlet of Luxembourg. We were amazed and marveled at the way some of the homes were built into the cliffs that hung over the small valley. It was raining that day, making it a perfect time for us to go underground and spend most of the day "ratting" throughout the tunnel system. It brought back to me, the memory of my Hong Kong tunnel experience.

In the late afternoon we crossed over a high suspension bridge, leading out of the valley and put mile 000,001.0 on the odometer. Our first destination was Munich, Germany, where I was supposed to get in contact with my friend Ruthie. We traveled through wooded hills, orchards and vineyards. At dusk we pulled out alongside a small stream on the back road we were traveling on and had our first meal and night out in my new camper. On the first day into our adventure it was delightful to feel so free with no place to be, no hurry, no fuss, no muss.

The next morning we drove into the city of Stuttgart, visited the Porsche Museum, had an early lunch of smoked-pork, broad beans and sauerkraut, washed down with a few steins of Bavarian beer. After a little more sightseeing, we drove a short distance out of the city and found a small campsite along the Danube River. Feeling warm, lazy and comfortable, we settled in for the night, thus, a short day.

Early the following morning, we were awakened by the bellowing moos of cows. Parting the curtains and looking out the rear window, I discovered that I had parked the van directly in the center of the path that they followed to their milking station. They were not too happy about our intrusion. They were somewhat confused, all bumping into each other in their rush to continue on their way. I jumped into the driver's seat, started the van and moved it. It was hilarious, and I could hear Dana back in the bed under the covers, laughing her head off. A few moments passed and the cows moved on their way, mooing their satisfaction. Dana got up and we had a breakfast of yogurt and fruit out of our small refrigerator and then headed out to the autobahn.

The autobahn was a real trip, going from a small country road onto a polished black ribbon of superhighway, where some could experience the feeling of flight transferred through the power of super tuned machines like the Mercedes, Ferrari, Porsche, Maserattis and Volvos but definitely not Volkswagen, as I soon discovered. Looking into my side mirror, I watched a small dot appear on the horizon behind me. Quickly that dot took shape passing me so fast he disturbed the air enough to blow the hat I was wearing off my head, from my driver's seat to the back of the van on to the bed.

"Whoooooosh," went the passing wind, followed by a momentarily loud roar, "Grauuuuuugh," that dissipated quickly, as the bright red Ferrari zoomed by - fast becoming a dot on the opposite horizon.

It happened so quickly that no words were needed. Dana and I just looked at one another with wide eyes. I adjusted the mirror to accommodate a position change, leaned forward and wrapped my arms around the steering wheel, let out a sigh and waited for the next surprise as we droned our way on down the road.

Nearing Munich, we followed signs directing us to the Hauptbahnhof, (Central Station,) figuring that there would be a good starting point to start to explore the city. Nearby was the business district where, hopefully, the office where Maria worked was located. We arrived a little before the noon hour, found a parking place and sat down at a sidewalk cafe to plan our strategy. We were impressed by the sophistication of the nicely dressed and nicely coiffed business people who strolled about - hair stylists, you know - we had to look.

The men were well dressed in tailored suits with close cut haircuts. The women, some of whom were dressed in skirted suits, others in fashionable dresses with matching accessories and high heels, sported fancy hairdos with every color you could imagine. We sat and let ourselves be entertained by the constant flow of traffic moving around us, a noontime promenade.

At our sidewalk café, the waiter spoke good English. He answered my inquiries and directed us to the nearby corporate offices. I left Dana to watch the van while I went to check on Maria's whereabouts. I was back within the hour.

"Guess what?" I said as I approached our table.

"She's not here!" Dana replied.

"Right. John shipped her back to the States the day before yesterday."

"He was probably jealous of the count."

"Right again, and I checked up on him, and he'd been transferred to Spain. Goes to show you, what might be the truth today - might not be the truth tomorrow - looks like we're on our own."

"Well, we're here, let's enjoy it. We probably didn't need her, anyway," Dana replied confidently. "Besides, we've got all those guidebooks you brought."

"Like I said, I like your moxie," I gave her round butt a loving, fun squeeze as we left our table.

We found an RV camping spot on the Isar River, spending the rest of the day and part of the next visiting the Deutsches Museum, one of the best science and technology museums in the world. Displayed within was a fantastic exposure to the powerful and explosive mechanical adhesion of the German empire to their machinery, tools, drills, mining equipment, ships, planes, engines, automobiles, etc. It made me wonder how they lost the war with all that advanced technology. That afternoon we watched a soccer game at the Exhibition grounds and enjoyed the evening twilight that illuminated the Famous Hall of Fame.

The next morning we visited a couple of the massive beer halls Munich is famous for. We were sorry we were too early for Oktoberfest, the festive ten-day celebration. On our way out of town, I satisfied my motoring obsession by visiting the BMW Museum, once again in awe of German prowess in their building of automobiles, motorcycles and aircraft engines.

That afternoon we arrived in Wolfratshausen, Germany, and camped by the Isar River. We found a beautiful little park with about twenty white swans floating in the stillness of the water. Dana immediately made friends with them by sprinkling bread on the lawn. School children on their way home stopped to visit with us, speaking broken English. I took pictures of them with my new Polaroid camera. They danced up and down in glee when I gave them a picture of themselves within sixty seconds of taking it. That evening we had a fantastic dinner at a local restaurant served to us on a silver platter. The total price: twenty marks (five dollars).

The next day, the morning light, softened by the rising mist coming off the river, and the honking of the geese, woke me around six a.m. Dana lay next to me, her deep breathing indicating she was still asleep. I slipped out from underneath the covers, pulled on the clothes that I had left in a heap at the bottom of the bed the night before, quietly slid the van's door open and ventured out. In the still air, I felt a certain calmness overwhelm me, along with a sense of belonging. "Was this what my mystic customer back in San Jose told me to be aware of?" I wondered.

I walked across the bridge into the main part of the town and was suddenly hungry; as my nostrils picked up the scent of fresh bread just out of the oven. I followed my nose, walked a city block straight, then automatically turned to my left, just as if I'd walked the same path every morning for years. Bang! There was the bakery, just as I thought it would be. A small tinkling bell announced my presence as I pushed the door open.

"Guten Morgen," the baker said, as he kneaded cream-colored dough on a large wooden table, his hands white with flour.

"Guten Morgen," I answered.

"May I help you in some way?" He asked in English with a German accent. I bent down and looked at all the fresh breads and pastries displayed in the large glass case in front of me. The aroma was overwhelming, and my salivary glands secreted involuntarily, forcing me to swallow. I couldn't wait to wrap my lips around some of that sweet dough. I left with my mouth stuffed with an apple strudel and a large brown bag filled to the top with goodness.

When I arrived back at the campsite, Dana was in the front seat putting on her makeup, using the mirror on the backside of the visor. She'd made some tea and we soon devoured the bag of pastries. After, we sat by the river and planned our route to Innsbruck, Austria, our next overnighter.

The VW purred right along as we crawled up and down through the mountainous regions of Gasthof and Watchensee, Germany. I was getting used to the shifting pattern of the transmission, finding out the best response I could get from the engine using the proper gears. We rolled right along, although the going was slow. Volkswagens were not noted for their power in those days, and - what the hay - we weren't in any hurry to get anywhere. We had until May 10th to get to Monte Carlo for our first Gran Prix race.

Coming over a pass, we wound down a steep curvy road with numerous S turns. Far below us we could see the lakeside town of Watchensee. The road straightened out so I slipped the transmission into neutral and coasted down the rest of the hill, testing the brakes to keep the speed in check. As we descended, the air whooshing in our ears, it felt a little bit like a free fall. At the bottom, the village nestled around a small cove. We crossed over a small bridge where a river borne from a thunderous waterfall cascaded out of the forested mountain and fed into the lake. We both craned our necks looking out at it through the windshield. It was breathtaking and noisy; the mist from it sprayed on the glass as we drove by.

We stopped at the lone hotel at the water's edge and had lunch. Afterwards, we wandered around the small shops that encircled the small-town square. It was a bright sunny day and very warm. We came on to a beauty salon, the top of its Dutch door opened. From within we could hear some singing. Out of curiosity, Dana and I both stuck our heads through the opening. Here was a male hairstylist performing his magic on a client, all the time dancing around her and singing happily away.

"Now, here's a man after my own heart," I thought.

He felt our eyes upon him, turned and motioned us in. "Come join the party," he said in perfect English.

"Cool!" I said, surprised at his invitation spoken in our tongue. I opened the door and Dana and I entered. He spun his client around and asked us, "What do you think?"

"Very nice," we said in unison.

"We're both hairstylists," Dana told him.

"I figured you for Americans by your dress. I studied in New York City for a couple of years and recognize the style. Where you guys from and what are you doing here?" he asked, all in one breath.

"We're from San Jose, California near San Francisco, and we're here to travel, observe, learn a little bit, but mainly to enjoy and catch a few Grand Prix races around the country," I answered.

Holding out my hand for a greeting, I continued, "Name's Don, and this here is my lady, Dana."

He took it with a firm grip and shook it hard. "Franz, Franz Hammerlin." Then he quickly hugged and kissed Dana. "Gotchur'self a beauty here," he said to me smiling.

"Oh, excuse me for a moment." He turned to receive payment from his client, booked her next appointment and escorted her out the door. He brushed his hands together and asked, "Now - what can I help you with? Directions? Information?"

"Well, we aren't looking for anything special, but if you've got any tips, we're all ears." I said.

"Let's go have a stein of beer," he suggested. "There's a nice place upstairs overlooking the lake. Come on, my treat."

Franz closed the door to his salon, hung up an "Out to Lunch" sign, written in German on it, and we trudged up a flight of stairs to the beer hall. We spent about an hour downing some awfully fine stout homebrewed beers, during which Franz showed us an off-the-beaten-path road to Innsbruck on our map and assured us it would take us through some most spectacular scenic countryside, putting us in to the city about the same time. He also connected us with another hairstylist friend of his in Innsbruck and promised we'd have a splendid time in his company.

Hugs and kisses followed and, with Dana navigating, we continued carefully on our way. We didn't travel far, however. The beers caught up with us. We found a little niche in the forest hidden from the road and camped for the night. Innsbruck would have to wait for another day. It rained that night; the pitter-pattering of the drops on the steel top of the VW lulled us to sleep.

Arriving in Innsbruck, we looked up Karl, Franz's friend. His salon was very exclusive, in the European baroque style. He had a very large staff; most of who spoke English making us feel right at home. After initial introductions and some small talk, he invited us to spend the night in his chalet located in the mountains overlooking the city. We followed his squat, fast little Porsche in our simpler version of German technology. He had to wait several times for us to catch up. We arrived just in time to view the alpine glow of the evening's sunset on the mountain range across the valley opposite us. In about an hour, several of his employees joined us.

Karl smiled at us and broke out a three-foot tall Turkish water pipe. "Do you mind?" He asked.

We silently shook our heads side to side, indicating approval. He filled the bowl with some fine Moroccan hashish and lit up. Soon the room was filled with sweet, gray/white smoke. That night we had one hell of party, smoking, dining, drinking, and dancing into the early morning hours. Hairstylists do know how to party, no matter what country they're from - or in.

The next morning our host treated us to a fabulous breakfast of cinnamon apple-filled crepes topped with fresh whipped cream followed up with a cup of freshly brewed coffee. During the meal, Karl asked us if we would mind dropping off a product to a mutual hairstylist friend of his and Franz's when we arrived in Venice.

Dana and I looked at each other with wonderment in our eyes, but after a moment I agreed to do him the favor. He handed me a suspicious looking - we thought - brown paper package about the size of a large book tightly sealed with scotch tape wound over and over itself in crisscross patterns.

He gave me the name and telephone number of our contact, shook my hand and wished us a safe trip. We hopped in our van and proceeded on down the mountain, stopping by the site of the Olympic torch and the ski jump. It had remained in place in remembrance of the 1964 Winter Olympics six years earlier. The jump was still used to train Austria's future Olympic hopefuls. We were impressed by the massiveness and sculptured engineering of the structure.

We made angels in the fresh fallen snow with our bodies and, giddy from the previous two-day's experiences, headed on to Italy.

Weaving our way through numerous mountain ranges, marveling at the sights that greeted us at every twist and turn, we entertained ourselves trying to sing along with the Italian songs that poured forth out of our little AM/FM radio. We stopped for lunch at a viewpoint and then took a short nap in the small bed in the rear of the van. I wasn't asleep very long when a noisy diesel truck laboring its way up the pass woke me up with a start, and I became anxious to get on our way. I dressed and strapped myself into the driver's seat.

Dana yawned and murmured, "I'm going to stay back here and watch the world go by." In the rear-view mirror, I watched her sensuously stretch her arms to the roof of the van. Distracted, I swerved the van, coming ever so close to the mountain almost scraping the paint. Rounding a bend in the road, an Italian border check station came into view.

"Uh, oh," I said to Dana, "Looks like a change in plans. You'd better get dressed."

I saw two soldiers come out of the little hut that they'd been sitting in. They watched us as we parked alongside the road. They were holding machine guns in their arms, the barrels pointing to the sky in the ready position. A surge of adrenaline hit my stomach and my mouth went dry.

Dana hurried to dress, slipping on a full skirt and a large sweater with a deep V-neck, exposing quite a bit of cleavage.

I started the van and drove up to the checkpoint.

"Buongiorno, Signori." I said with a smile.

"Buongiorno," the one with the corporal stripes said. "Could we see your papers and would you mind stepping out of the van?" He continued in broken English.

We handed him our passports and visas.

"Why did you pull over when you saw us?" He asked.

"I didn't see you at first, and she was desperate to go," I said, nodding my head towards Dana.

"Open the van," he ordered.

I slid the side door open. He pointed to the inside and his partner started to search the interior. The bedding was rumpled, and the air in the van was emanating Dana's sweet, sexy perfume. We hadn't had a chance to hit a laundry and change the sheets yet. The search was quick. They didn't seem to be too suspicious. I think they were way more interested in Dana's alluring smile and her come hither eyes. The corporal kept grabbing quick peeks at her cleavage, becoming less interested in the van.

Two more cars pulled up behind us. He called his partner out of the van, handed our papers back to us, said, "Grazie," tipped his cap to Dana and waved us on our way. We hopped in the van and Vamoose!

"Well, we lucked out at that check point, thanks to your charm and beauty." I said to Dana.

"They were Italian, and I know how they think, me being one," she said. Smiling at me, she offered me a demonstration, squeezing her breasts together making her cleavage more pronounced.

"Men," she sighed heavily, leaning over and planting a big one kiss on me.

Near dusk we arrived at the little medieval town of Klausen in the Eisack Valley of Italy. We parked outside the town alongside the Eisack River and had a simple evening meal cooked on the small two-burner propane stove that came with the camper package included in the van.

We'd been taking photos along the way with a Polaroid camera, a present I'd received from friends back in the States at our going away party. They'd also given us a picture journal with plastic inserts to place the pictures. Next to each insert was a placard to write down the specifics of each photo, its date, place, occasion, happenings, etc. Each evening I would record the events of that particular day, giving us time to reflect and something to talk about.

I was behind in my entries, and it grew dark as I worked away. Around nine pm we decided to go for an evening stroll and venture into the walled city. It was very quiet, most of the townsfolk having already retired for the night. It was a little eerie, and I held Dana's hand while we softly walked along the narrow cobblestone streets. Even the town square felt a little strange with its silence. In the shadows we detected the red glow of lit cigarettes. We were challenged by rough sounding voices coming from the same direction. Out stepped four young hoodlums, all dressed in tight Levis, and cut-off sleeveless T-shirts, their heads wrapped in black silk bandannas, each carrying a long stick. As they approached us, they tapped the sticks on the cobblestone while chanting, "Bellissima, Bellissima."

They had their eyes on Dana and started to circle us. Somehow, I didn't feel threatened - a little surprised at their advances - but not afraid. I wrapped Dana around behind me and spoke loudly, "No problemo, por favor, no problemo."

They seemed surprised at my outburst and laughed weakly at my challenge, probably because I was talking in Spanish, not Italian. They backed up a step or two, deciding what their next move might be. I stepped forward and yelled, "Vamonos," waving my hands in the air. They were a little young, and I think my outburst in Spanish surprised them. They decided not to mess with us and they backed off mumbling, "Okay, Americano, okay."

"Let's get out of here, while I have them convinced that I might be trouble," I whispered to Dana. I took her hand, which was sweating, and we returned to the van and drove out of town.

We drove until midnight, found a small dirt road leading off into a farmer's pasture, crossed a small stream, parked behind a grove of trees, turned out the lights and, breathing a sigh of relief, crawled into bed.

"This has been one heck of an adventurous day," I said.

"It sure was, honey, but we made it, thanks to you."

Dana gave me a hero's welcome that night. Afterwards, we fell asleep exhausted in each other's arms - me feeling the protector, her accepting the protection. I felt proud of myself for standing up to those guys.

Around two o'clock in the morning it started to rain. I woke up but only for a moment, acknowledging the change in weather, I rolled over and fell back asleep. Dana never stirred.

At sunrise the rain had stopped, but I could hear rushing water. I got up out of bed and opened the sliding door to the outside. The van was up to its hubcaps in swirling brown water. We'd parked in a dry arroyo the night before that was now beginning to fill with the night's rain runoff.

"Dana, get up," I yelled. "We've got to try to get out of here."

I didn't hesitate. I jumped behind the wheel, started the engine, put it in gear and slowly crept out of the streambed up to higher ground. Minutes later, a raging torrent of water came rushing through where we had parked, raising the dry bed area another two feet.

"Wow! Check it out! We just got out in the nick of time. Another forty winks in slumberland and we would have floated away."

Close to noon we pulled into Trento, a beautiful little city surrounded by the Italian Alps. We lunched on bread, cheese and wine, sitting on a park bench next to a wide canal diversion of the Adige River. The river's glass-like pond mirrored the bright colors of the stucco villas that ringed it. A fountain in the middle sprayed water twenty feet into the air in a wide fan-like pattern, the sun's rays radiating a kaleidoscope of brilliant colors. White and black swans paddled their webbed feet ever so slowly back and forth, creating V-shaped wakes behind their bulbous bodies. It was a midsummer's night dream, a fairyland, and we had a difficult time getting up off that park bench and leaving.

An hour later outside Trento we were laboring up a two-lane road that wound through a narrow gorge bisecting the mountains - a gateway through the Italian Alps, or the Dolomites. Below us a railroad track was cut into the steep granite mountainside and below that, the Adige River. Dana counted twenty-two tunnels that were blasted through mountain outcroppings that the trains disappeared in and out of - men and machines conquering the elements. Soon we broke out into a wide valley. The Dolomites literally shot out of the ground and reached straight for the sky. I was in awe of their height and steepness.

The next town we hit was Cittadella. We passed through and, on the other side we spotted a sign, Venecia 26 km. We were getting closer. After a bit we hit the main thoroughfare - Ponte della Libertà - that took us on into Venice.

It was the beginning of the weekend and the roads were crowded. Italian cars are smaller than most, and I felt like I was chasing a bunch of little bugs around. We got in line and went with the flow, arriving in Venezia around sunset.

The place was a circus of activity, and we were strangers in a strange land. Directly in front of us was a giant parking garage. I joined another line. Luck was with us and we were one of the last ones let through the tollgate. We wound our way up a circular ramp until we reach the uncovered top level, five stories above the ground. There was one space left, tucked into the far north end of the parking garage which we squeezed into. I turned off the engine and we took in the last of the sun's rays. The view was fantastic. We could see into the canal city and out to the sea beyond it. We decided to just hang out and had dinner in the van while the sun set over the Mediterranean.

We were changing clothes, getting ready to go into the city, when a rap-rap came on our window. I opened the door. Standing outside was a security guard who informed us that there was no camping allowed. I assured him that we had a place to stay and we would leave it unattended. He watched as we grabbed our backpacks, closed the curtains and locked up the van, but you could sense that he wasn't completely sure we were telling the truth.

"What are we going to do?" Dana asked.

"Well, first thing I'm going to do is see if we can get rid of this package we hauled all the way from Innsbruck." I pulled the slip of paper out of my billfold. "Ramone, no last name, 477-9083. Let's find a phone."

We found a booth and I dialed the number. No answer. I tried again, just in case I might have miss-dialed, still no answer.

"Shit!" I said. "Must be his salon number and they're already closed. We'll have to wait till tomorrow."

That night we roamed the city, watched the gaiety of the people, listened to the music that seemed to be everywhere, drank cheap Italian red wine and danced in the streets. Around two o'clock in the morning we snuck up the parking ramp, which proved to be difficult as we were both pretty lit from all the wine we had consumed and the excitement of being in Venice.

On the third level we almost ran into two guards who were having a smoke together in a little room next to the staircase. I peeked around the corner but could only see the back of their heads so I couldn't tell if one of them had been the one who had given us the warning.

We crept along the wall that hugged the staircase as they continued to smoke and talk. We'd just made it around to the stairs going to the fourth floor when we heard a third guard coming up from down below. He was whistling a tune in between his huffing, puffing, and grunting. He must have been the relief for one or both of the others. We took advantage of his noisiness to race up the two flights to the top and sneak into our van

We slipped into bed but didn't undress just in case we might be discovered. We waited breathlessly, listening. About ten anxious minutes went by. Then we heard the whistling getting closer to us. I was glad that I had pulled the curtains across the windows before we had left, hoping that it wouldn't look suspicious if we had to revert to this.

The whistling stopped right at the van. We could see the shadow of his head and hear his muttering as he shielded his eyes and tried to peer in. He pounded on the window and yelled, "Attenzione! Occupato?"

We held our breaths - both of our hearts were beating hard. Dana started to giggle, I had to hold my hand over her mouth. I knew she was drunk and was soon going to go into hysterics. Oh, my God!

"Attenzione! Occupato?" The voice grew louder and more demanding. He started to rap on the window with the nightstick he was carrying.

Again, " Attenzione! Attenzione! Occupato?"

He was growing more desperate as if he could hear our breathing and heartbeats. Finally, he kicked the side of the van, grumbled and went on his rounds.

Dana broke out laughing. "Attenzione! Attenzione!," she whispered. I prayed he didn't hear her. He didn't - he'd resumed his whistling, and it soon faded away.

"Dana," I whispered back, "You almost blew it for us."

"I'm sorry. It was just so comical - a frustrated little Italian security guard trying to scare up some imaginary action."

"I know and I don't blame you." I said. With that we drifted off to la-la-land, with me silently hoping that if either of us started to emit inebriating snores, we wouldn't be discovered.

The next morning we woke to the sounds of bells and whistles, music and singing. I slipped back into the clothes that I had hastily discarded the night before after the guard had left, jumped out of the van and peered out over the wall to the street below. There seemed to be a parade of some sort forming. Banners and flags waving from the top of tall staffs were being inserted into holstered, leather bands that hung off the waists of young men and women who were colorfully dressed in early 1700's era costumes.

Bands were tuning up and testing their instruments. Acrobats were jumping about, going through their routines and religious groups were milling around displaying placards of saints that hung from their necks. Dana sided up next to me and looked down. "Looks like a carnival," she said, matter-of-factly.

"Yup," I answered. "Let's go down, have some breakfast, then give this guy Ramone a call and find out what's going on." We grabbed our small daypacks, locked the van, and happily skipped our way down the ramp to the street below.

The Piazza Roma was directly below the Autorimessa. It was crowded with food stands. We started with sweet rolls and cappuccinos, which seemed to satisfy us momentarily. I found a telephone and rang up Ramone.

"Buongiorno, Ramone's," a sweet voice wafted over the line.

"Parla inglese?" I asked.

"Yes, I do. Can I help you?"

"Is Ramone in?"

"Yes, but he's with a client at the moment. Maybe I might be of assistance."

"I'm from out of town, and I've just arrived with a package from his friend Karl, who has a salon in Innsbruck."

"Oh, yes, Ramone spoke to Karl this morning and is anxiously awaiting the package. He needs it for the party tonight."

She called Ramone's name across the salon and rattled off something in fast

Italian. I could hear a distant voice yelling back at her.

"Ramone says to give you directions and have you come by. Where are you now?"

She gave me the directions and we headed into the heart of the city, the celebration going on all around us.

"I wonder what's going on? It's like a carnival or something." Dana asked.

"I don't know but look at all the flags flying from the tops of the buildings, and everyone seems to be in costume."

I was enthralled to be here on this day - at this time - in my life. As we walked next to the canal, I took Dana's hand in mine, giving it a slight squeeze. She smiled at me in acknowledgment. We crossed over the bridge, spotted the salon and went in. Immediately, we saw a tall, long haired, handsome Italian dude who was dressed in a bright, yellow flowered shirt that was stuffed in a pair of purple, silk, harem-like pants billowing out on top of his black and tan buccaneer boots with silver buckles that crossed over the ankles. He came across the floor and welcomed both of us warmly, placing his hands on our shoulders and giving both of us a kiss on each cheek.

"Ciao, my friends, so nice to meet you. Let me introduce you around, and then we'll go upstairs to my private quarters."

We shook hands, exchanging kisses like a couple of pigeons pecking one another, then climbed a spiral staircase up to a flamboyantly furnished studio apartment with a balcony overlooking the canal and street below.

"Pull up a pillow and have a seat," he said. "Do you have the package with you?"

"Right here in Dana's day backpack," I said, helping her slip it off her arms. I unzipped the opening and pulled out the brown paper wrapped package.

"I really appreciate you bringing this down from Karl. I didn't want to take the chance of the bottles being broken in the mail. They like to throw things around here in the Italian posts."

Dana and I cast a wondering glance at each other as he cut the tape off and unwrapped the package. He pulled out a couple of six packs of glass-bottled high fashion tints.

"Bellisima!" he exclaimed. "I need these for a couple of clients for the masquerade ball tonight in the Piazza San Marco.

"You mean to tell me that's all we were carrying down here - a couple of bottles of high fashion color!" I said astonished.

"Karl didn't tell you?"

"No, he never mentioned what was in the package. We smoked some hashish with him the night we spent in his chalet, and I just assumed that might be what we were transporting."

He laughed. "That rascal, he was just playing a game on you. He likes to play with people's minds."

"Well, he pulled one on us. We were sweating it all the way down here, not knowing what we were carrying"

Ramone rolled over laughing, tears coming out of his eyes. "Believe me. He would have never put you in that position. I've got to call him and tell him. He'll get a big kick out of your escapade."

"Shit, man," I said, feeling stupid. "Guess the joke's on us."

"Tell ya what. I'll make it up to you. You two have a place to stay?"

"No, we're camped out on the top of the parking garage," I said.

"Well, consider this place yours for a couple of nights. There's a hidden back staircase. I'll show you, and I'll give you a key to get in. Sound good?"

"Sounds great. More than we could ask for. Thank you," I said.

Dana leapt up and gave him a kiss. "Grazie Ramone, we'll love it!" She exclaimed, her eyes lighting up.

"Now, I've got to get back to work. When you come back, I'll set you up and, by the way, don't forget about the ball tonight. I have extra tickets. You'll be my guests."

"What's going on?" I asked.

"You've arrived just in time for Italian Liberation Day - the day you Yanks saved us from the German occupation during World War II. So, you'll fit right in."

"Ohhhhhhhhhh," we exclaimed together. "Way cool."

When we left the salon, after another round of cheek pecking, the day suddenly seemed much brighter. We put our arms around each other, laughing about the joke Karl played on us - if it was a joke, and we revelled in yet another stroke of good luck of being treated to something special from total strangers in our hair styling profession. We spent the next few hours kicking around the winding maze of back streets and canals, shopping for European-style clothing, trinkets and artistic jewelry which, when added to our ensemble, altered our appearance as we went along.

In the late afternoon we stopped at an outside cafe on the edge of the Piazza San Marco for some bread and cheese and a glass of wine. The Piazza was alive with an international mixture of people. Catholic nuns leading small packs of school children weaved among locals and tourists gaping at each other. Hundreds of pigeons fluttered from their statue perches to the cobblestone plaza, momentarily pecking up small bits of food dropped by the strollers, then filling the sky again with their coos and snapping wing movements. As we sat and watched the constant crowd change, four foreign tourists, with cameras hanging around their necks, emerged. They huddled close together, staring at us from about twenty feet away.

"Look, honey," I heard one whisper to her husband, "There's some real Italian gypsies. Let's see if we can get our pictures taken with them."

Overhearing the comment, I kicked Dana softly under the table and whispered out of the side of my mouth, "Let's see if we can have some fun with these people. Pretend you can't speak too much English."

"Okay," she whispered back.

They approached our table. "Excuse me, do you speak English?"

"No comprendo Inglese," I answered.

She started rattling off what perfectly, beautiful Italian gypsies we were. Could they take a picture with us? She asked.

"Peek-ture, peek-ture?" I said, imitating her movements, pointing back and forth, back and forth. Then, as if I finally got the picture, I said, "Oh si, si, peek-ture, peek-ture," inviting them to gather around us.

They were overjoyed, smiling and arranging poses, the women on my lap, Dana on the men's laps, everyone hugging each other and finally, a picture of just the two of us "Italian gypsies" together as a couple. I thought it would be all over after our portrait was shot. But apparently, they were having such a good time; they pulled an adjoining table close to ours, which we all gathered around calling a waiter over to have him take a group photo.

We sat around for a moment, trying to communicate with each other through badly broken English and hand signs. Finally, it got to be too much for me. I broke out laughing, saying, "All right, everyone, it's been fun so far, but I've got to confess we're not really authentic Italian gypsies. We're a couple of hairdressers from California here on holiday just like you."

They went silent, their eyes growing wide with amazement as they exchanged glances. Then the woman who'd instigated the whole encounter broke into laughter exclaiming, "Well you sure had us fooled. But, as far as I'm concerned, you'll always be the gypsies I met in Saint Mark's Square on Italian Liberation Day. Now, let us buy you a bottle of wine and we'll visit awhile."

We reintroduced ourselves to our newfound friends from Johannesburg, South Africa, and took more photos on into the early evening when we had to finally excuse ourselves. They gave us their addresses and made us promise that if we ever got to South Africa that we'd look them up and spend some time with them at their beach house on the Cape of Good Hope. We promised, bid our adieus and went on our way - with another connection in life to explore - if we ever got the chance.

Arriving back at the salon, we were just in time to experience the last two of Ramone's fantasy hairdos he had created utilizing the brilliant colors that we'd brought down from Innsbruck.

"Wow, look at you guys!" Ramone exclaimed, when we walked through the door. "You look like a couple of local gypsies."

"So, we've been told. Wait till you hear the rest of the story," I said chuckling.

"Well, let me finish up here. Then I'll familiarize you with the studio upstairs. Meanwhile, why don't you get your stuff from your van, and then you can hang out here for a couple of nights." As he spoke, he laid a final film of hair spray from a large aerosol can over the towering sculptured creation he'd administered to the highly colorful, party-going client's head. A fine misty fog of liquid hardener drifted in the air around her head. She held a plastic shield over her face as the lacquer settled, setting the fantasy-do into an unmovable object.

I thought that I'd hate to have to take that apart, brush it out, and wash it, having experienced the same process many times back in my salon in San Jose. That evening and for the next two days we were immersed in a world of fantasy. Costume parties were everywhere. You couldn't round a corner without being treated to something festive. I wanted to hang out, but we had a schedule to keep, so we trucked on down the road.

For the next twelve days we were on a whirlwind. We fell in love with Florence and spent three days there. Using our guidebook, we found a campground situated high on a hill tiered with olive trees 500 feet from the Piazzale Michelangelo, which featured a beautiful Loggia built in the 16th century. It cost us a measly three American dollars a day to stay there. We had our own little spot among the trees overlooking the city. From our vantage point we could see the Arno River and the famous Ponte Vecchio Bridge.

The campgrounds also had little huts about the size of overgrown dog houses that backpackers could rest in for a dollar a night. There was a building built into the hill that housed toilets, showers, a small cafe and a store. But the main attraction was a huge deck that cantilevered out over a falling stream trickling down to the river below. In the evening it came alive with bright lights and disco music. Dana and I feverishly danced a night away there, fueled by bottles of Italian red wine.

On the deck we also met our first fellow travelers, Shawn and Trinity, who had flown over on the same flight as we had ten days before. They had just spent time in Zurich and were on their way to Rome. We sat around, drank beer and exchanged stories of our adventures. Theirs, however, were quite calm compared to ours. We had a fine gourmet dinner together, which they paid for in trade, having me cut their hair on a stool under the olive trees. A good hairstylist in those days was like being a celebrity and often led to a multitude of invitations to private estates, dinners, airplane rides, special events, lively parties and romance. Who could ask for anything more!

Florence became the focal point and the beginning of our cultural education in cathedrals and early Italian Renaissance history. True, we'd visited and viewed museums, churches and other points of interests along the way in Luxembourg, Germany, Austria and Venice. But in no way did these other immense Rococo structures, built by centuries old craftsmen, often erected in perilous conditions, capture our full interest until Florence.

The Cathedral of Florence is one of the largest churches in the world, covering two city blocks. Its construction was started in the year 1296 AD and it took 140 years to build. The exterior is done in white marble from the quarry in Carrara and green serpentine from Prato. We loved the towering bronze doors called "The Gates of Paradise" that decorated the entry to the baptistery.

One of our favorite sculptors was Bartolommeo Ammannati, who sculpted the fountain of Neptune, a huge marble statue meant to resemble Michelangelo's "David." Though beautiful, it was unsuccessful since it didn't have a finished look, and the Florence locals dubbed it "The Pasty One." But we loved it.

After a few days of playing the tourist scene, we were "cathedraled out," and we slipped back into the hippie mode for the rest of our stay. That fit us better.

One day I played my blues harmonica, joining two other street musicians, a guitarist and a conga drummer on the Ponte Vecchio Bridge. We placed a hat upside down in front of us, threw a few of our own dollars into it and started playing. Pretty soon we had a crowd in front of us. We jammed most of the afternoon and then split the pot of $82 among the three of us.

I took my share and treated Dana to a most wonderful meal at a highly recommended restaurant just around the corner from the bridge. We experienced the most delicious lasagna, raviolis and veal parmesan we'd ever tasted. It was a perfect last evening. The next day we traveled into Tuscany to the town of Siena.

Siena sits on a small hill, the interior surrounded by medieval walls. Its streets branch out from a central hub, somewhat like a giant wagon wheel. The plaza in the center, Piazza del Campo, is home to the Palio, a 16th-century pageant that traditionally features a fast and furious bareback horse race. Unfortunately, we were two months too early to partake in the festivities that would happen on July 2.

Next to the Palazzo Pubblico, or Town Hall, is an elegant Gothic structure, the Torre del Mangia. It has great views from the top, but you've got to climb 503 steps to get there. We were completely out of breath when we reached the observation platform; our pounding hearts rang in our ears, momentarily creating a natural high.

We each leaned through an embrasure that ringed the top and gazed over the countryside and the Piazza far below us. From that vantage point we created our own Palio. We imagined we could hear the roar of the crowd cheering on their favorite steeds and their jockeys. Round and round they raced, some slipping on the cobblestones, sending themselves and their riders to the ground, some into the crowd. Mayhem ruled, somewhat like the running of the bulls in Spain, a frenzy fired by the consumption of huge volumes of wine. The crowd cheered loud. I shook my head and my make-believe world disappeared.

"Wow, I'm thirsty," I said to Dana, breaking the silence.

"Me, too."

I took her hand and we raced down the curved stairs, the force of gravity pushing us like a free fall. We were at the bottom in a few minutes and continued running together until we reached our van parked in a dirt lot outside the city's walls where we each gulped down a bottle of water.

"Let's head to Rome," I said, breathlessly.

"Let's," she agreed. That night we camped next to Lake Sansari, about 60 km from Rome.

The next morning around 11:00 o'clock, we hit the outskirts of Rome and worked our way into the city. It was like dropping into a time warp, with old and new mingling together. As we joined the swarm of small cars and motorcycles, we slowly drifted past the Arch of Constantine built in 312AD.

We funneled down to a circular road that encompassed the Colosseum, which was built by 100,000 Hebrew slaves in eight years from 72 AD to 80 AD.

I circled it once, then angled off to my left onto Via Mecenate. A park sat off to the left. I couldn't believe my eyes when I spotted a rusty, worn-out camping sign partially hidden by an overgrown bush with an arrow pointing the way. I turned into a palm-tree lined narrow street and there it was - a small haven hidden behind the park in the middle of the city. A strange location, it appeared to have been there forever, the city ignoring it as it grew up around it, leaving it hidden and obscure, on a one-block long street named Via Giovanni.

"Giovanni, I love it," I said, turning into the driveway framed by an arbor covered with vines where a small yapping dog greeted us. I noticed that most of the campers seemed to be long-term, usually a bad sign for drop-ins like us. There were, however, a couple of vacant spots. I wondered if the people were just gone for the day.

I shut off the engine. It was very still where we were. But all around the perimeter, hidden by a ring of ancient Cypress trees about thirty feet tall, the constant tempo of moving traffic drifted in. A stooped-over, older fellow with a beard wearing round, tinted John Lennon-type glasses, emerged out of a faded blue VW microbus. "You guys looking for someone?" he asked.

"Just looking for a place to light for a few days," I answered, hopping out of the van.

"Well, normally the old man who owns da joint don't let many people stay here. But Rob and Billy Jean left early this morning for the beaches off of Costa del Sol, and you guys look pretty cool. I'll tell him you're old friends of mine - see what I can do - my name's Jim. I've been coming here for nigh on seven years now. Let me go wake the old fart up. What are your names?"

"Don and Dana," we yelled after him in unison.

"Well, just hang out." He disappeared behind a dilapidated, rickety screen door that hung off the entrance to a small whitewashed stucco one-room house. I glanced over at Dana and crossed my fingers. We shut the van's doors and leaned up against the front of the van but only for an instant. The screen door squeaked, and Jim bent his way through the doorway back out into the courtyard. A scruffy, unshaven, shrunken Italian papa, about 75 years old, followed in his shadow, scratching his unruly head with hair that stuck out as if he'd just put his finger in an electric socket.

"Come va? Come va?" He asked, giving us a smile. He hitched up his pants, snapping his suspenders over bare white hairy shoulders. His potbelly hung over the waist band, the top button undone. His feet were bare, wide and flat. He shuffled closer, rapidly rambling on in his native tongue. He walked right up to Dana and gave her kisses on both cheeks. When she returned the gesture, his eyes lit up, his arms raised to the sky in admiration. I knew right then and there we were in.

Jim translated the old man's glee and pleasure. "He loves your old lady. She reminds him of his deceased wife. He'd love to have a pretty woman hanging around a few days. It'll cost you 20 lira a day and a bottle of wine."

"Deal," I said to Jim and, in the same breath, "Grazie," to the old man. We shook hands and Papa motioned us over to a small spot under two lemon trees. I hopped into the van and pulled into the spot. We'd lucked out again.

After hooking up to the Spartan but adequate facilities, we spent the remainder of the day cleaning up our living quarters, doing laundry and being introduced around.

It seemed as if we had fallen into a commune of sorts. That evening we all gathered together and shared a meal, each contributing a portion of a mixed bag of taste delights. After, while passing around bowls of hashish, they shared with us the knowledge of their travel experiences, music and philosophies. We felt very warm and secure, part of a family of the Timothy Leary dropout society. We were playing the part day to day with whatever it required of us to be accepted into these different realms of life. We were living in a dream, experiencing the adventure as it unfolded before us, knowing it was a temporary deviation from the working world, and we savored every minute of that freedom.

For the next three days we roamed Rome, did the Vatican thing, visited the Catacombs, hung out on the Spanish Steps in the Piazza Di Spagna, enjoyed demitasse cups of espresso with croissants and got involved in the middle of a political riot. That happened when we were sitting at a sidewalk cafe early one evening in the Piazza Campo Dei Fiori, one of Rome's most enjoyable squares, just relaxing amidst the picturesque food and flower stands. All at once, we were in the middle of total chaos. Young radicals adorned with black arm and headbands, their faces painted half black and half white, rushed by carrying lighted torches and strike signs. I was knocked out of my chair as a barrage of riot police came around the corner. I grabbed Dana and we flattened ourselves against the wall. The police, dressed in black combat gear, helmets faced with plastic and carrying shields and night sticks, slammed into people who couldn't get out of the way fast enough in their hot pursuit of the demonstrators.

It happened so quickly it scared us, disturbing an otherwise peaceful evening. The proprietor of the espresso shop came out, picked up the fallen chairs and tables, shook his fists and mumbled to us not to be alarmed, that it was normal and happened all the time. Someone was always going on strike, and Italians - well they were just naturally hotheaded. We finished our coffees and left, thankful not to have been caught up in the turmoil. We'd heard tales of other travelers like ourselves who had been beaten and robbed when they ended up in the wrong place at the wrong time. We took the hint - time for us to leave.

At dawn the next day we left to go further into the boot of Italy, hitting Naples, Pompeii, the Amalfi Drive and the Isle of Capri in a three-day whirlwind.

We took the direct route south on the highway and 240 kilometers later we topped a rise and dropped down into Naples just as the sun was dipping in the West behind us, illuminating the bay of Naples in brilliant light. Out in the harbor we could see both American and Italian war ships anchored on a mirrored surface, their gray surfaces tinted by the purple, pink, red, orange hue of the twilight. Inland, out in the distance, the coned tip of Mount Vesuvius 4,190 feet above sea level still shone brightly with sunshine.

We skirted the edge of the city, sticking to the water's edge. After driving about 10 km around the bay, we ran right into the little town of Portici, a suburb of Naples, where we spotted a pizzeria and pulled over. We discovered a small blurb on the back of the menu, written in English, Italian, and French, describing the history of pizza making, and telling us that pizza originated in Naples in the 18th century. We ordered the traditional Margarita pizza topped with tomatoes, mozzarella and fresh basil, which featured the red, white and green colors of the Italian flag in honor of Queen Margarita. The proprietors prided themselves in presenting the crusted delicacy in an art form and we were impressed, but also famished. The palette of color disappeared off the tin plate, along with a few beers. I paid the tab, left a nice tip, hopped back into the van and drove about a mile down the road where we checked into a campground for the night and promptly fell asleep.

The chirping of sparrows woke me early the next morning. I slipped the curtains aside and peered out. Mount Vesuvius loomed out right before my very eyes, as we were less than 5 km from the ruins of Pompeii on the south side of the volcano. I woke Dana. We ate hurriedly, left the campground and arrived at the ruins early, before the tourist buses arrived.

It felt special to be the only two walking around the ancient city excavated from the volcanic ash that buried it in 79 AD. Through the digging, scraping and brushing efforts of many, how life was lived almost two thousand years before had been revealed. We walked through roofless homes, their four walls still housing their occupants lying where they died. Respectfully, I whispered a prayer in reverence.

Around ten o'clock, other people started filtering in, their voices breaking the serenity that Dana and I had enjoyed for the last hour and a half.

"Let's go. I've had enough," I said.

We shed our coats walking back to the van as the day was warming up fast. I hopped into the driver's seat, rechecked my map of the area, and headed back out onto the highway, 28 kilometers southwest was Sorrento.

"Let's grab an early lunch there," I said, leaning over and pointing out the spot on the map to Dana.

"Okay," she answered with a smile.

Dana had been most agreeable on the trip so far. She was beautiful, always smiling, had a good attitude, dressed chic and looked to me for direction and advice. People were often taken with her beauty. Put that together with my gift of gab and sense of humor and we could handle almost every situation. Traveling as a couple automatically made us acceptable in many social circles. Being hairstylists; artists of sorts, attractive, energetic and somewhat mysterious, we didn't have the appearance of regular tourists. We seemed to be drawn into special cliques nearly everywhere we traveled. Once again, we seemed to have been "Born in the Right Time." ~

CHAPTER 31: THE MEDITERRANEAN

As we silently dropped into Sorrento, a small, genteel resort for the fashionable elite, only the whisper of a warm, humid, soft wind fluttered by the side mirrors of the van. We both gaped out the windshield, our necks craned forward, not wanting to miss a moment of what our eyes beheld. Sorrento's fabled cliffs loomed above us on our left, their gray-white faces reflecting silver streaks of fractured light caused by the angle of the sun, which at that moment was bouncing off the surface of the sea foam green tropical body of water on our right.

Drifting down the serpentine incline, we hit the last curve, a sharp hairpin changing our direction 180 degrees and putting us once again on flat terra firma. I was immediately drawn straight to the water's edge, where I pulled into a cobblestone parking area facing a sandy beach. I shut off the motor, its 4-cylinder gurgle replaced by the faint murmur of lapping waves. Dana and I each hopped out of our side of the van and ran around to the nose of the van and met. Elated to be near a seaside, I lifted her up in the air and swung her around in circles. Her chocolate black-colored hair swished in an arc behind her as she tipped her head back, her eyes to the sky, laughing. She was quite a beautiful sight. After a half a dozen spins, dizziness dropped us to the soft sand. We hit the ground still embraced, the world spinning around and around in our craniums. Together we lay there and laughed, just like a couple of kids, the sky above us still spinning in a fast, hazy circle. After a minute it slowly folded back into one image.

A short, wrinkly faced, old man holding the reins of a beautiful dapple gray horse hitched to an Italian pleasure cart stood by watching us, his eyes squinting and a smile on his face that spread from ear to ear. A gray felt cap was tipped back on his head and the sunlight lit up his brown mahogany face as he enjoyed our antics.

"Bravo, bravo," he cried, cupping his gnarly, fish line-scarred hands into a clap. As I was helping Dana up from the sand, he grabbed a flower out of the vase that hung off the side of his cart, dropped the reins of his steed to the ground, walked over and gave it to her.

"Grazie, grazie!" she exclaimed, giving him a hug. The remainder of the day evolved quite nicely from that moment on. We toured the town in the pleasure cart, ate at a fine Italian restaurant owned by our driver's son and took the afternoon hydrofoil boat out of the bay of Sorrento over to the Isle of Capri.

Capri is probably one of Italy's loveliest places and we were on our way there, day tripping along in a dream, or so it seemed at times. Soon, one mass of jutted cliffs gave way to another as the boat's twin hulls sliced into the smooth water surface of the Marina Grande of Capri, pulling into its mooring. The gangplank dropped and we disembarked. We walked down the heavily beamed pier. The planks were stained blue/black, and reddish/ purple, caused from years of sloppy spillage from the gas cans that filled the tanks of the small motor launches that hired out to the Grotto Azure or Blue Grotto, Capri's biggest tourist attraction.

As we strolled down the length of the pier, the guides to the Grotto hailed us from their small boats. The boats were filling up fast with tourists who had come over with us on the hydrofoil. We picked a slim, young, handsome, tanned youth of about twenty years of age. Actually, I think he picked us because of Dana. Roberto offered Dana his hand to board, which she took. I jumped in after her and we were on our way.

Out in the bay, we shared some wine, bread and cheese that we had brought over from our van in a backpack. Roberto was inquisitive, chatting like a magpie. He thought we might be a couple of movie stars on holiday from the United States. He was searching and we didn't want to disappoint him, so we played it to the hilt. That's when I realized that he was playing us as much as we were playing him. He told us of a hike we should take to the Villa Jarvis, built during Roman times by the Emperor Tiberius. He turned towards the cliffs towering above the water and pointed out the "stairs of a thousand steps."

"You can pretend you're goats," he said, laughing, "When you climb those stairs to reach the villa."

As I peered up at the challenge, I heard a loud slap behind me. I turned, startled to find that Roberto had pinched Dana on her derriere in that playful way Italian men were known for.

"Aha, caught!" I said, pointing my finger sternly at him. Embarrassed, he bowed his head and apologized. I reached over and punched him on the arm playfully and said, "No problemo, no problemo." He smiled innocently.

"Oh, you Italian boys," Dana said, as she touched his hand, indicating to him that we were cool about what he'd done.

Roberto made up for his folly by extending our trip for an extra half-hour. His commentary and expertise on the Grotto added to the experience. I tipped him well.

The afternoon continued to be mystical. After the Blue Grotto, we strolled the Piazzetta, window-shopped and took in the street scene. Around 3:30 we took step No. 1 on our climb up to the pinnacle of the island where we wanted to be for the sunset, which we had heard was spectacular.

I helped Dana adjust her daypack on her back, and we started our ascent. The rocky path of a thousand steps wound around the face of the cliff where the view grew in its intensity and beauty. We took our time, stopping often to catch our breath, as the climb was somewhat exhausting. After a while it became apparent to us that we had the path to ourselves, others choosing to take the more mundane way to the top via the scenic bus. We climbed higher. Now we could see the tour boats to the Blue Grotto bobbing on the water far below us. As they moved about, their wakes penciled small white lines behind them in the otherwise deep blue ocean. We moved forward and up.

"Look here," I said to Dana, pointing out a scratching on the granite face of the cliff. "It says, Joe, New York, 1945. Probably one of our soldiers who was here during World War II."

"Yeah, I wonder where old Joe is these days." She answered.

Finally, our hearts pounding out of our chests, we reached the top, placing our final step onto a wooden platform with a railing that guarded the edge. From that vantage point we could see two gulfs, the gulf of Naples to the north and the gulf of Salerno to our south. We caught our breaths while we immersed ourselves in silent thought, taking in the beauty of our surroundings.

We hopped across a grassy patch of turf that bordered the view platform and stepped onto the road that came up from below just as an old diesel bus labored its way up the last grade. We stopped and watched as it passed in front of us. Hanging out of one of the windows was our Blue Grotto guide, Roberto. A bright smile lit up his face when he saw us. He waved and called out, "Signore, Signora, Prego." He tucked his head back into the bus and yelled something to the driver. The bus stopped, its air brakes letting out a loud "whoooosh," and he hopped off.

"Hey, you guys, you made it up. Bravo, bravo," he said in thick English. "Come on, I'll show you where to see the most beautiful sunset." He took us to a restaurant his father owned.

No words could describe that evening. We dined on scallopini, fried raviolis and eggplant stuffed with ricotta, consuming at least a half-gallon of red wine along with it. After sunset we danced to piped-in music, consisting of mostly Italian love songs - Ah, amore - then we took the bus back down to the Piazzetta, singing our hearts out all the way.

At the pier, the ferry's horn was wailing the five-minute-before-departure warning; it was the last ferry of the day. We boarded the hydrofoil, the gangplank was raised, it was "Arriverderci, Capri."

We watched the lights of the island dip into the ocean behind us as the hydrofoil raced back to Sorrento. Dana and I sat close on a small bench near the bow. I held her hand; it was the only expression we needed to offer each other. We disembarked around midnight, walked a short distance to the van waiting for us where we left it, and re-entered reality once again.

I patted Dana's behind as she entered the van and said, "Why don't you grab some shut-eye. I'm still a little wired. I'd like to drive up the coast a little bit 'til I get tired."

"You won't fall asleep and drop us off a cliff, will you?" She asked, yawning.

"Don't worry, I wouldn't end this adventure with a tragedy. You're in good hands."

"Okay. Love you."

"Love you, too." I closed the door, hopped up front and slowly, very slowly, headed down the coast toward Amalfi.

I didn't last very long. The soft drone of the engine was singing me to sleep. My eyelids started drooping about twenty minutes into the drive. Ahead, the moonlight illuminated a silver strand of beach as I rounded the tip of the peninsula that jutted out from the mainland. I saw a camping symbol with the words Playa Campanella on it. It was deserted, quiet and welcoming. It seemed to say, "Stop here, spend the night, enjoy the moment." I did. Dana was already sleeping as I slipped into bed totally exhausted. ~

CHAPTER 32: CÔTE D'AZUR

The next morning at dawn's first light I was awakened by the clash of the steel sliding door hitting the end of its track. The stuffy air inside immediately changed as a warm sea breeze wafted through its portal. I peeked out from the covers. Dana was sitting on the floor's edge, her feet in the sand outside the van, naked, except for a pair of diaphanous, blue silk panties barely covering her derriere. I heard her sigh as she stretched her arms high over her head, taking in the sun's comforting warmth.

"Lovely, it is," I commented, breaking into her thoughts.

"Isn't it, though," she answered, "And what a pleasant surprise to wake up this morning and find ourselves alone on this beach with no cares, no woes, only this delightful scene."

I broke out our beach chairs and set them near the water's edge, where we had a breakfast of yogurt and croissants topped off with a cup of mint tea. While we sat, I studied the map and planned our trip up the coast on our way up to Monaco. We wanted to stay in this little piece of paradise forever - but - as with the Isle of Capri the day before, we had to keep on truckin on.

It was May 5, 1970. We had five days to reach the tiny principality of Monaco for the Monte Carlo XXVIII Grand Prix Automobile Race. It would be our longest continuous drive, horseshoeing us up and around the Gulf of Genoa that encircles the Ligurian Sea.

I scooted the van back up on the narrow two-lane road that clung precariously on the edge of the cliff side where we were again in awe of our surroundings. The first town we hit as we traveled along the sparkling coastline was the small fishing village of Positano. Like a page out of a fairytale, it's a jumble of pastel-colored houses clinging to the mountainsides as it cascades down to the sea. This town was the prettiest along this stretch of coast. It seemed to attract a certain group of people who found that the relaxed and friendly atmosphere compensated for the sheer effort it took to move around its narrow vertical stair-stepped streets.

Houses and boutiques, heaped up like the Anasazi Indian dwellings of our Southwest, were perched along the cliff faces. The beach below was the town's main focal point, with a little promenade lined with a multitude of cafés. We walked down to it and had an early lunch, watching the people and letting the world go by.

Midday we continued on our way, passing through the town of Praiano on the way to Amalfi. I wished we had had a sun roof to gaze through, as my neck seemed to have stretched a couple of inches longer with my constant craning out of the windshield, my nose almost touching the glass trying to capture all the beauty.

Amalfi was a charming maze of covered alleyways and narrow byways straggling up a steep mountainside. Here and there would be a tiny vineyard or an apple or plum orchard tucked into a cranny and held back by rock walls on unbelievably small plots of land. We stopped for lunch and breathed in its fresh air. As we traveled further south into the town of Ravello, famous for its noble villas and gardens, we realized that we hadn't allowed ourselves enough time to truly enjoy the splendor of these quaint little towns. If we had known how quickly we both would have become attracted to the area, we would have planned this part of the trip a whole lot differently. I promised myself that someday I'd return, which - true to promise - I have.

The Amalfi coast drive with all its twists and turns, slammed us with an array of visual surprises, providing for us the most dramatic and breathtaking scenery we had yet experienced in all of Italy. I know - I've said this before - but that's just the way it was!

Dana and I had both traveled in our sports cars up and down the famous Highway 1, experiencing the beauty of the Pacific coastline from Monterey down through Carmel and Big Sur onto its end in Morro Bay. We had always thought that drive was the most beautiful in the world until we felt the magic of this roadway. We reached Salerno and emerged back onto the main highway, drifting out of wonderland back once again into the frantic rush of things, faced with a long drive north up the boot to our next destination, Pisa.

It was a long tedious drive that day with dark clouds and rain. So, it was a good time for us to catch up with each other, one on one, so to speak. While we scooted up the highway, we spent the time talking about our recent adventures, what fun we'd been having and the surprises that might lie ahead. When we reached the confluence of the two highways just below Rome, I cut off to the left and back to the coast. Dana excused herself and went back to the bed to read and I lost myself in the driving. I could feel that we were both comfortable being immersed within our own mind's quiet time. That night we camped in a grove of trees of off a small country lane just outside of Pisa

Early the next morning we drove into Pisa. The weather was chilly, cloudy and miserable so we quickly took in the town's main attraction—the famous Leaning Tower. We climbed its stairs to the top, once again experiencing the law of gravity in defiance as we leaned one way going up and the other way coming down. As we left, Dana took a picture of me next to the structure comically leaning over at the same angle.

That night we ate at a small pizzeria, then continued on a few kilometers further north to the small town of Viareggio, where we camped for the night. The next two days would be a driving marathon as we raced around the remaining northern coast of Italy, eager to reach Monte Carlo for the race. ~

CHAPTER 33: GRAND PRIX OF MONACO

The day before the race we pulled into the outskirts of Monaco and within minutes the whole scene changed. Rounding a corner in the road, we were exposed to a horseshoe-shaped harbor, nestling within the regime of Prince Rainier and Princess Grace. We instantly knew we had entered the world of jet setters. Here in the principality was a getaway for the rich and famous and home to the most important Grand Prix race on the European circuit. We pulled off the road onto a rock-walled viewing area to savor the moment.

Out in the distance, on a knoll, sat the Palace of Monte Carlo. It rose like a crown above the Mediterranean, a pleasure dome lifted from a fairytale book.

Port Hercules, a semicircular harbor, sat at the city's edge. Within it, all lined up like a parade of toys, was a flotilla of luxury yachts, every one of them painted the same color, white. Many were large, expensive, ocean-going vessels driven by powerful diesel engines. Others were less ostentatious; smaller sailing vessels also painted white, their lacquered hulls reflecting the bright sun-spots that bounced off the silver blue water.

"Looks like Toyland down there," I said to Dana.

"Doesn't it, though, and it looks like a fun place to pretend to be somebody different. Who and what would you like to be while we're here?" She inquired, all giddy like.

"Let's pretend to be television soap opera actors from Hollywood. That might get us some action." I suggested.

"Okay, we can pull that one off, no sweat," she agreed.

"We're going to be in a fabled kingdom by sea where drivers from all over the world come to compete in the Grand Prix. We're going to be part of the whole scene that we'll probably never see again in our lives. Here we'll live each moment in the present - no past - no future," I philosophized.

We leaned across our seats, meeting in the middle, and kissed each other. My heart and soul were both filled with satisfaction as I pulled back onto the road and continued towards the city. I had hardly driven a few kilometers when I noticed some activity going on up ahead. A young couple, a man with a hammer in his hand and a woman with a paintbrush and a can of paint in hers, were hopping into an earlier version of my Volkswagen van, which was painted in bright psychedelic colors. I looked over in their direction as I drew closer and I noticed a large piece of cardboard nailed to a tree. Written on it, the rough letters still dripping with fresh wet paint, was a single word: GATHERING. Just like a homing pigeon dipping its wing in a turn, we fell in behind them and followed.

Their engine popped and farted out blue smoke as it slipped down a winding palm tree-lined lane down onto a small, hidden beach. My heart raced with anticipation.

"Looks like our kind of people," I said to Dana, as we entered into an oasis of the apparent gathering."

I pulled into a spot next to the van I'd just followed down the hill and hopped out.

"Hey, man, what's happening?" I asked.

"We're happening, man, that's what's happening," he said with a quick wink in his eye, and then he continued to ramble on in his lightly feminine, high-pitched voice.

"It's a gathering, man, a gathering of the Rainbow People." He winked again and stepped out of his van. "We've invaded one of the most valuable land speculative sites in the world. A country, only three kilometers long, that pays no income tax - a free world - that alone should tell you something." He winked again. "So we've claimed this spot, in this particular moment of time as ours." He winked again.

He came over and embraced me. He reeked of patchouli oil fragrance, an odor that was becoming more and more predominant as we traveled further down the coast.

Stepping back, his hands on my shoulders, he held me at arm's length, looked me in the eye and said, "Welcome, join us, and not to worry - we've been promised immunity of invasion from the local gendarmes. I think they'd like to keep our type all in one spot - knowing where we are. Besides, we got the best of the deal 'cause there's not a place to stay in town. There's some sort of big race going on, and it has the place filled to the brim with the crème de le crème."

"Well, hey, we're in," I said, accepting the invitation. "Let me introduce myself and my lady here." I pulled Dana over into my arms. "This here's Dana - I'm Don. We're traveling through Western Europe, following the race circuit. We're from San Jose, California."

"Out of sight, Mark and Bonnie, we're from Big Sur, Monterey. Hell, we're almost neighbors. After you settle in, I'll introduce you around to some of our other fellow wanderers." He winked again.

Jeez! By this time I began to wonder if he had some sort of an affliction or something in his eye or was it just his way of being friendly?

"That'll be great, but first I'd love to run into town to the L' Automobile Club de Monaco and get passes to tomorrow's race. That's what we're here for, the Grand Prix, the big one."

"Hey, Don, don't sweat the small stuff. Leave your van. Besides, it'll be a real hassle in town. We got an old Vespa, runs on one cylinder, very reliable, and you and your old lady can tool into town on it." He winked again.

"Whoa, hold on now, that's the ticket. Kind of like Cary Grant and Audrey Hepburn in 'Roman Holiday' I said, accepting his offer and pumping his hand in gratitude."

After we were introduced around and I got the van ready for the next few days of camping, we hopped our butts onto a well-worn, banana-shaped seat with white cotton stuffing hanging out of its ripped sides in a faded, robin's egg blue Vespa with a bad case of "beach rot" and headed back up the hill on into town.

As soon as we hit the upper road that bordered the coast, we were forced into a steady stream of quick maneuvering traffic. Dana squeezed my upper body and held tight as I played dodge em cars with a mixture of crazy Italians, Spaniards, Germans, and Frenchmen and whoever else were racing around this little town of Monaco.

We'd checked out how to get to the automobile club and now Dana was yelling the instructions to me from a small white piece of paper she held in her hand.

"Left here, then a fast right, there's a little park over there, and it's on the left."

The Vespa coughed and sputtered with the two quick turns, its gasoline being shushed around, upsetting the float level on the carburetor.

"Oh, there it is, Don," Dana pointed. "Pull over."

"I can't see a spot. They're all full," I said.

"Well then, just double park for a moment and I'll hop off."

"Okay, let me get you some money real quick here for the tickets, and I'll circle the block a couple of times," I said, reaching into my back pocket for my billfold.

"My treat," said Dana. "I'll meet you here in the same spot in a short while, okay?"

I moved out slowly, getting my bearings as I watched Dana skirt across midday traffic. I must have spent the whole of the next hour stopping and starting, yelling and being yelled at, and basically protecting my life as traffic snarled around me. It was very nerve racking. Finally, after about the ninth time going around in a circle, I saw Dana running towards me coming from between two big trucks parked in unloading zones. She was waving her hands in the air, a big smile on her face. She slid onto the back while I was still in motion.

"Go, Donny, go. And, boy, do I have a surprise for you," she said.

"Okay," I said. "Lay it on me."

"Let's go for a cappuccino first," she said, giving me a squeeze.

A car pulled out of a parking spot directly in front of me. Perfect timing. I pulled in and hit the kill button. The tired engine gasped one extra weak revolution. I shoved the key deep down into the front pocket of my Levis, took Dana's hand and grabbed the two wrought iron chairs at a small cafe that the occupants of the car who had left us the parking spot had vacated. We sank into the still warm, round cushioned seats, and ordered up a couple of cups of cappuccino.

"So, tell me," I said, looking up at her from the brim of my cup as I blew on its surface to cool its contents.

"Ummmm good," she said, in turn, sipping hers ever so carefully, and holding me in suspense for another moment.

"Dana! I'm waiting."

"I met a man," she started, "But don't be jealous or take this in the wrong way. Promise?"

"Promise," I said.

"Okay, so I'm standing in line with a 100-lira note in my hand when I feel a tug on the bandana tied around my head. Annoyed, I turned, ready to blast whoever was being so forward, and I come face to face with my neighbor's son, Perry Edwards. Anyway, he's here filming the race for CBS. He knows who you are from a conversation with my mother at a cocktail party. He said she mentioned that her daughter was wasting her time, running around with this hippie hair stylist, chasing car races in Europe when she should be home cultivating her future and her security with some young lawyer or doctor. Then, guess what?"

"What?"

"He gave me these." She reached down into the space between the skin of her breasts and the inner layer of her bra, pinched her fingers onto the silver white nylon cords that laid there like coiled snakes and pulled out two CBS media pit passes.

I took them in my hand and checked them out. "Wow, they'll get us in anywhere."

"One catch," she said.

"What's that?

"I might have to go out with him after the race."

"Hey, no problem," I said, "It'll be good for you."

"You won't mind?"

"Well, a little bit."

She smiled that special Dana smile with those big double-layered false eyelashes fluttering the air. We left the café and did a little shopping for dinner that evening.

It was that night that things started to change between Dana and me. It seemed that we had agreed silently, understanding one's needs, to let each other go for a while, a pact of temporary freedom with no love lost. We began an "open relationship," joining in on another part of the hippie free love movement.

The next day, Sunday, May 10th, was race day, the 28th running of the prestigious Grand Prix of Monaco. We grabbed a shuttle bus that was running people back and forth to the 'Circulaire" (protective fencing) which surrounded the track. We found the media gate and proudly displaying our special passes, entered the world of the elite. After locating Perry at the CBS filming trailer, where he was perched on top of its roof, I left Dana to do what she needed to do and I went on to roam around the pit area.

Everyone was friendly. I met the infamous Graham Hill and Jackie Stewart standing next to his red and white Formula One. The air was filled with electricity as the pre-race activities were going on. Prince Rainier and Princess Grace had just arrived in their throne boxes at the start/finish line to a thunderous applause. Strung around the 180-degree hairpin turn, flags of all nations were moving like waving handkerchiefs in the breeze that blew in from the bay.

Helicopters whopped the air above us, cameramen hanging precariously out of the open doors capturing the action of the crowd below them. In the yacht harbor, horns, bells and whistles were sounding off. And on top of every mast and off every fantail there flew more colorful flags and ensigns. The day was beautiful - a little cool - but bright sunshine sparkled off the silver blue bay. It was a perfect day for racing.

For most of the morning and early afternoon, the high-powered cars had been in and out of the pits, circulating the track, practicing, testing their equipment and warming up their rubber. Ferraris, Maserattis, Bugattis, Lotus and other Formula One cars gave everyone a preview of the power output of their high revving engines, reaching over 250km/h (160 mph) in the straightaway coming out of the tunnel.

An hour before race time, the cars were called in and an eerie silence hushed over the scene as last-minute preparations and adjustments were made in the pits. The air was tense as the drivers readied themselves for the 3:30 sharp start, a tradition since the race's beginning in 1929. We waited. The minutes ticked on by. Finally, the silence was broken by the music of the Monaco National Anthem played over loudspeakers that were strategically placed around the whole circuit. The crowd rose to its feet as the music reverberated off the buildings that form a natural amphitheater around the harbor. Goosebumps rose from my skin.

Three military jets flew over, diving down to the surface of the ocean and then pulling up just in time so that the power blast from their afterburners disturbed the water in such a way to create a crater on its surface, pushing the water high into the air. Dangerous - but spectacular! I figured that they knew what they were doing. As they disappeared in the distance, the disturbed water fell back to the surface like mushroomed waterfalls. The crowd went wild. What a show to start the race.

I heard a loud "DONG". I glanced at the large ornate 17th century Victorian clock that adorned the fascia of the building directly above the Prince and Princess's canopied and draped thrones. It was 3:30.

In the middle of the track, the starter leaped into the air with his silk green flag and when he and the flag touched its surface, they were off. He stood there, high upon his toes, flapping the flag back and forth as anxious drivers in their machines raced by him on either side, racing for the first turn and the climb up the hill to the inner part of the city. The roar of 28 powerful engines, releasing close to 20,000 units of horsepower, reached a high crescendo, supercharging the crowd's enthusiasm.

The opening seconds of the Monaco Grand Prix are perhaps the most intense of any motor sport. The short sprint to the right-hand Sainte Dévote corner presents the drivers the first passing opportunity.

After ten laps or so, the field was spread out and the action was now throughout the course. Out in the distance I could hear the roar of the crowd, but I could only mentally visualize what might be happening. That's when I decided to leave the pits.

I exited through the gate we'd entered and immersed myself within the thronging crowd. It was truly very exciting! I worked my way up to the Grand Casino in the square and stood on the top step to the entrance under a royal blue canopy and watched each machine slide into the turn in front of it. As every car came by, the crowd in unison would stand on their tiptoes, oohing and ahhing, while their heads traveled from right to left and left to right as if watching a tennis match. During one of those crowd waves I felt a slightly stronger nudge on my left shoulder. I turned to see who had gotten so close and came face to face with familiarity.

"Steve Boecher?" I exclaimed, my face lighting up in total amazement.

"Yeager, you old salt," Steve answered, giving me a warm hug, his camera gear pressing against my chest.

"What the hell are you doing here, and where did you come from?" I asked.

"Hey bro, you know us old Navy buddies might just show up anywhere in the world these days."

"I know, but here?"

"What better place? We were both car nuts back in Honolulu, when we were roommates, and here we are almost nine years later, still car nuts."

"Hey, sorry I smashed you with my camera gear with my bear hug, but I'm here on an assignment as a roving cameraman with CBS."

"No shit! Do you know Perry Edwards, by chance?"

"Do I! He's the head of film editing with my crew here."

"Well, he's the guy who gave me this media pass." I held out the pass that hung on the cord around my neck

"God, what a coincidence. It really is a small world, isn't it? Well, I've got to pay attention here. I am working, you know, meet me back at the CBS trailer after the race, okay?"

"Gotcha."

"Steve Boecher," I thought, "Can't believe it."

After slamming down a piece of pizza and slugging down a local brew, I roamed the circuit catching glimpses of the action as I worked my way back to the pit area and the start/finish line.

A crash by the No. 5 car on the hairpin turn into a stack of hay bales slowed the action a bit, bringing out the yellow caution flag. A gate was removed from a side alley and the crippled car was pushed out of harm's way, and the race continued again at full force. The crash and the delay did prove beneficial to a couple of drivers, allowing them to close the gap during the caution lap.

Arriving back at the media gate, I pulled out my pass and held it up with my right hand waving it in the air and passed on through, back once again into true reality as the vibrations within the pits were ever so much stronger than on the other side of the fence. Here there was a lot more at stake: fame and money.

I reached the CBS trailer just in time to see the white flag drop, signaling the last lap. Everyone who had been sitting, rose to his or her feet. Those already standing leaned their bodies forward over the guardrails. We didn't have to wait long. Soon the resonance of the screaming engines exiting the tunnel onto the straightaway sang in our ears. The large crowd limited my view of the whole scene as I caught brief glimpses of the cars flashing by. With my head I followed their progress down into the left curve that would lead them into the right hairpin turn around into the straightaway and into my direct line of vision of the finish line.

My ears picked up each downshift heard behind me and I wondered who was going to show first. Then, in the apex of the corner, the leader, Jack Brabham, binds up and crashes into the wall. The Austrian Jochen Rindt, driving for Team Lotus, capitalizes on his error, taking the win; this would be the last victory for the famous Lotus 49.

The air was filled with elation and some disappointment with the final result. Jochen Rindt's win would go down in Grand Prix history. Everyone on team Lotus was jumping up and down, giving each other high fives, slapping each other on the backs and hugging and kissing the pretty girls. It was quite the moment, the feeling - tingling and electric - I got goose bumps.

The race over, I worked my way over to an over exuberant Dana who was surrounded by the men of the CBS crew, each trying to get their lick in with her. Observing her antics, I chose to hang in the background until she got her ya-ya's entirely out.

After a while, things calmed down. The trophy cup and flowers were awarded to the winning team. Princess Grace did the honors, but they received no kiss from this lady, only a polite handshake. Her duty done, she stepped back to join her husband, the Prince, as a giant magnum of champagne was handed to the winner, who immediately popped the cork, shook the bottle and sprayed the exuberant crowd standing on the track below.

Soon the excitement dwindled and the crowd started to leave for home. Evidently, the CBS crew had a lot of wrap-up work to do and they left Dana standing there by her lonesome. She seemed suddenly lost and confused, her bubble burst, so I walked over to her, put my arms around her and said, "Let's go home."

She looked around and said, "Let's thank Perry first, okay?"

"Okay."

We walked up the perforated steel steps and entered the trailer's interior. The crew had popped some Budweiser's they'd had shipped over along with their camera gear. Steve had just returned from his roaming film assignment and Perry was buried in some paperwork.

I greeted them with a smile. "Hey, guys, great race. Just wanted to thank you ever so much for the opportunity to experience this first-hand."

"No problem, bro, but you can thank your lady there for being in the right spot at the right time," Perry said, nodding towards Dana.

I heard a beer can pop and fizzle and it suddenly appeared in my hand.

"Have a beer, Dino." Steve said, using my old Hawaiian beach boy nickname.

"Haven't been called that in a long time, Steve-a-reno."

"Nor me that." We clicked cans.

Dana looked at me quizzically and then back at Steve.

"Steve, this is my lady friend, Dana.

Perry broke in. "We're all meeting at the Grand Casino around nine this evening - hope you two can join us."

"Hey, we'll be there."

Dana and I caught the shuttle bus back to the beach just as dusk was approaching. When we reached our stop and hopped off the bus, I was replaying the experience. The humming drone of the high revving, powerful horse-powered engines were still deep within the cavity of my brain. The earth felt like it moved ever so slightly underfoot. For a moment it felt like I was still on the track. I took Dana's hand. She smiled up at me, kissed me and said, "Thanks, I needed that." We were back in tune with each other - at least for the moment.

We walked down the hill, skipping along and laughing about the day's events. Reaching the end of the pavement, we slipped off our shoes and socks, welcoming the coolness of the soft white sand after a day on hot pavement. Mark was lounging under a palm tree and waved hello.

"Hey, check out the celebs," he said as we approached the campsite. He got up from his rusted aluminum beach chair with its frayed, faded, blue and white plastic webbing barely holding it together and hugged us both. He winked. He then noticed my media pass, which was still hanging on the outside of my shirt. He took it in his hand, fingered it, turning it around to check out both sides, then let it drop back in place on my chest, tapping it a few times with his forefinger.

"Wow, here I was just joshing you," he drawled, "but media passes? You really are celebrities. Come sit down and tell me about it. Want a joint?" He winked again!

"Nah, we don't really do drugs, but let me go grab a beer out of my icebox," I said.

"I'm going to change into my swimsuit while you guys bullshit," Dana said.

I slid the door partially closed and went back to talk to Mark.

"Where's Bonnie?" I asked.

"She's meditating," he said, pointing towards the shoreline.

I could see her sitting cross-legged, arms stretched out in front of her, her upturned wrists resting on her knees, thumb and forefinger touching each other, staring straight ahead. She looked very peaceful and calm.

"That's one thing I could never get into," I said.

"Me, neither. I just get stoned, that's my meditation." He took a hit off his joint and blew the smoke slowly to the sky.

"Oh, what the hell," I said. "Give me a puff. I could use some - but only for medicinal purposes."

"Yeah, sure, medicinal." Mark chuckled, as he handed me the joint.

I took a deep drag, inhaling its sweet taste deep into my lungs.

"Tasty," I said. "Smells good, too."

"Afghanistan."

"Ummmm."

We sat around and chewed the fat for a while until the thought of a nice swim in the ocean broke me away. "Got to take a dip," I said. I left to join Dana in the water.

That evening we ate with Mark and Bonnie. They cooked up a wonderful vegetarian stir-fry and we provided a bottle of wine. After dinner I asked if we might borrow the Vespa to go into town to meet with our CBS friends.

"Take it," Mark said. "But be careful. The lights aren't too good."

Dana and I changed into what we thought would be appropriate clothes for the Grand Casino and headed back into town. Mark was right. The small light on the handlebar of the scooter was pretty dim so I had to hug the side of the road. Lucky for us there were overhanging streetlights that helped light the way.

We arrived a few minutes before nine and cruised by the front entrance checking out the Mercedes, Ferraris, Porsches, Lamborghini's, Citroens and other exotic automobiles parked along the circular drive.

I saw a couple other motorcycles, bicycles, and scooters parked around the side of the Grand Casino.

"Looks like employee parking. It'll probably be safe here," I said, scooting the Vespa into a far corner.

We rounded the edge of the building back into the bright lights of the Grand Casino lighting up its rococo turrets and its green copper cupolas. The Grand Casino, circa 1863, was quite spectacular at night. At the entrance we spotted our entourage standing on the top step waiting for us. They were all dressed up with sport coats and ties.

"Wow, you guys are all duded up," I said.

"Yeah, well, they won't let you in without a coat and tie," Perry announced.

"Shit, what am I going to do?"

At that moment, Jackie Steward, sans his favorite hat, with a pretty woman wrapped around his arm strolled by taking it all in.

"Got a problem, me lad?" He asked in his very British way.

"Yes sir, seems I don't quite meet the dress code."

"Follow me, I gotcha covered," he said.

Within a few minutes I reappeared, wearing a blue sport coat and plain black tie.

"Well, we're impressed," Perry said. "Guess it's who you know."

"He's a great guy!" I answered, and all together we entered the sanctum of the ultra-rich.

Bohemian crystal chandeliers hung from the ceilings. Paintings of voluptuous courtesans hung on the walls. It was like a scene from a James Bond movie. Wealth emanated from the pores of these people. It showed in their clothes, their jewelry, how they carried themselves, and their speech and even in the elaborate hairdos the women wore. Cigars, cigarettes and martinis were in the hands of the people crowded around the gaming tables. The baccarat table seemed to be holding the most interest, and I nudged Dana up close to take a peek.

Sitting on the dealer's right was a high society damsel of great beauty and apparent wealth. Diamonds sparkled from around her neck, wrists and fingers. She was dressed in a pure white, form-fitting gown, undoubtedly designed by some famous courtier. Holding an air of confidence about her that commanded everyone's attention, she slowly pushed thousands of dollars' worth of chips, betting on the cards as they exited the box. Two handsome, well-built men, attired in tailored Armani suits stood behind her at parade rest, their arms crossed behind them. Their bodies seemed to sway ever so slightly as their watchful eyes continuously scanned the room and its occupants, always returning to the woman and the action below them.

She was winning big and nonchalantly tossing a portion of her winnings back to the house. There was a mystical allure about her and, as the crowd grew, Dana and I were slowly shoved out of the picture. We wandered deeper into the Casino's elegantly decorated interior, its architecture reminiscent of some of the European palaces we had visited. We soon found more intimate rooms, all with their own gambling flavor–poker, roulette and other interesting games, some of Oriental descent. But it was the craps tables and its walls splashed with a riot of Rococo paintings that drew us in.

Still early in the evening, especially for serious gamblers, a fresh table was just opening up as two casino workers swished off its protective covering in one sweeping movement, revealing its green felt decorative dice rolling surface. It beckoned to me. I'm not that much of a gambler, but I did have some winning moments.

I stepped up to the table's rim and laid out the minimum bet on the line, took the dice in my hand, bounced them onto the felt a couple of times until they felt right and tossed them to the far end, turning up a winner on the first roll, "Yo, seven, come to Daddy."

Feeling good, I repeated the process, bouncing the dice off the tabletop enough to glance at their position. I set my bet, this time on the field, called it and rolled.

"Give me boxcars." Up popped a pair of sixes, paying me three to one. I heard Dana squeal next to me. My exuberance faded, however, when I crapped out on the next roll. With that I passed the dice and stepped back for a moment, letting the next shooter roll his best shot. He blew on the dice in his hand, shook them and yelled, "Come to me, baby!" and threw a winner. Money ahead, I decided to stick around and match his bets. He was hot. But, after a few good rolls I elected to quit while ahead. I collected my chips and cashed them in, stuffing a couple hundred bucks of the principality's local exchange into my pants pocket.

Leaving the casino, we roamed town and celebrated into the wee hours of the morning. We drank fine wine, ate great food and drank from our round-bowled, glass snifters filled with exquisite brandy. Around four in the morning, our arms all hanging onto each other for support, we staggered into the hotel where the crew was staying. Dana and I crashed in Perry's suite - at his insistence - while he went to share a room with one of the others. Entering the room we tore our clothes off leaving a trail to the bed, letting them lie where they dropped and slipped between clean satin sheets. It had been one hell of a long day; we'd been on the go for over 20 hours and a lot had happened. I don't remember falling asleep.

Noon, May 11th. We were startled out of our stupor by the sound of a gonging bell announcing the changing of the guard up at the palace. I leapt out of bed only to fall immediately back upon its surface, knocked down by a sudden rush of blood to my head from a massive wine and brandy headache. We got up very slowly and gradually came to life again.

After breakfast we went out on the small balcony that jutted out from the side of the building. We looked over its edge and spotted our friends below. They were packing up their gear into a couple of support vehicles that had pulled up in front of the hotel. I whistled to them. They looked around, then up.

"There they are," Steve said, spotting us. "How did you guys sleep?"

"Very well, thanks to you and Perry," I answered.

"Hey, last night was a treat," Steve continued. "We all really enjoyed the whole crazy scene. But we're out of here, on to a race in France, then Spain, then up to Brussels. What about you?"

"Well, first we have to return the Vespa, pick up our van. Then I think we'll continue down the coast for a while."

"Well, let me give you our schedule, and maybe we can connect again at one of the races."

Steve rushed up to the room and handed me a print out. I took the paper, scanned it quickly and said, "Looks like it might be Brussels." We all hugged and shook hands around. Then Dana and I beat it back to the Casino in hopes our little scooter hadn't disappeared into the night.

Lucky for us, the Vespa was sitting there waiting for us. I took out the key from my pocket, unlocked the steering fork and gave the kick-starter a pump and the little engine "popped to life" after emitting a little compression fart.

"Hop on, puss. Let's get back to the beach. Mark and Bonnie are probably wondering where the hell we disappeared to."

Dana chose to sit side saddle on the way out of town as we tooled off into the traffic back to the campgrounds. Everything was going along just fine until we ran out of gas about a hundred yards before we crested the last little grade that led to the road to the beach. We pushed it up the rest of the hill. Topping the pinnacle, puffing from the exertion, we hopped back on and coasted down the grade to the beach. With no compression to hold us back, I held the front brake handle tight, causing the tiny brakes to squeal in protest all the way down.

Mark heard us coming and got up from his rickety beach chair when we came around the last curve and into sight. "Ran out of gas, huh?" He said when we rolled off the pavement and onto the sand. "I could hear those brakes squeaking way before I could see you. I just knew it was my little Vespa. Been there myself a couple of times."

He chuckled. "You guys must have had a good time last night. It's almost the middle of the afternoon and we were getting a little concerned you might have been hurt or something."

Just then the Vespa's front wheel caught in the soft sand and down we went. Laughing, I picked myself up, helped Dana up and righted the scooter. "Nothing hurt here except my pride, and do we have a story to tell you, you won't believe it."

Later that night the four of us sat around the campfire discussing pasts and futures. We discovered that we had a lot in common and, ironically, were heading in the same direction with the same goal, the island of Ibiza. ~

CHAPTER 34: DOWN THE COAST

Anxious to get on our way, I woke way before anyone else, took an early morning swim to refresh myself and get my wits together, then rousted Dana out of the sack so we could move on out. We had a quick breakfast of yogurt and tea. Mark dropped by to reiterate the plan we had discussed the previous evening and we promised to try to meet up again in Alicante, Spain, where we would take a tramp steamer out to the island.

I started the engine and waved goodbye as we climbed up the hill and hit the road again. What a trip we'd been on! We'd just done the bay of Naples, the Amalfi Coast, the Italian Riviera, and we were about to enter France and its famous Cote D'Azur, the most built-up, overpopulated, over-eulogized, and expensive stretch of coast line anywhere in the world.

We drove out to the coast highway, the only exit out of Monaco, and proceeded a few kilometers down to Nice. The mountains were most spectacular, breaking their fall just a few meters from the coast before leveling off to the shore. We arrived in Cannes and got caught up in the crowds as we drove down the main promenade with its beach on our left filled with bikini-clad men and women and the hotels on our right, jammed with celebrity seekers, tourists, photographers, and wannabes. We decided it would be too much hassle to find a place to park and partake in any of the festivities, so we passed through and continued on to Marseille.

Marseille is a true port city with a trading history going back over 2,500 years. We roamed the harbor area taking in all of its busy activities, then drove up to the Basilica of the Notre Dame de la Garde, which was located on a high hill overlooking the city. After parking in the main parking area, we climbed up a winding staircase to an observation platform and viewed the city and its harbor through the eyes of the Golden Virgin, a beautiful sculpture of the Virgin Mary.

Off in the distance we could see a small island, which held the Chateau d'If, the evil island fortress that figured in Dumas' great adventure story, The Count of Monte Cristo. No one had ever escaped from there; most prisoners, incarcerated for political or religious reasons, went insane or died before reaching the end of their sentences. We took a few pictures, had lunch and continued our journey on to Gerona, where we spent the night in an olive grove that we happened onto, high in the hills. The next day we dropped down into the bustling city of Barcelona.

Barcelona, an attractive and stimulating city and the second largest in Spain, proved to be most exciting. We cruised into the city's outskirts, still hugging the coastline searching for a specific camping spot. We'd heard of a resort that was a favorite of the Europeans on holiday. As we passed the main harbor of Port Olympic, we saw signs directing traffic to the Playa de la Barcelona.

We traveled a little further down, skirting the main part of the city. On our right we passed a large municipal park that housed an old castle and a museum. A few kilometers past it we saw a little camping sign. It appeared to be what we were looking for with its palm trees and white sandy beach. I flipped on my left turn signal and turned into the entrance to the park. It welcomed us with a whitewashed concrete arch crowned with several different flags of nations of Europe. We pulled over next to the registration office and I got out. A few minutes later I came out with a map of the area to check out what was available. All the beach sites seemed to be taken and then I noticed someone pulling out of their spot. They waved us in. "We're really in luck," I said, and pulled into the spot.

"Oh good," said Dana. "Now can we settle down for a while?"

"You betcha!" I half sighed.

Before wrapping it up for the evening, we had a couple of hot dogs cooked over a small fire that I had built and briefly met our hippy looking, next door camping neighbor, Troy.

The next morning we woke early, at first light before sunrise, both with deep hunger pains in our stomachs. We crawled out from underneath the covers and I went straight to the little icebox and started pulling out our provisions.

"Yogurt, kefir, bread, peanut butter and jelly - not a very filling breakfast but nourishing. We'll have to make a grocery run today," I said, as I piled the ingredients for breakfast on the little pullout table. "Stay in bed and I'll make you a tray."

We ate breakfast, made the bed, cleaned the van, put on our swimsuits, grabbed our towels and went to the beach for a morning dip. The sun was just peeking over the horizon, a brilliant ball of orange/gold fire. The water was warm and soft to the touch. We swam out from the shore a good way, and then turned to look back at the view from a different perspective. Bobbing up and down, floating with the swell, we indulged in small talk while treading water and taking in the quiet serene scene when something brushed against my leg.

"Whoa, what was that?" I said.

"What?" Dana asked, her voice slightly panicked.

"Something brushed against my leg!"

Suddenly the water around us became alive, swirling with a school of small bait fish jumping out of the water, frantic to escape their hidden pursuer.

"Something has those fish panicked. Let's swim for the shore."

We pulled some strong strokes to get us to the beach fast. Our hearts were beating and, as we neared the shore, we could see small groups of people watching the morning feeding frenzy going on behind us in the sea. I spotted Troy, our hippie neighbor, standing on the beach frantically waving us in. We swam for him, not daring to look behind us. He called out to us, "Faster, faster!" Soon my right foot hit soft sand, then my left; I picked myself up and grabbed Dana's hand. We rushed out of the water and dropped to the sand exhausted from our swim sprint.

"You guys were lucky," Troy said, "There's a feeding frenzy going on out there. Turn around and look." The sea was alive with action and it had followed us into the shoreline.

"I should have warned you last night about early morning swims here in the bay. This happens most every day around here. It's scary, sometimes."

Troy proved to be a wealth of information for the area we were in. He'd been traveling for about a year and was heading in the same direction as we were. He had no wheels, just the pack on his back, hitchhiking or walking to his destinations. We told him we were heading down the coast to Alicante where we were to meet Mark and Bonnie, who would join us for a trip to the island of Ibiza. He said he was in no hurry to go anywhere and, if we didn't mind, would love to tag along with us for part of the way. Dana and I agreed that we could use the company and said yes.

We hung around Barcelona for about a week doing the usual, sightseeing, shopping, eating, swimming and, of course, partying. We visited all the architectural wonders we could, including the unusual designs of the famous Gaudi whose smooth movements were incorporated in iron, glass and cement. We visited galleries filled with Picasso, Miro, and Dali paintings. Wild!

As we strolled around the city we noticed that all the street names were in the Catalan dialect. We were still on cathedral overload after Rome, Florence, and Venice so we spent more time shopping, which in this particular city was most interesting and fun. As we bounced from shop to shop and from one side of the street to the other, the male clerks all went gaga over Dana and the young girl clerks goo-goo over me. In one day of craziness, we managed to rid my pockets of most of my Monte Carlo winnings.

The fantastic leather shops drew most of our attention. The styles, colors and textures were phenomenal, and the scent of fresh, new leather very provocative. The hawkers stood outside their shops and whistled or called out trying to entice us to step into their establishment.

At the end of the day, we strolled down the street in new attire. I, in a full-length Edwardian-style pigskin coat, and Dana in a pink leather mini skirt with a matching pink leather vest with a six-inch fringe hanging from it–she loved PINK! We were quite the pair and attracted an audience as we strolled. We loved the attention at this stage of our lives.

"Tom Jones, Tom Jones," a group of giddy uniformed schoolgirls called out to me. I was impressed. They thought I was the Welsh singer who was so popular at the time. They handed me their school papers and pencils for an autograph. I, of course, didn't want to spoil their illusions so I happily accommodated them while humming his latest hit "Delilah." It was hot wearing the coat, but I was having so much fun with my façade that I chose to leave it on most of the evening.

Discos were at the top of the rage list during the early '70s, and the Europeans took their dancing to the limits at these establishments. Dana and I loved to dance together; we had some good moves.

With our new threads on, we were starving for some action to fill out the night, so we hailed a cabbie and had him take us to the Palladium, one of the popular Barcelona nightclubs we'd heard about. The cabbie was duly impressed with our attire. He said the doorman at the club was his brother and that he would get us in the door.

"No worries, signore. You have a $20 American bill for my brother?" When we got there, he gave it to his brother who ushered us in, past a line of waiting patrons.

What a scene. The place was alive - a human ant farm filled with moving bodies gyrating on an under-lit revolving hard Plexiglas floor. The crowd was dancing trancelike to loud pounding, pulsating music that came from huge speakers suspended from the ceiling above. Dozens of strobe lights flashed a multitude of colors upon the dancers below, momentarily freezing their motions in stop action. I immediately obtained a contact high, and I could feel that Dana was equally possessed—so on to the floor to join the mass of moving humanity we went.

I took control and slowly moved us up closer to the main action in front of the stage where a DJ was performing his talent. Suspended from the ceiling were two caged semi-nude go-go dancers going through their motions - wild things. I was slightly taller than most of the male clientele and, dressed in the Edwardian pig skin duster, I guess I had a commanding appearance as no one challenged me as I slowly worked the two of us up to the stage. It took a while - excuse me, excuse me, sorry, excuse us.

We began dancing and, after a few wild, expressive dances, we had to shuck our outer attire. We placed my coat and her jacket up on the stage where they would remain in plain view of us and continued to release our inhibitions. Dana started to whoop and holler like an Indian, and her bizarre actions slowed the dancers around us. They gathered around us in a circle, swaying back and forth while clapping in time encouraging us to become even wilder. We satisfied their craving, dancing ever more suggestively until we were molded together, moving as one, again on the stage of life. Yahoo! Finally, that song ended and the crowd dispersed. We stood there panting and with that I thought we'd had enough excitement for the day, so I grabbed Dana's hand and our coats and dragged her through the crowd and out the front door. We hailed a taxi and had him deliver us to the campground.

After his lights disappeared down the lane, silence returned bringing a noticeable ring to our ears caused by the high decibels put out by that loud music. The smell from the sea and the flowers that hung off the vines that canopied our campsite - coupled together with the heat from our bodies - seduced us down on the soft sand to finish the foreplay we'd started back on the dance floor. It was ever so sweet. The next day we left for Alicante and the island of Ibiza, leaving Troy behind. He had linked up with a pair of babes from France who were traveling with backpacks - right up his alley.

Following the coast we took our time lounging here and there on small soft sandy beaches. It was a continuing holiday in paradise. As we neared Valencia, we started to catch glimpses of what lay ahead of us. Far out in the distance we could see tall white high-rise apartment buildings jutting into the blue sky looking like giant candles stuck in the sand. We were entering another favorite holiday spot of the Europeans who were drawn by the long white sandy beaches and crystal-clear waters.

As usual, we were winging it and had no real plan, so we cruised into the city's outskirts in a slow searching manner. We could see a few camping areas off to our right opposite the beaches, tucked away in little oasis of palm trees. Most were full so I decided to turn down a sandy road that seemed to wind around behind them. I followed it until we couldn't go any further, where we came upon a whitewashed, walled compound that not only seemed inviting, but also safe. When we reached the open gates to its entrance, we noticed a sign written in English that said, "Welcome Travelers—English Spoken Here." We pulled into a camping area, which was adjacent to a white-stucco five-story apartment building. There were a few people milling about and I stopped a couple to inquire about the place. After a moment, the man pointed over to the apartment complex. "The office is over there," he said.

We hopped out and went through the sliding glass door that led into a small sitting area with a reception desk. No one was about, so I rang the small silver bell that sat on its surface. A man came out of a small restroom behind the desk wiping his hands with a brown paper towel.

"Can I help you?" He said in a heavy English accent.

"I hope so," I said. "We're looking for a place to hang out for a couple of weeks, and we'd like to leave our van somewhere safe when we go over to the Isle of Ibiza."

"Oh, I think you've found your spot, old boy. Jon's the name," he said extending his hand in welcome. "And you've arrived just in time for the festivities."

"Festivities?" I questioned.

"Yes, my wife and I have recently purchased this," he spread his arms out encompassing the compound, apartment building and campgrounds, "And we're having a barbeque and friendly get-together this evening. Now, would you like a camping spot or would you like to get out of that van for a while and rent a room with a view?"

I looked at Dana, then back at him. "Both," I said. "How 'bout we go for the room tonight. It'll give us a chance to clean up the van a little and then we'll settle into the campground."

I signed the registration book noticing, as I did, Mark and Bonnie's names on the list. I prepaid for a week and we got some of our gear out of the van and climbed the stairs to the fifth floor. Finding our room, we opened the door and I immediately fell exhausted onto the bed.

"Wake me an hour before the barbeque," I said and promptly fell asleep.

I awoke to a pinkish hue on the horizon when Dana rousted me.

"Dinner in half an hour," she said, "and I've connected with Mark and Bonnie—they're anxious to see you."

We found the party in a far corner of the complex under a grove of palm trees. Red wine was being served and the crowd was already conversing rather loudly—mixed in with laughter. We spotted Mark and Bonnie talking with the bloke who'd checked us in. He had his arm wrapped around a pretty redhead, presumably his wife. Dana and I hugged Mark and Bonnie; they in turn, introduced us to Jon and Karen, our hosts.

We immediately felt at home and had a super time meeting the other guests, our new campmates. It was very communal—like the place we'd stayed at in Rome and at the beach in Monte Carlo—and we loved it. The next week we just hung out, strengthening our relationships with Mark, Bonnie, Jon and Karen.

We were in a great location on the Costa Blanca, and Jon just happened to have a speed boat moored at a small yacht club a few meters down the road at Cabo de San Antonio, so we went water-skiing.

They all were skiing the old-fashioned way on two skis. So, when it came my turn, I thought I'd show them some action. I immersed myself into the warm blue waters of the Mediterranean, got lined up and yelled, "Hit it." As soon as I popped up and got my bearings, I dropped one ski and slipped my foot into the rubber casing that was behind my foot on the other ski. And off I went jumping the wake and shooting a giant, water rooster tail, behind my ski on the sharp cuts. Everyone in the boat was applauding as I sailed over the calm water showing off my style, which I had learned a few years before back in California water-skiing on the delta waterways of the Sacramento River.

I worked into a real smooth rhythm while skimming over the clear water. As I watched the different coral formations slip by under my ski, I lost myself in the moment and dazed off and—"SLAM!"— down I went. The boat came around to pick me up.

"Quite a show, Don." Jon said.

"Yea, I just kind of lost it for a moment, though." I climbed aboard and cracked open a beer.

We partied for a week, cleaned up the van, made our plans to leave it with Jon and Karen, and packed our bags for our trip to the Isle of Ibiza. We checked the schedules for cruise boats, but most were expensive. Then Jon told us about an inexpensive tramp steamer that left at dusk and arrived at the island in the morning. When the night arrived for our departure, Jon bussed us down to the port. The four of us, packed out like foot travelers, boarded the steamer as the sun was setting.

We checked out our "staterooms," which were small iron cubicles with two rickety canvas bunk beds that hung out from the bulkhead on rusty chains. The mattresses and pillows were very hard, although they were covered with clean sheets and pillowcases; but you still had the feeling that they were probably covering old stains. A rusty toilet and small sink sat in one corner, and one tiny light was enclosed in an iron-crossed container on the ceiling. Everything was painted ship gray and the only saving grace was a small porthole above the upper bunk, which provided a bit of light but no ventilation. Our only source of air came from a noisy air shaft that peeked out from in between the equally noisy water pipes that passed through the overhead.

"Eeee Ech!" Dana expressed when she saw our quarters. "Maybe we should have taken the cruise boat."

"Maybe, but it's too late now, so let's try to make the best of it," I said, throwing my gear on the top bunk. I unzipped the side pocket of my backpack and pulled out a bottle of wine.

"Luckily, Jon and Karen gave us a couple of bottles of wine for a bon voyage gift. Let's take this one up to the main deck and look at the city as we leave port." The fresh air smelled wonderful as we came up from down below. We felt the ship lurch as a large tug secured to the fantail by a three-inch thick hemp rope began pulling the ship away from its berth. We went back to watch. As we did, the ship's steam whistle announced our departure, its scream echoing back from the concrete walls of the terminal. When we were clear of the dock, the tug let go of us, its own whistle sounding all clear. We heard a cling-cling from the steering house signaling for power. The ship's single screw started turning under us ever so slowly as we turned out to sea. Looking back at the city fading into darkness, we realized why the Romans had named this place

"Lucentum" (City of Light) as the skies above it were remarkably luminous.

"Pretty impressive, isn't it?" a voice from behind us said. Mark and Bonnie joined us, another bottle of wine in hand.

"Almost surrealistic," I said. "I can see now where Dali might have been inspired to create some of his works here."

"It does look like it's been splashed on a canvas, doesn't it!" Bonnie chimed in.

"Hey, Mark, let's grab a couple of those deck chairs over there and pop the corks on these wine bottles and watch till the last light fades in the distance," I suggested.

"Good idea. We'd better grab a couple before the steerage passengers take them all up. We'll have to give them up later so that they'll have something to sit on besides the hard deck as we cross over."

"Well, I don't know," Dana said. "I think I'd rather stay up here than spend the night down in that rat hole we have for a cabin."

"Isn't it awful?" Bonnie agreed. "I'm with you, girl."

We pulled the hard metal folding deck chairs up close to the fantail railing and sat down on them, put our feet up on the railing, and opened the wine bottles. We didn't have any glasses so we drank straight from the bottles. Mark had bought a pack of Turkish cigarettes to smoke to curb his dope habit, and we all took a puff. They were NASTY!

It grew a little cool around midnight, the bottles were empty, I had a headache from the strong tobacco and Dana was a little drunk and somewhat seasick—not a great combination. So, even though we didn't want to, we retired to our cells. We bid our friends good night, and I helped Dana stumble across the deck and down the stairs. I opened up the door and Dana went straight to the toilet, dropped down to her hands and knees, put her head in its bowl and lost it all. Oh, my God, she was a mess. I helped her into the lower bunk and left her moaning, while I went back up for some fresh air.

I roamed about for an hour observing the peasants trying to make themselves comfortable up on the open fantail. There were crying babies with their mothers, old people shuffling around with blankets over their shoulders and a few men watching a soccer game on an old black and white TV hanging off the bulkhead. I could imagine what it might have been like for the immigrants who crossed the ocean to Ellis Island in similar or worse conditions with only the belongings they could carry. I knew now what a tramp steamer really meant and vowed it would be my last time on one. Next time it would be first class, on a proper ship.

Finally tiring of the commotion up on deck and feeling it might be safe to venture back down, I left. It was quiet and dark in the small room when I opened the door. "Dana," I whispered. No answer. She was passed out, her breathing deep. Good, now maybe I could get some rest. I crawled up into the top bunk. The sound of the sea slipping by the heavy plates of steel that made up the hull of the ship soon lulled me to sleep–just like it did years ago on the aircraft carrier–the Kearsarge. Tomorrow I would greet another day, again, in another place. ~

CHAPTER 35: THE ISLAND OF IBIZA

The next morning, my brain in its semi-conscious state suddenly detected a change of light as it passed across my closed eyelids, waking me in the process. I felt the steamer slowing. Its propeller screw vibrated more as it made a sharp turn into port. A sudden shudder ran the length of the ship. It woke Dana. I detected a moan escaping from her parted lips that came from deep within her. I peeked over the edge of my berth down into her squinting, pained eyes.

"Rough night, huh," I commented.

"Oh, God," she said.

I swung my feet out and over the edge of the roped canvas bunk and lowered myself down to the deck. I went to kiss her, but she held her hand over her mouth.

"I think you might want to wait till I brush my teeth," she said. I agreed as I detected the stale smell of vomit.

"I was just trying to be comforting."

"Thanks, but why don't you go up on deck and let me pull myself together."

"Okay." I splashed some water on my face, slipped on my clothes and left her alone.

On deck, people were lining the rails as we entered the port. I saw Mark and Bonnie near the bow and joined them.

"Wow, check it out," I said as I gazed up at the 16th century walls that enclosed the town. "Looks like a fortress."

"Yeah, I read up on the history of this place last night and it seems there was always someone out there trying to conquer it, be it the Romans, the Carthaginians, the Corinthians or whoever."

"I think I'm going to like this place," I said.

"We've heard it can be pretty wild," Bonnie said.

"Well, we'll just take it as it comes. Where are you guys staying?" I asked.

"We've got some friends who have a small villa high on a cliff overlooking the sea, about 12 kilometers northeast of here called Villa Salada. We understand it's near some old Roman baths. What about you two?"

"Some pension called Playa Talamanca that Jon turned us on to in the Bay of Talamanca. He was kind enough to have called ahead for reservations for us, so I think we're covered."

The lines were tossed from the ship to the men on the dock who tied up the boat. A gangplank on wheels was rolled up and people began lining up to disembark.

"I'd better go down and get Dana and our bags. Don't leave before we can get some directions to where you're going to be."

"Okay, we'll wait."

I got Dana and our bags, and we followed Mark and Bonnie down the gangplank. A hint of Patchouli fragrance in the air hit my nostrils. "Hmm," I thought, "Must be in the right place."

We walked down the pier to the street and I wrote down the directions to where Mark and Bonnie would be hanging out. Look for an American flag, I was told. American flag? Seemed strange way out here in the Mediterranean.

"Okay," I said. "That shouldn't be too hard."

Dana and I hailed a taxi that took us to our hotel. We walked into a small lobby, registered and got an ocean-view room. Jon had done us well, although it was probably the most spartan of any hotel accommodations we'd had so far. It was totally white—white walls, white floors, white drapes, white towels, white bedspread, white sheets and pillowcases and a white tiled bathroom, all enclosed within a two-story elongated white Moorish design building. These people must be color blind, I thought.

I walked over to the window and opened the wooden blinds to look down at the beach. The white sand was dotted with brown bodies clad in bikinis, men in the briefest of briefs and women in small bottoms who, for the most part, were topless.

"Check it out," I told Dana, motioning her to come to the window.

She peered down at the scene and said, "Looks like I'll have to get myself a new bikini, doesn't it?

We spent the rest of the day at the beach just plain relaxing—finally. Dana loved the freedom of being able to expose her bare breasts comfortably, and I was totally enjoying their exposure. It seemed different somehow—freer; I guess you might put it. The two of us were feeling liberated in our new environment on this strange island seemingly lost in the middle of the Mediterranean Sea.

That evening, after a long shower and a short rest, we walked around the bay and into town. As we neared Sa Penya—a former fisherman's quarter now the center of Ibiza's nightlife—we could feel a change of energy in the atmosphere. Loud music, mostly rock and roll but in all different languages, screamed at us as we rounded a corner into the main hub of activity. We immersed ourselves in a flowing web of international cultures and peoples; all mixed together like a giant fruit salad. There was an English/Irish pub selling meat pies next to a Moroccan stand selling lamb on long wooden sticks. American hamburgers were being ravenously gobbled up right next to a French restaurant, where the patrons sat delicately picking at fancy plates of food looking like pieces of art, the ingredients formed into images of small plumed birds. Street vendors were selling a conglomeration of foodstuffs, trinkets and souvenirs. Clothing shops, boutiques, t-shirt shops and tie-dyed garments splashed in kaleidoscope colors were hanging off awnings everywhere.

We moved along with the flow, mesmerized by the carnival atmosphere. We noticed that marijuana, kef and hashish were all being smoked openly, casually being passed among individuals. As we strolled by one group of glassy-eyed Rastafarians, their heads wrapped in multi-colored knit hats and dreadlocks sprouting out from underneath them like threads of rope, a cigar-sized joint of "ganja" was passed to me. I refused – "Thanks but no thanks"– not knowing what else might be in it. Continuing on, we were amazed at the amount of drug paraphernalia that was being sold. Bongs and pipes of all kinds of shapes and sizes and rolling papers of all different flavors and colors were in every little shop.

And drinking? Same story. Everybody seemed to be consuming some sort of alcoholic beverage—wine, exotic cocktails, shots of Ouzo, Vodka, Tequila, Jack Daniels and, of course, beer suds from all over Europe. Never saw a Budweiser or Coors, which was okay by me. It seemed that whatever you wanted or desired was at your fingertips—a carnival of delights. These people were here to play and party—party the endless party.

Dana and I had never experienced a scene quite like this. We might have at one time thought that we were the party hogs, but this was so out of this world it made us feel like country bumpkins. We knew we'd better enjoy this experience to its fullest, so we jumped right in and melted into the scene.

We strolled the streets, sampling various foods along the way and grabbing a beer here or a glass of wine. Time just got away from us and it wasn't until long after midnight that we began to stumble back to our hotel. Our bodies and minds woozy from the evening's many consumptions, we strolled barefoot in the moonlight along the white sandy beach, completely enthralled and enraptured with our present surroundings.

The next morning we hurt. We had to force ourselves up out of the prone position. A shower revived us somewhat but what we really needed was some food. We made our way downstairs to a continental breakfast of orange juice, fruit, and croissants covered in jelly and jam then topped it off with a strong cup of black North African coffee. The breakfast was included in our room price, which was then the equivalent of $12.47 in American currency. Those were the days my friend—yes—those were the days!

After the meal, we felt a little better and decided that we'd better proclaim this to be a day of R&R. Back up in the room I slipped into my Speedo and Dana into her crocheted pink bikini. We gathered up a pair of white beach towels, some suntan lotion and a couple of books to read, stuffed them into a beach bag and headed down to the sugary sand.

It's a wonderful feeling to spend a day at the beach, no matter where in the world you are. Each has its own allure of sounds, sights and smells. That first step, when you place your foot onto that delightful grainy substance—the loose, gritty particles slipping between the toes of your bare feet—telegraphs to your brain the serenity of it all. You pause for a moment and take in a deep breath while observing the whole scene, surveying your choices of where to "light" for the day. You go to your spot, spread out your towel or set up your chair. Then you settle in and if you like that spot that's where you'll go every day.

That particular day we chose a spot next to a family of eight on holiday from Great Britain. We paid little or no attention to them, concentrating instead on reading, sunbathing and ourselves. About noon the father started rummaging through a large cooler that they had brought to the beach. He must have thought it was about time that we got to know one another. "Would you folks like to join us for a little lunch?" he asked.

I glanced over at him, then back to Dana. "Sure we would," she said, answering for the both of us. So we picnicked on the beach with them. During the next few hours we traded small pieces of our lives. They had spent holidays in the same place every year during the month of May for the past seven years. We became good friends for a short period of time and to this day I can still feel the love that they gifted us with.

After five hours in the hot Mediterranean sun, we excused ourselves from our newfound friends and went to our room for a cool shower, then headed into town to shop for a new bikini for Dana.

As we strolled along the promenade, the beach on our left and shops on our right, we came across a Vespa motor scooter rental agency. Ten minutes later, after showing them my International Driver's license and signing the necessary papers, we hopped on a bright yellow Vespa and were on our way. It's really wonderful how a new and different set of wheels can make you feel. The sense of knowing that you've just expanded your horizons provides a sense of release and new freedom.

Included in the rental was a detailed map of all the roads on the island, a city map and a full tank of gas, which the clerk at the store said would probably last us our whole vacation since the island wasn't that large – "About 41 km. from tip to tip," he said.

We headed to Dalt Vila, the upper town, winding our way up a steep slope to the cathedral square where we parked the scooter. We got off and peered over the walls that were built by the Emperor Charles V in the 16th Century. Looking down into the harbor and the sea beyond was breathtaking. From there we took a leisurely tour through the quiet meandering streets, checking out the small shops and art galleries. Later, at a small restaurant, we dined on a dish of basil, garlic and tomato angel hair pasta, dipping pieces of fresh bread into its delectable sauce while we sipped on a glass of red wine and watched the sunset from its patio. It was a very peaceful and serene scene, and from somewhere out in the labyrinth of the rustic medieval noble houses, a violin sang its evening song.

Day three: We packed up some fruit and water and decided to go find Mark and Bonnie. We headed out of town on the only highway to Sant Antoni de Portmany. About 7 km out, we connected with a road and turned right following Mark's directions, which also corresponded to our map. The road started to climb and the Vespa struggled a bit carrying the two of us. Another 4 km we came upon a small dirt road on our left that looked as if it went down to the water. A bit further we came upon a rise leading to a plateau that flattened out, opening a new vista to us. The road became very narrow, dusty and rutted. It crept precariously along the edge and seemed to be turning into nothing but a goat trail.

"Do you think we're in the right spot?" I asked Dana out of the side of my mouth, carefully keeping my eyes on the road.

"Well, Mark said it was out in the middle of nowhere." Dana replied. Just then she spotted a white structure out in the distance, an American flag flapping in the ocean breeze. "Oh, there it is."

I knew we'd found the right place as I spotted a couple of telltale VW bugs rusting away under a large willow-like tree. Comically, the tree seemed to be caring for the old relics as its branches, swaying back and forth in the wind, softly brushed the tops of the Beetles.

Approaching the villa, I honked the squeaky horn on the handle bar announcing our arrival. Instantly, from around the far corner of the building, came two pure white German Shepherds barking their disapproval of the surprise intrusion.

"Uh, oh, I hope they're friendly," I said.

"You'd better hope," Dana agreed, as I felt her tense up and grab me closer.

"Good dogs, good dogs," I pleaded.

"Junior, Jepson, HEEL!" I heard someone yell out with a stern command. The dogs stopped in their tracks, but that didn't stop them from showing us their fangs, letting us know that they meant to protect their territory.

"Stay still," the voice warned. We did.

Around the same corner came their owner. As he approached, he calmed the animals with an assuring touch. They whined slightly, licked their chops and lay down to watch us.

"You must be Don and Dana," he greeted us.

"We are. Sorry to cause a row," I said.

"It's all right. They were just doing what they were trained to do. We seldom get visitors out here."

"I can see why. Looks like it's the end of the road."

"It's the end, but with a new beginning," he added with a bit of his wisdom.

"My name is Eric. Welcome, come on in and meet the ole' lady," he said extending his hand out in greeting. He ushered us into the structure, it was as if we were suspended in mid-air, floating; for as far as the eye could see, a blue sapphire sea spread out before us into infinity.

"Debra, we have guests," Eric called out.

A body rose up off a chaise lounge out on the cantilevered deck, and a beautiful ebony black woman drifted into the main room of the house. I was taken aback, but I melted when she approached me and took me into her arms and whispered a warm "Welcome" into my ear. From that moment on, she held me completely under her spell.

Eric beckoned us out onto the overhanging veranda. We approached the wrought iron railing and peered over its edge. Far below, close to the water's edge, we could see two naked bodies relaxing in a water-filled crater carved out of volcanic rock.

"That's Mark and Bonnie down there. You ought to go join them," he said as he let out a loud whistle and waved to their now upturned heads. "Don and Dana," he shouted pointing to our heads.

"Send them down!" Mark's voice—somewhat muted by the crashing of the waves far below—drifted up to us on the wind.

"There's your invite, darlings," Debra breathed out seductively from behind us. "You tool on down der on your little Vespa, mon, and we be joining you soon." (Jamaican?) I wondered.

"Just go back to the last road you passed. That'll take you down to the baths," added Eric.

We smiled, hopped onto "Mellow Yellow," and off we went down to the Roman baths. I had previously read about these baths in a travel brochure on Ibiza. They were wonders of nature, carved out of the volcanic rock by thousands and thousands of tide changes that were prominent on this side of the island. They were discovered in the 7th Century B.C. by the Carthaginians who founded a colony on the island while under Roman rule. When the tide rises in the morning, the baths are flooded with fresh seawater. As the tides subside, the pools are filled to their brims, the water warmed by the sun during the day.

As we approached Mark and Bonnie, they rose up. Their deeply tanned bodies showed no tan lines and they glistened. We stripped the clothes off our bodies, tossed them to the side in a small pile and eased into the bath. It wasn't at all salty, as I thought it would be. In fact, it was somewhat sweet to the taste and had a faint aroma.

Our friends laughed in unison. "We have added a few special ingredients," said Bonnie. "Debra, our voodoo queen up there, has gallons of her special potion blended together in white jugs that we mix with the sea water neutralizing its salt content somewhat, thereby giving us an elixir of sorts. Kind of like this iodine, baby oil, and peanut oil mixture she gave us for tanning. She spun herself around in a half circle showing off the cocoa-colored shine her skin had taken on.

"When you get out of the baths, we'll spread it all over you," she said.

"Oh joy," I thought, just as Eric and Deb arrived.

"Hello, my darlings," Deb drawled. "We've brought you some culinary delights and liquids from the Gods."

She set down a basket of goodies with one hand and held up two bottles of vino up in the air with the other. Dana and I accepted a tulip-shaped glass full of the white intoxicator and, with that, everyone slipped back naked into the baths and the party began.

Two days later as we were putting along on the scooter to the Bay of Talamanca, Dana and I talked and laughed about our adventure here so far on the isle of Ibiza. Arriving back at our hotel room we spent that day most of the next doing the same. Around midnight of the second night we headed into town to The Cave, a late-night disco. It was rated as being the ultimate highlight of all the happenings on the island and, of course, Debra's eyes had lit up when we asked her about it. "Oh, darlings, you'll get totally lost in its craziness," she said.

The Cave's red neon sign cast a sinister light upon a large heavy planked and iron-hinged door. Outside, waiting for entry, was a line of bizarre people that looked totally outrageous in their costumes, makeup and hair. Earlier that day we had run into a buxom, redheaded, freckled-faced college dropout from Des Moines, Iowa, and she had programmed us ahead of time. She'd clued us in on how to get accepted into the club, so we had dressed accordingly. We watched as some were let in and others were told to come back later. As the line moved up, we waited with heavy anxieties. We chatted with the couple ahead of us, introducing ourselves. Miles and Jewel reciprocated with a heavy English drawl.

"So delighted to make your acquaintance. Miles Howard, actually people like to call me 'Lovely.'" The Amazonian creature next to him extended her hand back over her shoulder for us to touch as we moved forward in line. They were from England and they vacationed on the island often. When they found out it was to be our first experience at the Cave, Lovely flashed us back an amused smile.

"Well, by all means we have to make sure you get in. Join us; we'll become a foursome. I've got clout and persuasion," he added, waving a loose stack of greenbacks in his right hand. We moved up to the door. Lovely rapped and a small visitor-viewing window slid open revealing a small part of one's head with a large brown eyeball.

"It's Lovely here, it 'tis, with me bird, and a pair of hips from the States."

The window closed part way. "It's Lovely, the pimp," a knowing voice said.

"Let him in, and his friends, also," another said. The window closed, the door opened, we were in. But the "pimp" part made me wonder.

Once the door closed behind us we found ourselves in a foyer where we were again scrutinized. When they were satisfied that we wouldn't be any trouble, a big black bouncer who weighed about 350 pounds parted heavy thick burgundy drapes and we followed Lovely and Jewel into the inner sanctum of the club.

Wow!!! It was immense. We had entered a giant underground cavern that rumbled with circus-like activity. I had been to many nightclubs, discos, fancy dance halls, honkytonks, jazz hot spots, etc. etc., but this was the big daddy of them all. I felt Dana's grasp on my hand tighten. Reacting, I bent my head down to hers and said, "It is really wild and crazy—but it looks totally in control."

"Don't worry, I can handle myself. It'll be a funky time," she answered.

I felt my free hand being taken by Jewel and the four of us, linked together, slipped into the abyss and melted into the action. Our bodies automatically altered themselves into movements like an undulating wave as we immersed ourselves into the fluid crowd. One was all and all were one. We entered a large chamber off to our right and fell into a world of pulsating music emphasized by brilliant colors. Here was one of the biggest discotheques in the entire universe.

Our heads began moving up and down to the beat as we pressed ourselves into the crowd on a large flexible Plexiglas floor, entering the wild, weird, wonderful world of European disco. Flashing colored lights bounced up from underneath our feet, exploding into simulated water splashes when they hit the surface. From above, blue and silver strobe lights synchronized with the drumbeat flashed down on us like drops of dissipating rain. Entranced, I looked into Dana's eyes. I could sense that she was slowly drifting away from me. Her pupils were nonexistent as the blue and silver sparkles flashed off her corneas. Slowly, we were being stirred into a thick soup of humanity.

I looked around me; more heads were bobbing up and down, seemingly in unison and in all sorts of abandonment. Each different, some were crowned with bright yellow, pink, or purple-colored Afro wigs, others' faces were painted in wild colorful theatrical makeup. Some were costumed to the hilt and a few were almost bare-assed naked. A small group controlled the center of the dance floor, their bodies painted white specifically for the black light strobes. The blues danced off the whites enhancing their sensuous movements that were somewhat X-rated. I gazed around for eye contact and got hits from all corners—a smile here—a stare over there. Some I acknowledged; others, I ignored.

From around the perimeter of the cave's dome above the dance floor, a foggy mist was shooting out of small tubes hung from its craggy ceiling. Then from the sidewalls, low to the ground, light soap bubbles were blasting out from other hidden tubes. Soon the dance floor was awash with silver-blue rainbow-colored soap bubbles mixing with the foggy mist. They softly caressed our bodies, bursting upon contact and emitting a perfumed fragrance that drifted into the atmosphere.

At some time during my spaced-out observations, Dana's hand had slipped away and I was now holding on to Jewel's. Not that I minded, Jewel was indeed what her name implied and I fell into the burning ring of fire. We gyrated and grinded our bodies together, lost in a time warp of total insanity until we were drenched in perspiration. Sweet body odors drifted all around us mixed with exotic perfumes creating the musk smell of passion.

After what seemed to be a very long time, Jewel started leading me off the floor. Once out of the mass, we climbed up a flight of stairs carved into one of the walls. Above, there was a whole new system of smaller caverns holding a series of alcoves that ran along a corridor that traveled far back into the cave.

She evidently had a purpose and knew where she was going so I just let her drag me along. Why not? We passed people sitting on Turkish rugs smoking hashish out of water-cooled hookah pipes. I saw lots of couples making out and openly touching each other. There were attendants with drinks and silver trays of hashish, kef and other smokable drugs casually walking around servicing people's wants and desires. We took a hard left and then another and came to a dead end. There, sitting in a lavishly decorated Bedouin-style, shell shaped alcove, were Lovely and Dana. Damn!

Lovely fluffed up some large silk pillows and patted them, beckoning us to join them. We flopped down into the nest. He had a magnum of champagne cooling in a silver bucket next to him.

"Taste of the bubbly?" He pulled two cold glasses out of the bucket and offered them to Jewel and me. We accepted as he took the large bottle and filled our glasses and then refilled his and Dana's.

"To the night and whatever it may bring," he toasted, and we all clicked our glasses together and sipped the bubbly. The carbonated fizzed bubbles tickling our nostrils were a special treat. Lovely purchased some kef and we shared a water pipe, taking deep pulls on the lengthy tube that was filled with white smoke. "POW!!" It was smooth. Soon we were all floating. The rest of the night and into the morning was all lost in a time warp. All I remember is that finally I could hear less noise and I felt like I'd just missed the last train out of town. I picked myself up and had to shake Dana who had passed out. Lovely and Jewel were nowhere to be found.

"Dana," I half whispered. "Let's get out of here." I helped her up; she staggered and fell back into the pile of silk pillows pulling me with her.

"Oh, God," she said. "What truck ran over me? Did you get its license?"

"Funny girl. Come, try again." I got up and forcefully pulled her back to her feet. She wrapped her arms around me like a war casualty and, with her on my back, I dragged her through the cavern's passages. There were a few people still hanging on. Small Spanish women were sweeping and mopping around them. We reached the door to the foyer and a solemn-faced bouncer pushed it open for us.

"Had enough?" he asked.

"Yup," I answered walking past him. I pushed the big wooden outer door open and we were shocked with the day's bright, hot Mediterranean sun. It was 8 a.m. Sunday morning.

We trudged down the hill into the village and discovered a proprietor just opening up his restaurant. He scooted open it's bright, blue painted door with his foot while his hands latched it to the wall with a small hook. There were a few people standing outside, waiting to grab their favorite table. You could tell they were locals as they greeted the restaurateur, his wife and the waiter with hugs and kisses. We took the hint and followed suit. More impulsive hugs and kisses but accepted with warmth.

Another table and two chairs appeared from inside the restaurant for us and were placed on the small patio next to the locals. They completely ignored us and were quite loud and excitable. It was hard not to overhear their conversation. In my subconscious I picked up their jests and some of their names, as Dana and I tried to relate to the previous evening. We ordered Moroccan coffee with lots of raw sugar and goat's milk, a fresh fruit plate and two croissants.

Our neighbors were smoking Turkish cigarettes. Their second-hand smoke was drifting in our direction.

"Excuse me." I said to a turbaned-headed black woman. "Could I bum one of those from you? They smell rather sweet and would probably go good with my cup of coffee."

She looked down her nose at me at first and then tossed her head back in laughter.

"Oh, darlin', now I recognize you. You da one was wit Jewel on da dance floor last night. You do got da moves, darlin', you do got da moves."

She pounded the tight pack against her hand, slipped a smoke out and handed it to me.

"Careful not to inhale too deeply, darlin', they a bit harsh, unlike your American Marlboros" she warned.

"You know Jewel?" I asked.

"And Lovely."

"He got Dana and me into the Cave last night."

"That's good, darlin', tis sometimes hard for tourist types to get let in."

I lit my cigarette, took a drag and blew the smoke up into the air. "Not bad." I said. " A bit rough on the throat."

"Oh, you get used to them," one of her companions said. "Either that or pass out." They all chuckled.

"Where do you know Lovely from?" I asked.

"From da streets of London. I was part of his crib until I latched onto a sugar daddy." She smiled and put her butt out in an ashtray on the table. "But we be still best of friends, yes indeed."

"I wonder if we'll run into him and Jewel again. I'd like to thank him for last night. He pretty much treated Dana and me," I said, nodding my head towards Dana, who had remained silent during most of our conversation.

"I think he treated us because he wanted some of that hot Italian loving," she finally spoke up.

"Did he slip you a 'Mickey', my child?" she asked.

"All I know is that I passed out, and now I have one hell of a headache." Dana cupped her forehead into her palms and slowly shook her head.

"You got ta watch da little bugger sometime, but maybe you just had too much kef and champagne."

"Maybe," Dana answered.

"Well, maybe best you ask him fer yer self. Come to dis address tomorrow afternoon. We all be havin' a London farewell party. Lovely and Jewel, they be dere. You could surprise 'em, Okay?

"Okay," we answered in unison.

She wrote down an address on the inside of a book of matches and handed it to me. "You be wantin' to grab a taxi–it's a bit out of town."

"Oh, we got a scooter and a map. I'll find it." I said.

She and her group got up to leave. She took my hand in hers and asked, "Who should we say is coming?"

"Oh, I'm sorry. I'm Don and this is Dana."

"Pleased," she said. "Just say you a guest of Queen La Angelo. That'll get-cha in da door."

She squeezed my hand, turned and floated away with her entourage. I leaned back in my chair and let out a long sigh. "Small world."

"Isn't it, though," Dana said.

I paid the bill and we got up and left.

That day we just vegged at the beach. We were both exhausted from the previous evening's events and needed a full day and night to recuperate. The next night we did go to the party. This time it was at a mansion high on the cliffs overlooking the city and surrounded by high walls. We ran into Lovely, Jewel and Queen La Angelo just as we pulled up to the front door on the Vespa.

Turned out to be one hell of a party filled with celebrities and people from all walks of life and from many different countries. The food was exquisite; the wine—smooth. Marijuana and cocaine were the social drugs. After a while, everyone was high, but seemingly in control. Sophistication seemed to rule.

Around 6 p.m. someone yelled out, "Look down below in the harbor at the pier, Lovely, your ship has come in."

Everyone gathered at the arched openings in the fountain area. Looking down at the harbor, they raised their glasses to Lovely, Jewel, Queen La Angelo and the others who this bon voyage party was for.

"Let's go to town," someone else yelled, raising his glass even higher.

"Looks like the party's over," I said to Dana.

"No, Donald, you cluck. It's just moving."

We hopped on the Vespa and joined the parade down to the pier. We were all in grand spirits, yelling and laughing at each other as we raced through the narrow streets down the hill towards town and the pier. People jumped out of our way and hugged the walls as our crazy group cascaded past them. It was just like in the movies, 'The Great Race' or 'Chitty Chitty Bang Bang'. But here we were—right in the middle of it.

As we raced madly down the main boulevard along the seaside and turned onto the wooden pier, our exuberance was suddenly curbed. Blocking our way were Spanish soldiers. Some were standing guard over bundles of what looked like cotton bales wrapped in black plastic. They wore combat fatigues and hard helmets. They held semi-automatic machine guns across their chests. Opposite the steamer on the other side of the pier was a gray Navy PT boat. In front of it was a high-powered speedboat that was being unloaded of more bales. Six Moroccan men were on their knees on the dock. Their hands were tied behind them, and their heads were wrapped in black cloth. They sat on their haunches, their heads bowed—silent.

Our intrusion of the drug bust was not welcome. Before anyone realized what was going on, the soldiers standing guard over the bales turned toward us. We all slammed on our brakes. The wooden pier was worn from years of use and somewhat slippery for our sudden action. Cars slid sideways, bouncing their occupants about. The Vespa slipped out from under me when I hit the brake too hard, tossing Dana and me down on the dock. It disappeared over the side. Oh, no! Trouble!

I jumped up only to see it disappearing into the depths, its yellow body turning to green as it sank to the bottom. Commotion abounded and I was sure there was going to be a lot of explaining to do. I immediately sobered up, my head reeling from the fall.

The Ibiza police arrived, sirens blaring, lights flashing. Yelling in Spanish to the police, a soldier rushed up pointing to us and to the water where the Vespa had disappeared. He was very angry. The police responded by holding their hands up in front of him and yelling back. He backed off. They grabbed Dana and I by our arms and escorted us to one of the waiting police cars. We were shoved in the back and the door slammed in our faces. Dana and I looked at each other, panic in our eyes, speechless. We'd heard about American tourists disappearing for years in foreign prisons because of some drug deal or misunderstanding. It never had crossed our minds that we might ever be in such a situation, but here we were. Now what?

As we were being driven away I looked out the back window and saw Lovely, Jewel, Diana, the Queen and everyone else standing in a group arguing with the police and the soldiers. I wondered what would happen to them. The scene behind us soon disappeared, and I turned my head back to look into Dana's panic-stricken eyes. I took her hand in mine and gave her a weak smile. "It'll be alright," I said. "Try not to worry."

That night, largely due to the excitement of the drug bust and a total lack of communication between our languages, we spent the night in a jail cell. Here I was again—behind bars. But my main concern was Dana. She was quite attractive, I worried that some crazy sex-starved imbecile on night duty might try to put some moves on her. I didn't notice any women matrons around to guard her, and she was taken away from me to another cell in another part of the building. I protested but went unheard.

I didn't sleep at all that night. I just waited for daybreak to see what would happen. Around nine o'clock the next morning I thought I heard a familiar voice. I got up off of the hard bunk and peered down the hallway through the bars. A door opened and in walked Diana, our hostess from the previous night, with an official-looking person dressed in a gray suit with black pinstripes. Dana was close behind, escorted by a woman police officer.

They stopped in front of my cell and stood there with their hands crossed in front of them. The officer came around them and opened my cell. He motioned me out and I stepped out into the hallway.

Diana spoke. "This is Inspector Hernandez. He is a friend of mine. I have explained the situation to him. You and Dana are free to go. We apologize for any inconvenience that we may have caused you and Dana, but it was necessary to protect you from the military. It was a pretty touchy situation out there last night. Your friends have left the island and you are asked to do the same tomorrow, by boarding the ship back to Alicante. You may have the day to yourselves to collect your wits and pack your bags. We'll take care of the recovery of the Vespa and return it to the rental company. Do you understand? I think the party's over."

"Thanks for being our savior, and we appreciate your help," I half whispered through my embarrassment. They stepped aside, I put my arm around Dana, we walked down the hall through the station and out into the bright sunshine.

"See," I whispered in her ear while I kissed it. "I told you not to worry."

Back at our hotel, we took a good long, hot shower, cleansing ourselves of the stench of the cell's musty mattresses that we had spent the night on and clearing our heads of the events leading up to our custody. I had to hold and comfort Dana, as she was visibly shaken.

That was the third time I'd spent behind bars, enclosed within a 10 x 12 cell. But it was Dana's first feel of harsh reality. I talked her into putting on her new bikini and spending the rest of the day on the beautiful Mediterranean Isle of Ibiza casually lounging and sunbathing on the beach. It worked. The worries slipped away.

Next morning, after breakfast, we dressed for our voyage back to the mainland, packed our bags, paid our hotel bill and called a taxi to take us into town. The ship, the Alicante, was a little bit fancier than the last one–faster also. I secured a stateroom for the return journey, not wanting to experience the inconvenience and discomfort that we had had on the tramp steamer on the way over.

We arrived back on the mainland, late afternoon and grabbed a taxi ride back to the campground. Pulling into the park, we saw Karen watering the flowers outside of the office.

"Morning Karen, we're back," I sang out to her.

"Oh, it's you two. And where are Mark and Bonnie?"

"I don't know, probably back on the island. We were evacuated–asked to leave the island quickly–so we couldn't say our goodbyes. Besides, we had no transportation with our rented Vespa now deep in the depths, but that's another story." Jon made dinner for all of us and we filled them in on our experiences. We all had a good laugh; it was then that Dana and I realized we were ready to move on.

We weren't doing very well in chasing the race circuit, having found that there was much more to Europe than fast cars. It didn't matter since we were having the time of our lives. And, if we didn't get caught up in many more bizarre happenings, we might–just might–make the race in Brussels on June 7 and 8. It was now June 1, 1970. ~

CHAPTER 36: CROSSING THE PYRENEES

I fired up the VW. It coughed and spit for a moment or two, then caught its rhythm and smoothed out.

"Must have had a little moisture in the carburetor," I said to Dana as I put the van in gear and we rolled out of the campground. Jon and Karen were at the gate, waving farewell. "Thanks again," I called out, and we were on our way. We headed north towards the city of Zaragoza. A bit out of Valencia we picked up a hitchhiker, a Scottish lad by the name of Ian, a short spitfire of a man with an unruly head of carrot top-like red hair. Dana slipped into the rear camping part of the bus and I pulled over to pick him up.

"I want to thank you kindly," he said in a heavily accented brogue as he hopped in the shotgun side of the van.

"Just throw your gear in the rear with Dana," I told him. We introduced ourselves and continued on our way. He turned out to be rather interesting and very jovial, a welcome companion to our trip. He kept Dana and me in stitches for the first few hours until he drifted off to sleep. Dana was under the covers in the rear bed catching some zzz's also. I drove on in silence—it felt good.

I put in about three hours of listening to the drone of the VW's engine and running gear before I got tired and stopped at the small town of Huesca, a hamlet in the foothills of the Sierra de Guara Mountains. Ian wanted to buy us dinner to help pay for the lift. So, after a small discussion, we decided to have a picnic and enjoy the fading daylight. We stopped at a roadside market and bought a bottle of wine, a loaf of fresh baked bread, some meat and cheese and sat at a roadside table and watched the sunset. It was still and quiet, a magical evening in the Tena Valley near the center of the Aragonese Pyrenees.

After dinner Ian offered to relieve me of my driving duties. I hemmed and hawed, mulling over his offer. He sensed my reluctance and fished through a small pouch in the front of his backpack coming out with a leather billfold. Opening it, he pulled out an International driver's license, proving to me that he was a capable driver.

"Okay," I said. "I am rather tired of driving this bus and could use a break." I threw him the keys and crawled in the back with Dana and lounged on the bed. We passed through the little village and did some sightseeing as we bounced about on the old brick roadways. On the way out of town I spotted an old garage—next to it, in a junkyard, were some unusual automobiles from the '30s and '40s. I salivated as we drove by, as we all know by now how much I love cars, especially the older ones. We exited out into the countryside and began our ascent into the mountains. I paid attention to his driving for a while, then the wine and sleep caught up to me and I drifted off. There was only one main road leading up the valley to the village of Panticosa, a small ski resort located in the center of the Spanish Pyrenees Mountains, and I was sure he could drone his way up the hill, just as I had droned my way up from the coast.

I wasn't asleep but kept my eyes shut in hopes of drifting off. The sway of the van, as it slowly crept its way up and around the seemingly endless curves, finally lulled me to sleep. Then we were rudely interrupted by a sideslip and a tilt. A serious tilt! The engine died.

"What the hell's happening?" I yelled to Ian as I crawled over and grasped the sliding door handle. I twisted it to OPEN and it slammed backwards fast—too fast. At the end of its run, it banged loudly; its sound echoing in the darkness. Then silence. Then we heard it—a thundering rush of water. We had slipped off the road onto an inclined strip of grass, whose rock-hard cliff's edge dropped off into–Nowhere Land.

"Grab the flashlight, Dana, and hand it to me," I said as my heart raced. We were in trouble.

"Ian, you're a dead man," I said to him in disgust.

"I'm sorry, but I thought it was a bit of flat land to camp on. My eyes were tired, it was really dark."

I could see he was more terrified than I was so I decided I'd better get going and remedy this situation before it got any worse. We slowly made our way out of the van and up onto the road. I flashed the light around and surveyed our situation. "Seems like we're going to need some help here," I said. "Looks like its rear end is up against a tree and a large boulder. Lucky you didn't go 10 feet further 'cause we'd be sucking air in another world." We walked over to the noise of the waterfall and peered over the edge. Far below we heard the force of its power echoing back to us. Man, we were lucky. I was right–another ten feet and we could have said goodbye to Hollywood.

We went back on to the road and started to walk back towards the last town. We hadn't walked 10 steps when we heard a car coming down from the top of the pass. I caught the brightness of its headlights as it entered the far end of the concrete bridge that was directly up from our "camping spot." I stepped out into the road and waved the flashlight in a large circle. I heard the driver shift down two gears when he saw my signal. Still, he slipped by us with a fair amount of speed. I could smell rubber as he hit his brakes hard, the bright red taillights lighting the woods around us. He put the car in reverse and backed up to where he could see the van and us, his headlights lighting up the scene.

It was a black Citroen, that funny French car that can raise and lower itself. Inside were a man and a woman. I bent down to talk to them.

"We slipped off the side of the road, and I think we'll need a tow truck to get us back on the pavement."

"Let me take a look," he said in English with a thick French accent. He opened his door and got out.

"Hmmm," he said, crossing his arms in front of him and stroking his salt and pepper goatee with his right hand. "I think you're right. Hop into the back seat and we'll get you down into the village and try to get you some help."

I turned to Ian. "Stay here with the flashlight and see if you can secure the van a bit more. Find some rocks or big pieces of wood and put them under the tires."

"Okay, okay," he said, shaking his carrot top head up and down.

Dana and I got into the back seat of the Citroen, exchanged names, and the four of us roared off down the mountain back to Huesca. On the ride down we made small talk. The two took this route twice a month on business between Paris and Barcelona. He spoke French, Spanish, and English and promised he could interpret for us and get us aid. I thanked him immensely and mentioned the garage I had seen earlier in the evening.

"Yes, I know the one," Franck said.

It was getting well into the night, around 10 o'clock. The town was asleep when we bumped back onto the brick road that led us to the garage. Outside, sitting on the stoop of a small house that shared a common wall with the garage sat two old men hunched over, drinking, talking and smoking. They looked up with passive interest when we drove up. We all got out and Franck approached the two men, rattling off a greeting, and apology for the late intrusion. The two men looked at each other and conversed back and forth for a minute. Then, the younger of the two got up, flipped his smoke away, hitched up his coveralls and scratched his head.

"What's up?" I asked Franck.

"Well, it seems that they do have a tow truck. It's very old and works only sporadically. But they were tinkering with it the other day and it's running fine at the moment."

He pointed to the man shuffling around the corner of the garage. "He's going to warm it up a little, check a few things, get some chains and tools and help you folks out. His name is Diego and he wants the equivalent of $25 American for his service."

"No problemo. And thanks ever so much for your help," I said reaching out and shaking his hand.

"Yes, thank you!" Dana elaborated, placing a kiss on Franck's cheek. His eyes lit up and he said, "I'll go over the details with him one more time, make sure he really understands and we'll be on our way."

Franck walked us around to where we could hear a motor sputtering to life. The mechanic was leaning over into the engine compartment adjusting the idle and the air jets on the carburetor. It started to smooth out, as we got closer. Franck held him on the shoulder with one hand as he emphasized, once again, the importance of the mission to him, looking him seriously in the eye. The man stood and shook his head up and down with each sentence. Then Franck shook his hand, waved goodbye to us and continued on his way. "Good luck," he said as they drove away. His wife had slept through the whole episode, opening an eye–for a moment–every now and then.

We heard a clutch grinding behind us in the silence of the night, then a movement. The next thing we saw were two round rusty amber lights emerging from the dark garage lot. Diego stopped next to us and motioned for us to hop up and in. I helped Dana step up on the rusty running board. Since it creaked under her weight, I wondered what would happen to it when I stepped on it. I lifted myself up using the side rail attached to the cab, but the running board still groaned in protest.

The inside of the cab was no better. The gauges were filthy and dimly lit. The windows were dusty and smeared, the floorboards virtually non-existent. We could see the road passing by under our feet.

"Just great," I thought. "Now I have two strangers in my life that I have to watch closely–Ian and Diego.

We started our grind back up the hill. The truck was a 1932 Reo. It smelled of age, as did Diego. He chained-smoked, hacked, and talked to himself, grunting and groaning all the way. We figured that perhaps Diego wasn't quite all there, but he'd probably driven this road a thousand times and in lot worse conditions. So, we held on.

After a grueling hour and a half–the most unpleasant ride that I had ever experienced–we finally rounded the bend that had thrown Ian into the ditch and were surprised at what we saw. The whole area was lit up like a crime scene. There were at least four cars and one semi-truck, all with their lights on. The trucker had hooked a long chain onto his bumper and was about to back up and, hopefully, pull the van back on to the road. Everyone stopped what he or she was doing when we approached in the rusty relic. They looked at our vehicle like it was some strange iron monster emerging from the past. Which–by the way–it was!

I hopped out of the truck before it came to a stop and quickly walked up to the group. I saw Ian standing next to two men, one of whom I assumed was the trucker.

"Yo, Ian, looks like we aren't lacking for assistance, are we?" I said, as I approached.

"No, blimey, first one stopped, then another, and another, then the big rig. It's been rather chaotic for near on to an hour now. I mean with all these different languages and solutions to our dilemma, no one can make a decision. I'm glad you're back. They're afraid if the semi-truck starts pulling the van forward, the rear end might slip on the damp grass and slide down and over."

"We need another chain on the rear bumper pulling the other way to take up the slack. Let me get Diego's tow truck into position."

I started shouting instructions, augmenting them with hand motions. Everyone backed off and let me take over. After many Si, Si's, and No, No's, we finally got both rigs hooked up at a 45-degree angle to each other.

"Now," I told Dana, "You direct the truck, slow and easy, and I'll handle Diego."

Dana went and stood by the trucker's door as I did the same on the other end—next to the relic.

"Okay, everyone, let's try it." The engines started. Diego set his brake, put the gearbox in neutral and transferred the power of his engine to the tow lift mechanism. The trucker released his emergency brake and put his transmission in reverse.

"Okay, now, slow and easy."

Dana and I pointed our fingers in opposite directions, using hand signals for the go-ahead. The semi moved first, bringing the van a few feet closer to the road. Clang, clang, clang, the tow truck's large sprocket gear started collecting chain links one by one. It was working!

"Okay, STOP!" I yelled. "Ian, remove those rocks and pieces of wood you put behind the front wheels so they don't get in the way."

"Okay, SLOW AND EASY AGAIN!" I yelled, and we repeated the process. Nearer and nearer to the road the van came. Everyone was holding his or her breath and then it happened!

"BRIIIIIING!" The tow truck's gear slipped, and 25-30 links of chain slipped by its cog before Diego hit the brake.

"Ohhh!" you could hear a moan from the bystanders as their heads twisted to the sound of the VW hitting the end of the slack. "Karrrrrrrrumph!" It stopped, slightly teetering, hanging near to the edge.

"Ahhh," a sigh of relief rushed from the same. My heart also skipped a beat and Dana finished it off with a loud shriek! This all happened in an instant, but it held. Thank God!

We regrouped, and together we slowly inched that little bus up the hill. Everybody applauded as all four wheels once again arrived back on the blacktop.

I ran over, hopped in, started the engine and moved it as far on the other side of the road as I could get it.

We all gathered around, hugging, laughing, and wishing each other good luck and thank you. They drifted off into the night; we could see their lights bouncing off the curves far below, long after the sound of their engines had disappeared. Soon, we were all alone and once again we heard the thunder of the waterfalls.

"Let's get out of here," I said. We hopped in, fired it up and off we went to the summit. When we crested, we were close to the French border at the resort town of Panticosa, high in the Spanish Pyrenees Mountains. A hilltop restaurant, its red and blue neon lit sign muted in a fine mist created by hoar fog that drifted up from the opposite valley, provided us with just the right amount of illumination to allow me to pick a safe flat spot for us to park and get some sleep. Ian got out of the van with his thermal sleeping bag and went to find his own nesting place under a tree. I closed the van up tight after him, drew the curtains and Dana and I hit the sheets, safe but exhausted.

The next morning dawned to a spectacular view. Awakened by the call of cooing birds and cawing crows, I ventured out of the van as the early morning's sunrise was just peeking over the horizon. I was surprised to see remnants of concrete pillboxes dug into the side of the hills that overlooked the valley below. The World War II reminders momentarily took me back in time 25 years before. I stretched my arms high to the sky and with a large yawn and a shake of the head went back to wake Dana to experience the moment.

She slipped on the rumpled clothes she had hastily discarded on the floor a few hours earlier and rallied. Stepping out onto the terra firma, she matched my last motions, stretching, yawning, and shaking the sleep out of her head.

"We're right up here on top of the world, aren't we?" she said. "Look at that valley below us. There's a village down there with a beautiful church steeple." Just then Ian came up from the side of the hill to join us, his sleeping bag wrapped around him like an Indian blanket.

"Come on you two, I'll treat you both to an alpine breakfast," I offered.

The restaurant hut was very small, but warm and cozy inside. A fireplace at one end crackled out a soft welcoming sound, the dry pine logs emitting a fragrance that mixed well with the thick pieces of ham sizzling on the grill. The cook/waitress was the first to look up as we entered. "Buenos Dias," she greeted us, wiping the end of her blackened, silver steel spatula on the iron grease trap on the end of the grill.

"Buenos Dias," we chimed back.

A small group of locals were seated around a horseshoe-shaped eating counter. Their heads all turned away from their plates and cups of coffee as they gave us a curious look.

"Hippies," one grizzled, hunched old man mumbled as his gaze returned to the large white porcelain cup filled with steaming black liquid in front of him. The lady cook looked over at him and bombarded him with a scolding, shaking the spatula in the air at him. He put his lips back on the brim of the cup, still mumbling inaudibly under his breath

"Don't mind him," she said in broken English, the index finger of her free hand circling the sign for craziness around her brain. "You sit down by the fire and I'll get your breakfast order."

We moved around the counter and pulled the wooden chairs away from under the table, scraping them on the plank floor as their heaviness protested their being moved. We sat down and she brought over three old wrinkled, well-used, greased-spotted menus.

The corn cakes and ham that one of the patrons was devouring smelt divine, so I ordered up the same. Dana had scrambled eggs with goat cheese, and Ian went for the local porridge, a sort of oatmeal with heavy cream. All were delicious. During breakfast we gabbed about the events of the previous night, laughing at some of the incidents and drawing breaths of relief at others. Over coffee we discussed the trip down into the valley and our entrance into France. I mentioned the fact that I did have one contact to make in Paris and dug out a sheep-eared piece of paper from the depths of my billfold with Madame Chantal Larue's address and phone number.

Dana looked at me suspiciously. "How come you never mentioned this before?" she asked me.

"So much has happened on this trip that it had completely slipped my mind until a minute ago when Paris entered the picture," I fibbed, not wanting to disclose the fact that this woman had been popping into my mind for some time now.

"Uh huh," Dana uttered, disbelieving. "Just slipped your mind, I'm sure."

"Really, she's just someone who was a customer of mine once back at my salon. She was a visiting relative of one of my regular clients. She knew I was going on this trip and that I might be in Paris. She asked me to look her up if I was." I tried to be nonchalant.

"Uh huh," Dana uttered again, still not thoroughly convinced of my innocence.

Ian had slid his chair a little behind Dana. He looked at me and rolled his eyes as if to say, "You'd better leave this one alone."

I took the hint and said, "Well, maybe we'd better be on our way." We drained our coffee cups. I left a small pile of coins on the table that I was sure would more than cover the bill, we scraped back our chairs from the table, thanked the cook/waitress and left.

We retrieved Ian's sleeping bag, threw it into the van, loaded up and headed on down the road. We were in no hurry so we stopped in the village in the valley below to view the 16th century church whose steeple we'd seen from up above. There was a certain old-world charm about the whole village, and I felt very reverent and comforted as we walked off our breakfast around its tight winding streets, marveling at the unique architecture, a mixed bag of Spanish, French, and Bavarian tastes all blending together in unity.

The sun was bright, bringing out vivid colors of the surrounding mountains and countryside as we continued on our way. Once again we were in another country, France. Now it was Oui-oui instead of Si-si. We traveled on, passing through many valleys, one appropriately called the Cirque de Gavarnie as it was carved in a natural horseshoe shape with a 400-meter waterfall cascading down from the apex of a box canyon.

After a stretch of flat land, we drove into the mountains, stopping to soak our feet in the natural hot spring waters of Ax-les-Thermes, world famous for its therapeutic hot sulfur spring-fed waters. Arthritic people from all over came to soak their aches and pains away in its many health spas. We picked up an informational brochure and I counted more than 60 different pools and spas to choose from. We settled on a small public foot soaker fed by a pipe coming out of the side of an old stone bridge that crossed the Ariége River. It was soothing and relaxing, after we lunched at a sidewalk café, inhaling down quickly its fresh baked bread with cheese, grapes and red wine. The sun was at its peak and we sat back in the white plastic chairs and let it engulf us. The wine and food intensified the ambiance of the moment. I never wanted to leave this lovely, clean, friendly, wonderful town. I let my mind wander and for the moment this was home. I imagined myself in a past life living here, and this was my return visit. I was brought out of my daydreaming when Dana, antsy to get underway, shook me gently and said:

"Don, we should leave soon if we're ever going to get to Paris."

Reluctantly I pushed myself up from my slouched back position, sighed and said, "Okay."

Ian looked at both of us.

"Coming, Ian?" I asked.

He stretched and sighed, also. "No, I think it's as far as I'm going today, and maybe even the next day, and the next, and the next."

"I know the feeling," I replied, "I feel the same way."

We hugged and wished one another bon voyage and went our separate ways. ∼

CHAPTER 37: PARIS

Two days later, June 5th, we entered the teeming metropolis of Paris, a true metamorphosis from the serenity of the mountain town of Ax-les-Thermes. I joined the parade of traffic on the Avenue Des Champs-Élysées heading towards the Arc de Triomphe as Dana examined the tour book and the city map in search of a camping RV park that we'd been told about.

Horns, sirens, bells and whistles, and the clinking and clanging of public transporters engulfed our ears. The movement about us was erratic, but in order, streaming by me on all four sides, left, right, front and back. Keeping pace with the flow of traffic, while paying attention to the somewhat comical antics of the French drivers, was a total disruptive cultural shock.

"You found the way to the campground yet?" I asked Dana. "I don't think I can take too much more of this traffic commotion."

"I see a little red tent mark here on the map, next to the river about three kilometers further up the road," she said as her finger traced a line on the face of the map. "Turn left up here, any of these streets will take you to the river."

A few city blocks down we ran into a concrete barrier that ran alongside the River Seine.

"I guess I should turn right?" I asked.

"Yes, it should be along this street somewhere up ahead."

We went about half a mile along the river and found a little inconspicuous trailer haven hidden in a park-like atmosphere, nestled in between a row of apartment complexes, seemingly way out of place. We could see the small yellow flag out front with the image of a trailer appliquéd in black silk. I pulled in and once again was reminiscent of the spot we stumbled upon in the heart of Rome. Here was another off the beaten path hidden refuge, right in the middle of a major city. I spotted a tiny white house with blue shutters and a red tiled roof in the rear of the park. I pulled into an open space in front of it, and sure enough, there was a small red neon sign with the words No Vacancy shining above its doorway; the good news was that the No part wasn't lit up. Yea! I shut off the engine; the compression in its chambers backed up a revolution and farted it out one last gasp. The noise brought out the proprietor.

"Bonjour Monsieur," he greeted, a bright smile on his face.

"Bonjour, do you have a vacancy?" I asked.

"Oui, a tiny spot next to us," he said in perfect English pointing to the space.

I restarted the engine and pulled into the spot he'd pointed out. We got settled and I walked along a line of large bushes that bordered us from the house, back to its front door. I knocked softly. It was answered by a sweet voice from inside. "Entrée." I slowly opened the door and stepped inside. A beautiful curly-headed woman sitting at a small round, dining room smiled up at me.

"Oh, you must be the Americans that Jacques told me about," she said in broken English—unlike Jacques' perfect pronunciation. "He'll be right out, he's in the loo." She took one long last drag of the cigarette she was smoking and stubbed it out in a mother-of-pearl seashell that was being used as an ashtray.

I heard a flush and the bathroom door opened as Jacques came out still zipping up the fly on his pants.

"Oh, I didn't know we had company," he said rather nonchalantly. "Sit down, sit down." He rattled on, as he pulled a cushioned wrought iron chair away from the table and invited me to settle into it. He motioned to the woman seated across from me. "My wife, Mimi." I reached over and took her hand in mine and kissed it, the French way. "Charmed, I'm sure." I said smiling into licentious looking eyes. She fluttered her lashes answering playfully. "Merci Monsieur."

"My wife is a flirt." Jacques said with a smile. "It comes with the job. She's a dancer at the fabulous Crazy Horse Saloon—right here in good ole gay Paree."

"I 'ave to keep zee coo-stu-mers smiling," she added, rising up from her perch.

"Yes, you do my lovely, and you'd better be on your way," Jacques said as he patted her on the rear. "She does the early show, I don't like her out till all hours of the morning."

"Well maybe I'd better sign up and I'll be on my way," I said.

"If you'd like, come over later and we'll visit further. Mimi doesn't get home till a little after midnight," Jacques offered. "I would relish any new, or different conversation."

"Maybe I will, thanks," I said. I signed the register, paid him for a couple of nights stay, and went back to the van. Dana had our little tube all reorganized and she looked exhausted.

"I just had a little snack out of the fridge," she said, "now I'm going to take a siesta. These last few days have taken their toll on me."

"I know what you mean, but I've just been recharged by that wiry little guy next door and he's invited me back over to have a little gab session with him. I'm sure that he'll be an encyclopedia of information. I'll grab a quick bite and get out of your way."

Dana crawled between the sheets. I munched on a few vittles and left to go visit Jacques.

Jacques Belle was his full name. His father, a Frenchman, was a Minister of Finance in one of the French provinces where they had originated. The family had owned the property that the RV Park was located on next to the Seine River for over forty years. Their wealth came from a very large successful farm, whose profits were shared with the third-generation tenant farmer, most going to Jacques' father. No small wonder his father was Minister of Finance.

His mother was born and raised in England and Jacques had been educated in Lancaster, England, which explained his perfect English. He and Mimi traveled quite a bit. His cousin Charmaine shared the responsibility of running the park, allowing them to split their times to do so. They recently had traveled to Sun Valley, Idaho, to do some skiing, which he had been doing since he was four years old. He had a childhood friend now living there who had been recruited from the French alpine village of Chamonix to coach the American women's Olympic ski team. His name was Michel—they had become friends because of their mutual interest in skiing and automobiles.

Jacques drove a BMW. He said he loved the German technology in cars much more than the "Frenchies' toys," as he put it. He felt there was no comparison. He loved speed, in his cars, his women, and on the slopes. In fact, he was just that—a very speedy fellow. If you didn't know him, you might think that he was high on some drug. But he was just a high-energy type of person. He was probably one of the most articulate people I had ever met. His vocabulary was far beyond my reach, and I felt a dictionary would be very helpful in trying to fully understand what he was saying. So, during our conversations—I would fake it—uttering a timely uh huh, or an OK—and just let him ramble on. If I felt I needed to really know what he was trying to convey to me, I would ask him to please repeat it back to me, only slower, and in layman's terms. Then he would just beat around the bush in another direction. I never felt stupid; it was just that he was much more educated, or at least pretended to be.

Mimi was a city girl, born and raised in Paris on the left bank, the "artsy-fartsy" part of town. Her parents were both artists, her father a painter, her mother a stage actress, and Mimi had followed right behind in her mother's footsteps. She was very vivacious and had danced and acted all her life since the age of four. Her passion now was that she was one of the femme fatale performers at the infamous Crazy Horse Saloon, one of the few survivors of the heydays of the World War II supper club revues. Others in that realm were the Lido, the Folies Bergere, and the Moulin Rouge. It was considered then, as well as it is now, by many aficionados to be the best semi-nude show in the city, featuring on stage, variety acts and performances of many talented and beautiful women on. Mimi was also an avid skier, a clairvoyant and a professional masseuse.

I learned their whole life story in a period of little less than three hours. I don't know if he was trying to impress me or was just spilling his guts out. After all—he did have a captive audience of one—me. Also, the fact that we consumed a full six-pack of strong home brewed beer that one of his cohorts kept him supplied with, might have added to the looseness. I was just about to tell him a bit about myself when Mimi arrived back home.

"Jacques!" she said as she stepped through the door, her hands on her hips and a scolding look upon her face.

Oops, I thought, he's in trouble. I immediately exited, stumbling as I tripped on out to the van, and passed out as soon as my head hit the pillow.

"Jeez, you reek. Did you two boys have too much fun last night?" Were the first words to greet me the next morning. Dana was sitting on the van's floor with the sliding door opened, her feet on the ground and a cup of tea in her hand.

"You might say that," I answered, quietly.

"Mimi came over a moment ago and told me the state she found you two in when she came home last night."

"Yeah, well, we kind of got carried away drinking his home brew."

"And he talked your ear off, I understand."

"Yes, he barraged me with his seeming knowledge of a million things, especially the molecular structure of the spring water that went into the beer and the fermenting process."

"Well, she wanted to apologize to you for her flair-up and has invited us over for croissants and coffee."

"OK, I'll get up."

"The showers are over there." Dana pointed to a small white building hiding behind their house.

In the shower, I let the water beat against my brain until I felt the hot water suddenly go cold. That really brought me back to reality. I shut off its flow and wiped myself down while listening to the birds singing in the trees mixed in with the hum of the city, hidden from view. I slipped on a pair of shorts and a white tank top that I'd bought in Monaco. It had a Formula One racecar on it and the words 1970 GRAND PRIX of MONACO. Wrapping my wet towel around my neck, I grabbed my ditty bag and went back to the van, ready to meet another day.

Jacques, Mimi and Dana were sitting at a small round white patio table with a green, red and white (the colors of France's flag) umbrella shading them from the morning's sun.

"Come on over, my friend, and join us." Jacques said with spirit, beckoning to me with a wave of his hand. I dropped my toilet kit and wet towel off at the van and did so. As we sat and conversed, the park's other inhabitants one after another, stopped by to say hello and meet us.

"Quite the friendly little group of people you have here," I commented.

"Oh yes, Jacques is very good at profiling individuals within minutes of meeting them. He doesn't let just anybody hang out here," Mimi said, with a reassuring nod of her head.

"Well then I feel very fortunate that Dana and I have been accepted into the fold."

"And I liked the appearance you both presented when you first arrived," Jacques added. "Now what are your plans?"

"Some sightseeing for sure," I replied. "You know, the Louvre, the Arc de Triomphe, the Cathedral of Notre Dame, some nightlife, and we have to check our post as we haven't heard a word from anyone in the States for quite some time. Another reason I happened to be here for—is—there's a Grande Dame of a woman I met back in the States that I need to look up." Dana shot a sharp glance at me when I said I, rather than we, which I purposely chose to ignore.

"A Grande Dame? Interesting, what's her name? We just might know her," Mimi said.

"Her name's Madame Chantal Larue," I answered.

"Chantal Larue! But of course," Jacques blurted out. "She is a worthy dame of discreet years and optimum property. She is indeed the Grande dame of Grande dames."

"Really?" I said.

"Yes, really," Mimi elaborated. "She's quite the woman, well known among the elite of Paris, a baroness I believe, as she was once married to a man of title—now deceased. Her influences draw men to her even though she is now in her early seventies. She lives on the left bank in the luxurious hotel Relais Christine. It's on a quiet street between the Seine and Boulevard St. Germain. When her husband died, he left her the suite to reside in for the rest of her life. They do that now you know. She is the only permanent resident, treated like a queen from my understanding, as her living there is a draw to other influential peoples of her category. Jacques and I could run you by there if you'd like."

"Well I'm certainly not going to surprise her. Proper etiquette and all, but I would like to call her first to see if she remembers me and let her know I'm in town."

"We can do that. Jacques, go get the phone and bring it out here."

Jacques went into the house, returning moments later with a white antique cradle phone attached to a long line, which dragged along behind it. He set it down on the table.

I dug into my billfold, extracted the dog-eared slip of paper and handed it to Mimi.

"Why don't you let me call? I'm sure her man servant will answer, it'll be easier for me to get the information to her."

She dialed the number and spoke to someone in French. Mimi put her hand over the mouthpiece. "She's very tired, and now resting."

"Tell him we'll ring up again tomorrow around noon, if that's all right."

She passed along the message and told me that he said she would be expecting the call.

"Thank you for doing that. At least she knows now that I'm in town." I said.

"'Tis no problema," she answered, mixing her languages.

We finished our coffees while gleaning information from the two of them about the easiest way to get around Paris. Jacques gave us a Metro bus schedule, which would prove to be a great help, as Paris is a huge city. Next, he wrote down in French our present location, just in case we wanted to grab a taxi for a quick return. He added the location of the post office where our mail had been sent to General Delivery.

We each slipped a daypack around our shoulders. Mine held the usual items, camera, language translation booklet, a visitor's brochure, a change of outer clothing, some fruit and a bottle of water. Dana, never one to be without her makeup, stuffed hers with an assortment of cosmetic items, a change of clothing, an extra pair of shoes, a fold up floppy hat, and a sketchpad and pencil. She had recently decided to exercise the artistic side of her brain.

It was a beautiful bright sunny day. We were both excited to go out and mingle with the masses. We walked along the River Seine toward the Route de l' Hippodrome, one of the main thoroughfares where we could get transportation into the center of the city. As we strolled, we engrossed ourselves in the bustle of activity that surrounded us. Long, double deck tour boats with lounge chairs on both decks cruised by us on the river, loudspeakers calling out the points of interest as they slowly chugged along. There were pedestrians, motor scooters, small automobiles, souvenirs and food vendors everywhere we looked. When this city decided to wake up, it did it with a vengeance!

I saw a group of tourists, dressed in polyester suits, t-shirts with superfluous sayings printed on them, bright colored flowered dresses, strange hats, cameras hanging around their necks, and their noses stuck in information booklets, all gabbing away. They were standing in line along the side of a big black diesel bus, its engine softly idling away, slowly shuffling their way up to the stairs that led into its interior. I walked around to the front and saw a sign that said MUSEE du LOUVRE.

The uniformed bus driver, his black beret tilted off to one side, was standing on the sidewalk, his back to us, seemingly bored, smoking a cigarette, gazing off into space, not paying any attention to the loading. We spotted a couple with matching blue denim shirts on, with the word Minnesota and their first names, Betty and Bob, embroidered in red thread on their left front pockets.

"Dana," I whispered, "let's sneak on this bus. It's going to the Louvre, so we might as well start there."

Dana, always one to take a chance with me, snuggled closer to me and whispered, "Let's go for it."

"Disguises," I suggested, slipping on my dark sunglasses.

"Good idea," Dana agreed as she dug out her folded up floppy hat from her pack and pulled it low over her eyes.

We closed ranks behind the Minnesota couple. I nonchalantly started a friendly conversation with them. At first they looked back at us with wary eyes, but as soon as I told them I was from St. Paul, Minnesota, they readily accepted us as part of the group. With our backs to the bus driver, we shuffled along with the rest of them. A few stragglers fell in behind us, closing the gap as we blended in.

Boarding the bus, I headed straight to the back. The eyes of those already seated, followed our intrusion with curiosity. I remained totally optimistic, smiling and greeting them as we passed by. None said a word to us or questioned our joining them. We faded away into the far corner and slumped down in our seat, hoping the bus didn't hold a full load and we'd have to relinquish our place.

As the bus filled, low conversation floated around among the tour group. We remained quiet and snuggled up close like lovers. No one paid us any attention. As the last person got on the bus, the bus driver followed close behind. He immediately sat in his seat, surveyed the group with a quick glance in the rear-view mirror. Seemingly satisfied, he closed the door, pulling on the lever that extended out to it, released the air brakes, put it in gear, and we were on our way. As we pulled away from the curb, I saw him put an eight-track tape into a player above his head. A prerecorded informative tour in English came on, broadcasting knowledge and facts of special interest as we rolled along. The bus company must have done these tours a million times as the timing on the tape was perfectly synchronized to every attraction.

In between sites soft music would play, allowing our driver to add his little bits of trivia. His eyes would dart back and forth from the traffic to the rear-view mirror as he paid attention to his driving while delivering his narrative. Every time he did that, I swear to God, he was checking Dana and me out, trying to figure out from where we might have materialized. But then again that might have been just my guilt complex working overtime.

When we arrived at the Louvre, everyone piled out. Being in the rear, we were the last to leave. The driver was checking a list as we disembarked. He looked at us, then back at the list, then back at us, then back at the list. I could tell that he knew he'd been conned, but there was really nothing he could do about it. I could hear him yelling French obscenities at us as we hurried away and became lost in the crowd. I'm thinking, sorry!

The Louvre was a fascinating, artistic venture into the past. A quarter of a mile or more of Masters, long forgotten but still remembered. Slashes of color laid upon canvases in a thousand different techniques. The very floors softly echoing the sounds of reverence as we drifted down the halls. To tour the Louvre is to witness the unfolding of art history from prehistoric times to the twentieth century. It is renowned as one of the world's greatest and largest art museums, packed with treasures from all countries and civilizations.

I was enthralled with some of the huge paintings that adorned its many walls. I would set myself down on a viewing bench in front of one of them and allow myself to melt into the canvas, taking in its many messages. Dana would join me in this meditative study but would soon become bored and try to hurry me along—not allowing me to linger within my thoughts. I tried to explain to her that you just don't go to the Louvre to speed past the many major milestones of civilization. But we only had so much time and hunger was creeping up on us, so I finally conceded to limit our final viewings to the Venus de Milo, Winged Victory, and Leonardo de Vinci's Mona Lisa.

As I stood in front of the Mona Lisa, I became enamored with her smile. I walked to the left of her, and then to the right of her, watching as her gaze followed my movements. I felt at peace and let out a sigh of contentment, mirroring her expression. I felt her placidity.

Dana nudged me out of my trance. "Come on, we've seen the Louvre. Let's go eat and get our mail."

I gave in, my stomach suddenly commanding attention. We walked out into the bright sunlight, transferred back into the real world. In the square, a woman was covered with pigeons as she fed them corn and seed out of a brown paper bag. One sat on top of her head, two were on her shoulders, and two or three at a time were fighting for the perch on her wrists and forearms—to be closest to the hand that held the feed. They all changed places when she tossed the feed out onto the cobblestones. We watched for a moment as each one, equally frantic in their greedy rush to fill their crops, flew around her.

I grabbed Dana's hand and rushed her across the Rue de Rivoli, the street that bordered the Louvre, to a small café on the other side with sidewalk dining, where we could still watch the "Bird Lady" and the parade of humanity coming and going from the museum.

It felt good to sit down. We started with a carafe of red wine and a fruit and cheese plate. As we discussed the day's events, I felt a bit of negative energy coming from Dana. We ate lunch and had our carafe refilled. With a slight buzz from the vino, giving me courage to ask Dana if there was something bothering her.

"Yeah, I'm a little pissed off at you," she confessed.

"And why's that?" I asked innocently, although I had an inclination.

"Well, it seems that you don't want me tagging along when you have your rendezvous with that Madame person."

"It's not that I don't want you 'tagging along.'" It's just that I felt at the time when I was shampooing and setting her hair at my salon in San Jose a few months back that she was looking forward to entertaining me when I arrived in Paris. Besides, I had never really mentioned to her that I would have a traveling companion, much less that she would be a beautiful woman, such as you." With those last, well-placed words, Dana's anger faded some.

"And besides," I continued, "she's close to her seventies."

"You're probably right," she sighed. "You know how my Italian jealousy and temper can sometimes get the best of me."

I squeezed her hand and placed a kiss upon her lips. "It'll be for only one night, and I'll probably pick up on some clues to where I can take you to have a good time."

With that she returned the gesture. She seemed to be satisfied to let me go for one night. Of course, I never mentioned the fact that I had found Madame attractive, alluring, and very interesting for an older woman.

After lunch and before continuing our sightseeing, we took a short nap on the grass of a small park across from the café. When we woke up from our little snooze, we silently read our individual mail, kept the contents to ourselves, and then continued on our way.

There are far too many famous, historical attractions to see in Paris. To mention all that we observed would once again, seem like a travelogue, and I've already mentioned this before, as it seems that I could go on forever, so I'll only mention a few.

I marveled at the buttresses of the Notre-Dame Cathedral that soared into the sky along with its magnificent façade adorned with gargoyles that peered into your soul. The Arc de Triomphe commanded a bustling view of the city's traffic grid like no other, which we could see when we climbed its stairs to a height of 164 feet and looked down onto the Champs-Élysées and the multiple other avenues that intersected into the circle that surrounded it. Napoleon planned his triumphal arch in the early eighteen hundreds to celebrate his military successes, but as empires come and go, Napoleon's had come and gone for more than twenty years before it was finally finished in 1826. France's Unknown Soldier is buried beneath its archway. A flame is rekindled every evening at 6:30 in honor of France's fallen. From this vantage point, off in the distance we could see the Eiffel Tower looming into the evening's sunset.

We checked our tourist guidebook and decided to walk from the Arc de Triumph to the Eiffel Tower, a little less than a mile away. We walked down the staircase into the chaos we had been observing from above. A traffic control light allowed us and other pedestrians to cross over the busy intersection back into the main part of the city. We chose what we thought would be the quickest and easiest way to get to the tower. We choose the Av. Marceau, a street that would lead us directly down to the Seine. Reaching the river we turned right on the Av. de New York and strolled down to the bridge that was directly in line with the gargantuan steel structure. We crossed over the bridge stopping for a moment in the middle of the Seine to observe an evening dinner cruise boat that slowly drifted towards us. Observing the merriment on the boat below us, the dining tables covered in white linen with small candles lit on each one of them, I got caught up in the romance of the moment and pulled Dana close into me for a long lingering kiss. Lovers do it in France all the time.

My eyes were still closed when I heard the loud speaker on the boat directly below us announce "L'Illumination," immediately followed by a roar of oohs and ahhs accompanied by applause that echoed back to us as the boat passed under the bridge. Releasing Dana from my embrace, we turned towards the Eiffel Tower and watched as the breathtaking nocturnal illumination was ignited. Every girder was highlighted in glorious detail, all 12,000 of them, bringing the steel structure's enormousness ever more into perspective.

"Biggest lit Christmas tree I've ever seen," Dana said.

Holding hands, our hearts filled with excitement, we playfully skipped across the rest of the bridge and onto the plaza square that boxed the tower. Here we joined the romantics It seemed that when the sun went down, a whole different variety of tourists suddenly appeared, definitely much younger, better looking and more spirited. The beautiful people rule the nights in Paris and here we were in their midst.

If the Statue of Liberty is New York, if Big Ben is London and if the Kremlin is Moscow, then the Eiffel Tower is Paris. We could feel the electricity around us. It touched us wherever we roamed. We stood under its mass and peered up into its belly. Then we walked up three flights of stairs and caught the elevator to the top.

Here, at its pinnacle, as we gazed out upon the city, we saw why Paris lives up to its moniker, La Ville Lumière, the City of Light. It was the highlight of the day and it peaked our enthusiasm. I felt Dana shiver a bit and she let out a big yawn. I put my arm around her, smiled into her eyes.

"Had enough?" I asked.

"I think so," she answered.

We took the elevator down to the square where we wandered around for a bit, wanting to savor the moment just a little bit longer. There was a crepe vendor next to a beautifully lit fountain, and we decided to indulge in some local fare. We ordered a trio of taste treats, the crab, and the chicken and for dessert, the fruit. The crepes were delicious, thin but strong enough to hold their ingredients. Their flavor, soft and delectable, a wonderful mixture of country fresh eggs and milk, mixed with the perfect amount of flour and sugar. I devoured mine within moments. They just seemed to disappear off my paper plate. They were truly a French culinary delight. My mother, Rose, made them for us, when we were kids. And that's what she called them, "French pancakes." With that— we called it a day. A line of cabs sat alongside the plaza, we grabbed the one next up and I gave the driver the address that Jacques had written down for us. He acknowledged the information and off we went back to the trailer park and a warm bed. ~

CHAPTER 38: INTO A SEPARATE NIGHT

I shook Dana awake. "Dana, Dana," I said. "Do you know what day it is?"

"I think it's Saturday," she said sleepily, not concerned. "Why?"

"It's June 7th. We're supposed to be in Brussels today and tomorrow for the big race."

"Well, we blew that one, didn't we?" she sighed.

"Yeah, but we could probably get there tomorrow for the main event, 'cause I think today is just the time trials."

She propped herself up one elbow, brushed the hair out of her eyes and said, "You know it really doesn't matter to me. I'm perfectly happy right here in Paris."

"But what about the boys, Perry and Steve? Don't you think they'll be expecting us?"

"Maybe so, but I'm sure that the race is their first priority and the two of us are the furthest from their minds." Then she added cattily, "Besides, you can't forget about your rendezvous with your Madame Chantal Larue."

I leapt on her playfully, smothering her with reassuring kisses. "You're oh so right," I said. With that, we got lost under the covers.

About an hour later, after our tussle together, I left Dana by herself so she could freshen up. I crawled out of the van and stepped into the sunlight. It was a beautiful day and I thought "Dana's right, no need to go anywhere". Jacques and Mimi were sitting at their little patio table enjoying a cup of coffee and a cigarette together. (The French love to smoke.) They waved me over to join them.

"See you made it home alright last night. Did you two have a good time in the city?" Jacques asked, his eyelids moving up and down humorously, mimicking an old Groucho Marx trait.

"We did, we did. We cultured ourselves out."

I sat down and relayed the events beginning with the tour bus episode up to the finale, watching the Eiffel Tower light up the night.

"Well, you experienced about one-fiftieth of what there is to see and do in our city, but you did hit a few of the high points," Mimi said glancing down at her watch. "It's nearing noon, shall I make your call to Madame Chantal Larue?"

I thought for a moment, welling over in my brain if I should mention the fact that I had a traveling companion or not. Mimi glanced at me, waiting for an answer to her question.

"Sorry. I was just wondering when I talk to her whether or not I should ask if I could invite Dana along?"

Jacques broke in immediately. "That's totally up to you, but if I were you, I would take this ride by myself. I think that having another female present could put a damper on the evening."

"Why don't you go have your fling and we'll keep Dana entertained." Mimi added. (I love the French attitude.)

"Ok, dial her up." I said, feeling a bit more comfortable, now that I seemed to have Jacques and Mimi on my side. Mimi hopped up and went to get the phone, giggling as she went, seemingly just as excited to make the call as I was. She was back in a flash, phone in hand, trailing the long cord behind here. She sat down at the table, crossed her legs and dialed the number, winking assuredly at me as she did.

"Bonjour Madame." She placed her hand over the mouthpiece for a moment and silently mouthed the words to me, "It's her." Turning back to the phone, she said, "Je m' appelle Madame Mimi Belle. J'appelle Monsieur Donald Yeager. Comment allez-vous?" She paused for a moment listening to the reply.

"Very well, thank you, one moment, here's Donald," Mimi answered in English. She handed the phone over to me.

"Bonjour Madame." I said politely. From the other end came the same sweet, soft voice I remembered. She respected my lack of French language skills by speaking in perfect English. Her image popped into my mind as we started to converse. She said that she was extremely pleased that I had remembered her invitation. She said I was also fortunate as my timing was impeccable because she held in her hand at that very moment an invitation to a gala Artists Ball. My heart leaped. I love a party, which by this time—if you got this far into the book—is fairly obvious!

We gabbed on, reacquainting ourselves. She inquired on how my trip through Europe was developing so far and if it met my expectations. I told her that I hadn't had any real expectations, just sort of going with the flow, but if I had had any, they would have already been far exceeded. She chuckled on the other end and said, "I can assure you that this evening should satisfy your passions."

"My, my," I thought.

"Now for the details," she said and gave me her instructions. She and her manservant, Pierre, would pick me up that evening at the entrance to the park. I was to look for a black Citroen limousine and dress as artistically "funky" as I chose. We agreed on a time, 9:00 pm, a little early to attend the Artists Ball, she said matter-of-factly, as it would probably go on till sunrise, so she felt we should cocktail and dine together first. I thanked her for the opportunity to experience what I was convinced would be a most phenomenal evening—little did I know. We said our adieus and I hung up the phone.

Jacques and Mimi were looking at me over their now empty coffee cups. Mimi was the first to break the hanging silence.

"Well?" she said, flicking the cigarette ash to the ground. She took one long drag on it and stubbed out the butt in the ashtray in front of her, indicating that she had been held in suspense long enough. "Tell us."

"I've been invited out to dinner and to an Artist's Ball," I said excitedly.

"An Artist's Ball? Of course, we know the one, and indeed, it will be a "ball!" Jacques and Mimi exclaimed loudly in unison.

Their loud voices rang through the stillness of the park carrying back to the van. I heard the sliding door slam back against its stop and Dana came stomping out her hands on her hips, an astonished look on her face.

"An Artist's Ball!" She exclaimed as she approached us, a hint of jealousy resonating in her voice.

"Oh, oh." Mimi whispered, while rolling her eyes skyward, recognizing a woman's fury and disapproval.

Dana sat down hard in the chair opposite me, her eyes half closed in slits as she glared at me. "What's this about an Artist's Ball?"

I knew I was suddenly in big trouble. I explained, trying hard to downplay the event, but I knew it wasn't going to work. Her Italian temper wouldn't accept my casualness. My stomach turned as I realized that this just might be–the beginning of the end–of our relationship. I'd screwed up. I was soon to realize the meaning of the cliché, "Hell hath no fury like a woman scorned."

The remainder of the day was tense. Dana at first didn't mind me having a date with Madame Chantal Larue–well maybe a little bit. But now that there was an invitation to an Artist's Ball, it changed the whole picture. Dana was never one to miss a party; however, she was going to miss this one and she was feeling extremely slighted. And to make matters worse, she waved her mail in my face. "My mother sent me an open return ticket from Paris to San Francisco. She thinks it's been long enough that I've been traveling around Europe with a common hairdresser. She thinks I need to come home and get serious, you know, further my career, and perhaps marry someone more appropriate. Well, I thought, this is truly the icing on a flat cake, as I knew how much her mother's influence could control her.

We stuck to ourselves most of the day, with only blurbs of small talk between us. We ate an early dinner together in silence. I picked at my food since I was to dine out later that evening. After the meal Dana busied herself primping for her evening out with Jacques and Mimi. As her transformation took place, she began to hum to herself, seemingly satisfied with what she saw in the mirror.

"Happier now?" I asked, hoping to excite some pleasantry.

"Somewhat." She sighed as she applied the last touches to her makeup. She caked black mascara on her eyelashes using a small brush, and then applied her lipstick, first bright pink out of a tube then she outlined her lips with a liquid pencil of deep purple, very dramatic. She placed a fresh Kleenex between her lips to blot them and then popped them loudly as if to say, "There, I'm finished."

"See ya. Have fun," she remarked somewhat sarcastically, as she grabbed her pink-fringed leather shoulder bag off a hook by the door and sashayed out of the van on her way over to Jacques and Mimi's. I watched her walk away, her long black hair swinging in unison with her fringed skirt. I had to admit she was quite the sight. She would have no problem having fun tonight.

Left alone, which was a rarity in itself; I popped a beer and contemplated my navel. My mind was in a kind of haze, so I had another beer. I sat back taking in the moment and enjoyed my quiet time. After an hour or so, I came out of it. I jumped up and started to busy myself getting into costume. I was most indecisive, I must have changed my ensemble five or six times, mixing, matching, or mismatching, various clothing that I had bought while in Europe along with others that had come with me. I finally decided on the "Italian Gypsy" look, the same disguise that had fooled the South African tourists we'd met in St. Mark's Square in Venice sometime back.

Once attired, I stepped outside to check myself out in the men's public facility of the park, which had a much larger mirror and brighter lighting than the van. My tan had deepened, my hair was a bit longer, so I appeared even more gypsy-like in the costume. I had draped all the copper, silver, bronze and gold jewelry I could find, around my neck and on my fingers and wrists, which enhanced the saddle tan richness of my skin. I slipped on a pair of bloomed out blue and white vertical striped pants and stuffed their bottoms into a pair of brown leather high top boots crowned with two-inch black leather bands that I had bought in Barcelona. On my upper torso I draped a cream colored, soft woven, Moroccan cotton shirt with billowing sleeves that were buttoned loosely around the wrists with pearl white bone buttons. Around my waist I tied a black silk sash scarf, borrowed from Dana's wardrobe. I was quite the striking figure, if I must say so myself. Actually, I thought, taking in the time—1970, and the place—Paris, I was not totally caricatured. In fact, I thought I looked rather like a nicely dressed young gentleman, in his early thirties, with a splash of style. ~

CHAPTER 39: A PARIS NIGHT

As I stood under the arc light outside the main entrance to the trailer park waiting for the chauffeur-driven black Citroen limousine that would soon whisk me away to the bright Paris nightlife, I watched the fracture light that bounced off the waters of the Seine River from the arc lights that lit a bridge a short ways away. Soon the headlights of a low-slung vehicle appeared from around a corner a few blocks down the street and came in my direction. I looked at my watch, right on time, as I assumed this was my chariot coming.

I was right. Seeing my dark form silhouetted under the streetlight, the extremely shiny, slant-eyed exotic mechanical creature showed its true form as it emerged from the surrounding darkness. It stopped with its rear passenger door directly in front of me. In anticipation I stepped off the curb onto the pavement as the door silently opened before me like a page in a mystery novel. I bent down and entered the semi-darkness of its interior. I was greeted with the sounds of a popping cork and the clink of a glass.

"Good evening Donald," my hostess said from the darkness of her corner. Her black-gloved hand appeared out from the shadow holding a glass offering. I took it. "Merci." Another glass, her glass, appeared out of the void. Then her face, ghost like, shrouded by a black hooded cape that she wore, appeared from the shadows—we clicked glasses, toasting "Salut," as we looked into each other's eyes over the vessels' rims. I sipped and the aroma of truly fine Champagne emanated from the rising bubbles as they burst their flavored carbonation under my nose. Heaven!

She smiled at me and then turned forward, "Pierre, Let's start at Harry's Bar."

As we drove away from the curb, the Citroen seemed to float, riding above the roadway's disturbances. The ride was so smooth that I noticed the champagne in our glasses maintained their levels. A warm feeling swept over me. The sudden awareness of where I was—and whom I was with—made me feel very privileged, as these encounters sometimes only happen once in your lifetime. I remembered then some advice one of my patrons gave me long ago; "if you get an invitation, or opportunity to visit or discover something new—do it— if you don't, it may never be presented to you again—so here I am!

Madame Chantal Larue spoke. "Donald, you don't mind if I call you Donald, do you?"

"Not in the least, ma'am, as it does sound proper and all."

"And you can call me Lily, like the flower." We clicked our glasses again, this time in a mutual agreement.

"Ah Donald," she sighed with satisfaction. "It will indeed be gratifying to an old lady to introduce the Paris nightlife to such a fine young man. "Don't you agree, Pierre?" she said, turning forward and addressing her friend.

"Yes, Madame, it can be eye opening at times," he chuckled.

I caught his eyes looking at me through the rearview mirror. He was smiling. I was beginning to like this guy, and I started to feel more comfortable.

A bit later, we pulled up to the curbside at the entrance to Harry's New York Bar, a landmark that had become famous during the pre-war years. Regulars included American writers F. Scott Fitzgerald and Ernest Hemingway who had a running battle about who was the better writer of the two. It was sacred to Papa's disciples and cronies—a gathering place for all types of artists, poets and the early bohemian types during the early 1920's. It was where the "Bloody Mary" was first concocted, and it's still the headquarters of a loosely organized fraternity of drinkers known as the International Bar Flies (IBF.) The Cuban mahogany interior dates back into the mid-nineteenth century and was shipped over lock, stock, and barrel from a tavern on Manhattan's Third Ave. There was also a basement piano bar where jazz musicians jammed until the early morning hours.

Pierre slipped the transmission into neutral, pulled on the hand brake, and left the motor running. Three attendants suddenly appeared out of the woodwork and rushed to open our doors. Pierre stepped out first, instantly growing in stature. He tossed his black chauffeur's hat, Frisbee-style, back onto the driver's seat. He rolled his shoulders, rearranging the coat of his Italian silk suit, buttoned it and ran his hands through his thick, dark head of hair. He stepped back to take Madame's hand and escort her out of the car over to where I was waiting on the sidewalk. The entrance door opened for us. We stepped into a smoky, noisy New York bar, right here in the streets of Paris and were escorted to a table with a slight rise up from the original floor, our backs to the wall. We had a commanding view of all the comings and goings, a front row seat you might say. Immediately the maitre d' was upon us, bowing up and down, a wide smile rolling up both sides of his face—a Joker's smile! He greeted us rattling off a waterfall of the fastest French dialogue I'd ever heard through somewhat clenched teeth while rubbing his hands in circles. Madame extended her right hand, which he took delicately and kissed it. She then nodded her head in my direction and introduced me. I took his extended hand and shook it; it was limp, like a wet dishrag.

His salutations completed, he turned to the crowd, raised his hands in the air and clapped three times while chanting, "Lily, Lily, Lily!" A knowing few raised their glasses and answered the call, "Lily, Lily, Lily!" She acknowledged the notoriety with a smile and a wave.

"Wow!" I half whispered to Madame, "this is quite the show."

She leaned over closer to me and said, "Let me let you in on a little secret."

Evidently, Lily was Madame's stage name back in the late forties and early fifties when she was quite the celebrity torch singer, a white Josephine Baker.

Her stardom in the music world, her involvement in the arts and her charity work spread her warmth over the face of Paris like butter on toast. She had had many lovers and had married well.

Here I was sitting in the most famous bar in Europe with a Grande Dame and a man of mystery. I felt like I was in attendance in the court of a king and queen. A constant parade of people cow-towed to them, ambling by to say hello, some stopping long enough to sprinkle in bits of humor showing how much they both were loved. I remained silent, glued in place, a smile of amusement plastered on my face. I wasn't introduced to anyone; it would have been trivial, to say the least, even if I were. I felt slightly overdressed in my "Gypsy" outfit and didn't quite fit into this crowd. I mentioned this quietly to Lily and she pooh-poohed my fears saying that it was they who were intrigued with me. "Remember," she said, "sometimes silence is golden." She made me feel much better and, after a few vodka martinis, I again melted into the scene.

As it drew closer to dinnertime, my cheeks were getting sore from the constant smiling and my stomach was rumbling. As if reading my mind, Pierre motioned to an attendant standing in the shadows of the front door. I saw him nod his head and he left through the door. We sipped the remaining liquid in our martini glasses and left.

Outside, the street scene had changed. There was more hustle and bustle, more people filling the open-air cafes, all busy watching the promenade. There was definitely a buzz in the air. This was Paris by night. Our limo was waiting, the same three men holding the doors open for us. This time I walked around to the street side to get in while Pierre helped Lily into the curbside seat that I had previously occupied. He walked to the driver's door, slipped the attendant a small wad of French francs and dropped behind the wheel. He donned his hat, turned and smiled and said, "Dîner" and off we went.

"Well, that was an experience!" I blurted out as we drove away from the curb.

"Just the beginning my dear, just the beginning," Lily answered, giving my hand a little squeeze. She chatted away giving me a touch of history as Pierre drove down the Champs-Élysées to 17 av. Franklin D. Roosevelt, to the restaurant Lasserre's location. She was proud of her city and didn't want to leave me in the dark. I listened attentively.

"Lasserre, is one of Pierre's and my favorite eating establishments. It once was a simple bistro before World War II, a rendezvous for chauffeurs. When René Lasserre purchased it after the war, it was quite dilapidated but he had a dream—now it is a legend. I'm sure you'll enjoy the degustation you're about to experience, for René is a passionate chef. Pierre will drop us off; he has a spot up the street where he will leave the car. We will wait for him in the lounge."

Pierre pulled up to the entrance and a waiting uniformed doorman bent at the waist to open Lily's door. I let myself out and rushed around to take her arm and escort her inside. The reception lounge was decorated in Louis XVI style furniture with brocaded walls. The maitre d' stepped forward and took Lily's gloved hand and directed her to a salon chair. I glanced around at the surroundings. I could see the main salon through two large white doors; it was two stories high with a mezzanine on each side. The ceiling above was painted with lamb white clouds floating in a cerulean sky. I could see the tables in the restaurant set with fine linen, fine porcelain, crystal glasses edged in gold, a silver candelabra flanked by two ceramic white doves.

"OK." I hummed to myself. "This is great." But a small touch of regret strummed at the strings of my heart. I wish I'd brought Dana. My thoughts were erased when Pierre showed up. He took Lily's hand and helped her rise off the chair.

"Come, Donald," she said, "Let us wine and dine." The maitre d' escorted us to our table.

We walked down a long aisle, tables to our left and right. I noticed, as we passed the other diners, a few men stood up from their tables and gave bows of recognition. Others raised their wine glasses when we passed by. Lily acknowledged them with a nod of the head and a sweet smile. Pierre remained sober and I kind of just tagged along. Down at the far end was one semi-round booth, seats covered in red velvet—another special table—I presumed. Lily went in first taking the center, Pierre to her right, me to her left. We now faced back down the whole salon with all tables in full view, including the entry and lounge. Once again our backs were against the wall and, for the second time tonight, I felt that I was really with someone, or two, really special people.

The menus were offered to us and the folded napkins were unruffled and dropped softly unto our laps. "I'll send André with your wine list." The maitre d' said as he started to bow out.

"And Philippe," Madame said, stopping him. "Would you mind rolling back the sky? It's such a nice evening out."

"It's no problem, Madame."

"Your wine list? Roll back the sky? Was there more to this story?" I thought—

and as if reading my mind, Lily offered an explanation.

"This restaurant has a very large wine cellar. It holds some 18,000 bottles of wine, or more, very confusing. When my late husband died, he left me with quite a large private collection. My present residence doesn't have the capacity to hold all the wines—other than a few special token bottles. The rest, Pierre and I distributed among a few of our favorite restaurants around Paris. Naturally, we pay a corkage fee for the privilege of enjoying our own spirits, but we always know the quality is going to be sublime. As for the sky—watch as the roof rolls back to reveal the real sky. We shall dine by moonlight." And sure enough, there was the Paris night sky above us.

André came with the list and it took but a moment for Lilly to make her choice. "I choose a light Beaujolais for sipping while we make our dinner selections." She smiled at me while she pulled a small pair of folded reading glasses from her purse. "I suggest the truffle salad for a starter."

"A wise choice, Lily," Pierre said. It was the first time I heard him speak her given name.

My nose was stuck in the menu. It was all in French and I was trying to decipher a word or two here and there, to no avail. I knew truffles were sniffed out of the ground by special pigs held back on leashes so they didn't devour them immediately and that they were a true delicacy.

Dinner was indeed a culinary delight. After the truffle salad we moved on; Belon oysters flavored with Chablis, fillets of sole in puff pastry, veal kidneys flambé and pigeon André Malraux. Each entrée was fully explained to us as to its preparation and accompanying flavors and spices.

Four courses, two more bottles of exquisite wines, accompanied by pleasant and intelligent conversation brought us past midnight and into the first hour of the next day. It was undoubtedly the latest, longest, most relaxing and elegant dinner engagement I was ever involved in.

I sipped my brandy while Lily excused herself to "powder her nose" and Pierre handled the check. I reached over and touched the sleeve of his jacket. "Thank you ever so much," I said. He winked at me as he placed his gold-plated pen back into the left inside pocket of his suit coat. "It's Madame's pleasure, I'm sure," he said.

We left the table and made our way back to the reception area. As we reached the lounge, Lily came out through the red leather, ladies' room door. Strutting towards us, a wide smile on her face, she slipped on her black evening gloves and hung a black beaded purse on her left wrist. She carved a high "C" in the air with her right hand waving us out the door and said quite gaily, "Come on, boys, on to Le Bataclan!" Striding in next to her, one on each side, we wrapped her arms into each one of our arms and skipped out of Lasserre. The black Citroen sat at the curb waiting, its gleaming paint job reflecting the restaurant's lighted marquee behind us. I opened the door for Lily and let her in, following behind her, and Pierre went around to the driver's side.

We drove away from the city's main area into a remote working-class neighborhood on our way to the Artists Ball. We popped another bottle of cold Cristal Champagne, and Lily once again took over as my tour guide. This time however, I noticed she was much less reserved–in fact–she was quite like a college girl out having a good time with the boys. I observed also, that Pierre was probably going to be keeping a closer protective eye on her.

Le Bataclan was originally built as a Parisian Opera House and to this day it still house's various versions of the arts. The walls and the ceiling, Lily explained, still maintained their original baroque appearance, but other than that, it had been converted into a large disco hall, now catering more to the partying crowd, the jet setters, the hip and the outrageous. (I for one, just loved the outrageous creativity some of life's characters can come up with–to repeat–Outrageous!)

The streets became narrower and darker, more like alleys, as we neared our destination. Then we emerged out into a more open area and I immediately saw where we were heading. The facade of Le Bataclan was eerily lit up with two theatrical spotlights slowly moving back and forth in a semi-circle. Long lines of party hopefuls were standing outside in quest of entry. I was somewhat concerned when I saw the scene and wondered how we were going to get past the crowd, but I knew–of course we would. Bisecting the main entrance were red velvet swag ropes between gold stanchions that separated the average joes from the elite. In front were attendants with top hats, long waistcoats and white gloves greeting the private invitation holding guests. We pulled in line.

We moved up fast and were soon at the head of the line. Two attendants rushed to open our doors and we all exited. Pierre walked Lily around the rear of the Citroen, we linked arms and together we ascended to the roped off staircase–brightly decorated with multi-colored metallic streamers. You could feel the eyes upon you–we were stars. Entering the hall, we walked up another staircase, then around a curved corridor to a private curtained opera booth overlooking the dance floor below. Here again, due to Lily and Pierre's contacts we had an exclusive unobstructed view of the whole "happening." A waiter appeared immediately after we were seated with a silver ice bucket and more Cristal Champagne. I thought, "Oh mercy."

The scene below was unbelievable, as in the Cave on Ibiza. Again, I involved myself into the loud music, flashing strobe lights, and costumed characters of all different degrees of dress or undress. The dance floor seemed to move with the rhythm, and the beat of the music, the flashing bodies intermingling with each other, all flowing together, like a wave of liquid humanity, and I wanted to be a part of it.

As if reading my mind, Lily suggested I go below and join in the festivities. She broke out her opera glasses and said, "Donald dear, go join in. Pierre and I are only observers of this craziness, we'll keep some sort of tabs on you from up here." "Oh goody!" I thought.

I left them with my heart a-thumpin', to go roam around and see what trouble I could get myself into. I parted the curtains of our special box and walked out into the frenzy. My eyes were filled with a multitude of bizarre characters. The costumes, or lack thereof, were a feast to the eyes. Feeling like the gypsy that I am, I immersed myself into the human maze. Body contact was immediate, so I fell into the rhythm. I moved among the crowd dancing with whoever was receptive to my movements. Most of the contacts were spontaneous and short lived. I held that 'just passing through' attitude. A one-on-one, eye-to-eye, connection hadn't happened yet—until a bronze maiden with emerald green eyes and long flowing black hair latched on to me. She had only a loincloth on the bottom half of her body. The remaining skin surfaces were painted in suns and moons, feathers and flowers, snakes and scorpions. She had soft moccasins on her feet, feathers in her hair and her face was painted like a cat. Her small, almost boyish, firm breasts had lightning bolts streaking out from her raised silver colored nipples. I knew instantly that this woman had chosen me for a partner. My Gypsy look had evidently attracted her to me. Fortunately, she spoke broken English and we could communicate some. I felt—tonight I needed no other—this was satisfaction! Time slipped away, we danced wild, we danced slowly, we caressed each other, and we kissed. It was as if we were the only ones in this space at this time and then—BAM! It was over.

She touched my cheek with her hand, kissed me softly on the lips and whispered, "Au revoir, mon ami," she slipped away and disappeared into the crowd. I stood there for a moment, somewhat surprised and despondent. Lost, I allowed myself to be bumped around like a rag doll until I came back to my senses. I took a deep breath, worked myself through the crowd out of the ballroom, and back upstairs to our enclosed balcony seating.

I parted the heavy curtains and surprised Pierre and Lily in each other's arms. I knew there was more to that picture than what met the eye. "Now look at you two," I said laughingly. "I'm so glad to see you together as one."

"Life ripens with age, Donald, as does love. Sit here with us and enjoy the show from our perspective." I slid a cushioned chair close to them at the table. "Have another touch of the bubbly," she offered. Pierre reached next to him and pulled a cool bottle out of the silver bucket. "Opened, only a moment ago." He said.

"Thanks, I need it after what I've just experienced."

"We know," she giggled, waving her opera glasses in the air. "We've been watching you. You're quite the knave. But where's the girl?"

"She disappeared," I said, still amazed. "Just disappeared." I leaned forward and put my empty glass on the table.

She chuckled again. "Better keep his glass full, Pierre."

I borrowed Lily's opera glasses, and for the next half hour I searched in vain for a glimpse of my feathered beauty—nothing!

It was around four in the morning when Lily decided to call it an evening. I was totally in agreement. I felt as though I'd been run through the spin cycle of a washing machine. My head throbbed from the pounding, beating music and too much fine wine and Champagne.

On the way back to the trailer park both Lily and I fell asleep. When we arrived, Pierre doused the lights and drove back to the van, which during the course of the evening I had described to him. I felt the car stop and Pierre shook me softly. My eyes popped open and I heard him whisper, "Shhhhhh, don't wake her."

"Thank you, I'll call later." I whispered back and I slipped out of one door and into another.

Dana was sleeping soundly, her breathing quite heavy. I removed my smoky, damp clothing, wrapped a towel around my waist, grabbed my ditty bag and stepped out of the van. I hung my pants and shirt outside on a tree branch and went to shower off the stickiness that clung to my body. I took a long hot shower, taking the time to reflect on all of the events of the evening and trying to anticipate what might come between Dana and me within the next few days. The water started to turn cold so I stepped out of the shower, toweled off and went back to the van. I hung my damp towel over the back of the driver's seat, slowly slid the sliding door almost closed so as not to wake Dana and very carefully crawled into bed beside her. She never stirred. "Whew!" I fell asleep and, in my dreams, resumed dancing with my mysterious maiden. ~

Chapter 40: It's Over

Morning came to me around 10 o'clock. I reached over to caress an empty spot. Not surprising. I hadn't really expected a warm welcome. I parted the small curtains at the back of the van and peered outside. I could see Dana, Jacques, and Mimi sitting under the umbrella sipping coffee and laughing together. I tossed the covers aside, pulled on yesterday's clothes, put a baseball cap on my bad hair, and went to face the music.

"Morning, everyone," I said as I approached the table. Their conversation stopped and I received a rather cold stare from Dana along with neutral looks from Jacques and Mimi.

"Ummmm," I thought. "I'd better handle this one with kid gloves." I sat down.

"Well," Dana said, stretching out the well.

"Well, what?" I asked.

"How was your rendezvous?"

"Very interesting and very tiring." I said, attempting to downplay the extremely exciting evening I had just experienced. "And yours?" I continued.

"Oh, we had a Ball!"

With this vibe of contempt, Jacques and Mimi got up from the table. "Excuse us, we think we'd better leave you two alone for a while."

"Good idea," Dana said, urging them on their way. We sat silently for a moment until they disappeared into their little cottage.

"I'm leaving tomorrow mid-day. Mimi helped me book a flight this morning while you were snoring your head off and," she said, reaching into the side pocket of her shorts, "you can have this." She tore up her original return ticket on Icelandic Airlines and tossed it onto my lap. I glanced down at the fragments lying on my lap, took a deep breath and looked at her with sorrowful eyes, looking for forgiveness.

"It's your own damn fault," she said. "You were being selfish, pompous and arrogant. My mother's right. I have to get on with my life."

I said nothing, knowing an argument would only fire up her Italian temper. I was willing to concede. Then she softened a bit, knowing she'd gotten to me and reached out across the table and put her hand on mine.

"It's been a great ride, Donald, a great adventure and you've taught me a lot. I've learned a lot about myself and about you. Now it's time for me to move on." She looked at me with sad eyes and an expression I know matched mine. "I still love you, though." With that, she got up from the table and went back to the van.

I went for a walk along the river, needing to be by myself. After I thought about it for a while, I felt better. I'd lost a short love affair the night before and a long love affair today. I was batting zero here—I'd better get back to business.

I thought about the mail that I had received from California from Sandy, my salon manager. She had written that things weren't going smoothly and that it was important I return home soon or take a chance on losing my salon, my clientele and some of the girls who worked for me. I made a mental note to call Sandy and let her know I'd be home soon.

Wandering aimlessly, I happened upon a small plaza filled with bird merchants. The caged cooing of the white fantailed pigeons transported me to the days when I raised homing pigeons. There were birds of many colors, symbolizing their beauty; their songs, and happiness. I loved all the different species, but especially the songbirds that I could listen to and watch for hours.

I stopped to talk to one of the merchants who spoke English. He was grizzled, bearded, and tattooed, with a black patch over one eye, like an old pirate. He had traveled the Southern Hemisphere in search of his many-colored feathered friends. His birds came from Argentina, Costa Rica, Brazil, and South Africa. He favored the South American species because they seemed to be the most colorful, plentiful, and easiest to bring to France. We sat under his canopied stall and talked, drank wine and smoked Cuban cigars together. A small green parrot sat on his shoulder and pruned its feathers. His joyful deliverance of knowledge was just what I needed that day, so I planted myself and hung out.

Around three that afternoon, the bird merchants start closing their stalls. Some piled their cages in the back of small pickups. Others carried their cages on long poles strung out on the back of their necks and shoulders. I said goodbye to the pirate, and headed back to the trailer park, hoping I had given Dana enough time to finish packing for her flight back to the States.

When I arrived, I approached the van sheepishly and called out her name, "Dana?" No answer. I saw the sliding door was closed. I went closer and peered through the side window that was part way open. "Dana?" I heard the screen door slam shut behind me.

"Looking for your lost girlfriend?" Jacques asked.

"Kind of," I answered.

"She's off with Mimi, doing some last-minute shopping. She wanted to get something from Paris to take home to her mother. They'll be back for dinner–you know–your last supper." He chuckled at his humor. I groaned. He came over and put his arm around my shoulder affectionately. "It's okay, buddy. Many will come, but few will be chosen."

"Whatever that means–I've heard that one before."

"Oui - but it's true. Come on, let's have a beer." Jacques had wisdom beyond–a man after my own heart. ~

CHAPTER 41: GOOD-BYE EUROPE

Jacques and Mimi had not chosen sides, but each had taken one of us under their wings to ease the pain of separation. They were very compassionate and loving people and wanted to see us both happy. We spent the day mostly separated from each other, but when we did come together it was in the company of our two friends.

We had a nice farewell dinner. Mimi tossed a mean green salad with mango and poppyseed dressing. Jacques cooked up some shrimp on the barbecue. During dinner we consumed a couple of bottles of chilled Sauvignon Blanc that helped smooth any remaining tensions. Our conversation was casual, non-confrontational and very relaxing, setting the mood for Dana and me on our last evening together. I silently thanked them for their efforts.

Around 11, Jacques got up from the table, stretched his arms out and let out a large yawn. He blinked his eyes twice and said, "You guys go have a nice night together and we'll catch up with you in the morning."

We smiled at each other, feeling we were back together on the same wavelength again. We got up from the table, hugged our hosts, thanked them again and walked back to the van with our arms around each other. We had a tender night together and slept in, holding each other close, not really wanting to let each other go, savoring those last moments. Then came a rap on the door.

"Dana, time's running short. We have to leave fairly soon," Mimi said. We had decided that I would remain behind with Jacques while Mimi drove Dana to the airport.

"Well, looks like this is it," I said.

"Looks like," she answered hesitantly.

"I'll get out of your way so you can finish your packing."

"That'll be nice."

I slipped on a T-shirt and shorts, grabbed a towel and went to shower. After a few minutes, I heard the shower start in the women's bathroom and Dana's voice singing softly. I finished my shower, dried off, got dressed and went to Jacques and Mimi's outdoor table and sat down to a plate of fruit and croissants.

Jacques was reading the morning paper, hiding his face. When he heard the sound of the iron legs of my chair scrape the patio bricks, he dropped the paper, lowered his chin and looked at me over the rims of his rectangular-shaped, Benjamin Franklin reading glasses.

"And?" he asked.

"Everything's cool," I said. "She's back there in the shower singing."

"Seems like a good sign."

"Thanks to you two."

"You'd have done the same for us." He went back to his paper. "Have some breakfast."

Later, as Dana and Mimi were loading her luggage into the Fiat, it was as if we had all signed a contract, the terms of which were now being carried out. Dana was dressed nicely for the flight, wearing a new soft silk chiffon dress (probably the result of her shopping spree with Mimi) with five or six different layers of brightly colored cloth that tiered down off her waist. Her pink cowgirl boots peeked out from underneath. Her head was skull-capped in a bright red and blue striped scarf, wrapped in the gypsy style, knotted over one ear with the ends trailing down onto her shoulder. Oh, I was going to miss this girl—darn it!

She came to say goodbye. She hugged Jacques first and triple kissed his cheeks in the French tradition. "Thank you for everything," she said to him. Then she turned to me, batted her fake, feathered eyelashes, wrapped her arms around me, smiled big, and said, "Take care, big boy." That was that. She hopped into the Fiat and she and Mimi sped away.

Jacques never said a word. He just lifted his eyes to the sky, gave a large sigh, and went back to his paper. So did I, with another chapter in the lesson of life under my cap.

I decided to spend three or four more days in Paris by myself. I stayed pretty much a recluse for the first few days, keeping busy with my own preparations for leaving. I called Icelandic and booked myself into an earlier departure out of Brussels. I then called Franz at the Luxembourg auto agency where I had purchased the van to notify him of my change in plans. We set up shipping the van out of Le Havre, France. They would pick it up and deliver it to the docks for me—for a price, of course. I called Sandy and gave her my new return date and then contacted my friend Richard, who was picking me up at the San Francisco airport.

My tasks finished, I spent time with Jacques getting to know him better. He showed me photos of their skiing trip to Sun Valley, Idaho. I got excited about the area so he gave me some people's addresses and phone numbers in Ketchum and Sun Valley to look up if I ever got there. I saw Pierre and Lily again and we relived our special night out. We took Polaroid pictures of us for me to take back to her niece in San Jose. I spent the last weekend with Jacques and Mimi and then the day arrived. Jacques drove me to the train station.

I took the train to Brussels to catch my flight. When the first jolt of the train's movement hit me, I awoke to the realization that I was again on my way—yet another journey. A sudden sadness rushed over me. What did the future hold for me?

I partially planned what my next move was going to be when I got back to the States. When the train pulled into the station, I hired a cab driver to serve as my guide and take me sightseeing for one last time. He began talking as soon as we pulled from the curb and we became instant friends. Some people come into your life for different reasons. Some stay for minutes, some for days, others for a lifetime. This special man filled this - special day.

I boarded the flight on time, found my window seat and prepared myself mentally for a long droning flight. I had been somewhat irresponsible for quite some time, and now I had to gear up to face the daily grind. Little did I know how instrumental my wandering around Europe was going to be in reforming the rest of my life. The plane lifted off the runway and I watched the last lights of Europe disappear into the distance. With the blackness of the Atlantic Ocean now below us, I had only the reflection of my face bouncing back at me off of the Plexiglas window to gaze into. My mind emptied and, lost in space, I drifted off to sleep. ~

CHAPTER 42: DECISIONS

Now that I was back behind my chair in my San Jose hairstyling salon, I somehow didn't feel the same. Three months of freedom had instilled the wanderlust in me. I wanted to move on, to search for new adventures.

It was 1970 and so many changes were going on around me that I often found myself daydreaming. I would drift back to the past and then suddenly shoot into the future. Mechanically, I would go about the haircuts, roller sets and comb-outs that I had done a thousand times before. I needed a change, a new challenge. Mrs. Jones at 9 on Friday morning, Mrs. Smith at 10. Same people every day. Boring! I knew there was something more for me—out there!

Turning the chair away from the mirror so my client couldn't see my eyes looking out at the world outside, I would automatically indulge in light, polite, mostly meaningless conversations that I had heard over and over before.

Across the street, on Saratoga Avenue, things had changed drastically since I left for Europe. Gone were the once beautiful plum and peach orchards. Also gone were the small fruit stands that stood in the shade, boasting the bounty of the immigrant laborers who picked the crops for the other immigrant landowners, who were now being forced out of their small farms by the swelling land values. Instead, progress met my eyes. I use that word heavily since it made my heart feel heavy. The new gas station, the new McDonald's, the new Taco Bell, the new shopping mall, etc., etc., etc! It was mind-boggling how heavy equipment (like those giant yellow D-9 caterpillars that I kept seeing everywhere) could level generations of peaceful prosperity and replace them with a new world of commerce and chaos. The singer, Joni Mitchell, said it all in her song: "They paved paradise to put up a parking lot."

That evening as I locked up the salon, I looked towards the west. My eyes rose above the imposing McDonald's golden arches and Taco Bell's giant red bell to search for the distant ridgeline of the Saratoga foothills that crown the horizon of the Santa Clara Valley. Less than a year ago, I could have made out the outline of every tree on that ridge. Now they were but a blur, standing like silent sentinels lingering there shrouded by dense grayish white and dirty blue smog.

I guess it all started somewhere in the late sixties, but now moving into the seventies, the invasion of Middle America into the Santa Clara Valley and its surrounding area was at a peak. According to statistics the number of new phone hookups during the month and other data indicated that the population increased by about 350 people per day! More people meant more homes and more shopping centers; so more orchards fell, just like dominos, all in a line. A few held out for longer but, as the suburbs grew up around them, they also fell.

Within one decade, the valley ballooned by 400 percent. Silicon Valley, Lockheed Missiles and Space, and the semi-tropical climate contributed to its explosion. Trying to stay ahead of the suburban sprawl, I moved further and further out into the countryside. I was now commuting over an hour each day to and from work driving along Blossom Hill Road, the first road I had driven on when I arrived from Hawaii nine years earlier. When I first observed the valley from this vantage point, it was thick in bloom and alive with color. A floral pallette of whites, pinks, oranges, reds, and lavenders splashed within the greenery greeted the eye then. Now it was a sea of tiled roofs.

I realized I didn't want or need city life any more. My European adventures proved to me that there was much more to life than what appeared on the surface. I would begin my search for a better life, a place that hadn't been discovered yet, one that had an easy going, relaxed attitude, preferably a fun-loving resort town in the mountains. That made me think of Sun Valley, Idaho–the town Jacques had mentioned.

That evening, driving home just after dusk, I experienced a sorrowful event that accelerated my relocation search. I had worked on 22 clients that day and was very tired. I turned off Blossom Hill Road onto Highway 101 and headed south towards my apartment complex, hidden behind two massive peach orchards, where I normally entered down the middle. Somehow, I was distracted and sped past the entrance. Realizing my mistake, I pulled into the gas station down the road and headed back. Something just didn't look right and then it hit me. Both orchards were gone, blown away in the breath of a day! Turning down the now wide-open lane no longer flanked by leaves of green, I scanned the scorched earth in total awe.

Down in the far corner of the now barren ranch land, deep in the evening's last shadows, sat four D-9 cats and a giant earthmover trailing a huge spiked drum. They looked like well-fed monsters resting after a satisfying day of gluttonous ravaging. Scattered in large piles, backlit by the last light of the day, were the remains of the two orchards, their twisted, crushed, splintered limbs reaching out as if in pain. Soon they would be torched, their leaves never to recycle ever again the oxygen and chloroform they had been sharing with the atmosphere for the last 50 or 60 years.

I was devastated. Another farmer's fruit growing life ended— just to make room for the new Californians. Beauty and life soon to be replaced by black-top asphalt and another tract of homes. This time it was too close to home. I shouted out loud: "That's it! I'm out of here. On to Sun Valley." ~

BOOK FOUR

CHAPTER 43: MOVING ON

Once I'd made the decision, I got the ball rolling. I took a trip to Sun Valley to check it out. When I traveled there in June, the mountain, deserts, and plains I drove through were in full bloom. The landscape was starker than the area I had come from but it held its own beauty. I'll never forget the first time I topped the crest of Timmerman Hill and viewed the Camas Prairie and the Wood River Valley below me. It was picture book material. The green pastures and golden grain fields spread out across the prairie floor until they reached the foothills of the valley. The Wood River, like a silver streak, shimmered in the sunlight as it meandered its way through the valley. In the distance were three snow-capped mountain ranges: the Sawtooths, the Pioneers, and the Boulders.

I was instantly hooked. The view reminded me of a similar scene I had seen in Austria. I dropped down into the prairie and drove on up the valley. About an hour later I arrived in the small cowboy and ski town of Ketchum, Idaho, at the base of Mt. Baldy—Sun Valley's ski mountain. I booked a week's lodging at a small motel with a hot springs swimming pool, unpacked my bags, and went out to discover what this little mountain ski town had to offer.

Ketchum had one stop sign on the corner of Main Street and Sun Valley Road. Main Street, six blocks long, had two grocery stores, a drug store, a post office, a bank, one ski shop, a log cabin motel with a hot springs pool, two gas stations, three restaurants, six bars and an old casino. I stood at the corner and observed the action. It was Friday night around five. Most people were streaming into the Pioneer Saloon, a local's favorite. I walked through the swinging doors. It was packed to the hilt, everyone munching on the complimentary happy hour chicken wings and prime rib bones, a Friday night tradition.

I squeezed sideways up to the bar between a pretty brunette and a handsome blue-eyed man dressed in Levi bib overalls. "Excuse me," I said. "Need to order a beer."

"Let me buy you one. Where are you from?" the man said.

"The Bay Area," I said.

"Are you?" the brunette on my left said, breaking into the conversation. "So, are we, are you moving here?" she continued.

"Thinking about it."

"What do you do?"

"I'm a hairstylist."

"Oh? My husband, John, who just bought your beer, is also; we have a salon on Sun Valley Road, about two blocks from here."

"Need a job?" he asked.

"Sorry, we didn't introduce ourselves." she broke in. "I'm Sandi, John's wife. We were just talking today about him getting some help. The area is growing, and he can't keep up—has to turn people away. That's not good, you know."

"No, it's not. Maybe I can help out."

We had dinner together—a great cut of prime rib, large, juicy and succulent. I gave them a quick rundown on my hairstyling abilities and, the rest, like they say, was history. I knew it was meant to be.

By the end of the week I had a job at his salon, The Tonsorial Parlor. I also fell so in love with the area and its people that I decided this was where I'd like to relocate. I put a deposit down on a 450-square-foot loft condominium located on the Warm Springs side of the mountain in a place called The International Village. It was my first real estate investment.

Excited about my purchase and my decision to move on in life, I drove back to San Jose, and in three months, I sold my salon and prepared for the move to Sun Valley. I celebrated my 31st birthday at a going-away party that my friends threw. The next day I was on my way in my 1937 Cadillac, towing a small enclosed trailer filled to the brim with personal items and two Siamese cats, Bon Earth and Madame. Wagons Ho! ~

CHAPTER 44: THE WRAP UP

The next 40-plus years hold some of the most exciting and interesting adventures I have had—adventures that I continue to enjoy as we speak. I have been fortunate to have had the intuitive sense to "break out of the box" and discover the world, traveling to many more foreign lands including Tahiti, Australia, Sicily, Italy, Costa Rica, Peru, Panama and Chile. I've returned to Hawaii numerous times and traveled down all four coasts of Mexico. I've flown in quite a few private airplanes, including personal jets. I became an expert deep powder skier and learned how to play two more instruments, guitar and piano. I've performed my music on stage with some well-known names. I've also acted in three movies; in one, I even had a speaking part and have recently became a Thespian, with five comic Shakespearean plays under my belt. I contracted, designed and built with my own hands two beautiful homes, including all their landscaping. I must have planted over 200 trees in that time, and I'm still digging holes in the ground. I've created many metal sculptures and canvas paintings that adorn both the walls of my home and those of others who love my work. I've captured some special moments on film. My love for automobiles has always been with me. I've built at least three hot rods and two custom cars. I've had two near death experiences that made me love each moment I remain here on earth. And I've written this book.

I was indeed BORN IN THE RIGHT TIME and blessed with good luck and good fortune. I attribute my good fortune to a number of things: my birthright and upbringing, my Navy service, my move to San Jose, Calif., and becoming a hairstylist, and my relocation to Sun Valley. And, finally, my marriage of 33 years to my loving wife Laurie, whose love, understanding, and direction has made me the man I am today.

I've led an active life, full of some outrageous activities. What did it all mean? I would like to share some of my thoughts and advice with you, dear reader.

Automobiles

What red-blooded American boy (or girl, nowadays) hasn't fallen in love with their father's car? The family automobile is usually the first choice of the son or daughter since it is closest to home and readily available. And who is going to give you your first driving lesson? Often, it is your father. He might start you at an early age just sitting on his lap and placing your tiny hands on the steering wheel. That's how it all started for me, when my father took me to the Minnesota State Fairgrounds for my first real lesson. Driving an automobile, feeling the freedom, and having a love affair with the world's most popular toy–I feel–is one of the key steps on the ladder of life.

Adventure and Meeting People

The scent of adventure does not appeal to all, but to those who fear not, it becomes almost an obsession. To travel and discover, to become part of the whole world with its many diversified cultures enables you to understand your own self as well.

"People who need people are the luckiest people in the world," sang Barbra Streisand. If you are lucky, people come into your life every day. Some may only stay a moment, some a few hours, days or weeks, others for months and years, but very few are there for a lifetime. A passage in Chuck Yeager's book, (no, no relation) tells how his father determined that if a man dies and has 10 lifelong friends who will stand at his gravesite, he would indeed have lived a fulfilling life.

If every day you could meet one new person and learn at least one new thing, then you have achieved more than most and added more riches to your memory bank. For me, every day is a new day and I try to live in present time and be present. To live and to give, to find honesty within yourself, and to focus, are tools to use to find that everything you need in life will be drawn to you.

Success

When opportunity knocks, open the door. When someone extends an invitation to you and the timing is right, accept it or the moment might slip away and you may never receive such a chance again. Part of my success in life has been from "grabbing the moment." By being an open individual and not being regimented, I can move forward. When I find myself stuck in routine, performing the same action, day after day, I try to find that one special thing that can alleviate the pattern, while still maintaining my reliability and responsibility.

My Hairstyling Experience

Being a popular hairstylist, my chosen lifetime career, and a successful salon owner taught me other life lessons: how to be a businessman, a fair employer, and an entrepreneur. Every day standing behind the chair was a learning experience for me. I had a captive audience but, often, I was the captive. I've always been one on one with my clients, gaining their respect, trust, and admiration. Some I took under my wing; others adopted me. Some had personal troubles and therefore sought my advice, compassion, and understanding. I assured them what they told me would be held in highest confidence–like the priest in a confessional.

My main objective was personal styling and I thrived on being instrumental in helping my clients maintain their present image or in other cases change them completely, uprooting them from looking like everybody else. I loved helping to explode their hidden beauty with a new look and often a change in attitude.

Women love their hairstylist, men appreciate their barber/stylist and lucky me, I was able to capture both ends of the deal. My enthusiasm for my profession and my ability to meet most people's expectations opened the yellow brick road for me. My work offered me the opportunities to immerse myself into many different realms. The spectrum runs wide from the lowest echelons in the poorest ghettos that could hardly pay for my services to the multimillionaires who live in their mega mansions and fly in their private jets.

Women

I love women, needless to say, as they have always been an important part of my life. I'm guessing that was one good reason I became a hairstylist. But even way before that at the tender age of 13 when I had my first kiss, I knew women would be one of my obsessions. I am enamored with their voices, their softness, their beauty, and their minds. Women seem to offer much more clarity in life than men do. I'm like the big rooster, his wings spread wide, with all the little chicks hovering underneath for his protection. That's how women make me feel, the protector, the entertainer, the Romeo. Maybe that's why I've experienced so many wonderful romances in my life—some to cherish, others to have little or no memory of.

The Navy

Although my induction into the Navy happened under rather peculiar circumstances, it undoubtedly was one of the luckiest breaks I had in my early life. The Navy offered me the means of escape from a life that was turning into a series of wrongdoings. My juvenile delinquency was beginning to run rampant and the Navy provided me with the opportunity to escape from leading what could have been the dull humdrum life of a lower middle-class worker. Instead it led me into a life of travel and adventure, starting with the first time I boarded the train out of St. Paul en route to boot camp, beginning my discovery of the world outside my childhood bubble.

Last Words

Life itself is a journey and we as individuals have control of our own destiny. We must learn from our present and past experiences, both good and bad. We must use our street smarts. Being born in the right time, in the right place, and of good parents all contribute to who and what we might become, but it still is up to us to make the right decisions in life. When we realize that we only have one body and one mind that we alone dwell within and treasure that as a God-given gift, only then can we achieve the peace and tranquility that accompanies that learning. ~

Thank you, dear reader, for making the journey with me. I wish you a life of adventure and happiness as you live life to the fullest.

Don Yeager

✳✳1959✳ U.S.A.: Alaska, Hawaii Achieve Statehood • Eisenhower

State Of Hawaii | City and County of Honolulu | **OPERATOR'S LICENSE**

No. P **333923**   This certifies that the person named and described below has been licensed by the Examiner of Chauffeurs, of the City and County of

Date Issued **11-3-59**   Honolulu as a **automobile**

Restrictions **none**   operator under the provisions of the Laws of

Name **YEAGER, DONALD RICHARD**

Address **VR-21 Barbers Pt.**

Date of Birth **9-29-39** | Sex **M** | Weight **182** | Height **6'**
Month Day Year | | lbs

Color Eyes **blue**

**THE
NAVY
DAYS**

Honolulu/Waikiki

**VR-21
Transport
Squadron
Barber's Point,
Hawaii**

INDIVIDUAL SURVIVAL CHECKOUT CARD

**USS Kearsarge CVA 33
West Pacific Assignment**

Made in the USA
Columbia, SC
25 June 2021